Thami al-Glaoui

Edinburgh Studies on the Maghreb

Series Editors: Allen James Fromherz and Matt Buehler

International Advisory Board
- Amira Bennison
- Aomar Boum
- Francesco Cavatorta
- Mounira M. Charrad
- Irene Fernández-Molina
- Jonathan Hill
- Frédéric Volpi
- Katja Žvan Elliott

Books in the series (published and forthcoming)

Geopolitics and Governance in North Africa: Local Challenges, Global Implications
Sarah Yerkes (ed.)

Thami al-Glaoui: Morocco's Greatest Pasha
Orit Ouaknine-Yekutieli

International Influences on Tunisian Democratisation
Pietro Marzo

edinburghuniversitypress.com/series/estm

Thami al-Glaoui
Morocco's Greatest Pasha

Orit Ouaknine-Yekutieli

EDINBURGH
University Press

*To Yuval, my partner, my best friend, my love.
And to our children, the lights of my life, Omri, Gal, and Shoham.*

Edinburgh University Press is one of the leading university presses in the UK. We publish academic books and journals in our selected subject areas across the humanities and social sciences, combining cutting-edge scholarship with high editorial and production values to produce academic works of lasting importance. For more information visit our website: edinburghuniversitypress.com

© Orit Ouaknine-Yekutieli, 2024, 2025

Edinburgh University Press Ltd
13 Infirmary Street
Edinburgh EH1 1LT

First published in hardback by Edinburgh University Press 2024

Typeset in 11/13 Source Serif Pro by
Cheshire Typesetting Ltd, Cuddington, Cheshire

A CIP record for this book is available from the British Library

ISBN 978 1 3995 2067 6 (hardback)
ISBN 978 1 3995 2068 3 (paperback)
ISBN 978 1 3995 2069 0 (webready PDF)
ISBN 978 1 3995 2070 6 (epub)

The right of Orit Ouaknine-Yekutieli to be identified as author of this work has been asserted in accordance with the Copyright, Designs and Patents Act 1988 and the Copyright and Related Rights Regulations 2003 (SI No. 2498).

Contents

List of Figures	vi
Acknowledgements	vii
1. Introduction: The Last Lord of the Atlas	1
2. A Loyal Servant of Two Empires	20
3. The Glaoua Tribe on River Seine	57
4. The Age of Conspiracies	97
5. 'He is the Jews' Friend'	134
6. Erasure and Revelation: Telling al-Glaoui from the 1960s to the Late 1990s	166
7. 'I am a Moroccan and a Berber': al-Glaoui and Amazighness	193
8. Reconciliations	204
9. A Never-ending Story	228
Bibliography	243
Index	274

Figures

1.1	Entrance to the Kasbah of Telouet	2
2.1	Map of Morocco, 1930	22
2.2	Thami al-Glaoui hosting Ernest Vaffier, who arranged the evacuation of the Glaoui brothers and their troops from Oran to Tangier	28
2.3	Thami al-Glaoui meeting with his uncle Si Hamou at the Telouet Pass	41
2.4	Thami al-Glaoui wearing his French decorations during a visit to France	42
2.5	Thami al-Glaoui arriving at the French army camp at Bou Yahia during his 1922 *harka*	45
2.6	'His Excellency Si el Hadj Thami Glaoui, Grand qa'id of the South, Pasha of Marrakesh, Grand officer of the Légion d'honneur'	52
3.1	'Al-Glaoui at the Grand Hotel'	76
4.1	Thami al-Glaoui	119
4.2	Thami al-Glaoui and Martinaud-Deplat, French minister of justice	122
5.1	Al-Glaoui at his palace's gallery where he received guests	155
5.2	Rabbi Makhlouf Abu-Haseira welcomes Pasha al-Glaoui	159

Acknowledgements

The writing of this book was made possible thanks to many people and institutions to whom I am incredibly grateful.

First and foremost, I wish to thank my parents, Vivian Melki-Ouaknine and Yosef Ouaknine, who let me in on their real and imagined journeys to their memories, worlds and homelands. I am thankful to them for letting me share their longing and sense of place, and for the deep curiosity in people and history they instilled in me.

I am wholeheartedly grateful to my spouse, Yuval, for limitless discussions surrounding the writing of the book, for travelling together with me along the mental and physical routes this research had taken me, for reading numerous drafts of the manuscript, and for giving invaluable advice which infinitely improved the book.

I am highly indebted to my children, Omri, Gal, and Shoham, and to my sister Hadas, with whom I discussed many topics in this volume and who exposed me to critical challenges and insights with their great openness and intellectual curiosity. I also thank my other family members, Ilai, Hanna, Chen, Greg, Idit, Alain and Yael, and particularly my grandson Nur, who brought joy and happiness as the writing reached its final stage.

I was blessed to benefit from the excellent guidance of Iris Agmon, my MA and PhD adviser, who became a friend and family for life. She accompanied the development of this project since its inception as an MA dissertation and has been a source of encouragement and inspiration ever since.

The research and writing of this volume were made possible through generous funding from the Israel Science Foundation (ISF) Research Grant no. 337/16, 'The Caïdal Lords of the Atlas – Caïdalisme, Colonialism, and Post-Colonialism in Morocco and

Beyond', and Ben-Gurion University's Dr Sam and Edna Lemkin Career Development Chair in Middle East Studies. The research of specific parts of the book was also supported by ISF Research Grant no. 2050/19, 'Morocco under Vichy Rule'.

In addition, I am deeply grateful for the constant backing of Ben-Gurion University and its Middle East Studies Department. Throughout this research, I also got the support of Oxford University and Tel Aviv University post-doctoral fellowship at St Antony's College, Oxford; a post-doctoral fellowship at Tel Aviv University; and the Lady Davis post-doctoral fellowship at the Hebrew University, Jerusalem. I am also thankful for the BGU Rich Foundation Grant for promoting women in academia, the Université Internationale de Rabat, Sapir College and the Chaim Herzog Centre for Middle East Studies and Diplomacy.

Incredible friends advised, encouraged and shared their immense knowledge with me throughout the writing process. Aomar Boum, with extreme generosity, always offered guidance, immense support, good ideas and advice. Avi Rubin guided me through the book's proposal stage with great friendship and patience. Haggai Ram instructed me in the world of academic book publishing. In addition, Avi and Haggai offered constant and unfailing support throughout the upheavals of academic life. I am grateful to Daniel Schroeter, who was always a source of inspiration, sharing his materials with the most extraordinary generosity and offering indispensable advice. Dror Zeevi opened my view to many additional aspects with his incredibly broad knowledge.

I am grateful to Nimrod Hurvitz for the numerous discussions and consultations, and to Yigal Nizri who always gave unique counsel and backing and was there to encourage in moments of distress. I greatly thank Ehud Toledano, who read the manuscript and gave significant comments that helped to situate al-Glaoui's case within broader intellectual and regional contexts. I am also profoundly obliged to Joëlle Bahloul, whose work set a brilliant academic and personal example for me in addition to being a most precious friend.

I was fortunate to have a group of best friends accompanying me while writing this book and beyond. Aliza Uzan Suissa, with whom I can talk about everything and laugh at everything. Bat-el Danzig, who in addition to being a great friend, also eased the way through the complex administrative crossroads surrounding the book's production. Rachel Damri, who so often cheered me up and shared her unique expertise in the academic world.

I was also fortunate to have had the friendship and guidance of my excellent friends and partners from the Forum for the Study of Jews and Christians in Muslim Cultures and from many other activities: Haya Bambaji-Sasportas and Menashe Anzi.

A few scholars and dear friends were a constant inspiration for me, offering unique outlooks for looking critically yet humanistically at occurrences and processes: Ella Shohat, Haviva Pedaya, Amnon Raz-Karkotzkin, Khalid Ben Srhir and Jamaâ Baïda.

I am deeply indebted to Ruth Ginio and Lynn Schler of BGU Africa Centre, for their partnership, and grateful to Ruth for sharing with me ideas about colonialism and post-colonialism in Africa.

Akin Ajayi edited this book brilliantly and improved its style, arguments, and narratives. Amy Klein-Asher also contributed to editing an earlier version of one of the chapters.

I am grateful to the devoted and tremendously friendly staff of Edinburgh University Press, who led me through the publication process: Emma House and Louise Hutton, commissioning editors; Isobel Birks, assistant editor; Bekah Dey, who designed the cover; and Eddie Clark, managing desk editor. Three anonymous referees read and commented on the book, improving its arguments. Matt Buehler and Allen James Fromherz are series editors for 'Edinburgh Studies on the Maghreb'. Lel Gillingwater put a final touch on stylistic matters in the text. Kate Kent meticulously indexed the book.

I am indebted to the staff of the many archives I worked in. Special thanks are due to Jamaâ Baïda, the director of the Archives Du Maroc; Damien Heurtebise, the archivist in charge of the French protectorates in North Africa at the French Diplomatic Archives at Nantes; Haya Milo of the Israel Folktale Archives. Sydney Corcos graciously shared materials from his family archives with me. Paul Dahan facilitated my access to sources in his archives.

Many dear colleagues and friends contributed information, advised and guided me to additional sources. Guy Burak, librarian for Middle Eastern and Islamic Studies at New York University, helped me locate rare books and turned my attention to valuable sources. Rabbi Shlomo Zalman Miara shared with me his vast knowledge of Jewish Morocco and photographs from Marrakesh. Brahim El Guabli shared memories of his family's Amazigh history. Miko Gabai told me his family's lore from al-Glaoui's days in Marrakesh. Sydney Assor directed me to significant sources. Jean-Pierre Eckmann was incredibly kind in helping me establish contacts with the descendants of Albert Berdugo. I am also thankful to the inhabitants of Telouet, who shared memories, stories and insights, to numerous informants in Morocco and elsewhere, the Berdugo and the Assaraf families and Museum Dar El Basha in Marrakesh.

I am indebted to my student assistants, Mohamed El Hamdaoui, Yona Abeddour, Eden Sulimani and Fana Abu Hamed, who participated in this research.

Many thanks to my colleagues at the Department of Middle East Studies at Ben-Gurion University of the Negev who have provided an intellectual home: Aref Abu-Rabia, Yoram Meital, Relli Schechter, Muhammad Al-Atawneh, Daniella Talmon Heller, Yoni Mendel and Yair Horesh. I am also very thankful to other members of the BGU community over the years, who became familiar with my work in Morocco and about it: university presidents Rivka Carmi and Daniel Haimovich, rector Chaim Heims, deans Amit Schechter, David Wattstein and Nirit Ben-Aryeh Debby, Faculty of Humanities and Social Sciences administrative units' directors Avital Edri and Yael Mashiach Karadi; BGU Research and Development Department and especially Helen Abutbul.

Many others have contributed, helped and encouraged me in numerous ways, and I am truly grateful for their ongoing friendship and support: Tzvi Ben-Dor; Samir Ben-Layashi; Raphael Ben-Shoshan; Shaul Ben-Simhon; Simon Ben-Simon; Kawtare Bihya; Najia, Leila, and Haja Amina Bouarfa; Henriette Dahan-Kalev; Samia El Glaoui; Avraham Elharar; Yuval Evri; Dani Filc; Tania Forte; Moshe Gershovich; David Goeury; Tourya Guaaybess; Meir Hatina; Alma Heckman; Kobi Ifrach; Jackie Kadoch; Samuel Kaplan; Liat Kozma; André Levy, Saghir Mabrouk; Bruce Maddy Weitzman; Jessica Marglin; Rachel Milstein; Salima Naji; Richard Pennell; Michael Peyron; Tami Sarfatti; Avi Shlaim; Tal Shuval; Lior Sternfeld; Victor Vyssotsky; Jimmy Watt; Michael Willis; Fruma Zachs; and Meir Zamir.

I am incredibly thankful to all these friends, additional family members, and many others who wished to remain anonymous yet know their part in this story and my sincere gratitude.

1
Introduction: The Last Lord of the Atlas

During a recent conversation with a friend, I mentioned in passing that I was about to finish writing a book about Pasha Thami al-Glaoui. The friend, born to a Moroccan-Amazigh family who have lived in the diaspora for many years, contacted her family to ask what they know about the Pasha. The response was immediate. She contacted me soon afterwards, to say:

> You should have seen their reaction. It was like asking them to reveal their most taboo secret. I could sense the fear and hesitation. I asked them what they knew about the Pasha, and all the answers I got were preceded with caveats: 'they said', 'the urban legends say', 'we heard' ... Unsurprisingly, this character was not taught in history classes![1]

This family's reaction, in 2020, was not very different from what I had experienced repeatedly during my research into the Glaoui story over the last few years. Older people who remembered him, or who remembered stories recounted by their parents, claimed that he was frightening, ruthless, brutal and incredibly rich. Reports in old journals revealed that he was often to be found surrounded by celebrities: Winston Churchill and Charles de Gaulle, Charlie Chaplin and Simone Berriau. As I became drawn to my subject, eventually deciding to write about it, I was warned time and again that the topic may still be considered sensitive. Perhaps I should consider researching something else? This only piqued my curiosity further. In time, I realised that comments like this are but a part of al-Glaoui's story, intricately connected with the 'facts' about his life.

My fascination with the story of Thami al-Glaoui began while I was carrying out interviews in old *qsur* (fortified villages) in

Figure 1.1 Entrance to the Kasbah (castle) of Telouet. Drawing by Ernest Vaffier (Vaffier 1917: 30). Modifications have been made to the original image.
Courtesy: Bibliothèque de l'Institut national d'histoire de l'art, Jacques Doucet collections, 174 U 1.

southern Morocco, studying past relationships between Muslims and Jews in those places. Among these *qsur*, in the mountainous village of Telouet, a ruined castle stood prominently, presenting a brilliant contrast between its past grandeur and the present emptiness and neglect. The enormity of the empty structure, belied by signs of its former splendour, seemed to conceal a secretive story (Figure 1.1). The allure of the castle's tale grew even larger as I progressively learned about the life of the man whose story was associated with it – Thami al-Glaoui, once the great *qa'id* (tribal leader) of the Glaoua tribe, who populate the region of Telouet.

My first steps into the subject were slow, as people were not willing to reveal more about him than a few scattered remarks. Within the immediate bibliography about the Pasha, the most accessible and known source is a 1966 book describing Thami al-Glaoui's rise and fall, *The Lords of the Atlas*. By the 1960s, the book's author, British traveller-writer Gavin Maxwell, had encountered similar problems while undertaking his own research. Maxwell's biographer wrote about this process:

> It was one thing to have an idea; it was another to find one's way through the labyrinth to the secret at its heart. The recent history of the Glaoui was a matter of great sensitivity in Morocco at that time, and the government was only too anxious to forget the whole episode. The facts of the matter were largely locked away in the inner recesses of the Royal Court, or in the memories of the surviving members of the Glaoui family, and it was not easy for a prying investigator from the West to gain access to them. Unfortunately, Gavin had chosen the wrong moment to try. (Botting 2000: 265)

The story of Thami al-Glaoui was everywhere and nowhere. It was well known yet disturbingly elusive; critical for many, but at the same time under-told.

Thami al-Glaoui (1879–1956) was the leader of the Glaoua tribe, and Pasha of Marrakesh between 1912 and 1956. His name is connected in Moroccan history with the concept of the *qa'idal* system (or, as the French colonisers called it, *caïdalisme*). In this system of rule, as practised in Morocco during the pre-colonial and colonial periods, the central administration delegated powers to regional rulers (*qa'id* in Arabic; *caïd* in its French transliteration). The *qa'id* collected taxes and often exercised de facto local authority on behalf of the administration, in return for a certain percentage of the revenues thus collected.

Stretching the authority bestowed by the *qa'idal* system to its limits, al-Glaoui managed to extract enormous power from his status. After defeating or succeeding other *grands caïds* (the French term for the senior Moroccan *qa'id*s operating as part of the *caïdalisme*), by the 1930s he had become the third most powerful person in Morocco, after the Sultan and the French Resident-General. Moreover, in 1953 al-Glaoui was a member of the small circle of people who instigated the deposition of Sultan Mohammed V and his exile by the French. Three years later, in what some have since described as the apogee of his life, al-Glaoui changed course, calling for the Sultan's return and for Moroccan independence. Pardoned by Mohammed V, al-Glaoui died a short time later, missing Morocco's Independence Day by a few months (Abun Nasr 1987: 370–1; Peyron 1999; Yasin 2003; El Glaoui 2004; Samama 2006; al-Buzidi 2007; Boum and Park 2016).

While the basic information about al-Glaoui is clear, the sheer volume of tales about him, jutting out at different tangents, is perplexing. It seems that the production of these narratives never actually ceased; they have continued to evolve before our eyes, an amazing dynamic interweaving stories, storytellers and histories.

Hence, this book is a study of the story of al-Glaoui, and the multiple ways in which it has been told. The goal of this book is to investigate the Pasha's biography as a cumulative story, its creation outliving its protagonist and its authors, emphasising the interdependencies between the figure, the story and the storytelling. Together, these characterise history as an ongoing amalgamation of historical action and acts of storytelling, challenging the notion that the latter two should be considered as separate entities.

My goal is to clear some of the fog that surrounds the biography of Thami al-Glaoui, combining this with an analysis of its manifold tellings and retellings. Thus, beyond the new data and perspectives it presents about the person, this book also reflects on his story and the various ways in which it has been told; how it continues to evolve; how it has affected processes within Moroccan and French histories, and was in turn affected by these processes; and its contribution to a more nuanced understanding of the telling and writing of history.

By merging al-Glaoui's biography with the many differing narratives about his tale – and with the life stories of the authors who wrote about him – this book seeks to offer a fresh perspective on major processes of twentieth- and twenty-first-century Morocco, and the colonial empires involved in these processes. These include the creation of colonial modernity, and the traumatic shifts from an imperial world order into nation-state configurations and global post-national formulations. Finally, I also seek to rescue al-Glaoui's memory from the simplistic and reductionist interpretations that certain historiographies have proffered.

Making al-Glaoui Great Again

Thami al-Glaoui's history and life story, as well as specific episodes from his life, were, and continue to be, told by many storytellers in various ways and from numerous perspectives. By 'storytellers', I refer to the broad diversity of people who have written or spoken about him: be they al-Glaoui himself, novelists, journalists, administrators, researchers, playwrights, poets, family members or common people. The numerous verbal utterances that they have produced in various media manifest the intimate link between story and history (a concept already discussed by scholars such as White 1973; Veyne 1984; de Certeau 1988) – an association demonstrated by the fact that many languages use the same word to denote the two concepts. The French and German examples of *histoire* and *geschichte* which, respectively, mean both story and history, are rather well known. But effectively, Arabic and Hebrew offer similar, though less colloquial instances. In Arabic, *rwaya* (رواية) means a novel and a story on the one hand; but on the other hand, it also means tradition (in the sense of traditions passed down from generation to generation) and a narrative. In Hebrew, *hagadah* (הגדה) means telling; it also refers to the telling of historical-cum-mythic happenings, such as the Passover Hagadah, which tells the story/history of the Exodus of the Israelites from Egypt. The history–story link is, thus, universally inherent. In order to exist, history requires a storytelling mechanism which supplies the process that translates a past into a narrative.

The translation of history into a tale brings about additional, yet inevitable, interpretive elements: giving explanations and meanings to the told past (White 1978: 81–100; de Certeau 1988: 6), singling out 'events' and arranging them as 'causes and effects', accentuating certain facts and silencing others. Different narrators tend to deduce different causes, effects and events, conveying them in connection with their own unique perspectives and aims. When history becomes 'a storied form of knowledge' (Munslow 2019: 16), its narration can also assume literary characteristics, such as tragedy, adventure, romance or farce (White 1978: 86; Stone-Mediatore 2003: 22; Chartier 2011: 1) – dramatically enhancing a particular point of view about past occurrences.

The research presented in this book explores how deeds are told, probing into the extent to which action and tales are intrinsically intertwined, constantly producing and reproducing each other. I analyse events that indeed happened: people who were really born, robbed or killed, houses that were truly built or destroyed. Simultaneously, I examine the narratives describing these events. These, not so rarely in the case of al-Glaoui, do not match. In some cases, they clearly contradict each other, creating ongoing chains of inter-textual stories and histories. Disagreements of this form are particularly thought-provoking, as they emphasise the twists and turns of historical narratives and worldviews. I consider such cases throughout the book, such as the differing accounts of the 1912 rescue of French prisoners in Marrakesh by al-Glaoui (Chapter 2); the 1950 *Mulud* (the Prophet's birthday) celebrations at Mohammed V's court, the breaking point in the relationship between the Sultan and al-Glaoui (Chapter 4); the supposed Amazigh cavalry attack staged by al-Glaoui against Fes and Rabat in 1951 (Chapter 4); and more.

In storytelling, the expectation is that a story will have an ending. This expectation originates in the inherent human aspiration for finding order in a world that is seemingly chaotic (Stanzel 1992: 112). Accordingly, a story is often invented as a means of setting order to a set of otherwise disorganised events. As Juan Fernandez puts it in his *Story Makes History, Theory Makes Story*, 'narrativity is a way of giving a first theoretical structure (interpretation) to the historical material, through *naming* events and objects, and *plotting* sequences of events in meaningful wholes' (Fernandez 2018: 98–9; italics in the original).

Al-Glaoui's story contradicts these expectations, in that it lacks an ending and is highly fractured and disordered. Endurance and mix-ups characterise the story's ongoing spread from the beginning of the twentieth century to the present. It expands across diverse tracks, including books, videos, websites, blogs, newspaper articles, lectures, conversations, plays and rumours.

The story-history that this book offers studies these endurances and disorders in order to learn the dynamics that create such an ongoing multi-track historical narrative, and the specificities of the form (see a similar approach at Stone-Mediatore 2003: 3, 5).

In order to study the routes that a story has taken – including this book, which is another 'brick' in the construction of the Glaoui tale – I examine numerous sources about al-Glaoui, towards which I pose a number of questions: what new information and opinions appear on the scene? Which events and actors are selected as 'leading' in various tales, and why? What literary devices do the authors use to make their point? What metaphors are used, by whom, and to what end? And, how are the stories structured?

The book makes the point that authors and readers of narratives about the Pasha were almost always 'in dialogue' with earlier and contemporaneous texts about him, maintaining through these what could be described as a virtual conversation with the Pasha himself. Gavin Maxwell's book (discussed in Chapter 6) disputes, from beginning to end, an earlier volume about the Pasha written by Gustave Babin (Chapter 3) – which itself communicates with al-Glaoui and with contemporary and earlier texts (Chapters 2 and 3). Abdelilah Benhadar's play (Chapter 8) creates imaginary conversations between al-Glaoui and other actors, while heavily relying on Babin's text (Chapter 3). In this sense, al-Glaoui's accumulative tale exhibits what Genette described, using the metaphor of the palimpsest: 'On the same parchment, one text can become superimposed upon another, which it does not quite conceal but allows to show through' (Genette 1982: 397; as translated by Clark 2009: 131). Across the following chapters, I explore how texts imitate and transform older ones; I examine the ways in which previous texts are used to gain new meanings; and I investigate how all these inform the broader goal of studying relationships between stories and histories.

Thami al-Glaoui lived through one of the most turbulent periods in the history of modern Morocco: beginning with his rise to power at the end of the pre-colonial era, as a key player in shaping the country through the colonial period, and finally reaching the end of his life in a symbolic association with the rebirth of independent Morocco. As detailed above, al-Glaoui's death did not reflect the end of 'telling' him. Texts and stories about the Pasha have continued to be written, intensifying in number and variety within the last three decades. The study of such a lengthy period thus examines stories from a lengthy time span, reflecting multiple periodic genres, discourses and historiographies.

Pre-colonial Moroccan historical texts (mainly referred to in Chapter 2) were written mostly by chroniclers appointed by the Royal Court (for example, al-Nasiri) to record the sultans and their deeds (El Moudden 1997; al-Mansour 1997: 109–10). Accordingly, al-Glaoui, who was at the beginning of his rise to power towards the end of the pre-colonial period, is rarely mentioned in these chronicles. Texts by French authors from the beginning of the twentieth century to the end of the French Protectorate – which frequently refer to al-Glaoui – were more ethnographic in nature and studied multiple aspects of Moroccan society (for example, Beylié 1909; Barthou 1919; Le Glay 1923; Montagne 1924; 1930; Bel 1938). However, these ethnographies, beyond being academic treatises, also nurtured the ruling apparatus; their data was primarily intended to facilitate colonial French ambitions. A nationalist strand within Moroccan historiography appeared in the 1930s and has intensified consistently since Moroccan independence in 1956 (for example, Lahbabi 1975; Laroui 1977; 'Ayash 1986). This strand sought to decolonise history by preferring local sources to colonial ones. It severely critiques French historiography about Morocco, and all partnerships with the French – including, of course, al-Glaoui's collaboration with the colonialists. Despite the fact that the *qa'idal* system was abolished with Moroccan independence (Boujrouf 2005), its memory, and especially al-Glaoui's role within it, turned in post-colonial nationalist historiography into a concrete example and a literary metaphor of betrayal, corruption and brutal feudalism (for example, Abun Nasr 1987: 382; Zebib 1995: 180–7; Hammoudi 1997: 129–30; Filali 2014). This negative attitude derived from the acts of violence and exploitation committed by al-Glaoui against many Moroccans, his resentment of the nationalist movement and, especially, his role in the plot to depose Mohammed V.

The temporal sequence of these historiographies does not necessarily mean that they substituted each other. Often, earlier concepts and data are embedded within later narratives, and some strands prevail into later periods. For example, after Morocco's independence, some historiographies, especially those written by non-Moroccans, continued to portray a colonial spirit (for example, Hoffman 1967; Waterbury 1970; Bidwell 1973). Contemporaneous and later Moroccan accounts are definitely non-colonialist; even so, many of them up to the present day continue to reproduce some colonial representations. Moreover, in its mission to erase past colonial historiography through the creation of negative images of the same topics and basic questions, nationalist writing has sometimes (unintentionally) magnified colonialist voices (Burke 2007: 1).

Many academic texts representing different approaches to local history and society other than the pre-colonial, colonial and nationalist historiographies, have been published since the 1960s. These include anthropological, sociological, Marxist, gender studies, postcolonial theory, subaltern studies and microhistorical approaches (for example, Geertz 1968; Gellner 1969; Gellner and Micaud 1972; Hart 1972; Maher 1974; Brown 1976; Dwyer 1978; Berque and Pascon 1978; Geertz, Geertz and Rosen 1979; Rosen 1980–1; 1984; 1989; Pascon 1986; Mernissi 1987; Miège, Zaki and Habi 1992; Daoud 1996; Hammoudi 1993; Ennaji and Gellner 1994; Ben-Srhir 2005; Boum 2013).

In the investigation of al-Glaoui's story and history, awareness of these approaches, and their time-specific vocabularies and rhetoric, can facilitate what contextual analysis defines as 'the intents' of their authors (Hall 2017: 244–5). At the same time, the study of texts related to the Pasha demonstrates that their reception has frequently been disengaged from 'the authors' intents', creating many – and often incompatible – trajectories, in a pattern resembling Barthes's observations in *The Death of the Author* (Barthes 1967). For example, although Gustave Babin addressed his book to the early 1930s French community in Morocco as an attempt at its rectification (Chapter 3), 'interpretive communities' (as coined by Fish 1980) of his text eventually came from a much wider spectrum of readers, with very different agendas: adherents of the nationalist Moroccan parties (before and after independence, Chapters 4, 5, 6); novelists such as Gavin Maxwell (Chapter 6); critical Moroccan documentary and fiction authors, since the end of the 1990s (Chapter 8); researchers like me in the present time; and current bloggers. This course of affairs not only represents a phenomenon that should be reckoned with while examining texts, but in the realm of this study is regarded both as the history and as the dynamics through which a historical 'story' constantly produces new meanings.

At the beginning of this chapter, I described the difficulties encountered by Gavin Maxwell while researching his book on the Pasha. Maxwell's persistence eventually paid off, with his volume published in 1966. Two years later, simultaneously with the publication of the French translation of his book (Maxwell 1968), another book about al-Glaoui was published in France (Le Prévost 1968), possibly a response to Maxwell's anti-French perspective (see Chapter 6). However, this short burst of publications died out quickly, followed by almost thirty years of silence during which almost nothing substantial linked to Thami al-Glaoui was published. It seemed, for a while, as though his story was fading away, an overlooked episode in the backyard of Moroccan history.

But this amnesia was temporary. Since the late 1990s – a point in time which coincidently (or not) corresponds with my own 'discovery' of the topic (Ouaknine-Yekutieli 2003) – al-Glaoui's story has resurfaced, accruing new publications and public debates. This resurgence has intensified apace, with new editions and translations of old books, the publication of new volumes, and the emergence of many public debates in the press, the performing arts and on social media.

While the Moroccan nationalist discourse continues to condemn al-Glaoui and the *qa'idal* system, alternative narratives – particularly popular with descendants of the ancient *qa'idal* lords – have appeared in the last two decades (for example, El Glaoui 2004; al-Glawi 2004; Goundafi 2013; El Glaoui 2017). These narratives tend to highlight the contribution of the grand *qa'id*s to Moroccan unity, their overall loyalty to the ruling dynasty, and their resistance to colonialism (Ayt al-Katawi 2013). Next to this new historiography, another recent discourse establishes its importance in the context of Amazigh *qa'idal* histories within the struggle over *Amazighité* (the French term for Amazighness, often used in Morocco as well: for example, Willis 2008; Maddy-Weitzman 2011: 160; Hagan 2013: 196).[2] Thus, many new trajectories of al-Glaoui's story seem to be emerging, moving towards making him great again.

Storytellers

My search for stories about al-Glaoui encompassed many available sources: from books, through newspaper articles, archival sources and online social media, to interviews. The latter were conducted mainly with 'ordinary' people who remembered al-Glaoui, or who told me about the ways in which the Pasha of Marrakesh is remembered, and his story told in their own families. These include people in both Morocco and in the various Moroccan diasporas all over the world. For ethical reasons, these sources remain anonymous in the text.

Existing books which focus on the Pasha include volumes by Gustave Babin (first edition 1932, second edition 1934), René Janon (1953), Gavin Maxwell (1966), Jacques le Prévost (1968), Albert Berdugo (1996), Abdessadeq El Glaoui (2004), and 'Abdellatif Jebrou (2005); as well as a short pamphlet composed by Thami al-Glaoui himself (al-Glaoui 1933), and an unpublished report, labelled 'secret' at the time, prepared by the French Indigenous Affairs officer Paul Schoen (1938).

These books present multiple perspectives about the Pasha, and represent milestones in the development of his story. The majority are what Magnússon (2017: 313) has described as 'ego-documents' – significantly transmitting the aspirations, frustrations and life views of the authors through writing, in this case, about al-Glaoui. For instance, Babin's rage over the collapse of his private colonial dream, allegedly al-Glaoui's doing, brackets his text (Chapter 3). Berdugo's feeling of having been undervalued at al-Glaoui's court, and thus failing to fulfil his potential, filters through his writing (Chapter 5). Likewise, Gavin Maxwell's melancholy over the loss of his upper-class Scottish family's status – part of the general decline of European aristocracy in the first half of the twentieth century – buttresses his enchantment with al-Glaoui's nobility, and his sorrow over the latter's collapse (Chapter 6). Thus, by writing their tales, storytellers were rewarded with the opportunity for catharsis, an opportunity to let go of personal distresses (Arendt and Young-ah Gottlieb 2007: 264). Still, their narration did not only bring about 'therapeutic' rewards. Reporting and holding knowledge about 'the Moroccan' – the more mysterious, exotic and 'opposite-self' the persona of the writer, the better – determined and substantiated the positioning of these authors as skilful and authoritative storytellers within their communities of readers, as discussed in the Said-ian observation of 'Knowing the Oriental' (Said 1978: 31–48).

Along the history of the Pasha's story, some of the books written about him have been re-published over the years. Babin (1932) had a second edition published in 1934; Maxwell (1966), which was translated to French in 1968, has had a series of English re-issues, the last in 2012. However, the greatest wave of republications has been in Morocco since 1999. In that year Babin (1932) was translated into Arabic (Babin 1999), followed by new editions of Le Prévost (2013 [1968]) and of Maxwell's French version (2016 [1968]) – all reprinted in Morocco. The new editions were accompanied by new original Moroccan texts (El Glaoui 2004; Jebrou 2005; Benhadar 2010). Collectively, these demonstrate the astounding reawakening of al-Glaoui's tale in contemporary Morocco (this is discussed in detail in Chapter 8).

The 'voices' heard in these books, up to a point in common with national archival documents (see below), represent only a thin stratum of the social classes (in contrast to social media writers; Chapter 8). These are the voices of authors connected with the state – the colonial (Babin) or the post-colonial (Abdessadeq El Glaoui) – or those of professional journalists (Babin again, Janon, Le Prévost, Jebrou, and Berdugo during a certain phase of his life), playwrights (Benhadar) and novelists (Maxwell).

Comparing these books against archival documents highlights additional aspects. In the case of archives, it is a conventional wisdom that the perspectives of their documents are limited by measures of categorisation, silencing and control, embedded in the archival structure and enforced by various other aspects (see below). Much of this applies to books as well, but in a different manner. Apart from the a priori limited opportunity of one becoming a published author, there are also various forms of publication-related considerations that attach to the final outcome. In the cases studied here, these include marketing aspects dictated by publishers, or governmental censorship – as was the case with the banning, for a time, of Maxwell's book in Morocco (Chapter 6).

The censorship of published material was not enacted by institutional powers alone. As Maxwell reports, following the 1932 publication of Babin's *Son Excellence*, adjudged to have defamed the Pasha, al-Glaoui tried to make this book disappear in any possible way that he could – buying out the stock from the publishers and anyone who may have had a copy of it, stealing it from others, even burning houses in which he believed that the book was present (Maxwell 1966: 174–6). Whether a true account or a flight of fancy on Maxwell's part, this reveals something of how al-Glaoui was perceived. People were ready to accept that the Pasha was capable of acting this way; Maxwell, with his unique storyteller's skills, was attuned to his readers' eagerness for such stories, and propagated the apocryphal tale. The purported biblioclasm creates intertextual links with fifteenth- and sixteenth-century Iberian and Italian autos-da-fé and book burnings, in which Jewish and Muslim books were burnt (Raz-Karkotzkin 2005), and with Heinrich Heine's oft-quoted pronouncement: 'Where they burn books, they will ultimately burn people as well' (Heine 1908: 21). In Heine's play *Almansor*, the person who made this proclamation was a Muslim, referring to Christian acts; however, Maxwell's narrative transfers the action to a Muslim burning a Christian book. Al-Glaoui thus becomes an allegory for uncontrollable and primordial Oriental vindictive forces – which, by extension, could be understood as transferable from books to people. Such to-and-fro movements between authors, readers and connotations shape al-Glaoui's story as a never-ending narrative.

As my research for this book proceeded, it became clear that al-Glaoui, a highly influential Moroccan leader during the colonial period, should be seen not only as shaping local and regional circumstances, but also as affecting metropolitan realities while concurrently being shaped by them. The observation that colony and metropole should be treated as a single field of analysis is common to historiographies of the last few decades (for example, Said 1993; Cooper and Stoler 1997; Conklin 1997; Cannadine 2001). However, this view has recently been broadened; the current challenge for historians is to locate colonial histories within larger, global contexts (Burke 2014: 8). The call to global history reflects a rejection of previous points of observation, which tended to favour nation-state frameworks, monographs of specific locales, and micro-histories which ignored broader interdependencies. This new orientation seeks to transcend borders, studying an interconnected world in which things, people, ideas, capital, commodities and institutions are in constant flux and exchange (for example, Saunier and Iriye 2009; Chartier 2011: 8; Beckert 2015; Conrad 2016: 5; Schayegh 2017; Ram 2020).

Accordingly, the simultaneous discussion of the history of al-Glaoui and the history of his story, as components of a grander meta-history, occurs within multiple scales of observation: from micro-history (for example, Ginzburg 1980; Zemon Davis 1983), deriving historical insights from analysing al-Glaoui the person and his deeds, to global history, seeing al-Glaoui, the stories about him and their authors, as participants in global processes and productions. Such an approach makes it possible for global and micro-histories to reinforce each other (as practised, for example, by Bischoff 2017: 135–6; Robisheaux 2017: 4–5).

Al-Glaoui's life story forms the backbone of this book. But the book simultaneously explores the biographies of people who wrote about him. Studying biographies has recently gained momentum in historical research, to a degree that some have identified a current 'biographical turn' in historiography (Meister 2018: 2). This turn to biographies stems from the capacity of the form to reveal much, not only about their protagonists, but also about the world that they lived in, their interactions with others, and about micro- and macro-historical processes (Nora 1987; Levi 1989; Margadant 1996; Nasaw 2009). In recent historiography about Morocco, historical biographies are especially common. Daniel Schroeter (2002) builds his historical narrative on the life story of Meir Macnin; Susan Gilson Miller (2006) develops historical observations in charting the life of Moroccan scholar Muhammad as-Saffar, and later, those of Nelly Cazès Benatar (Miller 2021). Similarly, Sahar Bazzaz studies (2008; 2010) Muhammad bin Ja'far al-Kattani and Muhammad al-Kattani; Etti Terem (2014) works her inquiry around al-Mahdi al-Wazzani; Jessica Marglin (2016) develops historical insights from figures such as Shalom and Ya'akove Assaraf. This book takes the biographical turn a step further, investigating several interlacing biographies in sync. Beyond the grand life story, that of Thami al-Glaoui, it also investigates the biographies of the people who wrote about him: the French Paul Schoen and Gustave Babin, the British Gavin Maxwell, the Moroccan Albert Berdugo and Abdessadeq El Glaoui, and others. The stimulus for this kind of exploration is the idea that a broad view of all these figures, who were products, representatives and instruments of three empires – the Sharifian (Moroccan), the French and the British – and who were to witness a global transition to a post-imperial, decolonised, national world order, might enable a better appreciation of the history of al-Glaoui and of the ways in which it has been told. The simultaneous scrutiny of multiple biographies challenges political and cognitive limitations. By making it possible to discern patterns of thought crossing borders between people, countries, metropoles and colonies and creating comprehensive narratives and discourses, it shows global effects in action.

The Archive as a Storyteller

A large part of this research 'listens' to 'stories' collected in archives. The archives consulted were the Moroccan National Archives (Archives du Maroc); the French diplomatic archives at Nantes (Archives Diplomatiques de Nantes); the Quai d'Orsay archives (Archives du Quai d'Orsay); the British and the American National Archives; the French National Library's digital library, Gallica; and some smaller archives and collections.[3]

Stepping into these archives to locate and study stories about Thami al-Glaoui was a challenge, because they have been a priori shaped by measures of selection, exposition and restriction dictated by political and other considerations, and reflect a range of power relationships (as elaborated by, for example, Foucault 1972; Richards 1993; Derrida 1996; Hamilton et al. 2002; Stoler 2002; Kaplan 2002; Moore et al. 2017, and others). Records and documents pertaining to al-Glaoui were scattered among multiple domains and files. In some cases, these had been sealed for set periods; some of these limitations, fortunately, lapsed as the research progressed. My archival investigation, thus, sought to piece together a life story which had experienced a kind of 'explosion', its fragments scattered across numerous archival locations and folders.

Gathering the pieces in order to reconstruct a story was a meandering task, all the more so due to numerous insights accrued along the way about how such archival materials should be treated. Some post-colonial calls discredit the very institution of imperial archives, on the grounds that they have little to do with the lives of ordinary people (Clancy-Smith and Gouda 1998: 1–2). Others, on the contrary, claim that the deliberate neglect of colonial archives radically reduces legitimate points of view while attempting a social, political or historical analysis of previous colonies (Burke 1998: 7). Concomitantly, other perspectives, such as Laura Stoler's reading 'along the archival grain', propose that researchers also turn the gaze beyond the documents – onto the officials who created them, and to the 'epistemic anxieties' which might have guided their ways of thought and expression (Stoler 2002; 2009; Grangaud and Oualdi 2016: 150–1; Ouaknine-Yekutieli 2017).

With regard to al-Glaoui, studying the archives – and not just the texts and documents – led to important insights. While inquiring into how specific documents made their way into the archives, it became clear that a large measure of chance played a role in the order in which I was eventually to encounter them in the various national depositories. Documents relevant to al-Glaoui had accumulated across the colonial period in numerous protectorate offices in Morocco – unsurprising, given that his activities interacted with many branches of the administration (for example, Secrétariat general du protectorat; Direction des affaires politiques; Service des affaires indigène). Each of these offices archived its documents with varying degrees of consistency. Throughout the forty-four years of the French Protectorate (1912–56), periodic administrative reforms took place, during which some offices were merged while others were split. These organisational changes necessitated the transportation of boxes of archived documents between colonial offices across Morocco and Algeria – a risky operation, as far as the preservation of stacks of papers is concerned.

When Morocco eventually secured its independence in 1956, the separate archives of all the protectorate's divisions were transported to the French Embassy in Rabat. There, after several months of collection, the documents were split between France and Morocco. The material considered by the French as politically sensitive was sent to France, while that which was considered 'innocent' remained in Morocco. The decision concerning what to transfer and what not was sometimes influenced by practical considerations, such as the quality of the documents' storage – dossiers likely to fall apart were, on the whole, not removed (Heurtebise 2007). The evaluation of what was 'sensitive' mainly depended on the judgement of protectorate officials, who along the years had marked much of the paperwork they produced with stamps designating degrees of confidentiality and importance: 'Secret', 'Very Secret', 'Urgent', and so on, not unlike the patterns identified by Stoler in the Dutch Colonial Archive of Java (Stoler 2009: 27–8). These markings, originally intended to draw attention to specific issues, became the basis for the subsequent cataloguing of the documents, and their division between archives.

One such case, elaborated in Chapters 2 and 3, is that of French Indigenous Affairs officer Paul Schoen. As part of his training, in 1938 Schoen wrote a *mémoire* (equivalent to a MA thesis) about Thami al-Glaoui. Schoen marked his report as 'top secret' – and thus contributed to the future restrictive measures applied to it in the archives, which practically and allegorically added to the sense of intrigue surrounding the Pasha's story. Schoen explained his judgement by quoting his superiors' comment that 'too often the Pasha of Marrakesh appears to know what is said about his subject' (Schoen 1938: 1). But it may be assumed that a sense of 'documentary awareness' on Schoen's behalf was also involved – an assessment of how he would be judged or remembered when future readers evaluated his assessments.

Hence, the recording of al-Glaoui's documents in different offices, their subsequent division between countries and the secrecy that shrouded the archival processes relating to some of them all introduce a sense of mystery to the story of the man who, even before the creation of the archival depository, had managed to blur administrative and epistemological distinctions, and to create contradictory impressions.

The case of al-Glaoui portrays the degree to which the stages of sorting, combined with political judgement as well as randomness, has shaped the archival records in France and Morocco from which present historians seek to reconstruct aspects of the past. The officials who create the policy, and its memory – the distribution of the narrative in archives, the arguments and the place of the archivists – all form a part in the creation of a historical story, comparable to historiographic encounters and historic research. In a broader sense, these processes also add nuance to grasping certain aspects of the mechanisms of colonial modernity, and to gaining awareness as to how conceptions about them were shaped.

Beyond the national depositories, archives belonging to al-Glaoui and his apparatus would have been highly informative in my task. However, as far as I could tell, these were confiscated by the Moroccan government at independence, and have remained inaccessible since (Perrier 2017).[4] Some documents belonging to al-Glaoui were copied and subsequently published in books written by his former secretary Berdugo (1996), and by the Pasha's son, Abdessadeq El Glaoui (2004). But this selection is rather small.

On Loyalty and Betrayal: Telling the Story of Morocco's Greatest Pasha, Thami al-Glaoui

The book consists of nine chapters. The introduction and conclusion aside, each chapter deals with a discrete period in the life of al-Glaoui up until his death in 1956, or with a stage in the posthumous lifespan of his ongoing story to the present day. Each chapter also discusses a major work about al-Glaoui, written either during or about the period covered within the chapter. These discussions sometimes take the form of imagined dialogues exploring specific themes, between al-Glaoui and the authors of the publication in question, or between the authors of the publications themselves.

The ability to imagine such dialogues rests on the condition that telling al-Glaoui was often a tool used by authors to assert their claim to various issues, ranging from justice, loyalty, betrayal and truth, to colonialism, nationalism and *Amazighité*. These assertions of the authors, when juxtaposed against al-Glaoui's texts and deeds, supply the material and context necessary to construct virtual exchanges of views, ultimately allowing for a broader presentation of al-Glaoui, his worldview and his tale.

As the narrator of this book, I shape the discussions and conversations by juxtaposing each main publication against documents written by or about al-Glaoui, and with analyses of central events and discourses of each period, relevant historiographies and various features of storytelling. The complexity which ensues enables the extraction of al-Glaoui and the various authors' voices, thus permitting them to 'communicate' with each other on the relevant themes.

This choice, to present additional figures and their tales beyond the leading hero, reflects the constant evolution of al-Glaoui: not just as an individual, but also as a story made and told by other people, themselves reciprocally shaped by the act of telling him. Furthermore, the fact that these authors are not only Moroccan, but also French and British, emphasises al-Glaoui's hand in broad, global processes. Accordingly, the heroes of the book are, on the one hand, al-Glaoui and the authors who wrote about him, and on the other hand, the numerous stories generated and shaped in a process of constant creation. The two perspectives complement each other, calling attention to a protagonist who was sometimes silenced and who sometimes silenced others, and who is definitely underrated as a central pillar of Moroccan history.

Gavin Maxwell described the last moment of al-Glaoui's life as follows:

On the last morning, 30 January 1956, with his family united around him, he rallied himself and spoke with great lucidity. To *Caid* Brahim he said, 'Listen, my son, take care of your brothers, and our friends, and the people of our houses and our lands. Look after their interests to the very end. When you have an enemy, watch him – I've had plenty, and I know.' A quarter of an hour later he made his last effort and pronounced the *chahada*, the profession of faith, *La illa Lah Mohammed rassoul Allah* – 'There is no God but Allah and Mohammed is his Prophet.' Then the heavy eyelids closed, and he did not regain consciousness. The Lion of the Atlas, the Eagle of Telouet, the Black Panther, the Mountain Gazelle, the last of the Lords of the Atlas, died at 11.30 a.m. aged seventy-eight. (Maxwell 1966: 262–3)

This dying speech of al-Glaoui is almost certainly Maxwell's invention. Nevertheless, it has not been questioned by any reader up to now. Was it accepted because Maxwell was such a good storyteller, or because the expectation was that al-Glaoui indeed would have uttered such poetic last words? And if indeed it was invented and then accepted, how much of what we know of al-Glaoui (what we think we know) might similarly be the creation of storytellers and myth-makers? What indeed are the relationships between this story (and others) and the actions of the characters they describe? And, finally, what do such cases reveal about the relationship between story and history?

As we continue our story, we shall turn the gaze in the next chapter to the emergence of Thami al-Glaoui's figure and legend, and to the acquisition of the first motifs associated with him and with his telling thereafter. Continuing to use Maxwell's narrative as a trailer projected on to the screen, we shall rewind sixty-three years back from al-Glaoui's deathbed scene. The picture dissolves, and a windy, snow-capped, rugged mountainous landscape appears.

Notes

1. Personal communication.
2. The Amazigh (Berbers) are considered the indigenous population of North Africa.
3. Gallica is available at <https://gallica.bnf.fr/> (last accessed 17 August 2023). Other collections I consulted were Collection Dahan-Hirsch; Centre de la Culture Judéo-Marocaine, Brussels; Sidney Corcos's collection; and the Dov Noy Popular Story Archive in Israel.
4. Jean Lefévre reported, in May 1957, of the confiscation of 'very important' documents from al-Glaoui's palace, and explained that some documents were placed in the French archives, but remain unreachable. Centre des Archives diplomatiques de Nantes (henceforth CADN) file 1MA/282 100: 'Jean Lefévre: l'occupation du palais de l'ancien pacha aurait permis le saisie de documents importants', 3 May 1957.

2

A Loyal Servant of Two Empires

Mountain Rescue in the Atlas

Gavin Maxwell's *Lords of the Atlas* (1966; see Chapter 6 for more about the book and author) – the starting point for many non-Moroccans of their acquaintance with Thami al-Glaoui – describes the 1890s kick-off of the Glaoui brothers' astonishing rise to power with the following tale:

> In that autumn of 1893, when what little remained of the Sultan's army was struggling upward through the snows under a canopy of ravens and vultures and with a rearguard of jackals and hyenas . . . Madani and Thami al-Glaoui heard of the approach of the defeated Sultan's army . . . Madani, having called upon his tribespeople for their ultimate resources, wanted no misunderstanding. The Sultan must be welcomed, and welcomed as he would wish . . . inside five hours he [the Sultan] and his army were installed at Telouet . . . an endless banquet at which course succeeds course . . . long after the guests can eat no more, lasted all through the night . . . By some unguessable means Madani found the resources to prolong this situation for several days, while the Sultan recovered his strength . . . On the day before the imperial *ḥarka* struck camp and set out for Marrakesh, the Sultan showed his gratitude. He made Madani his personal *khalifa*, or representative in the region, giving him nominal command of all the tribes between the High Atlas and the Sahara, and the *caidat* of Tafilelt itself. Of infinitely greater significance, he made him a present of a considerable quantity of modern arms and ammunition. The exact amount of this armoury it is now difficult to establish, but it included the 77mm bronze Krupp

cannon, the only single heavy weapon in all Morocco outside the imperial Chareefian Army. (Maxwell 1966: 47–50)

Bathed in an aura of Oriental glamour, the scenery of the Atlas Mountains, and the 'barbaric' blend of inherent generosity and brutality, the literary topos of 'Thami al-Glaoui as rescuer' emerges for the first time – in this early case while he operates as his older brother Madani's deputy in rescuing the Sultan's exhausted convoy. From that event on, historiographies about al-Glaoui returned, time and again, to the theme of the loyal servant coming to his lord's rescue in moments of peril. This topos, which cuts across different contexts and times, recurs as a basic motif in tales sympathetic to al-Glaoui – and likewise as a point for his antagonists to refute.

The excerpt from Maxwell introduces additional elements that recur in subsequent narratives: the Moroccan court and its intricate relationships with the local *qa'ids*; southern Morocco's harsh landscape; foreign intervention in the country; and a generous measure of Oriental décor. This paragraph projects all these elements on the faraway mountain pass of Tizi n' Telouet,[1] 70km south-east of Marrakesh and 2485m above sea level (Figure 2.1).

Tizi n' Telouet and the mountain range around it was controlled by the Glaoua, one of many Amazigh tribes living in the High Atlas (El Glaoui 2004: 10; al-Buzidi 2010; El Glaoui 2017: 26–7, 31–2). The tribe had served the 'Alawi court from at least the time of Mawlay Isma'il (1672–1727),[2] who bestowed the patronym Mézouar upon 'Abd al-Sadeq al-Glaoui, the chief of the tribe in his time.[3] The Glaoua maintained a good relationship with the court throughout the eighteenth and nineteenth centuries, while simultaneously controlling the surrounding area and tribes on behalf of the *makhzen*.[4]

In the nineteenth century, Mohamed al-Mézouari al-Glaoui was nominated *qa'id* by Mawlay 'Abd al-Rahman (1822–59). The appointment was reaffirmed by his successors, Mawlay Mohammed IV (1859–73) and Mawlay Hassan I (1873–94). When Mohamed al-Glaoui died in 1886, Madani, his eldest son, succeeded him as chief. Across this era, the family accumulated significant wealth from the taxes they collected at the mountain pass – a major route channelling the Saharan trade into western Morocco – and from their control of regional salt mines (El Glaoui 2004: 7–13; al-Buzidi 2010: 87–9; El Glaoui 2017: 60–5).

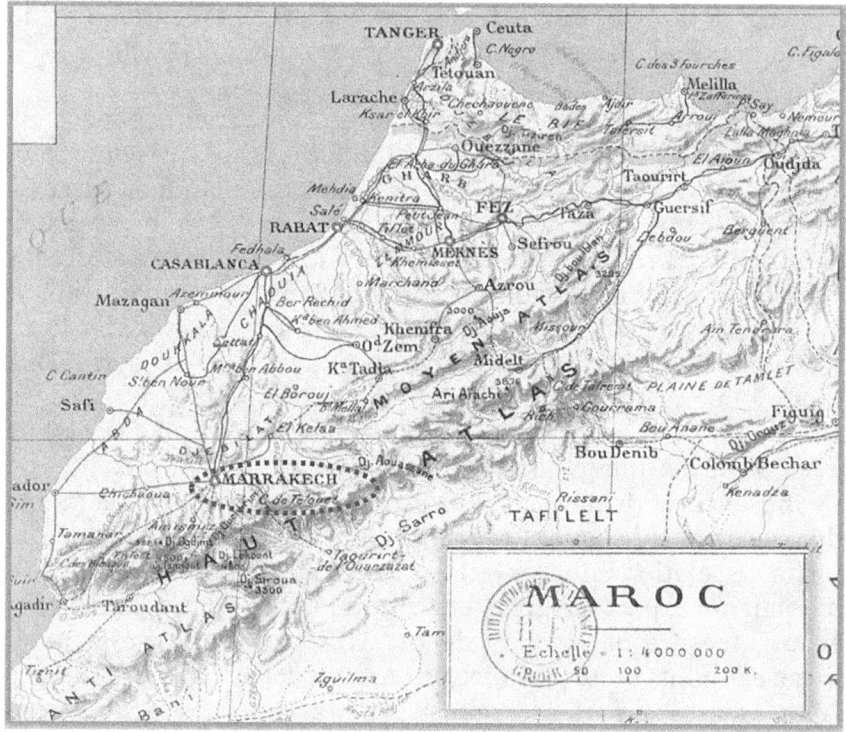

Figure 2.1 Map of Morocco, 1930. Marrakesh and Tizi n' Telouet (C. de Telouet) are marked with an ellipse. Modifications have been made to the original image.
Courtesy: Bibliothèque nationale de France (henceforth, BnF).

In 1893, the year in which the rescue story unfolded, the charismatic Sultan Mawlay Hassan I (1857–94; r. 1873–94) had attempted to consolidate and reorganise the Sharifian Empire. He was confronted with numerous challenges: Europeans, and especially the French, encroaching on his territory; a significant national debt, due to long years of European manipulation and inefficient tax collection; rebellious tribes; and occasional droughts. Nevertheless, he pushed forward with the reform programme initiated by his father, Mawlay Mohammed IV (al-Nasiri 1954; Touzani 1979; Afa 1983; al-'Arabi 1989; al-Bazaz 1992; Ben Srhir 2005: 206–59). As part of this endeavour, he reorganised the empire's administration and reinforced his army, personally travelling around Morocco accompanied by a huge armed *mahalla* (convoy) in order to exercise his sovereignty – a performance of magnificent generosity, edged with a show of power that the local tribes could not resist (Nordman 1980–81; Rivet 2012: 292). As he travelled across his country, Mawlay Hassan gave away presents, nominated *qaʾids* (Goundafi 2013: 26–7, 31) and delegated some measure of sovereignty to his subjects. The last was on the condition that they remained loyal to the court, transferred taxes to the *makhzen*, and that they send troops to support him in times of emergency (Pennell 2000: 98–100). The practice of granting territorial rights to multiple *qaʾids* might have been used to maintain a certain degree of competition and rivalry between the *qaʾids*, who would in turn uphold the ruler's dominance (Gottreich 2016: 230).

In 1893, Mawlay Hassan's *mahalla* approached the High Atlas, on its way back from the Sahara after a particularly demanding voyage. The journey had taken its toll on the Sultan's health. According to the story, as the *mahalla* progressed, Madani al-Glaoui sent out a convoy to meet it at Ferkla, some distance from Telouet. According to Paul Schoen (1938: 16–17), Madani placed 100 camels and as many mules at the Sultan's disposal, then accompanied the royal convoy for twenty-five days (note that such numbers are a common literary code for indicating a large measure (Stewart 2018), thus signalling a storytelling pattern rather than an attempt for accuracy). Clearly, Madani invested a lot – or, it is told that he spent a lot – on this splendid opportunity to host the Sultan.

According to the tale, the highlight of the encounter was a reception hosted by Madani at Telouet, where the Sultan and his entourage rested for several days. One can assume that during his stay at Telouet, Mawlay Hassan would have made the acquaintance of Madani's fifteen-year-old brother, who was assisting in organising the complex reception while attentively learning the art of leadership and obedience. This young man was Thami al-Glaoui, protagonist of this volume.

Forty years after the publication of Maxwell's book, pro-monarchical Moroccan historian ʿAbdelkarim Filali provided a much less dramatic version of the same event,[5] inserting for good measure a somewhat derogatory description of the brothers' roots:

> Al-Glaoui was a Tasawati in origin, the name deriving from the Tasawat valley, from which his father departed after he was a shepherd ... He and his people were chased by the strong hatred in the region towards those who were called

the Haratin.[6] They moved to Telouet near the valley of Zu'aitar, to where they fled after suffering from the harassment of the Sanhaja Berbers who were still looking at the coloured Haratins with a look of ignorance and contempt ... He [Madani] was nominated for this post because he guided the royal convoy ascending from Tafilalet on the road to Marrakesh after it lost its way, and when asked to which people he belongs, he answered: Glaoui. After asking for his affiliation, the chief leader [Mawlay Hassan] nominated him to the sheikh of the people to whom he belonged. (Filali 2006: vol. 11, 283–4)[7]

According to the popular versions of the story, towards the end of his stay the Sultan expressed his gratitude and trust in Madani, twenty-seven years old at that time. He re-declared him his *khalifa* (deputy) for the Todgha, Tafilalet and Feija areas,[8] granted him control of the fertile Tazert region, and presented him with a Krupp cannon and a supply of ammunition (Schoen 1938: 16–17).

This cannon has come to occupy a special status in stories about this encounter. Not all the narrators necessarily position it in terms of a token of gratitude. For example, Paul Pascon (1981) suggests that the Sultan left it at Telouet due to the difficulties involved in transporting it in winter, as he had done with another cannon left with the *qa'id* of Demnat.[9] The expectation was that he would recover both cannons at a later time. But due to his untimely death, the Sultan never did retrieve his cannons.

Whatever the reason for leaving the Krupp cannon with Madani, the significance that this anecdote gained far exceeded the weapon's firepower. Boum and Park (2016: 207) propose that the cannon's real impact was as a symbol of power. This symbolism was probably well propagated throughout the High Atlas at the time, attaining worldwide recognition when it became a motif of later tales about al-Glaoui (for example, Maxwell 1966: 47–50; Le Prévost 1968: 20; Pandolfo 1997: 215; Yasin 2003: 8–9; El Glaoui 2004: 12; Porch 2005: 162; Lahnite 2011: 83; El Glaoui 2017: 66). In these later narrations of the encounter, the cannon signified the shift in the status of the Glaoua: from a remote mountainous tribe to a powerful entity intimately linked to the *makhzen*.

Considering the Krupp cannon anecdote from other perspectives affords additional interpretations. A German-made cannon left in a remote Moroccan *qsar* – and one made by a leading artillery manufacturer of the time (Grant 2007: 10) – underscores the global aspect of the Tizi n' Telouet encounter. While but a single weapon, its story fuses elements of Moroccan, German, French and British histories.

Unlike the long-departed participants in the encounter, the famous but rather small cannon still exists. It was deposited in 1938 at Kasba Taourirt in Ouarzazate (Schoen 1938: 17), where it has been on display ever since. The still visible serial number of the cannon makes it possible to locate the weapon's records in the Krupp archives in Germany. A short entry indicates that it was 'the third of a batch of seven 8,7 cm field cannons L/24'[10] sold to Morocco in 1884.

But to gain a better impression of the Tizi n' Telouet encounter, one must go even further back in time. Upon his accession in 1873, and having witnessed his predecessors' military defeats at Isly (1844) and Tetouan (1860), Mawlay Hassan decided to modernise his military. This action was a part of a discourse and engagement in reform that encompassed much more than the military, also taking in the Moroccan intellectual and religious circles of the time (Harakat 1994; El Mansour 1996: 54; Terem 2014: 51–6). In practical terms, this was a process that reverberated throughout the Islamic world, from the Ottoman Empire and Iran in the east to the Sharifian Empire in the west (İnalcik 1976; Shaw and Shaw 1977; Enayat 2013; Rubin 2017: 1–2; McDougall 2018).

Mawlay Hassan dispatched ambassadors to Europe to purchase the most up-to-date weapons, and to organise military training for his new army. Select Moroccan cadets were sent to study in European military schools, and hundreds of soldiers set out to Gibraltar to be trained under British officers (Ben Srhir 2005: 247–64). Mawlay Hassan also handpicked Harry Aubrey de Vere Maclean, a retired Scottish officer, to lead the ongoing instruction of his Moroccan soldiers on their return home. Maclean proved to be so successful in this role that he remained in the Sultan's service until the latter's death (1894) and continued to serve his successor Mawlay 'Abd al-'Aziz until 1907 (Ben Srhir 2005: 259; Filali 2006: vol. 5, 399).

Besides being a military instructor, Maclean was also a liaison between the Moroccan and British courts – and, in effect, a British agent operating in Morocco (Ruxton 2018: 306). He learnt Arabic, was granted the rank of *qa'id askari* (military commander) and became known in the Moroccan court as Qa'id Harry Maclean (Stearn 2006). Wearing the Moroccan army's uniform, he joined Mawlay Hassan's frequent *mahallas*, and was probably present at the Tizi n' Telouet rescue incident as well (Maxwell 1966: 39).

Manoeuvring between the European powers trying to manipulate the situation for their own benefit via their consuls and agents, Mawlay Hassan I purchased weapons from multiple sources: Belgium, Italy, France, Britain and Germany, as well as the United States (Ben Srhir 2005: 247–64). The Krupp cannon, emblematic of the rise of the Glaouis, was a part of this acquisition's spree.

Hence, the basic ingredients of the tales subsequently told about al-Glaoui merged at Telouet in the winter of 1893: generosity and domination, intricate relationships between the court and local elites, European military involvement and colonialist aspirations, winds of reform, and the fierce forces of nature. These are incorporated within the grander global 'stories' of the time, thoroughly described and analysed by academic constructs such as dependency theory (for example, Baran 1957; Ghosh 2017), colonial modernity (for example, Barlow 1993; 1997), Orientalism (for example, Said 1978), and the analysis of imperialism (for example, Said 1993; Cooper and Stoler 1997).

The Dramatic Arc

Shortly after leaving his hosts at Tizi n' Telouet, Mawlay Hassan died unexpectedly (1894). Because the accession to the throne of his fourteen-year-old son, Mawlay 'Abd al-'Aziz, had the potential to trigger a severe dynastic struggle, chief minister Ba-Ahmed Ben Musa took control of the government, immediately suppressing all resistance. He ruled Morocco as regent on behalf of Mawlay 'Abd al-'Aziz for six years, directing his efforts towards preserving the administrative apparatus and suppressing tribal revolts (Abun Nasr 1987: 306; Filali 2006: vol. 5, 397–404).

Mawlay 'Abd al-'Aziz eventually acceded to the throne in 1900. He was immediately confronted by a series of problems: French incursions into Moroccan territory, the failure of his own reform programme,[11] and a growing economic crisis (Bentaleb 2004; Lahnite 2011: 28). Despite his attempts to ground his decisions via numerous consultations, such as with the Fes Council of

Notables (al-Khadimi 1986; Terem 2014: 44–9), his efforts failed. To make things worse, in the autumn of 1902 a full-scale revolt, named the Bouhmara Revolt, after its leader, erupted in the Rif Mountains of northern Morocco. The revolt was to last almost seven years (Bekraoui 1980; Khalufi 1993).

As part of the pact between the court and the great *qa'id*s of the south (in addition to the Glaouis, these also included Taïeb Goundafi, Abd al-Malek Ben Mohamed al-M'tougui and Miloud Ben al-Hachmi al-Ayadi), Madani and Thami al-Glaoui were often called upon, with their troops, to assist in fighting rebellious tribes (Bentaleb 2019: 88). In 1902, they were summoned to confront Bouhmara (El Glaoui 2004: 7–13; El Glaoui 2017: 75–81). However, ʿAbd al-ʿAziz's army suffered repeated defeats. The Glaoua did not evade this fate: despite Thami's personal distinction in the battlefields, they were overpowered and had to be evacuated by sea, on a French boat that took them from Oran to Tangier (Figure 2.2; Vaffier 1917; Schoen 1938: 82). Glaoua leader Madani was injured in these skirmishes. On his return to his territory near Marrakesh, he was further embittered by the realisation that he would not be rewarded by Mawlay ʿAbd al-ʿAziz for his loyal support and personal sacrifice. This disappointment was aggravated when the neighbouring *qa'id*, Taïeb Goundafi, was compensated for the costs he had incurred in the course of the same war (Goundafi 2013: 40). Accordingly, Madani changed course and began to plot against the young sultan (Schoen 1938: 24; Abun-Nasr 1987: 310; El Glaoui 2017: 80; Bentaleb 2019). In future narratives – especially the anti-al-Glaoui ones – this course of action was understood to attest to the brothers' supposed trait of being inveterate 'conspirators' (Goundafi 2013: 43). As the Sultan's army crashed to defeat, the French continued to raid territories in the south and east of Morocco. These actions intimidated other European powers, at the time at the climax of their Scramble for Africa (Chamberlain 2013), leading to swift political action in Europe. A series of inter-European summits led to agreements validating French penetration into Morocco, in exchange for concessions to the other colonial powers elsewhere. France signed bilateral pacts with Italy (1900), Spain (1904) and Germany (1909 and 1911), and the *Entente Cordiale* with Britain in 1904, all guaranteeing French hegemony in Moroccan affairs. Particularly significant was the Algeciras Agreement of 1906,[12] which increased European economic and political power in Morocco and weakened Sultan Mawlay ʿAbd al-ʿAziz, who was

Figure 2.2 Thami al-Glaoui hosting Ernest Vaffier, who arranged the evacuation of the Glaoui brothers and their troops from Oran to Tangier in 1903 (Vaffier 1917: 28). Modifications have been made to the original image.
Courtesy: Bibliothèque de l'Institut national d'histoire de l'art, Jacques Doucet collections, 174 U 1.

rapidly losing support in his own country (Chamberlain 2013: 83–4; al-Karuri and Sadeq 2016).

Local rivals frustrated by regal indifference to their efforts in the Bouhmara Revolt and by other issues related to the tax reforms – particularly the Glaoui brothers – approached the Sultan's brother, Mawlay 'Abd al-Hafidh, and asked him to lead a popular revolt. 'Abd al-Hafidh agreed; in 1908 he was declared the new sultan by the *ulama* (scholars of Islamic law and religion) of Marrakesh. Immediately upon his ascension to the throne, he proclaimed a jihad against the French. In the ensuing struggle between 'Abd al-'Aziz and 'Abd al-Hafidh, which lasted a few months, the former was abandoned by the remnants of his army and was forced to abdicate (Abun-Nasr 1987: 312; Bentaleb 2019).

While events were unfolding on the ground, historiography and storytelling were taking shape. From his deposition onwards, 'Abd al-'Aziz was described by many narrators as a spoiled child who, despite genuine goodwill, had been tricked into wasting huge sums of money on personal follies (for example, Galland 1913: 120–1; Harris 1921; Filali 2006: vol. 5, 397–404). For many Europeans, this image was a useful signifier for all Moroccans, and was consequently adopted as another justification for colonial action. If the Moroccans and their sultan were acting like children, then a chaperone was needed. As stated by Gabriel Galland (1913) in *Le Maroc: un empire qui se réveille*,

> With the most limited foresight, the Moroccan is just the man of the moment: the past does not leave deep traces in his memory, and the future hardly concerns him. Have we not seen Sultan Abd-el-Aziz sacrifice his throne to his passion for European amusements which plunged his compatriots into indescribable stupor? (Galland 1913: 120)

French colonial storytelling propagated a notion of a Moroccan decline, which could only be repaired by European intervention (much like the contemporaneous Orientalist discourse on the decline of the Ottoman Empire; Kafadar 1997–8). This rationale would be reversed a few decades later by other storytellers, however. French colonialism, which explained itself as rescuing Morocco from pre-colonial decadence, came to be presented in post-colonial discourse (see Chapters 4 and 5) as 'the decadence' which Moroccan nationalists should set out to abolish. Hence, the motif of 'rescue from' became the cornerstone of multiple narrations. Each narrative adopted the image of 'the saviour' to promote its own heroes. A similar literary script was applied to recounting the French colonial empire, the Moroccan nationalist movement and the deeds of individuals like the Glaoui brothers.

Simultaneously with the evolution of these meta-narratives, Thami al-Glaoui's story was receiving its first brushstrokes. From a storytelling perspective, the clock started to tick with the 1908 overthrow of Sultan 'Abd al-'Aziz, an act which signalled the onset of the dramatic rise of the Glaoui tale's arc. In this screenplay, the arc's climax arrived in 1956 when al-Glaoui gained the necessary power to trigger the much grander dethroning of a legitimate sultan – which, inevitably, led to his own downfall. In this framework, storytellers recounting al-Glaoui's tale from the mid-1950s onwards marked the deposition of 1908 as a prophecy to be fulfilled: having done it once, he will do it again (Le Prévost 2013 [1968]: 284; Berdugo 1996: 104).

The Wily Wardens

Madani al-Glaoui played an active role in proclaiming Mawlay 'Abd al-Hafidh as the new ruler. This time, he was promptly rewarded by being nominated to war minister and Grand Vizier (El Glaoui 2017: 95–107). Nationalist Moroccan historian 'Abdelkarim Filali described this event thus: 'Mawlay 'Abd al-Hafidh had taken Madani . . . as a hunting device and as a door-guard to chase dogs and thieves' (Filali 2006: vol. 11, 283).

Filali, like Maxwell forty years before, uses animals as metaphors to emphasise his point (for such literary uses, see Baker 1993: 4–5). Here, the Glaoui brothers are portrayed as chasing away predatory (and impure) animals trying to harm their masters: dogs for Filali, ravens, vultures, jackals and hyenas in Maxwell's case (1966: 47). Regardless of the tone – loathing in Filali, appreciative in Maxwell – each rhetoric depicts the brothers as those who 'clear the way' for their masters. However, the dramatic sense is intensified because the animal metaphor subtly implies that they themselves were also no more than tamed beasts – superficially loyal, but capable of treachery.

In Mawlay 'Abd al-Hafidh's round of new appointments, Thami, by then thirty years old, was appointed Pasha of Marrakesh. Hammou, Madani's brother-in-law, became the governor of the territories south of the Atlas. Thus, by 1909, the Glaouis were inching closer to the central orbit of Moroccan political life. Such a repositioning also brought about intermarriages. Madani married Lalla Zineb, the daughter of al-Mokri, a chief *makhzeni* and later the Grand Vizier of Morocco throughout the protectorate period (1912–56). Zineb's sister was wed to Sultan 'Abd al-Hafidh, who also married one of Madani's daughters, Lalla Rebia (Arnaud 1952: 245; El Glaoui 2004: 7–13, 95). Thus, the Glaouis reached a status by which they became committed to the *makhzen* by way of blood ties too.[13]

'Abd al-Hafidh managed to gain broad popular support by promoting an uncompromising stand against the European encroachment and espousing armed struggle. In its first stages, the Hafidiyya, as the new regime was called, seemed successful. The Sultan suppressed the Bouhmara Revolt, created a new *makhzen* in collaboration with the High Atlas leaders, and began to re-establish governmental authority in the peripheral regions. However, as time passed, his relationship with Madani al-Glaoui worsened (El Glaoui 2017: 107–16). After the mishandling of an Amazigh uprising, and under pressure from the French, the Sultan removed the Glaoui brothers from their posts and proclaimed another *qa'id* – Goundafi – as his representative in the south. These actions once again set the brothers against the ruling monarch (Schoen 1938: 30; Maxwell 1966: 104–21; El Glaoui 2017: 116–33; Bentaleb 2019: 91).

According to historian Richard Pennell, Madani's response to his removal by the Sultan was a whisper: 'He has dropped me. May God drop him' (Pennell 2000: 151). The wish materialised very quickly. In 1911, the French army continued its advances in south-eastern Morocco, with Spain invading in the north. Given the dire situation, 'Abd al-Hafidh had no choice but to follow in his deposed brother's footsteps and sign new loan agreements with European powers to fund efforts to reinvigorate his army and administration. These loans were accompanied by the signing of a treaty with France and Spain in 1911, which included some punitive clauses for Morocco. Concomitantly, the popular support that the Sultan had enjoyed evaporated. The demanding months of jihad increased tensions between the government and the tribes, with the renewed cycles of tax collection further exacerbating these (al-Khadimi 2009).

At the beginning of 1912, tribes around Fes rebelled against the *makhzen*'s tax collectors and the military reform, and they besieged the city. The French sent a task force to Fes, ostensibly to support the Sultan and protect the city's European residents. In such circumstances, with central Morocco practically taken over by the French, 'Abd al-Hafidh had no choice but to sign the Treaty of Fes (1912), which transformed the *makhzen* into a French protectorate. As if that were not enough, a few months later 'Abd al-Hafidh was forced to leave Morocco, succeeded by his brother Mawlay Youssef (Abun Nasr 1987: 313; Gershovich 2000: 55–8; Wyrtzen 2015: 21–2).

Marrakesh: Another Rescue

Soon after his appointment, Mawlay Youssef restored the Glaoui brothers to their respective pre-coup positions. Madani was again *qa'id* of large territories in the south, while Thami returned to his post as the Pasha of Marrakesh (Schoen 1938: 30–1). However, large regions in the south were displeased with the French takeover. Fierce opposition consolidated under Mawlay Ahmed al-Hiba, son of the late Ma' al-'Aynayn, who had been one of the fiercest fighters against the European colonisation of Morocco and the Western Sahara (Ma' al-'Aynayn 2005). Al-Hiba, who declared himself the legitimate sultan, created alliances with tribes disadvantaged by the transition of power to Mawlay Youssef, and managed to take control of the Anti-Atlas region. From this power base, he marched on Marrakesh in 1912, where he received homage from all local leaders, including the Glaoui brothers (Schoen 1938: 32–3).

The French could not tolerate such insubordination. Announcing a mission to rescue six French citizens trapped in Marrakesh during al-Hiba's takeover, a military column led by General Mangin approached the city. The advancing column clashed with al-Hiba's forces en route, succeeding in driving them away. Noting the changing fortunes, many local qa'ids swiftly switched their alliances from al-Hiba to the French. In the ensuing drama, another narrative of loyalty and rescue wove itself into the story of Thami al-Glaoui.

It would seem that when al-Hiba captured Marrakesh, Thami al-Glaoui hid in his palace the six French citizens whom Mangin had set out to rescue (Schoen 1938: 35–8). Some commentators after the fact, such as Gustave Babin, questioned the veracity of this story, claiming that al-Glaoui had made it up in order to win the favour of the French authorities (Babin 1934: 45–58). Babin's allegation, it should be noted, was a part of a broader campaign against al-Glaoui. Although the next chapter is dedicated to describing and analysing this conflict, al-Glaoui's response to this specific allegation is worth mentioning here, because it marks out the place that rescue stories gradually acquired in the discourses appended to him.

In his debate with Babin, al-Glaoui not only vowed that his version of the rescue at Marrakesh was truthful; he also claimed that a few years earlier, he and his brother had rescued another French citizen. Al-Glaoui was referring to an incident from the pre-protectorate period, and the kidnap of the French explorer Marquis de Segonzac in southern Morocco (Zimmerman 1905: 285). Al-Glaoui claimed that after a few days of uncertainty regarding the fate of the missing Marquis, he and Madani had located him, successfully negotiating his release with his kidnappers.[14]

Paul Schoen, a French officer of the Bureau of Indigenous Affairs, supported al-Glaoui's account of the Marrakesh event, contra Babin's. Moreover, he added that two other Moroccan notables – Milud Ben al-Hachemi al-ʿAyadi and Driss Ould Menou – also helped in the rescue of the French prisoners, and in supporting the forces of General Mangin generally.

A special note should be made of the first of these two, al-ʿAyadi (1880–1964). Al-ʿAyadi was the leader of the Rhamna tribe throughout the colonial period (Iburki 2000). His biography shares striking similarities with al-Glaoui's, albeit without quite reaching the opulence of the latter. The similarities between the two, along with the fact that their territories converged, led to al-ʿAyadi being presented in various narratives almost as al-Glaoui's mirror image or 'doppelgänger', a common trope in the literary terminology.[15] From the literary point of view, because the two resembled each other so much, their appearances together in certain scenes tended to emphasise the importance of these scenes. Al-ʿAyadi's appearances in al-Glaoui's narratives, hence, can be considered as an imaginary signpost, with the directions: take heed, something important in the plot occurs here. The Marrakesh rescue was the first of such instances.

After discovering that many of the *qaʾid*s had left him, al-Hiba fled Marrakesh. As the French column approached, Thami al-Glaoui ventured out of the city, heading a delegation of notables dispatched to welcome General Mangin. Accepting al-Glaoui's support and thanking him for protecting the French subjects, Mangin validated his position as the Pasha of Marrakesh, similarly confirming Madani's status as the *qaʾid* of the areas south and east of the Atlas (Abun Nasr 1987: 370–1; Pennell 2000: 149–50).

The rescue story of the French citizens, which resonates with the Tizi n' Telouet rescue anecdote that opens this chapter, reinforced the Thami al-Glaoui's image – a trustworthy vassal, ready to venture forth gallantly to rescue his lords if called upon. This recurring theme cuts across virtually his entire life, both in his actual deeds and in the fictions created by or about him. The adjectives 'loyal' and 'trustworthy' – together with their antonyms – became essential elements in the characterisation of Thami al-Glaoui in the texts to come.

In the context of the 1910s, the concept of 'rescue' had additional significance extending beyond al-Glaoui and his public persona. As noted earlier, this was deeply embedded in the discourse of the period, serving as a driving force for military and political action. The French citizens caught up in Marrakesh provided a pretext for General Mangin's campaign – which, in addition to their rescue, created an opportunity to assert French sovereignty. This campaign practically replicated the French military action in Fes a year earlier (May 1911). This was initiated ostensibly as an expedition to rescue French subjects trapped in that city, but in fact was intended to capture Fes, Meknes and Rabat, and ultimately to enable the establishment of the protectorate.

The concept was even broader, however. As discussed above, one key justification by the French for their *mission civilisatrice* was that their conquests were in fact intended to save millions of Africans and Asians from barbarism, decadence, tyranny and disease (Conklin 1997: 1–10). Thus, the *mission civilisatrice* was more than a strategy – it was also a way of narrating a story. As such, the rescuer image that became appended to al-Glaoui was but one part of a wider contemporary dialectic in which all sides – Moroccan and French – were deeply invested. Being 'a rescuer' became the literary detergent used to launder other acts, and a basic motif in al-Glaoui's characterisation.

Theatricalising the Self

Concurrently with the consolidation of al-Glaoui's image, there was another figure operating on the same stage cultivating the multiple attributes that would be connoted with it in contemporaneous and subsequent narratives: Marshal Hubert Lyautey, France's first Resident-General of Morocco. Lyautey's historiographic impact was so significant that a mere five years after his appointment to command the newly established protectorate, his actions were already considered part of a well-thought-out project, dubbed *la méthode Lyautey*. Lyautey's 'method' involved a constant combination of politics and power. He retained the Sultan, his government, and local hierarchies; but he also restricted their powers, simultaneously 'pacifying' the country. Presented as the establishment of law and order, this 'pacification' was a euphemism for military takeover (Bernard 1917; Rivet 1996; Puyo 2012: 86).

Lyautey's method envisioned a double division of Moroccan society. The first was between Arabs and Amazighs; the second between the so-called *bled siba*, 'the land of dissidence' mostly populated by Amazighs, and *bled makhzen*, the land under central government rule, which had a larger Arab population.

Lyautey and his administration made the calculation that the Amazighs would become natural allies of the French if they were cut off from the Arabs and from 'Islamic fanaticism' (Slavin 1998: 131–2; Guerin 2011). To rally the Amazighs to his cause, Lyautey enacted to so-called 'Berber policy', intended to nudge the Amazighs to surrender to the *dawla*, the protectorate administration, rather than to the Moroccan *makhzen* (Burke 2014: 137–9). Concurrently, he promoted a rule by which 'Berber law' and practice were given precedence over the *Shari'a* (Islamic law; see Chapter 3) in Amazigh areas, and he pressed the Sultan to publish an edict upholding the Amazigh right to an independent judiciary system.

Within this setting, the Glaoui brothers must have seemed like a trump card to Lyautey. Not only did they rescue French hostages; they were also *bled siba* Amazigh leaders who had demonstrated their willingness – and ability – to defy Arab authority as personified by the previous sultans.

Lyautey met the brothers a couple of months after General Mangin's triumphant entry into Marrakesh, when he arrived in the city to greet the French troops and local notables. On that occasion, he awarded each brother the title of Officier de la Légion d'honneur, in recognition of their assistance in the Marrakesh rescue affair (Schoen 1938: 38–40, 101). French historiography hailed this act and praised Lyautey's wisdom, describing the event thus: 'By delicate attention, General Lyautey gave his own cross to Si Madani, and Colonel Mangin his own to Al Hadj Thami' (Cornet 1914: 82).

In the succeeding years, the links between Thami al-Glaoui and the Resident-General strengthened. Lyautey showered medals and honours upon al-Glaoui, who reciprocated with gifts and routine congratulations on the Christian New Year and 14 July (Bastille Day).[16] Beyond honours, al-Glaoui became the main supporter of the French in their pacification of southern Morocco (see below). He also personally assisted Lyautey in a number of initiatives, such as the establishment of a military school for the children of local notables in Meknes in the early 1920s (Gershovich 1992: 233).[17] Lyautey, for his part, helped al-Glaoui with various personal issues, such as arranging special schooling for his sons,[18] and assistance in securing housing for his extended family.[19]

It did happen that Lyautey had cause to rebuke al-Glaoui on occasion, such as when the latter paid an unauthorised visit to the deposed and exiled Sultan Mawlay 'Abd al-Hafid.[20] However, such events did not harm the relations between the two. Years later, after Lyautey's death, al-Glaoui demonstrated his most sincere appreciation to the first Resident-General by participating in a drive to fund monuments dedicated to his memory in Morocco.[21]

Al-Glaoui's actions suggest that Lyautey became a role model with respect to at least some aspects of his conduct, such as in the realm of public relations. Historian Paul Rabinow illustrates Lyautey's outstanding expertise in this domain, commenting that his

> 'mise-en-forme' (fashioning) of all aspects of life – from his dress, to his marriage, to his home, to his team, to the architectural forms of the protectorate – was orchestrated with increasing agility and desperation. Lyautey had integrated a theatricality of self, work, authority, and order into his political strategy. (Rabinow 1989: 284)

Al-Glaoui followed suit.

Never Truly at Home: Paul Schoen's Narration of al-Glaoui

A *mission civilisatrice* couched in scientific knowledge was the keystone for the French colonial endeavour in general, and for promoting the policies in Morocco in particular. From their arrival in North Africa, the French gathered immense data about the area, disseminating this across numerous publications. This corpus included descriptions of the country and its inhabitants from ethnologic, ethnographic and folkloristic perspective (for example, Beylié 1909; Bernard 1921; Montagne 1924; Bel 1938; Marçais 1946). Complementing this 'cultural colonialism' (see Said 1978; Cooper and Stoler 1997; Conklin 1997), multiple Arabic texts were translated into French and made available to a broad public of European researchers and readers (Burke 2014).

The French academic project in Morocco, which began early in the twentieth century with the Mission scientifique du Maroc (Scientific Mission of Morocco) in Tangier, was intensified under Lyautey. Upon his appointment, he decided to move the mission to Rabat, and to shift its focus to the study of the Amazighs. Accordingly, the Comité d'études Berbères (Committee of

Berber Studies) was founded in 1915, and began to publish an academic journal, *Les Archives Berbères*. The new institution covered Amazigh ethnography and history as well as the study of Amazigh languages, and soon became instrumental in shaping the 'Berber policy' (Burke 1972: 195–6; 2014: 133–6; Lahnite 2011: 101–75). In 1920, Lyautey established the Institut des hautes études Marocains (Institute of Higher Moroccan Studies). In addition to publications, the institute also developed a training curriculum for prospective field functionaries, or *officiers de service des affaires indigène* (Indigenous Affairs Service officers; Miller 2013: 101–2). This programme required its students to study Arabic and Tamazight, Arab literature, culture and law, and to submit a thesis that further expanded French knowledge about the country's customs. Upon graduation, these students were hired as colonial administrators; among other tasks, they acted as 'advisors' to local leaders (Brett and Fentress 1997: 190; Slavin 1998: 135–6).

A distinct strand in the Glaoui's storytelling corpus emerges from the unique writing genre of these *affaires indigènes* officers. The best example is a *mémoire* composed by Paul Schoen. Although Schoen's research about Thami al-Glaoui was published after the events described in this chapter, I have decided to present it here because it depicts the prevailing discourse of the indigenous affairs officers that had accumulated since the beginning of the protectorate, and because information from Schoen's 1938 thesis on al-Glaoui is cited throughout this chapter.

Schoen was born to a French Alsatian family in 1900. He enlisted in the French Air Force in 1920 and became an airborne observer. In the Rif War of 1920–6 (about the war, see 'Ayash 1992; Boutabqalt 1997), his plane was shot down; Schoen survived the crash, found his way back to French lines, and was awarded a medal.[22] In 1928, he joined the Affaires indigènes du Maroc in Marrakesh as a lieutenant of the infantry,[23] with responsibility for the region of Amizmiz (circa 50km south of the city). In 1934, he was promoted to captain of infantry,[24] and three years later was assigned to the area of Tiznit, where he was put in charge of the bureau of the Ida Oultit tribal area in the far south (Annuaire 1937: 20). His post involved administrative work with occasional military action, such as commanding a Moroccan unit (*goum*) during the final pacification battles in the Anti-Atlas.

As part of his ongoing training as an indigenous affairs officer, Schoen wrote a 220–page dissertation on Thami al-Glaoui, analysing a rich bibliography about the Pasha alongside multiple classified intelligence documents. Following the acceptance of the dissertation in 1938, he was transferred to the Affaires indigènes d'Algérie, to serve in its Information and Studies Department. During the Second World War, after the liberation of Algeria from Vichy rule, Schoen resumed combat activities as commander of the 9th Algerian Zouave Battalion. His unit participated in military operations in Corsica, Provence, Alsace and Germany. In the last he was injured and was awarded additional medals for his conduct. After the war, Schoen returned to Algeria and created the Service des liaisons Nord-Africaines (North African Liaison Service). Attached to the governor's civil cabinet, the office collected information on Muslim politics, researched the local population, advised the government, published monthly bulletins and an annual report, and organised quarterly meetings. Paul Schoen's son Yves, who also became an army officer, was killed in a military operation in Algeria in 1959 – a fact that prompted Schoen's return to France a year later. In France, Schoen created and directed L'Association des anciens des affaires Algériennes (The Algerian Affairs Section Alumni Association), for veterans of his former Algerian offices; the Comité national pour les Musulmans Français (National Committee for French Muslims), which helped Muslims who had collaborated with the French in Algeria to settle in France; and the Bureau d'aide aux Musulmans Français (Office of Aid to French Muslims). Paul Schoen died in 1984 (Faivre 2002).

Schoen's biography represents a lifelong embodiment of the ideal French colonial soldier-researcher-bureaucrat, as cultivated by Lyautey and his methods (Puyo 2012: 89). He was highly knowledgeable, very opinionated, very involved, and a person whose advice was sought by the top colonial officials. Yet his life story betrays the sense that he was never truly at home anywhere, instead living in a perpetual state of in-betweenness. Schoen comes across as a man caught in an imposed borderline situation; in a forced love–hate relationship with the people he was supposed to care for, to study and control – not all that different from Lyautey himself.

With regard to al-Glaoui, Schoen's (1938) *mémoire* (dissertation) is a very detailed study.[25] Beyond the impressive academic knowledge on display, it also presents a political analysis proposing various paths of action vis-à-vis al-Glaoui (more on this in Chapter 3). Reading this document against the grain highlights its arrangement for purposes of colonial control; reading it 'along the archival grain', to borrow Stoler's (2009) terminology, displays the creeping anxiety in the French administration that al-Glaoui might develop into a great danger.

From a storytelling perspective, Schoen's text creates a distinct air of suspense and tension. Suspense is built into the manuscript since – as the author repeatedly asserts – lives and fortunes are at stake. But the reader reaches the end with no clear resolution: will al-Glaoui remain loyal, or will he turn his back on the French? Will he survive the next year? If not, who will back the French when he is gone? The narrator leaves the reader with no clue as to the end of his tale, but rather with a slight sense of apprehension and suspense.

Schoen was one of many French officer-researchers. Each focused his *mémoire* on a different theme; collectively, these dissertations constitute a distinct storytelling genre, drawing from academic, political, military and administrative perspectives, but also conveying feelings of uncertainty and danger – together with a sense of commitment that, for many, would last long after they had left the colonies.

The Warrior

Our storyline, diverted for a while from al-Glaoui's immediate biography, now returns to 1912 and Marrakesh. Directly after granting them both the title of Officier de la Légion d'honneur, General Mangin encouraged the Glaoui brothers to embark on grand *harka*s (military campaigns) against dissident tribes. The first of these was against the Mesfioua. After vanquishing them, the brothers were directed to a greater *harka*, organised in collaboration with the Sektana and Qa'id Goundafi, this time against al-Hiba, the pretender to the throne. In this mid-1913 campaign, Taroudant, the city where al-Hiba sought refuge, was captured. He managed, however, to escape to the Souss (Schoen 1938: 42–4).

The local forces worked hand-in-hand with French units, who, after each new victory, placed the captured areas under the control of their collaborators and co-opted the local leadership into their system. This method, the *caïdalisme* (*caïd* being the conventional French transliteration of *qa'id*), gave some senior *qa'id*s permits to collect taxes from tribal populations in their territories. In return, they were expected to be the loyal collaborators of the colonial administration in these areas (Montagne 1930; Schoen 1938: 46; Perkins 1981: 91–6; Yasin 2003; Lahnite 2011: 13–22). Years later, this policy was described by post-colonial historiography as a cynical colonialist approach, one that severely scarred the texture of Moroccan society. In 'Abdallah Laroui's words, 'throughout the Maghrib the policy was to make the old local élites collaborate in the work of colonisation by transforming them into a parasitic class' (Laroui 1977: 340).

As the 'pacification' battles were taking place, the Great War broke out in Europe. Resident-General Lyautey received an immediate order to withdraw his troops to the harbour towns, and to stand ready to transfer them to France. While figuring out how to obey this order without creating a military vacuum in Morocco, he decided to send a French delegation to Marrakesh to inform the local notables on the events in Europe, and get a sense of their loyalty. According to reports of the meeting, after the French representative's address, Madani al-Glaoui – speaking on behalf of all notables – announced that they were the friends of France and would remain loyal to her. Shortly afterwards, Madani gathered his family and announced to its members that this was the family's stand on the issue (Schoen 1938: 45). A generation later, Maxwell added his storyteller's touch to this tale, stating that Madani concluded his speech by informing his relatives that if anyone objected, 'there [are] dungeons at Telouet, from which, once entered, no prisoner had ever emerged either alive or dead' (Maxwell 1966: 147). Once again, the Glaouis justified their image as the saviours of their masters – and Maxwell as a master storyteller. Counting on Madani's promises, Lyautey sent most of his French units back to France but took care to replace them with Senegalese troops (Schoen 1938: 45).

Due to the war in Europe and the burden it created – and also due to the French military disaster at the Battle of El-Herri (near Khenifra in central Morocco) in which more than 600 French, Senegalese and North African soldiers were killed in a skirmish with Moroccan dissidents (November 1914; Gershovich 2000: 102–8) – the French decided on a two-year pause with respect to military action south of the Atlas. The Glaouis, however, continued to expand their territories in that area, especially under Hammou's leadership (Figure 2.3; al-Buzidi 2010).

Figure 2.3 Thami al-Glaoui (on the right) meeting with his uncle Si Hamou at the Telouet Pass.
Source: *Les Annales coloniales: revue mensuelle illustrée*, 1 January 1929, p. 1. Photo Flandrin (Casablanca). Modifications have been made to the original image. Courtesy: CIRAD.

In 1916, Madani and Thami resumed their *harka*s on behalf of the French, first setting out against the revolting Ftouka and Oultana tribes in the environs of Demnat, and then venturing on additional *harka*s with some French military support. Internal French circulars praised Thami al-Glaoui's loyalty and reported on his bravery in these battles. However, beyond the glorifying text and material gains, the frequent campaigns took their toll. In a mid-1930s letter to the Resident-General, Thami al-Glaoui described the immense loss of life during that period as a sacrifice to fulfil the French goal of 'pacifying' the country.[26] Al-Glaoui referred only to the Glaoua dead; but if all tribes involved in those battles are taken into account, the cumulative loss of Moroccan lives and property must have been extremely high (for example, Yasin 2003; Mutafakkir 2007: 7–9; al-Buzidi

Figure 2.4 Thami al-Glaoui wearing his French decorations during a visit to France, 14 February 1921.
Source: *Agence Rol. Agence photographique (commanditaire)*. Modifications have been made to the original image. Courtesy: BnF.

2010; Sussi 2014). The reality of inter-tribal wars was indeed common in the pre-colonial era. But in the colonial period, the involvement of the French military, together with the Glaoua's increasing power, led to truly exceptional human loss.

The battles continued; Madani's favourite son was killed in combat in 1918. Stricken with sorrow, Madani died a couple of months later (Schoen 1938: 47–50; El Glaoui 2017: 157). Following his death, his responsibilities were transferred to Thami, who was now nominated Qa'id of the Glaoua. In his new role, he continued to lead his troops in combat, collecting French honours and medals on the way (Figure 2.4).[27]

A text accompanying a 1917 medal he was awarded read:

> El Hadj Thami Ben Mohamed Mezouari El Glaoui, Pasha of Marrakech, rushed, in the Battle of Tizi on 11 April, to the

rescue of encircled parties, jostled by numerous enemies. Charging at the head of his riders ... in a brilliant counter-attack, he re-established the combat. On 17 April, at Oued Tiguinit, he ... charged with a sabre, defended his forces that were lower in number, exposing himself with the most admirable bravery, killing with his hands several adversaries, finally repelling the enemy, and taking several of its horses and guns. Throughout this day, he has not stopped fighting in the front row, showing himself even superior of his high reputation as a battle commander and 'a man of powder'. (al-Glaoui 1933: 7; my italics)

Al-Glaoui once again justified his image, that of a saviour and a fearless warrior.

The award of medals was often accompanied by an exchange of acknowledgement letters between al-Glaoui and the higher echelons of the French administration in Morocco, further bolstering his prestige. A study of these letters reveals narrative forms that would, in time, have an effect on future representations of al-Glaoui.

During this period, al-Glaoui wrote many of his letters to the authorities in Arabic. These were then translated into French at the French Protectorate offices. A comparison of the original texts and their translations reveals that at least until the 1920s, significant discrepancies existed between the two versions. In the translation process, the text was reformatted into the official format favoured by the French, which necessitated (among other things) placing the sender and receiver's names in different places than in the Moroccan format. As part of this reformatting, many of the platitudes and honorifics expressed in Arabic were cut out, replaced by a few brief words in French. Take for example the following paragraph by al-Glaoui:

My heart is full of joy and my mouth is filled with gratitude. May your excellence be indulged in permanent glory, happiness, popularity, nobility, blessing and abundance. May you continue to rise, advance, prosper, and be blessed with longevity. Please accept my sincere gratefulness and gratitude from a candid heart to a beloved person.[28]

But in the French version, this was translated into the equivalent of 'I would like to express my thanks, asking you to accept my wishes aspiring to make a beloved person happy.'[29] However, more glaring – and critical – discrepancies emerged in the actual content of the missives. For example, in a 1919 letter in which al-Glaoui thanks the local French commander for the medal he had just been awarded, he describes the medal as a Sharifian 'Alawi Order decoration granted by the French government. Thus, it was not a French but a royal Moroccan award, with the French playing the role of an intermediary in its delivery. But the translation, which the French command eventually read, omitted the reference to the Moroccan court, describing the decoration as 'a high distinction awarded by the French Government'. Also, while al-Glaoui's letter thanks the Resident-General without mentioning him by name, the translator added in the text forwarded to his superiors: 'General Lyautey'.

These discrepancies, also evident in other letters,[30] reflect Moroccan and French cultural and procedural differences, as well as deliberate decisions made by the translators. These minor differences may have seemed rather insignificant at the time of writing. However, as time passed, the divergences between the original and the translation opened pathways for different future narrations. Such dissimilar accounts were not merely 'different stories' but carried significant political and legal import. For instance, in order to reach a decision in an intricate judicial case connected to al-Glaoui in the mid-1930s, the metropolitan French legal system had to determine who had awarded al-Glaoui his decorations – Morocco or France. This was necessary to determine his legal status, and whether he should be considered a Moroccan or a French official for the purpose of the legal proceedings. In practice, he was a servant of the two empires spanning the sea separating Morocco and France. The contradictory representations set out in the letters made the court's decision even more difficult (for more about this legal struggle and the ensuing debate, see Chapter 3). Narrations as mediators of ideas thus interfered with political and judicial actions. Here, constructed 'stories' were translated into legal performance, to be added as points of reference for future discussions about the boundaries between colony and metropole.

The last *harka* personally led by al-Glaoui was against the Ait M'hamed, in 1922 (Schoen 1938: 56–7). Coincidentally, this campaign was the scene of the first encounter between Thami al-Glaoui and the protagonist of the next chapter – Gustave

Figure 2.5 Thami al-Glaoui arriving at the French army camp at Bou Yahia during his 1922 *harka* (Babin 1923: figure 7). Modifications have been made to the original image.
Courtesy: BnF.

Babin. The latter had joined the French command group of this mission in order to produce a propaganda book promoting the French pacification project (Babin 1923) and was a personal witness to al-Glaoui's last military field campaign (Figure 2.5).
Babin described al-Glaoui as arriving with a force of between 8,000 and 9,000 men and six cannons (Babin 1923: 8). His conjecture was that this battle had been conceived by the latter as vengeance for the death of Madani's beloved son (Babin 1923: 25–6). However, and despite Thami's personal courage, the battle ended in failure. The enemy stronghold in Hansali (near Beni Mellal in central Morocco) was not captured, and twenty-two fatalities were recorded among the Glaoua (Babin 1923: 37).

The frequent raids between 1913 and 1922, together with the continuous fabrication of stories, official texts and press reports about al-Glaoui's combat skills,[31] boosted his aura in both French and Moroccan circles (for example, Cornet 1914; Kabbaj 1927 in Mutafakkir 2007: 143) and was echoed much later in Moroccan Jewish stories about him (Chapter 5). Louis Barthou, a minister in several French governments between 1894 and 1934, wrote about Thami al-Glaoui in 1919:

> In the Atlas Mountains these were the qa'ids and pashas who under our guidance and control fought and defeated the hostile tribes. The old Grand Vizier Madani Glaoui, an outstanding and prestigious man, a real leader, organised the area of Demnat and broadened his influence all the way to the Todgha. His brother Hajj Thami Glaoui, the Pasha of Marrakesh, had taken a year later the same political direction of the all-powerful family. He is also a leader. Received by him in his beautiful palace, with the extravagance of a lord of a great race, I was able to appreciate his qualities of a fine Muslim scholar, his penetrating sophisticated mind and his attachment to France. Since 1912 he fights on our side. He is said to be a magnificent warrior. It was he who in September 1912, after the incident of Sidi Bou Othman, *rescued* in Marrakesh the French prisoners held by al-Hiba. Later on, he took part, with the reinforcements he brought from all his estates, in all the policing actions operated in the High Atlas region as far as Taroudant. The [World] War did not undermine his loyalty. In 1919 he gave us the biggest service. In a new revolt at Tafilalet organised by Si Muhamed Nefruten the Sharif of the Sahara, he recruited ten thousand men and led them to battle. Despite the cold and the snows that blocked the mountain passes, he crossed the High Atlas with his army and arrived in the Dades and Todgha valleys, until he met our forces at the Ziz. He defeated the Ait-Atta, made them compliant, organised all the regions through which he had passed, and dispersed the harka of Si Muhamed Nefruten. His good military conduct won him, in March, the High Officer Cross of the Honorary Legion. (Barthou 1919: 79–81; my italics)

Barthou's text is illustrative of Thami al-Glaoui's emergence as a significant, indeed semi-legendary figure, while at the same time encapsulating the principles of French policy in southern Morocco: indirect rule through the grand *qa'ids* who, in return for suppressing anti-French resistance, received excessive esteem, various emblems, and a free hand in running private armies and co-opting vast territories to their own ends. The text also reflects the discourse of the period, which – a short while after the pyrrhic French victory in the Great War – was filled with references to battles and bravery in combat. The practical expression of this narrative was the rising value of Thami al-Glaoui for the French, and the consolidation of his image, on both sides of the Mediterranean, as a mythical warrior of unrivalled qualities.

Harun al-Thami

As his prestige rose, Thami al-Glaoui was invited to France together with a few fellow grand *qa'id*s – including his doppelgänger, al-'Ayadi – to join the victory ceremony commemorating the end of the Great War, held in Paris on 14 July 1919 (al-'Atri 2018).[32] Two years later, he visited France again, and this time was received by President Poincaré. His charismatic personality and generosity won him a community of fans in Paris, soon nicknamed 'the Glaoua tribe on Oued Seine' (see Chapter 3). Al-Glaoui's second visit to France was followed by a visit to London, where he met with Prime Minister Lloyd George – an act that raised concerns in the French administration about his total loyalty to France (Schoen 1938: 54, 84–95, 114).

As he became known in wider circles in Europe, al-Glaoui invited European leaders and celebrities to visit his Moroccan estates. They responded enthusiastically and were highly impressed by the Oriental splendour and décor of his palaces and his generous hospitality. In 1923, for instance, British health minister (and future prime minister) Neville Chamberlain, together with the Morocco-based British journalist, writer and traveller Walter Harris, visited al-Glaoui in Marrakesh. They were welcomed in a grand reception arranged by him and by al-'Ayadi. On that occasion, Harris even promised al-Glaoui the protection of the British, should ever he need it (Schoen 1938: 115).

Simultaneously with his military pursuits, travels and international networking, al-Glaoui was continuously occupied with maintaining and promoting his local power base. He took close care of his relatives, attending to their material needs,[33] and he was frequently called upon to deal with various domestic tensions. He married six wives and had several concubines. Some of these marriages were contracted to foster links with Moroccan elites. For example, his wife Lalla Zineb, widow of his brother Madani, was the daughter of Grand Vizier al-Mokri; while another, Lalla Fatma, was the daughter of the former minister of war, Mehdi al-Menebhi.[34]

Beyond his close family circle, al-Glaoui felt an obligation to the current and past sultans of the ʿAlawi dynasty, despite obvious French dissatisfaction about his behaviour. He maintained contact with the deposed sultans ʿAbd al-Hafidh and ʿAbd al-ʿAziz,[35] exiled in France and Tangier respectively. In a similar vein, he paid constant tribute to the reigning sultan and maintained active contact with his fellow grand *qaʾid*s and other Moroccan political and religious figures.

Thami al-Glaoui was also an active businessman. He both bought and confiscated property –sometimes with French consent, and sometimes without.[36] He effectively was the ruler of Marrakesh and its environs, collecting taxes, nominating and removing local *qaʾid*s and judges.[37] Yet, despite his accumulation of wealth and ever-growing powers, he was still considered a civil servant, as a state-nominated pasha. For example, he was required to ask the central administration for permission before travelling abroad for medical treatment.[38]

To manage such an extensive range of activities, al-Glaoui established a court that included his *khalifa* (deputy), Ahmed al-Biaz; a personal aide by name of Hajj Idder; and bankers, consultants, translators, secretaries, cooks, drivers, servants, and many others (Schoen 1938: 157; El Glaoui 2004: 19–124; Katz 2006: 254).

Simultaneously, somewhat reminiscent of the image of royal courts, al-Glaoui presented himself as a man of letters. He had in his palace a large collection of rare manuscripts, religious and scientific books, and hosted and supported poets and musicians (Amenzou, 2000: 59; Mutafakkir 2007: 5, 9). It was also propagated that he knew the Quran well and could recite several of its commentaries by heart (Anuzul 2005). An idea of the impression that al-Glaoui and his court made in those years can be gleaned from a poem written by anti-colonial Egyptian poet Badiʿ Khayri (an active participant in the 1919 Egyptian Revolution against the British; al-Hamamsi 2012) after visiting the pasha:

> I longed for Marrakesh in my departure,
>   and the Maghreb became my place of residence
> And if you do not know,
>   what people know about the Pasha, known as al-Thami
> . . .
> How many countries' delegates
>   aspire to him, the one whose status is self-made

Travel the land from the plain and wilderness,
   even if it is a thousand-year march,
Kind with an unparalleled generosity
...
Marrakesh succeeded Baghdad before,
   and succeeded the throne of Harun al-Thami.
(selected lines from Khayri 1922, in Mutafakkir 2007: 141)

Thus, in the popular imagery al-Glaoui was compared with the eighth-century Abbasid caliph Harun al-Rashid, and his renowned court and legendary library in Baghdad. To the list of topoi attached to al-Glaoui, such as the 'saviour' and 'warrior', were now added signifiers such as 'generous', 'erudite', and 'self-made' – all adding to his majestic aura.

Maintaining his court required significant resources and was often beyond al-Glaoui's means. From the 1920s on, he was constantly in substantial debt to individuals, firms, the Sharifian state and the French Protectorate (more on this in Chapter 3). One way of meeting his financial demands was to extract even more taxes from the population under his rule. This, inevitably, instigated considerable antagonism among the tribes (Schoen 1938: 70; Chekblog, n.d.).

Fear

Noting growing resentment towards al-Glaoui, several French officers stationed in southern Morocco began to be concerned. Alarmed by his growing influence, his contacts with declared anti-colonialists (such as the Egyptian poet Khayri), and noting his inability to meet his debts, they suggested that the protectorate authorities replace him as soon as possible. Nevertheless, these recommendations were never taken seriously, due to more pressing issues. The outbreak of the Rif War in 1920 and the subsequent replacement of Resident-General Lyautey occupied the attention of the local and metropolitan French administrations (Schoen 1938: 60–3; Rivet 1996: 279–310). Given these more troubling issues, it would seem that despite his drawbacks, the French needed al-Glaoui – especially for as long as the 'pacification' of southern Morocco remained incomplete. For example, before the large 1922 *harka*, for which the French desperately needed al-Glaoui's help, they decided to clear some of his debts, purely on political and practical grounds.[39]

Preserving al-Glaoui and his status did not mean that the French hesitated to confront powerful local leaders, including some of the 'Lords of the Atlas'. In that very same period, they cut off support to al-'Ayadi,[40] and ended the rule of Goundafi (in 1924; Goundafi 2013: 112–13) and then Metougi (in 1928), partitioning the lands of the latter two, with the spoils largely accruing to al-Glaoui (Schoen 1938: 59–63).[41] Al-Glaoui was therefore a strategic choice made by the French.

This did not mean that the French granted al-Glaoui free rein. The French authorities continuously monitored his personality and loyalty, checking constantly how 'useful' he was to them. A confidential French document written in 1924 under the sub-title 'Attitude and Manner of Service' reported that Thami al-Glaoui was a

> Grand native chief of an impeccable straightforwardness and full of courtesy. Very affable and very hospitable. Very sensitive to honours, fond of pomp and luxury. Having an analytical mind. Very intelligent. Very far-sighted, fine and cunning diplomat. Hyper-active, judging people and things very quickly with a lot of good sense. Very aware of his value and of the accuracy of his views. Very compliant. An accomplished war-leader. A peerless organiser. Energetic. Very hard with his inferiors and much afraid of them. Very jealous of his authority. Very ambitious but very flexible. Knows how to let go of the rope when he is convinced that he will take it again when he wants to. An extraordinary master of himself and sometimes very violent. Very open to our ideas. Will evolve in the directions addressed by a generous spirit. Firm, attentive and tenacious. Of a proven loyalty. Political collaborator of the first order to the leader who will know how to impose on him the necessary influence, . . . [having] knowledge of things Glaoua in particular, and Moroccan in general.[42]

Thus, in the mid-1920s, side by side with the public portrayal of Thami al-Glaoui as a heroic supporter of the French mission, appreciative yet circumspect evaluations of his personality were emerging within the administration. Even so, the French believed, in typically colonialist fashion, that they held the keys to manipulating him to their ends. As proof that their judgement of his loyalty was correct, French officers noted that al-Glaoui did not use the opportunity of Abdelkrim al-Khattabi's revolt in the Rif (1920–26; 'Ayash 1992; Boutabqalt 1997) to switch allegiances. Al-Glaoui remained loyal despite al-Khattabi's anti-French propaganda, which had been broadcast across Morocco. It is likely, nevertheless, that various thoughts did cross his mind, as he maintained contact with al-Khattabi (Schoen 1938: 66) – but, for the moment, and from the French point of view, he remained trustworthy and useful.

The Rif War was a challenge for the protectorate as a whole. At a certain point during the war, Riffian rebels moved from the Spanish zone into French controlled areas and began to approach Fes ('Ayash 1992). Real doubts began to be voiced in France about Lyautey's ability to handle the unfolding situation. Accordingly, the French government decided to go around him, appointing Marshal Pétain, hero of the Great War, to lead the colonial army in suppressing the Riffians. Facing humiliation, Lyautey chose to resign in 1925 (Rivet 1996: 296–310; Singer 1998: 147; Miller 2013: 117).

Lyautey's successor, Théodore Steeg, did not subscribe to his predecessor's vision. Instead, he established an Algerian-style regime in Morocco, which (among other things) accorded much more power to the French settlers (Slavin 1998: 128; Guerin 2011: 371). Ignace Lepp, the anti-imperialist French writer, wrote thirty years later that from that moment on, Lyautey's inspiring ideal of 'Berber policy' turned into a 'revolting' Machiavellian divide-and-rule approach (Lepp 1954: 66).

Taking advantage of a request made by the Foreign Office in Paris to explain rumours of conflict within al-Glaoui's family (between Thami and his nephew Madani), Resident-General Steeg prepared, in January 1928, a broader review of how he envisioned al-Glaoui fitting in within the reform programme he was promoting:

> The Rifian affair settled, the Glaoui remained the only great native chief of the South. His power, his prestige, and his pride were at their apogee. Everything had helped to increase them; the obliteration of his rivals; the services rendered during the crisis; the liberties which the circumstances had allowed him to arrogate to himself.
> With the good order everywhere restored, and the Moroccan evolution accelerated by the growing development of French activity, as the advantages of the feudal regime became more pronounced, its evils seem all the more shocking.

Figure 2.6 'His Excellency Si el Hadj Thami Glaoui, Grand qa'id of the South, Pasha of Marrakesh, Grand officer of the Légion d'honneur'. Source: *Le Radical*, 14 October 1928, p. 5. Modifications have been made to the original image.
Courtesy: BnF.

> The time of the reforms cannot be delayed . . . but we must make sure that al-Glaoui becomes the first collaborator in these reforms . . . But what the reason dictates to the Pasha . . . his pride of a feudal does not endure . . . His nervousness betrays him in everything that touches or seems to affect his prestige.[43]

A shift in the plot was thus under way. Since Steeg's residency, and especially after the Rif War, the French had begun to establish indigenous affairs posts and offices within the Glaoua territory, manifestation of their control of al-Glaoui. The establishment of a post at Telouet particularly upset the Glaoua, but the French insisted on it (Schoen 1938: 68–9; Yasin 2003: 176). Even so, al-Glaoui was far from being an outdated Moroccan feudal lord.

His exceptional management, networking and public relations skills brought him much closer to France, and even to being French. While the French were conspicuously constructing an outpost at Telouet, al-Glaoui, unnoticed, was buttressing his outpost in Paris, as will be detailed in the next chapter.

Narrating al-Glaoui's First Decades

From the 1890s to the mid-1920s, as al-Glaoui turned from the teenage brother of a *qa'id* to a grand *qa'id* and pasha in his own right, the first topos, relating to the narration of his image, were created. Most prominent among these were motifs such as 'rescuer', 'warrior', 'wily warden', 'generous' and 'erudite'. While these referred specifically to him, these descriptors were at the same time part of broader contemporary discourses, such as the literary positioning of the French colonial enterprise as a rescue mission, or the wide distribution of stories praising bravery in battle, circulated globally in relation to the Great War.

During the period discussed in this chapter, specific storytelling formats relating to the Pasha were becoming popular. Such formats included reports penned by French officers, correspondence between al-Glaoui and the colonial administration, and praise poems written about the Pasha. These formed the base for future intertextual narratives and will be explored further in the following chapters.

In order to emphasise certain observations about al-Glaoui's story and history, in this chapter I have also referred to yet-to-come narrations. I set a 'literary signpost', indicating the future deposition of a sultan and al-Glaoui's subsequent fall, in order to expose the dramatic arc created by his tale. Likewise, quotes from later writers were used to underscore common metaphors and historiographies. Elaborating on all these and moving into the next phase in al-Glaoui's biography, the next chapter will begin with a short detour from the figure of the Pasha to one of the people whose storytelling about him represented a new narrative style – Gustave Babin.

Notes

1. Previously known also as Tizi n' Glaoua, and currently called Tizi n' Titchka. *Tizi* means 'mountain pass' in Tashilhit, the local Amazigh dialect.

2. The ʿAlawis are the royal dynasty that have ruled Morocco from 1666 to the present day. *Mawlay* is a prefix of respect, added to the name of a person believed to be a descendant of the Prophet.
3. Robert Montagne asserts that the name derives from *zwour* in Tamazight (an Amazigh dialect) and means 'precede': 'the *amzwar* is the one who is asked to be the first to do an important or a difficult act, because he has a lucky-charm' (Montagne 1930: 222, n. 2, as quoted in El Glaoui 2017: 35).
4. *Makhzen* is an abbreviation of *bled makhzen*, literally 'land of order', and refers to land under the effective rule of the sultan. Its antonym is *bled siba* – 'land of dissidence'.
5. About ʿAbdelkarim Filali, see al-Ashraf (2013).
6. Southern Morocco is home to a large population of blacks, the Harratin. They are descendants of slaves originally brought from sub-Saharan Africa to serve the local tribes, who were partly mixed among the Amazighs (Hoffman 1967: 13). In the past, these groups lived under the patronage of local tribal organisations, including many Amazigh tribes, and were considered inferior by those tribes (Hart 1972: 53–5) – an attitude reinforced during the colonial period (see Chapter 3).
7. All translations to English in this volume are mine, unless otherwise stated.
8. *Khalifa* literally means a replacement, in the sense of a deputy. Originally, the title was reserved for the leader of all Muslim believers after the Prophet. In Morocco, the term was applied also to lower-ranking officials.
9. The cannon was on display in a central circle in Demnat until a few years ago. See <https://www.atlasscoop.com/news23045.html> (last accessed 17 August 2023).
10. Source: HA Krupp, S 1/WT 1/4, p. 26 (letter from Krupp archives dated 9 September 2018). Hence, Maxwell misidentified the cannon as a 77mm.
11. The main reform was the introduction of a single standard tax, the *tartib*, literally, 'arrangement'. This was a tax on agricultural incomes and was intended as a replacement for Islamic taxes (Cherkaoui 2000: n. 2).
12. Austro-Hungary, Belgium, Britain, France, Germany, Holland, Italy, Morocco, Portugal, Russia, Spain, Sweden and the United States.
13. Such marriages were also arranged between the families of the *qaʾid*s, to foster local political alliances (Lahnite 2011: 48).
14. CADN 1MA/282 95, 'Monsieur l'ambassadeur résident général de France au Maroc', p. 4.
15. For the term and its literary uses, see Humann 2018: 2.

16. CADN 1MA/282 95, Thami al-Glaoui 'à son excellence le Maréchal Lyautey', 17 December 1924; Thami al-Glaoui 'à monsieur le Colonel Huot', 20 July 1924; 'de la part du Maréchal Lyautey' to Thami al-Glaoui, not dated.
17. CADN 1MA/282 100, 'rapport du Pacha Hadj Thami', 19 August 1921.
18. CADN 1MA/282 100, Lyautey to 'mon cher ami', 12 October 1924.
19. CADN 1MA/282 96, Thami al-Glaoui 'à son excellence monsieur le Maréchal Lyautey', 24 April 1923.
20. CADN 1MA/282 100, Lyautey to 'mon cher el Hadj Thami', 12 September 1923.
21. CADN 1MA/282 96, 'Le Général de Division Catroux commandant de la région de Marrakech, à monsieur le ministre plénipotentiaire délégué à la résidence générale', 4 February 1935; CADN 1MA/282 100, 'Le Général de Division Catroux commandant de la région de Marrakech, à monsieur le ministre plénipotentiaire délégué à la résidence générale', 8 February 1935.
22. *Les Gaulois*, 6 October 1926; *La Liberté*, 12 October 1926.
23. *Journal officiel de la République Française. Lois et décrets*, 9 July 1928, p. 7653.
24. *Journal officiel de la République Française. Lois et décrets*, 8 March 1934, p. 2433.
25. The dissertation is currently deposited at the French diplomatic archives, folder CADN 1MA/282 95.
26. CADN 1MA/282 95, Thami al-Glaoui to 'Monsieur l'ambassadeur résident général de France au Maroc', p. 9.
27. For example, CADN 1MA/282/95, Thami al-Glaoui 'à monsieur le Général Maurial', 8 April 1919; Thami al-Glaoui 'à son excellence le Général Lyautey, résident général', 11 April 1919.
28. CADN 1MA/282/95, Thami al-Glaoui to General Maurial, 'Ḥaḍrat al-muʿaẓam as-sayid mudīr al-umūr al-ahliyya wa-al-istiʿlāmat al-ʿumumiyya', 8 April 1919.
29. CADN 1MA/282/95, Thami al-Glaoui 'à monsieur le général maurial direction des affaires indigènes', 8 April 1919.
30. For example, between CADN 1MA/282/95, Thami al-Glaoui to Colonel de la Bruyère, 'Saʿadat al-qāʾid al-muḥtaram as-sayid al-kulūnel', 5 April 1919, and its translation: 'Le Pacha el Hadj Thami à monsieur le colonel de la Bruyère', 5 April 1919.
31. For example: 'Au Maroc'. *Le Bonnet Rouge*, 23 June 1917, p. 1; 'Mangin et le sud du Maroc'. *L'Action Française*, 11 January 1919, p. 2; 'Notre action au Tafilalet contre le Semlali'. *Le Temps*, 16 January 1919, p. 2.
32. 'Les Préparations pour le fêtes de la Victoire'. *Excelsior: journal illustré quotidien: informations, littérature, sciences, arts, sports, théâtre, élégances*, 8 July 1919, p. 2; and CADN 1MA/282 97.

33. CADN 1MA/282 96, Thami al-Glaoui 'à son excellence monsieur le Maréchal Lyautey', 24 April 1923.
34. CADN 1MA/282/100, 'Le gérant de l'agence & consulat général de France à Tanger, à monsieur le commisaire résident général de France', 19 July 1918.
35. CADN 1MA/282 100, 'Le Maréchal de France Lyautey le commisaire résident général de la République Française au Maroc, commandant en chef, à monsieur le ministre plénipotentiaire délégué à la résidence générale', 12 September 1923.
36. CADN 1MA/282 96; this folder holds various documents from 1915 to the early 1920s concerning commercial contracts arranged by al-Glaoui – some of which upset the French.
37. CADN 1MA/282 100, Thami el-Glaoui to Colonel Huot: 'Saʻadat raʼis idārat al-istiʻlāmat al-ʻumumiyya as-sayid al-kulūnel...', 14 July 1925; Thami el-Glaoui to Marshal Lyautey 'Fakhāmat al-māreshāl al-alʻẓam al-muqīm al-ʻām as-sayid al-general Lyautey dāma ʻizzan...', 16 July 1925.
38. CADN 1MA/282 98, Thami al-Glaoui 'à monsieur le Général Catroux commandant la region', 30 July 1931.
39. CADN 1MA/282 97, 'Général Daugan à monsieur le juge de paix', 27 June 1922, CADN 1MA/282 97, 'le Général Daugan commandant la région de Marrakech à monsieur le juge de paix', 18 August 1922.
40. CADN 1MA/282/100, 'Lettre du Caïd el Ayadi', 19 February 1914.
41. See also the *dahirs* (edicts) giving al-Glaoui control over groups of Rehamna and Metouga: Ministère des affaires étrangères, Fond: Maroc, Série: DACH, Article: 133, 'Le Colonel Huot, directeur des affaires indigènes à monsieur le conseiller du gouvernement, directeur général des affaires Chérifiennes', 11 December 1925.
42. CADN 1MA/282/95, 'Feuille de renseignements concernant: El Hadj Thami ben Mohamed el Mezouari', 24 January 1924.
43. CADN 1MA/282 100, 'Le commisaire résident général de la République Française au Maroc, à son excellence monsieur le ministre des affaires étrangeres, Paris', 16 January 1928.

3

The Glaoua Tribe on River Seine

Gustave Babin

Gustave Constant Babin was born in 1865 in the commune of Rezé, a suburb of Nantes in the Loire-Atlantique department in western France, to carpenter Gustave Babin and his wife, Mrs Constance Lebeaupin.[1] His early childhood passed under the cloud of the French defeat and humiliation in the 1870–1 Franco-Prussian War, which climaxed with Germany's annexation of Alsace and Lorraine. The social context of this defeat likely had an impact on his later mindset: significant class conflict, demographic decline and economic depression that lasted until 1897 (Mayeur and Rebirioux 1994: 42–71).

The Third French Republic emerged from the aftermath of that war (in 1870; Gildea 1996: 1). The nineteenth- and early twentieth-century governments of the Third Republic ran economic reform programmes aimed at protecting French agriculture and industry from international competition. As such, France was a part of a reform discourse running across the continent and its adjacent regions, from Morocco in the west to the Ottoman Empire and Iran in the east (Chapter 2; and, for example, İnalcik 1976; Shaw and Shaw 1977; Enayat 2013; Davison 2016; McDougall 2018). In 1878, the government initiated the Freycinet Plan, an ambitious public works programme intended (amongst other things) to extend the reach of the Third Republic to rural France; by the turn of the century, the French economy had fully recovered (Jones 1984: 16; Haine 2000: 124). Within the opportunities that had opened up, the young Gustave Babin, twenty years old in 1885, took up a job with his hometown's bridge and road service.

The France of this era was cresting a wave of optimism. French imperialism was at a high; Paris, the capital, was a global cultural, political and scientific centre – themes all extravagantly celebrated during the 1889 World Fair (Mitchell 1989). Yet, a year later, a wave of anti-Semitism spread across the country, culminating in 1894's Dreyfus Affair (Cahm 2016). In addition to its sociopolitical impact (Lebovics 1992: 19), the affair also revealed the dramatic power of the press, with much of the debate unfolding in newspaper pages (Émile Zola's *J'accuse*, for example). The French press had indeed enjoyed a remarkable surge, with daily newspaper sales quadrupling between 1858 and 1870, doubling again in the next decade, and then increasing by a factor of 2.5 between 1880 and 1910 (Haine 2000: 126). With an urgent demand for ambitious writers and reporters, Gustave Babin left his job at the bridge and road service in 1893 and began to write for the French newspaper *L'Illustration*.[2] He relocated to Paris, the heart of France's renewed economic, political and cultural life, in 1895, and began to write for a second newspaper, *Le Journal des Debats*.[3]

Following the grandiose 1900 Paris Exposition, Babin – who had developed a keen eye for art and architecture – wrote a series of articles about the exposition for *Le Journal des Debats*,[4] and published a critical monograph about the exposition, *Après faillite, souvenirs de l'Exposition de 1900* (After Failure, Memories of the 1900 Exhibition; Babin 1902). The book criticised the selection and exhibition of the architectural projects at the exposition, with one exception – the monumental gates of the exhibition, designed by his friend, the architect René Binet. This text provides evidence of the incipient critical writing style that would characterise his future writings.

At the turn of the twentieth century, the French government managed to achieve one of the Third Republic's key goals – the separation of the republican state and the Catholic Church (Larkin 2014). This achievement complemented a general atmosphere of optimism, deriving from economic prosperity, technological, scientific and cultural innovations. Despite this optimism, militarism and international tensions grew considerably in connection with the so-called New Imperialism (Cooke 1973), specifically the Scramble for Africa (Chamberlain 2013). The Third Republic expanded into what became France's largest overseas empire in history (Popkin 2013: 197). These expansionist tendencies inevitably collided with other European colonial ambitions, leading to conflicts like the Fashoda Incident, between France and Britain (in 1898; Brown 1970), and German–French clashes over Morocco in 1905 and 1912. To resolve these tensions, a series of agreements and meetings were convened: the Congress of Berlin in 1878; the 1884 Berlin Congo Conference; a French–British agreement in 1899; the *Entente Cordiale* of 1904; the Algeciras Conference in 1906; and understandings between the French and Germans in 1912 (Andrew 1968; Joll and Martel 2013: 49–86; al-Karuri and Sadeq 2016).

As the focus of European conflicts shifted to Africa and Asia, Europe enjoyed a relatively peaceful period. Alongside the glamour of the belle époque, economies recovered, technology developed, and trans-European mobility increased (Rowe 1999: 199–201; Popkin 2013: 191–200). Within this mood of openness, Gustave Babin found himself travelling the world as a press correspondent, reporting from Russia, Portugal, Tunisia and Morocco to an eager and curious French audience, writing on a wide array of subjects.[5]

When French forces invaded Morocco in 1912, Babin was invited to join the advancing army and report on its victories. Accepting the call, he authored a book titled *Au Maroc, par les camps et par les villes* (In Morocco, through the Camps and through the Cities; Babin 1912), which described the lives of French officers and soldiers during the military campaigns in Morocco. This publication was probably commissioned by the protectorate's first Resident-General, General Hubert Lyautey, who secured the services of traveller-writers, photographers, poster-painters and movie producers to publicise and justify France's colonial presence in Morocco (Otero-Pailos 1998: 24).

As the Great War broke out, Babin, almost fifty years old, returned to Europe and worked as a war correspondent for a number of journals. He also published a book about the Battle of the Marne (*La Bataille de la Marne*; Babin 1916). Babin's wartime activity earned him the *Légion d'honneur* and the *Croix de Guerre*.[6]

His profile on the rise, Babin published articles in many newspapers and magazines, some outside France, such as *Current History* (Babin 1919). Some sources suggest that he also qualified as a lawyer at around this time (Maxwell 1966: 174; Chafik 2000: n. 21), but this information is uncertain.

In 1922, Babin was summoned once again to Morocco, this time to report on the French pacification project south of the Atlas, being advanced with the help of the local *qa'id*s.

Subsequently, he published *La mysterieuse Ouaouizert, chronique d'une colonne au Maroc* (Mysterious Ouaouizert, Chronicle of a Column in Morocco; Babin 1923), also commissioned by the Resident-General. Babin encountered Thami al-Glaoui for the first time then, the latter one of the tribal leaders fighting alongside the French. Babin's first impressions of al-Glaoui were relatively positive (al-Glaoui refers to this later; al-Glaoui 1933: 2–3). Nevertheless, Babin was to write later that even then, his impressions of al-Glaoui were bad, but that he did not write negatively about him out of respect for his hosts. However, he claimed, a diligent reader of the original text would have discerned his true feelings (Babin 1934: 111). A specific French source even maintains that for a while in 1922, Babin was employed by al-Glaoui, assisting him in issues of journalism, and that, following a disagreement, the two parted ways.[7]

Inflation rose in France in the 1920s, even as the country's economy boomed. To meet the demand for manual workers, France recruited almost two million foreign labourers, primarily from Eastern and Southern Europe (Haine 2000: 147–50). Within this prevailing socio-economic context, Babin judged that the time was right for him to settle in Morocco. He set up home in Casablanca, established an independent French-Moroccan newspaper called *L'Ère Française* (Balafrej 1933: 6), and acquired an interest in various businesses. It was the last, it seems, that sparked his conflict with al-Glaoui.

The Imperial Storyteller

Babin enters our story because his views about al-Glaoui became pivotal in the development of the Pasha's tale. Most of al-Glaoui's subsequent storytellers refer substantially to Babin, even translating his key text into Arabic in 1999 (Chapter 7).

Babin's impact was significant, due to his unique status as a producer of texts for and about the protectorate. Babin did not arrive in Morocco a novice. When he settled in the colony in the late 1920s, he had almost thirty years' reporting experience. Beyond this, he had, at the age of a little over sixty, very defined views on ideological and moral issues. Opening up his own newspaper in Casablanca, bearing the auspicious name *L'Ère Française* (The French Era) suggests that he arrived with the belief that France was on the verge of leaving a major mark on Morocco – and that he wanted to be a part of this.

In making his new home in Morocco, Babin was entering familiar settings. He knew many people in the country: from both the French administration and the local population, Moroccans and French settlers alike. However, by 1927, the person in charge was no longer Marshal Lyautey, who Babin admired, but a successor who rudely abandoned the former's vision.

One can surmise that Babin was exhilarated by his new adventure, especially after being encouraged to move to the colony by two French businessmen and royalty, the princes Murât and Essling, who had interests in numerous entrepreneurial initiatives in Morocco.[8] No doubt, Babin hoped to make money. But he had also arrived with a sense of purpose: to fix the grand French *mission civilisatrice*, which, in his opinion, had floundered somewhat since Lyautey's resignation. Babin felt particularly suited for such a mission, given his experience as an 'imperial storyteller'.

The concept of the 'imperial storyteller' was coined by the researcher Ambreen Hai, who assigned it to Rudyard Kipling – *the* storyteller of colonial India. In relation to Kipling, Hai asserted that the metropole needed such storytellers, although, however, people in the metropole and colony also feared the subversive potential of the very same storytellers. Hai maintained that imperial storytellers were vulnerable and powerful at the same time – with useful, but simultaneously threatening potential, due to the critiques they raised concerning imperial realities (Hai 1997: 603).

Babin embodies these very qualities. As a 'storyteller' recruited by the protectorate, he indeed wrote two volumes praising France's presence in Morocco (Babin 1912; 1923). However, the founding of his own newspaper in Casablanca revealed another side to him. Despite generally tending towards justifying the existence of the protectorate, Babin did not hesitate to criticise its ways of action. Whilst a priori appropriate, the protectorate, in Babin's opinion, was prone to malfunctioning for a number of reasons – the main one being how the French had enabled the expanding influence of Thami al-Glaoui.

Writing about the French colony in Vietnam, Nicola Cooper was able to identify French imperial storytellers in this setting as well. Cooper describes their challenges to the colonial administration's mismanagement. Instead of recommending an end to colonial rule, these writers hoped that proper reform would return French rule to its 'original' benevolent and just nature (Cooper 2001). Babin was oriented towards a similar goal – saving the French Protectorate in Morocco from moral and actual collapse. The first step towards this, he thought, was the immediate deposition of Thami al-Glaoui.

The Poisoned City

In mid-1927, a year after establishing *L'Ère Française*, Babin started a campaign in the press against Thami al-Glaoui with a special column in his newspaper, *Chronique du Sud* (Chronicle of the South).

Published every few weeks, the column publicised a series of allegations against al-Glaoui. A July 1927 dispatch informed readers that al-Glaoui had made up the story of rescuing the French hostages in Marrakesh in 1912 (see Chapter 2).[9] A month later, Babin reported on al-Glaoui's tyrannical rule of Marrakesh, noting his disrespect to prominent European leaders, manifested by actions such as bringing people like his *khalifa* (deputy), Ahmed al-Biaz – or even worse, his Jewish secretary, Sam Berrimoj – to meetings with French officials. In his column, Babin appealed to the newly appointed local member of the French National Assembly, Ernest Lafont, to examine the finances of the Moroccan colony, and to cut off all financial support to al-Glaoui due to the latter's misconduct.[10]

On 1 October of that year, Babin reported that al-Glaoui had secured dishonest financial gain and claimed that a citizen who had not paid his taxes to al-Glaoui had been sent to jail.[11] The following month, Babin changed the column's name to 'Dans la Ville Empoisonné' (In the Poisoned City). In a report titled 'Fake: The Use of a Fake', he accused al-Glaoui of forging documents in order to secure ownership of a property in Marrakesh. In that column, Babin made another appeal to Ernest Lafont:[12]

> Mr Ernest Lafont will decide if the Republic, if France, intends to continue covering with the tricolour flag, protecting with its cannons, at the cost of serious risks, the abominable regime of corruption, rape, robbery, torture and killings, introduced in 1912 with the advent of Hadj Thami Glaoui, or if it is resolved to put an end to it.[13]

Responding to Babin's fierce attacks, the French administration decided to formally investigate some of the accusations.

Two days after publication of Babin's November 1927 column, the administration ran an internal audit to see if forgery had indeed played a role in the transaction reported in Babin's article. The investigation, however, determined that all was above board.[14]

In his study of Moroccan journalism, the historian Jamaâ Baïda notes that Babin's articles created the impression that he was driven by a passion for justice, which led him to criticise what he considered a feudal state crushing and oppressing Marrakesh and its environs (1996: 166). However, Baïda argues that the affair was more complicated. It appears that al-Glaoui and al-Biaz (his *khalifa*) had had a dispute with a certain 'Abd al-Hakim – who happened to be a long-term acquaintance of Babin (Maxwell 1966: 174; Baïda 1996: 166). Al-Glaoui, in his capacity as Pasha, incriminated 'Abd al-Hakim in November 1926 and sentenced him to jail. In response, Babin decided to help his friend, in his words 'a brave and excellent friend, the most French of the Moroccans, a friend who is like a fellow from the homeland' (Baïda 1996: 167).

Watching Babin's attacks gain momentum, al-Glaoui responded. As Pasha, vested with legal, political and administrative powers (Hoffman 2010: 873), al-Glaoui chose the law courts as his preferred arena by suing Babin. In a courtroom discussion about a month and a half after the publication of Babin's latest article (on 23 December 1927), Babin unexpectedly changed course. While he had never been compelled to back away from statements he had made throughout his career, he said, this time it was necessary. He had been led into making errors by bad informants; what he had published was completely erroneous, and he wished to apologise for this (al-Glaoui 1933: 4; Baïda 1996: 167).

Pleased with his public repentance, al-Glaoui's lawyer asked for the case to be closed. Embittered by the affair, Gustave Babin stopped publishing *L'Ère Française* and left Morocco. However, Baïda claims that Babin's public repentance was only a manoeuvre to protect his friend 'Abd al-Hakim from further harm (Baïda 1996: 167).

The confrontation between the two was far from over, though. Babin and al-Glaoui, both multi-faceted individuals, were proficient in different discursive tools of the period: pungent journalism on the one hand, the apparatuses of law and rule on the other. They were to clash again.

Al-Glaoui and the 'Berber Edict'

The global economic crisis of the late 1920s, which hit France in late 1929, only made its effect felt in Morocco after some delay (Sauvy 1969: 21–2). The effect was severe, however, primarily because it coincided with a series of droughts and locust swarms. The immediate outcome was a rapid rise in unemployment and a dramatic decline in family incomes. Farmers in rural areas either resorted to nomadism or migrated to the cities, settling in huge *bidonvilles* (shanty towns). The crisis did not pass by the French *colons* (settlers) either. However, they were able to protect themselves by exerting political pressure on the authorities, who annulled their debts and gave priority to the sale of their products in France. With these privileges, the settlers were able to ride out the harsh situation (Pennell 2000: 219–26).

From these stressful conditions a Moroccan nationalist movement emerged, in part the consequence of the socio-economic contrast between coloniser and colonised. Its ideology combined ideas common to similar movements in the Middle East and Algeria, with a local element of devotion to the ʿAlawi dynasty. In 1930, the movement was still small, but its influence steadily expanded in the big cities (El Qadéry 2010: 7; Zisenwine 2010: 9–12).

An unexpected boost for the nationalist movement was provided by the promulgation of the Dahir Berbere (Berber Edict) in May 1930 (Azaoui 2018). French colonialist researchers have claimed that from the onset of the protectorate, Moroccan society was characterised by a fundamental dichotomy. On one side were the *bled makhzen*, an Arab community, considered obedient to the central rule, inhabiting the large cities and the plains; on the other the *bled siba*, the rebellious Amazigh tribes populating the mountainous areas and the Saharan oases (Burke 1972: 177–8). The perception was that in order to improve their control over Morocco, the colonialists needed to drive a wedge between the Arabs and the Amazighs, and then encourage the latter to align with them. The Berber Edict, intended to encourage such a division, introduced a range of reforms; the main contribution these made to community life was the abrogation of *Shariʿa* (Islamic) law in Amazigh communities (Nelson 1985: 110–1; Eickelman 1989: 220; Maddy-Weitzman 2001: 29; Azaoui 2018).

The French were not prepared for the intensity of the resistance to the edict. Led by nationalist leaders Hassan Wazzani and Allal al-Fassi, the protesters claimed that the edict contradicted the Treaty of Fes; that the protectorate sought to cut the Amazighs off from Islam and to convert them to Christianity; and that Amazighs were as Moroccan as the Arabs, despite linguistic differences. The nationalists also rejected a colonial separation that associated Moroccans with the traditional and French with the modern. To drive their point home, the protesters directed attention to the fact that the so-called 'modern' French Protectorate had strengthened traditional Moroccan institutions such as the grand *qa'ids* and the leaders of the Sufi *tariqas* (orders; Hammoudi 1997: 13; Pennell 2000: 215). Al-Glaoui was the perfect example for this claim: a grand *qa'id*, a member of the Tijani *tariqa*,[15] and a key collaborator with the French (Abun Nasr 1965; El Adnani 2010).[16]

As if to further vindicate these allegations, in May 1930 al-Glaoui backed French attempts to suppress the anti-Berber Edict demonstrations, ordering the large-scale arrests of protesters (Eickelman 1992: 102). Historian and anthropologist Dale Eickelman cites Hajj 'Abd ar-Rahman, a rural *qadi* (judge) from southern Morocco and the protagonist of his book *Power and Knowledge in Morocco*, in connection with these events:

> A few days before the Berber proclamation, a messenger came to me from [my elder brother in] Bzu. He said that something big was going to happen in a few days and to stay away from it by remaining in the hostel. I didn't know what it was. I thought that perhaps it had to do with a film the Jews were making. I remained in my rooms, but many of the other students went into the streets to demonstrate. Soldiers (*makhaznis*) from the pasha arrested many of them and took them to prison. Later, much later, some of the men of learning went to the pasha to plead for the students' release, and most of them were. I wanted to continue my studies and these demonstrations had nothing to do with my studies. (Eickelman 1992: 103)

In addition to the serious protests, the protectorate had another major concern during this period: the ongoing resistance in south-eastern Morocco, in regions yet to be 'pacified'. The most problematic area was Jebel Saghro, the heart of the Ait-Atta tribe. Confronting this resistance, the French launched a large-scale operation in 1930. The fiercest battles took place at Jebel Bougafer, in the Saghro mountain range; resistance gave way in 1934 after intense combat, the French receiving substantial support from al-Glaoui and his forces.[17]

With the fall of Jebel Bougafer, France's conquest of Morocco was finally complete. The two sides counted their dead in the tens of thousands. But these were mostly Moroccan, as most of the French casualties were Moroccan *goumiers* – soldiers in local units created by the French (Hart 1972; Dunn 1977; Pennell 2000: 216; Gershovich 2000: 188–9; Maghraoui 2009: 55; Campbell 2018).

A 50 Million Franc Affair

Al-Glaoui was not overly affected by the economic crisis or the turmoil surrounding the Berber Edict. However, his significantly expanding official apparatus, his extravagant way of life and his responsibilities towards his extended family, together with his other obligations, necessitated resources beyond his earning capabilities. By the late 1920s he was in debt to individuals, firms, and to the state.

Seeking to help al-Glaoui repay his debts – and probably also in recognition of his support for the French cause during the anti-Berber Edict protests and the pacification battles – the Sharifian state agreed to borrow the sum of 50 million francs from the French La Caisse de Dépôts et Consignations (the Fund of Deposits and Consignations).[18] Via a second contract, the Sharifian state transferred this sum to the Pasha of Marrakesh in two payments of 25 million francs each, to be repaid in twenty-five annual instalments. The Sharifian state served as an intermediary, providing security for the Fund of Deposits and Consignations. Specific real estate holdings of al-Glaoui were designated as a guarantee for the loan.

The size of the loan can be grasped by comparing it to other loans taken out by the Moroccan state during that period. In general, two types of state loans could be obtained in such circumstances: direct loans, to finance state activities, and indirect loans, made to other bodies and guaranteed by the Moroccan government (as in al-Glaoui's case). Between 1922 and 1932, the total sum of direct loans borrowed by the Moroccan state was 1,702,284,101 francs. Al-Glaoui's loan was 2.9 per cent of this sum – more or less the same as the sum total of all state loans granted to the Department of Agriculture, Commerce and Colonisation between 1922 and 1932 (to compare, the Department of Public Works used 71 per cent of the state loan; Barbe 2016: 79–81).

Among the considerations that al-Glaoui made before taking the loan was his involvement in a project initiated by the protectorate's administration – the creation of a 'reserved quarter' – a prostitution zone – in Marrakesh (Harries 2016). The idea was to create something similar to the Bousbir prostitution quarter in Casablanca, which had been constructed by the protectorate and started operating at about the same time (Staszak 2015). The motivation for constructing a state-sponsored reserved quarter was to improve hygiene and decency in Marrakesh by concentrating its approximately 1,000 prostitutes in a controlled area. In order to begin this operation, the authorities asked al-Glaoui to negotiate the purchase of the necessary area, for an inclusive price of 10 million francs. Al-Glaoui began to put the necessary transactions into effect, probably envisioning potential future revenues – which, not incidentally, would help with the repayment of his 50-million-franc loan.

In 1932, the protectorate abandoned the reserved-quarter plan due to a lack of funds, in effect giving al-Glaoui one of the 10 million francs that he had allegedly spent. However, the two sides disagreed about how much was due to al-Glaoui for his expenses on the project, and the rate of interest to be paid on each side's debts. From al-Glaoui's point of view, his losses in that project had directly impacted his ability to make full returns on his 50-million-franc loan (Schoen 1938: 162).

Regardless of the losses from the cancelled project, the debt created by the loan steadily increased. Committed to making his payments, the Pasha imposed a *ferdh* (an irregular tax) on the tribes in his territories (Lahnite 2011: 30, n. 21).[19]

The case of this loan replicates, albeit on a smaller scale, a means by which France achieved its supremacy in Morocco, and a tactic adopted by other colonial powers – a policy of debt creation (for example, Sebti 2013: 41; Barbe 2016: 93). The usual scenario of such processes was that once 'trapped' by the huge loans, the borrowers (whether states, organisations or individuals) would eventually have no choice but to surrender their property or independence to the lender. As the 1930s progressed, al-Glaoui seemed headed in this direction. However, things were to turn out differently (see Chapter 4).

The negotiations for the 50-million-franc loan and its realisation, as well as al-Glaoui's involvement in almost all business initiatives in southern Morocco (beyond the 'reserved quarter', he had an interest in an initiative to open a casino in Marrakesh, and in various mining and agricultural enterprises) triggered a new wave of newspaper attacks against him.

This time it was the left-wing French-Moroccan newspaper *Le Cri Marocain* that began to run a column about al-Glaoui, titled 'Le Roi du Sud' (the King of the South). The column was written by Carette-Bouvet, the newspaper's founder and editor. Carette-Bouvet, who was also a member of the Human Rights League, and a staunch critic of the protectorate's policies (Rollinde 2002: 46–7), used his column to accuse al-Glaoui, and the French administration, of abusing the French justice system and of acting tyrannically.[20]

This set the stage for Babin's return.

The Appearance of *Son Excellence*

In December 1932, a routine check of incoming parcels at the Marrakesh post office uncovered a suspect delivery, addressed to a Bashir al-Ghezouli. The package contained several printed proofs, marked up in pencil, followed by the word 'Morocco'. Reading through the documents, the customs officer recognised the text as excerpts from Gustave Babin's articles against al-Glaoui and the protectorate authorities, published a few years earlier in *L'Ère Française*. The parcel's franking revealed the code PARIS 6I-R.086 – the area of Paris where Babin lived at the time.[21]

The officer decided not to withhold the package, but informed General Catroux, the French commander of the Marrakesh region, of his discovery. Catroux forwarded this note, with additional commentary, to the Resident-General. General Catroux checked whether he should inform al-Glaoui about the find; at the same time, he ran a check on Bashir al-Ghezouli. Al-Ghezouli, of Tunisian origin, was a member of the entourage of Qa'id al-'Ayadi. He had also served previously as representative of Gustave Babin and his friend 'Abd al-Hakim Tounsi, in a land transaction in Guedmioua (an area south-west of Marrakesh).

From a storytelling perspective, as noted in the previous chapter, sudden appearances of al-'Ayadi in al-Glaoui's plot signposted a focal point in the tale – the convergence of actors towards a dramatic climax. And indeed, albeit lacking our perspective, back in 1932, General Catroux – a distinguished French officer with a brilliant future ahead of him – also sensed impending turmoil.[22]

Seeking an explanation, Catroux promoted the idea that the delivery of the reprints was probably one aspect of a (presumed) conflict between al-ʿAyadi and al-Glaoui. It was suggested that the former, who Catroux considered a man of 'extreme pride', was deeply offended that the protectorate had given al-Glaoui a 50-million-franc loan yet turned down his own request for a loan. Catroux suspected that al-ʿAyadi wanted to force al-Glaoui to plead with the French, on his behalf, for a mortgage – with the threat that non-cooperation would lead to the publication of Babin's scandalous claims against him. Another possible explanation was that it was Babin who was behind this affair, either as vengeance for past slights or to extort money from al-Glaoui.[23] Already, a set of stories were being conjured up to make sense of the sequence of unexplained occurrences.

A few weeks later another parcel arrived at the Marrakesh post office from Paris, this time addressed to al-ʿAyadi himself. The officer in charge opened the box and was surprised to find a copy of a book: *Son Excellence: le Maroc sans Masque* (His Excellency: Morocco without a Mask). The author was Gustave Babin. Marked as printed in December 1932, the book bore a personal dedication to al-ʿAyadi, written by Babin. Catroux informed the Resident-General of this new development, asking for guidance: to confiscate the new parcel as well as the earlier reprints (which had already been released), or to allow the parcel on its way and to see what developed. He decided upon the second – and easier – option and informed the Resident-General that in the meantime, Bashir al-Ghezouli had been seen visiting al-Glaoui. Catroux hypothesised that al-Ghezouli could be playing a double game and concluded that al-Glaoui was probably already aware of developments. Again, a narrative was invented to make sense of the ongoing series of events, and to justify the path of action decided upon. Specifically: if al-Glaoui already knew about the slanderous publication, then why should the General trouble himself to inform him of his suspicions?

Son Excellence (Babin 1932; in this study, I consulted the second edition, dated 1934) presents Babin's allegations against al-Glaoui, in graphic language full of detail and rich in metaphors. According to the book, al-Glaoui was an imposter who had invented heroic deeds for his own self-aggrandisement. He kidnapped people, exploited orphans and widows, stole property from the weak, revenged himself on others, murdered, disrupted justice, terrorised people, and destabilised French rule in Morocco in a way liable to upset French values – even in France itself. In the book, Babin adopted the role of a missionary on a crusade to expose 'the real face' of al-Glaoui and the Frenchmen collaborating with him – to save France and Morocco.

Beyond promoting the book in France, Babin distributed the text to notables in France and in Morocco.[24] The book triggered a series of articles in the metropolitan newspaper *La Tribune de Paris*, further elaborating on Babin's allegations.[25] To further bolster the book's popularity, Babin sent clips of these articles to numerous personages in Morocco and France.[26] Seizing the opportunity, *Le Radical Franco-Marocain*, a Moroccan newspaper published in Rabat, published excerpts from Babin's book as well.[27]

Babin's book was received enthusiastically by the Moroccan nationalist movement, whose growth had accelerated after the promulgation of the Berber Edict. One of its leading spokespersons, Ahmed Balafrej – an editor of the nationalist newspaper *Maghreb* – soon afterwards wrote an article in support of Babin (Balafarej 1933). On a later occasion, he also praised Babin's former newspaper, *L'Ère Française*, saying: 'This newspaper served us, those who had begun learning the French language, as a practical school, since it was the only well-written newspaper at the time, and it also had other advantages' (Baïda 1996, 168).

Press Storytellers

The reignited conflict between al-Glaoui and Babin spread into a domain which had witnessed a substantial boost in 1930s colonial Morocco – journalism. The form of the conflict no doubt owed its origin to the evolution of French political culture after the French Revolution – which, according to historian Otto Scott, could not have occurred without the press. As he puts it:

> The press played the role of Author of the Event. It invented incidents and conceived legends. Most of these are now so deeply embedded in textbooks – such as the myth that the

Bastille was stormed by an enraged populace – that they cannot be removed. (Scott 1978: 4)

At the beginning of the twentieth century, France was home to a vast array of politically charged newspapers,[28] the most extreme using venomous means to promote their ideological goals.[29] In Morocco, at the onset of the protectorate,[30] Lyautey formulated local press legislation to prevent the publication of anti-French propaganda by foreign powers and to block extreme journalists from undermining the protectorate. The push for this legislation came from the fear that the press could transform itself into an anti-government weapon. One of the first editors of *Es-Saada* – the government newspaper, published in Arabic – observed that journalism was a dangerous weapon in inexperienced hands; Moroccans had not yet reached the stage in their development that would enable them to deal with this threat appropriately (Baïda 1992: 68–70).

In addition to preventing unwanted activities, the colonial administration took a keen interest in using the press to disseminate the government's desired self-image. Towards this aim, it founded newspapers such as *La Renaissance du Maroc*, presenting the protectorate's policies and subtly criticising aspects of political life in the metropole. Their delicate message, in Lyautey's time, was that his conduct in Morocco had succeeded in creating a civil morality (allegedly) absent in France (Slavin 1998; Otero-Pailos 1998: 24–6).

Until the end of the Great War, Morocco's press was tightly supervised. When this supervision was loosened, newspapers – especially those representing French *colons* – frequently, and publicly, attacked the protectorate's administration and its practices, demanding various privileges for the *colons*. In one extreme case targeting General Calmel, commander of the Casablanca region, the general suspended the offending paper for fifteen days and sued the editors. However, the editors were exonerated by the judges (Baïda 1992: 73).

Attacks by the press were not reserved for low-ranking officials, but also targeted the Resident-General as well. Bidwell comments that Lyautey was accused of multiple transgressions, ranging from claims that he was gay to insinuations that he took bribes. The accusations created such a poisonous atmosphere that Lyautey considered resigning more than once (Bidwell 1973: 27). As in the case of *Son Excellence* appearing as part of the Babin–al-Glaoui conflict, books were sometimes published alongside the newspapers' articles, as for example Henri Labadie-Lagrave's *Le mensonge marocain: contribution à l'histoire «vraie» du Maroc* (The Moroccan Lie: Contribution to the 'True' History of Morocco; Labadie-Lagrave 1925), a major defamatory attack on Lyautey.

The administration tried several strategies to stop these attacks. One was to purchase the offending newspaper, reaching an agreement with its editor to leave Morocco. Another was simply to expel the editor, as was the case with *La Guêpe Marocaine*, a paper established in Morocco in 1920. Its editor, Jourdan, sought out scandals and threatened to publish them unless his silence was bought. In 1922, Jourdan, with his Tunisian partner Ben-Amor, tried to instigate a conflict between Muslims and Jews in Morocco. This situation presented as far too dangerous to Lyautey, who decided to expel the editors. A third way of reducing press attacks against the government was the creation of press corporations, who refrained from attacking the administration and received preferential treatment in return (Baïda 1992: 76–88). Some of these corporations also ran newspapers and companies in France, exemplifying the intensive links that developed between metropole and colony over time.

Babin's writing style, in both *L'Ère Française* and his book, shared the offensive discourse common in the metropole and among the French colonial milieu of the 1920s and 1930s. In Babin's view, being critical of the administration and its representatives was the essence of the journalistic mission. His book discusses journalists who betrayed this duty, distinguishing conscientious reporters (like himself) who reported the truth from those who were mouthpieces for others or merely stupid (Babin 1934: 70). As evidence of his professional success, Babin quoted a letter he received from a Moroccan reader:

> I gladly see, he wrote me in the beginning of his letter, that you give in your newspaper *L'Ère Française* . . . an important and a compulsory place for the real history of Morocco, and about the accurate opinions about the people of today. (Babin 1934: 62)

Babin identified a certain naivety among French journalists in Morocco. Charmed by invitations for mint tea at his palace, their naivety left them easy prey for al-Glaoui's manipulations. In Babin's opinion, these journalists were to a large extent responsible for the myth of al-Glaoui (Babin 1934: 69).

Babin did not spare the administration either. He accused it of silencing the press, fearful that journalists would scare the public with their sensational revelations – even though this, that is, exposing wrongdoing and incompetence, was precisely the role of journalism. In bringing up this point, he referred to the loan al-Glaoui received from France, stating:

> However, Parliament must have ratified this broad philanthropy, some evening, at the end of the session, with twenty deputies in the room, sure friends of course, and paid dear enough to mobilise – unless one has once again broken the law in any way. But you also know if the newspapers are now well styled; if there is any new scandal below, we will have commandingly urged them not to frighten us. (Babin 1934: 267)

Babin reported the case of the editor of *Es-Saada* instructing a reporter to remove a report praising one of al-Glaoui's victims. To keep silent, he concluded elsewhere, is tantamount to collaborating in al-Glaoui's crimes (Babin 1934: 232).

Side by side with his criticism, Babin praised the few French-Moroccan newspapers that were not silent. He cited *Le Réveil du Moghreb*, which published articles about al-Glaoui's immoralities in Marrakesh, calling it 'the poisoned city'; *Cri Marocain*, which had published accounts of al-Glaoui's difficulties in repaying the 50-million-franc loan; and *L'Atlas*, which reported on corruption cases involving al-Glaoui's nephew.

From a contemporary point of view, Babin's ideas conform with the principles of a free and ethical press, as articulated, for example, by the International Federation of Journalists (IFJ) in its 1954 Bordeaux Declaration.[31] Yet, and again from a contemporary perspective, it appears that even with his call for decent journalism, Babin's ethical stand was rather restricted, given that he backed France's immoral colonial rule, and was an advocate of racist categorisations (see below).

Babin was brave in confronting someone of al-Glaoui's standing. But he only did so from the safety of France. Somehow, it was his fellow journalists who eventually found themselves facing al-Glaoui in the law courts.

In Response to a Scandalous Campaign

Even before the incident with Babin, al-Glaoui was aware of the power of the press. For a period in the 1920s, he had used the services of l'Argus de la Presse, a French company that aggregated data from newspapers on behalf of people or bodies who wanted to know what was being published about them.[32] Simultaneously, recalling Lyautey's use of the media, al-Glaoui hosted receptions for international journalists at his palaces, part of a drive to globally boost his image as an Oriental 'noble savage' (West 1932: 215).

When Babin extended his newspaper attacks into a full-length book, al-Glaoui retaliated with a twenty-two-page response, *En réponse à une campagne infâme* (In Response to a Scandalous Campaign; al-Glaoui 1933). The booklet presents a lengthy account of his services on behalf of France, cited as proof of his devotion to the French cause (see more about the booklet below). At the same time, he sued the newspapers who had slandered him: *Le Radical Franco-Marocain* in Morocco, and *La Tribune de Paris* in France. Here, al-Glaoui's actions resembled those of the Resident-General in similar circumstances.

Al-Glaoui also turned his hand to publishing, for a while running an independent newspaper called *Shams el-Janub*.[33] It is thought that at the end of the 1930s, he had also bought four French-Moroccan newspapers (Maxwell 1966: 180).[34] Thus, defying the colonialist notions of distinct abilities and roles in relation to 'the coloniser' and 'the colonised', al-Glaoui constantly switched roles and confounded expectations. One moment, he was an Oriental Pasha; the next, a European-style politician and businessman, employing available modern 'toolkits' to achieve his goals. Some observers, like Babin, were astounded to discover a native Moroccan comfortable with using the press – one of the symbols of French enlightenment – for his own ends, duplicating the work-patterns of French politicians and corporations.[35]

This notwithstanding, al-Glaoui's favoured arena was the legal system, where thanks to his roles of pasha and *qa'id* he would have felt much more 'at home'. The spectrum of legal options available to al-Glaoui was substantial. During this period, several legal systems operated in Morocco, creating a status often described as legal pluralism (Rosen 1999: 92–3; El Qadéry 2007: 32–6; Marglin 2017: 12–14; for a description of a similar situation in colonial Algeria, see Christelow 1985). These systems included *Shari'a*, managed by *qadi*s (judges) appointed by the Sultan, which dealt with inheritance and land cases. Alongside it, pashas and *qa'id*s presided over criminal cases, in their capacity of managing-officials within the Sultan's civil administration. In the countryside, there was also a customary law system (*'urf*) applied by local courts (*jama'a*), which presided over cases that in urban areas would have fallen under the jurisdiction of the *Shari'a* courts. In addition, as a colonial entity, a French legal system operated in Morocco. This dealt with economic issues and cases that involved Europeans, or Europeans and Moroccans; the overarching principle was that no European should be subject to the jurisdiction of Islamic law (Bidwell 1973: 271–2; Pennell 2000: 173; Bédoucha 2000).[36]

Al-Glaoui, in his roles of pasha and *qa'id*, was a part of the local judicial system (Schoen 1938: 96). He managed a *mahkama* (court) in Marrakesh responsible for criminal cases concerning the local population. Maxwell writes that in these courts, al-Glaoui's verdicts were delivered orally. No written records were kept, and Maxwell argues that al-Glaoui's court was free from French supervision (Maxwell 1966: 183). Bidwell claims that in territories under the effective rule of al-Glaoui, he encouraged the establishment of *Shari'a* courts instead of the customary-law courts, because he found the *qadi*s easier to control than the tribal leadership (Bidwell 1973: 265). Babin made a similar claim, adding that al-Glaoui manipulated the French legal apparatus; he described an investigation of a murder case, which (according to him), was executed by a direct order of al-Glaoui. Babin concluded his discussion with the following words:

> The indigenous investigation conducted under the leadership of His Excellency el Hadj Thami el Glaoui has, obviously, only one goal: to mislead French justice, to divert punishment from the true criminal, to stifle the suspicions which, from the first hour, have arisen, to silence the formal accusations ... (Babin 1934: 236)

Beyond being a judge in his own court, al-Glaoui was also involved in multiple lawsuits, as both suer and sued, thanks to his numerous business dealings.[37] In such instances, he had

Figure 3.1 'Al-Glaoui at the Grand Hotel' (Photo Traverso).
Source: *Le Journal des étrangers,* 25 September 1932, p. 9.
Modifications have been made to the original image.
Courtesy: BnF.

the support of several lawyers representing him, including the Moroccan Jewish lawyer Félix Guedj.[38]

By 1933, judging from the available evidence, al-Glaoui was all set for a legal campaign against Babin.

The Battle in Court

The French colonial administration learned of al-Glaoui's intentions to go to court at the end of 1933.[39] Al-Glaoui approached General Catroux, commander of the Marrakesh region, demanding the right to suppress any 'defamatory' statements levelled against him in the territories under his command. He stressed the fact – in a form of a veiled threat – that the Marrakesh area was tranquil, and should remain this way.[40] The general immediately summoned the recently appointed Resident-General,

Henri Ponsot (in office from August 1933 to March 1936) to Marrakesh to meet with al-Glaoui.[41] At the meeting, al-Glaoui argued that, as he was a public figure who had consistently supported the French, it was France's duty to stand by his side.[42] Al-Glaoui added that he was certain that there were legal avenues that could be used by the protectorate to influence the outcome of his cases in the courts of Rabat and Paris.[43]

Henri Ponsot responded in a patronising manner, informing the French foreign office: 'I answered the Pasha that I regret he did not inform me beforehand about his intentions, because I had estimated that the juridical move that had begun under these circumstances fitted neither the time nor the place.'[44]

There was a precedent for al-Glaoui's request: the French administration had stood by his side in earlier cases.[45] But being attentive to the new Resident-General's tone, al-Glaoui answered:

> Since I am not familiar with the French law, I thought that it was within the Resident-General's authority to put an end to this matter. I understand that it does not work this way and therefore I have to apply to the French legal authorities.[46]

Accordingly, al-Glaoui and his lawyers prepared to sue the newspaper editors who had defamed him. Their strategy was to emphasise his loyalty to France and to the Moroccan Sultan – which meant that allegations made against him applied equally to these distinguished entities as well. The documents prepared for the trials quoted, verbatim, citations accompanying the various decorations he had been awarded by the French between 1916 to 1925.[47] Simultaneously, al-Glaoui approached the Sultan; after noting the historic loyalty of his family to the 'Alawi dynasty, he requested the Sultan's support.[48] Following these steps, al-Glaoui re-appealed to the Resident-General,[49] asking that he exonerate him and punish the slanderers, in coordination with the Sultan.

Information about the impending trial was published in the French press in late 1933, alerting the metropolitan administration.[50] The Foreign Office wrote urgently to the Resident-General in Morocco, asking for an explanation, and ordered the General Security Office in Paris to collect information about the defendants' preparations for the trial.[51]

Following the request, the Resident General in Morocco prepared a secret position-file summarising the affair.[52] General de la Baume, the author of the file, concluded that while there might be some truth in Babin's allegations, the claims were exaggerated. He noted that the situation in Morocco, as well as the local mentality, should be taken into consideration; the behaviour that Babin complained about represented the general anarchy that France had met in Morocco (an often-cited French colonial cliché, usually used to justify the *mission civilisatrice*). De la Baume recommended careful consideration of the political consequences of supporting al-Glaoui. Al-Glaoui had assisted the French in very substantial terms, after all, and remained an exceptionally loyal ally. Thus, he concluded, it seemed necessary to support him. General de la Baume ended his report by observing that as the French had consistently demonstrated their appreciation for al-Glaoui, it would be remiss to abandon him now. De la Baume strengthened his evaluation by citing General Catroux's recommendation letter, which led to the approval of the 50-million-franc loan to al-Glaoui.[53]

Based on this position file, Resident-General Ponsot communicated his evaluation to the Foreign Office in France,[54] adding that he had attended a meeting with the Sultan on this topic. He summarised his report by noting: '[P]eople of authority here [meaning the Sultan and his court] are worrying very much, and this anxiety may severely impact their behaviour. From this perspective, the timing of Pasha al-Glaoui's lawsuits is not too good.'[55]

Resident-General Ponsot also tried to discover what was going on in the corridors of power in the metropole, and the information that the head of the General Security Office in Paris had discovered.[56] He managed to secure this information from Lucien Saint, a friend who also happened to be a previous Resident-General in Morocco and was now a French senator.[57]

Meanwhile, and in contrast to the metropole where the legal process moved slowly, issues in Morocco progressed apace. The lawyer representing the editor of *Le Radical Franco-Marocain* claimed that his client had been led into an error by one of his partners. The editor published an apology, al-Glaoui accepted his regret, and the case was closed.[58]

Just as the cases in Morocco were being settled, and it seemed that the incident was about to be put to rest, Babin stirred things up again by sending Resident-General Ponsot the updated 1934 edition of *Son Excellence*.[59] Simultaneously in France, Georges

Grilhé, the editor of *La Tribune de Paris*, published more short notes denouncing al-Glaoui.[60]

Al-Glaoui now turned to Paris, seeking leave to sue Georges Grilhé at a French *tribunal correctionnel* – a court of first instance, which adjudicated criminal offences. The defendant's lawyers resisted this move, seeking instead to have the case transferred to the *cour d'assises*, a departmental court. The reason for this was that the first option would be heard behind closed doors, while the other would be in open court, with a public jury.[61] Bizos, Grilhé's lawyer, rationalised the request on the grounds that al-Glaoui was a French functionary, and thus the case should be heard in the open. Al-Glaoui's lawyers disagreed, claiming that their client was a Moroccan functionary.[62] The court agreed with the latter, rejecting Grilhé's appeal to have the case moved to the *cour d'assises*.[63]

Three months later, the Paris *tribunal correctionnel* heard al-Glaoui's lawsuit for the first time and reached an interim decision. It stated that the accusations made by Grilhé were directed at a functionary of the French government, working in its service and carrying its decorations, and not a private person. Therefore, because 'the file did not contain any element that will enable an evaluation of this perspective', it was crucial to clarify the legal status of the Pasha: 'only when this becomes clear the lawsuit can be discussed.'[64]

The Foreign Ministry set out to fulfil the court's request, requesting legal opinions from its offices in France and in Morocco.[65] The answer from Morocco was that al-Glaoui was undoubtedly a Moroccan functionary.[66] The Sultan had appointed him, and the French Resident-General had accepted this nomination. Concerning the French war decorations, the protectorate office indicated that al-Glaoui had never commanded French troops, but only Moroccan ones performing *harka*s alongside their French counterparts; it was the combined action of both troops that had brought about the pacification.

The question of al-Glaoui's status was not an awkward one, since (as detailed in the previous chapter) different narratives about his affiliation had become established through, among other things, the inaccurate translation of his letters at the protectorate offices in the 1910s. For example, while al-Glaoui's original Arabic text had thanked the Sharifian Empire for the medals he had been awarded, the French version delivered to their commanders stated that he thanked France for granting him the medals. Thus, what may have seemed an innocent textual mismatch turned out to be the basis for a crucial legal decision.

As the legal proceedings became more intractable, the attorneys representing both sides met and agreed on an out-of-court settlement (Maxwell 1966: 176). I was not successful in determining the precise terms of this settlement; what is clear, however, is that defamatory comments about al-Glaoui in the press ceased.

Al-Glaoui's actions, particularly his lawsuits, testify to his mastery of the maze that was the legal system in colonial Morocco and the metropole. Legal pluralism is often conceived as a controlling device wielded by the coloniser, leveraging the vagueness, blurriness and overlaps created by multiple systems to its own ends (Christelow 1985: 3–4; Shahar 2012: 134). The conflict between al-Glaoui and Babin demonstrates, however, that in this case, manoeuvres were effected by *all* the actors, and in multiple directions. Al-Glaoui knew 'the rules of the game', demonstrating a talent for manipulation amidst complexity. Simultaneously, as other cases indicate, French administrators in Morocco used the multiple legal options against not only the colonised, but also against other French groups: settlers, commercial firms who had fallen out of favour, and even groups in the metropole (see similar observations in Merry 1991: 891).

A Round Table on Truth and Loyalty

The detailed texts produced during the battle between al-Glaoui and Babin provide enough contextual material for an imaginary dialogue between the two – the topics in dispute more abstract and theoretical than the specific details of their clash, but nevertheless at the heart of their conflict. I propose one such debate on a specific issue about which the two were in utter disagreement, namely the basis of a person's integrity: truth or loyalty.

Babin's opinion on the topic is clear from the subtitle of his book: *Le Maroc sans Masque* (Morocco without a Mask). His basic premise is that there is 'a truth' about Morocco, but that this is camouflaged and that it is his duty to reveal it. Babin frequently connected 'truth' with 'historical truth'. In his book, he quotes a letter he received from a Moroccan reader of his newspaper, thanking him for giving in his newspaper 'an important and necessary place for the *real* history of Morocco' (Babin 1934: 62; my italics).

Revealing the 'real history' is a motif that runs throughout Babin's narrative. For example, in the chapter titled 'The Rescuer of the French' (Babin 1934: 45), Babin discusses al-Hiba's takeover of Marrakesh in 1912 – the event during which al-Glaoui supposedly saved French citizens caught in the city (Chapter 2). Babin claims that the tale of rescuing the French hostages was a myth, one that had so become entrenched in the consciousness that it had become impossible to convince anyone that it never occurred (Babin 1934: 45). Babin, thus, proposes a critical examination of history in light of the documents presented in the chapter, in order to determine 'the truth'.

Related to truth is justice. The French, according to Babin, arrived in Morocco in the name of justice. Their goal was to save the Moroccan people, and to grant them a noble ideal: that of French justice. (Sometimes, he also uses an analogous term, 'French order'.) Babin's ideal falls well within the French colonial discourse of the *mission civilisatrice*, whose claimed goal was to spread the 'superior and just' French culture around the world (Lorcin 1995: 171). As a part of this discourse, the French arrived in Morocco in order to remove the cruel tyranny of a crumbling empire. Babin contends that the French had promised justice to the Moroccans, but that this noble objective had turned into a lie, thanks to people like al-Glaoui and his French supporters (Babin 1934: 8).

Babin's central claim is that al-Glaoui, and those French whom he had corrupted, were preventing the 'good' French from implementing the ideal of French justice for the Moroccans. What was happening in practice, Babin writes, is that 'the French hold the horns of the cow while [al-Glaoui] milks it' (Babin 1934: 136). Or, as he wrote elsewhere, criticising corrupt elements within the protectorate apparatus: '[T]he protectors, the civilisers, the servants of cleanliness, of justice, of progress, of so many sublime nonsense-proclaimed-sacred in generals' orders of the day, and the oratories of civilians, have allowed to survive, protected and perpetuated these barbarous customs' (Babin 1934: 140).

Thus, Babin, the colonial storyteller, positions himself and al-Glaoui at the two opposing ends of the discourse: one an honest man who stands for the truth and justice, the other a corrupt man whose avowals are but a lie.

In a study of cultural hybridity, colonial authority and performance in colonial India, Benton and Muth (2000) quote a scene from Forster's (1928) *A Passage to India*. The scene in question describes a trial in a British colonial court, with both British and Indian litigants. At a certain point, the prosecutor presses one of the witnesses, a British woman, 'to say the truth'; she begins her speech with the words 'I was raised to say the truth.' The implication is that the judges *must* accept the testimony of a British woman, because she understands the sacredness of an oath and the value of truth. However, the testimony of a native – even a Brahmin scholar – is suspect. The Indian way of thinking was conceived as cunning in its very essence, and a native would be unable to appreciate – much less provide – objective testimony (Benton and Muth 2000: 9).

Son Excellence presents a markedly similar concept. It is based on the idea that Babin, as a Frenchman, has the natural disposition to see 'objective facts' and 'historical truth', while al-Glaoui cannot. Babin knows 'the truth', and shares this with his readers; al-Glaoui hides and distorts it.

In my imagined dialogue between al-Glaoui and Babin, one would then be prompted to ask al-Glaoui something along the lines of: do the concepts of 'truth', 'historical truth' and 'objective facts' also represent, for you, such essential components of appropriate conduct?

Al-Glaoui's voice on this issue can be heard first and foremost through his *Son Excellence. En réponse à une campagne infâme: quelques documents* (al-Glaoui 1933). The twenty-page booklet – in fact, the only publication authored by al-Glaoui – reveals some of his self-image and his broader standpoints. The booklet is basically a chronologically arranged collection of excerpts, with almost no accompanying text. It includes selected quotes from Babin's texts, excerpts from the honours received by al-Glaoui, and copies of letters that the latter had sent to the Sultan and the Resident-General. Al-Glaoui's response to the question of 'truth' can be clearly deduced from the claims he raises in this booklet, namely:

1. Babin is disloyal and inconsistent in his views.
2. I am completely loyal to the Sultan and to France.
3. I deny Babin's accusations of cowardice on the battlefield.
4. I act as a representative of the French and the Sharifian administrations, as can be seen from the honours I have accepted.

Al-Glaoui's reaction does not aspire to expose any 'objective fact' or 'the truth', except concerning his bravery on the battlefield.

What appears to be the most fundamental claim concerns one's place within a patronage system in which unreserved support is expected in return for total loyalty.

His more direct answers to Babin would have been, thus: first, I am entirely and consistently loyal to the Sultan and to the French administration; and second, I do what I do as a Moroccan and a French functionary, and this proves the appropriateness of my conduct. 'Truth' is also involved – Babin is a liar, and I am truthful; but this is secondary to the main issues, which are loyalty and reliability.

Two different worldviews emerge thus. Babin's baselines are 'facts' and 'truth', while the basics of al-Glaoui are 'loyalty' and 'trustworthiness'. Taken on their own imagined terms, the men were faithful to distinct sets of values, both essentially linked with discourses that they belonged to: the rhetoric of the French Third Republic on the one hand, Moroccan imperial aphorisms on the other.

Al-Glaoui's concepts, are also evident in Lawrence Rosen's observations about the theme of 'negotiation' in Morocco:

> [T]ake the issue of trust in Islamic law and Moroccan society. Moroccan social relations rest on the negotiation of bonds of indebtedness among persons who have gained control of their passions by the development of their reasoning powers through religious education, dependence on people who are themselves attached to others, and by demonstrating how reliable they are once they have given their word. To address the question, then, of when is a bargain made by solely emphasizing the use of a technical form promulgated by the courts would run counter to ordinary sense about what makes a person trustworthy. (Rosen 1999: 91)

Yet, Babin's and al-Glaoui's differing views on these matters do not necessarily delineate emblematic 'French' or 'Moroccan' cultural approaches but are very much an effect of their corresponding positions. For example, French field colonial administrators often saw things much like al-Glaoui – a patronage system that is a priori reciprocal, with the two sides obliged to each other.[67] At the same time, executive staff distant from the field – like functionaries in the French Foreign Office in Paris, or even Le Ministre Plénipotentiaire Délègue à la Résidence Générale de la Republique Française au Maroc (the Minister

Plenipotentiary Delegate at the General Residence of the French Republic in Morocco) in Rabat – used Babin-style dichotomies more readily.[68] But, for them, unlike Babin, the discussions about al-Glaoui's image were not theoretical ponderings but actual and tangible policy-making.

Frenchness Matters

The mixing of people is an inherent characteristic of colonialism. As concerns French colonialism, people from the colonies migrated to France; French citizens settled in the colonies and 'creolisation' often occurred – as with, for example the French West-African *métis* (Ginio 2017: 1). In these multiple contexts, identity with its manifold aspects became pivotal in matters such as property rights, individual and legal status, self-imagining and power relations. During the period of the Glaoui–Babin encounter, the height of French colonialism, French society was accordingly possessed by identity politics. While the right-wing espoused racism and hailed the colonial project, other French circles, such as the Negritude Movement of migrants from the colonies, challenged French colonialism (Forsdick 2004; Brown Spencer 2006: 117–19). Facing these contestations, the government strived to present the colonial project as a great success. One measure taken to this effect was the 1931 Colonial Exposition – itself severely criticised – which presented the achievements of colonialism (Lebovics 1992: 51–97; Holland 2003: 160). While not stating as much formally, the presentation in the exposition of the many 'others' ruled by France effectively served to define who is 'French'. In that context, 'true' Frenchness emerged as an 'essence that no Jew, foreigner, or person of color could ever share' (Conklin 2000: 229–30).

Steeped in this atmosphere, Babin was deeply involved in identity politics and very sensitive to definitions of Frenchness – which, in time, became another hot-spot in his critique of al-Glaoui.

As early as the first chapter of his book, Babin accuses al-Glaoui of fabricating his genealogy to link himself with the Prophet's family. Babin describes al-Glaoui's claim as absurd because, by definition, *shlukh shurafa* cannot exist. *Shurafa* – descendants of the Prophet, who was Arab – must be Arab, and not Amazigh (*shlukh* referring to people of Amazigh descent). Babin asserted that not only was al-Glaoui not an Arab but, even as an Amazigh, he was of a lesser status, given that his racial background was mixed with that of the black population. Babin then presents another al-Glaoui fantasy: a genealogical link with the sixteenth-century Saʿadian sultan Mansur al-Dhahabi,[69] which Babin describes as a foolish claim invented to establish religious prestige (Babin 1934: 16–19).

Babin, as his text reveals, had firm views about racial hierarchies. For him, beyond the differences between the French and the Moroccans, the Moroccans themselves were not equal. Arabs stood at the top of the domestic hierarchy, followed by the Amazigh, with the blacks and Jews at the bottom (for his opinion about Jews, see Chapter 5).[70] As described above, in their Moroccan project the French sought to separate Arabs and Amazighs for purposes of control (see, for example, Burke 1972). Babin, it seems, accepted this distinction; but unlike the administration, which favoured the Amazighs, he accorded the Arabs higher esteem.

But what enraged Babin the most was not al-Glaoui's alleged attempts to present himself as descendent of a local elite, but his encroachment on Frenchness. For example, Babin describes the French General Daugan bidding al-Glaoui farewell on the former's departure from the Marrakesh area in the early 1920s. Al-Glaoui allegedly told Daugan: 'You can go away and be assured that during your absence I will be ... at least as French as you are' (Babin 1934: 68). Babin expresses his bewilderment at al-Glaoui's rudeness in proclaiming that he was French – especially to a French general.

A French journalist who interviewed al-Glaoui and was charmed by his personality, infuriates Babin even more. In the interview, the journalist asked al-Glaoui if one could remain reassured by the quiet from the southern tribes. After being reassured that the tribes would remain quiet under his control as they had been during the Great War, the journalist expressed his conviction that al-Glaoui was indeed a loyal friend of France. Here al-Glaoui interrupted, saying: 'No ... I am French, and if France is struck, it is as if I am attacked too' (Babin 1934: 70). Babin states that the interview is full of lies and deceits. But for him, the worst of it was al-Glaoui's claim, 'I am French' (Babin 1934: 72).

Babin's theory is that from the moment al-Glaoui presented himself as French, chaos ensued. Not only was it unclear where 'Moroccan' ended and 'French' began, there was a real risk of

Moroccanness invading the very heart of France. Al-Glaoui had crossed the lines; he was presenting himself as a Frenchman, using the French legal system, buying off French functionaries, sending his sons to be educated in France,[71] and even 'tempting' French women.[72]

Most troubling for Babin was the fact that al-Glaoui had created a political lobby in Paris to advance his interests. Contemptuously, Babin describes them as 'the Glaoua tribe on Oued Seine'.[73] Its very existence symbolised the incursion of the colony into the metropole – a fusion that, from Babin's viewpoint, dangerously blurred the border between coloniser and colonised.

This 'Glaoua tribe on Oued Seine', in Babin's descriptions, presents a group of gift-loving members of parliament and businessmen who had promoted al-Glaoui's immunity (Babin 1934: 9). Babin was especially disappointed by Steeg, the ex-French Resident-General in Morocco (1925 to 1929), suggesting that instead of embedding French order in Morocco, he had only acted for personal gain. Babin suggests that Steeg focused on French rather than Moroccan politics, and thus was overly preoccupied by what 'the Glaoua tribe on Oued Seine' might think of him (Babin 1934: 11–12). Any member of the French apparatus in Morocco who dared complain of any evil in the colony, Babin claims, would be exiled by the Parisian 'tribe' (Babin 1934: 32).

Al-Glaoui, Babin continues, bought off an ex-senior official of Lyautey's administration; with his assistance and the backing of 'the Glaoua tribe on Oued Seine', he was able to secure the 50-million-franc loan. This was twice the entire debt of all the French settlers in Morocco, who, incidentally, had applied in vain to the administration for help. Babin describes how French personalities and officers had begun to acknowledge the measure of the problem and tried to warn the administration of al-Glaoui's machinations, to no avail. He refers to Henri de la Martinière, who had expressed his negative opinion about *caïdalisme* – adding that no one listened to him. Babin writes that 'perhaps the report [by de la Martinière] still exists at the Foreign Office if the people of the Glaoua tribe on Oued Seine did not manage to sneak it out of there' (Babin 1934: 89). General Daugan had delivered a plan for a discreet solution to the Glaoui problem, Babin says – replacing civilian rule with a military administration. However, this did not happen thanks to General

Steeg, who was in constant fear 'of the terrible tribe on the banks of Oued Seine' (Babin 1934: 90).

Al-Glaoui, in this telling, exercised influence over events not only in the colony but also in France. For people like Babin, this was inconceivable. He could accept a French politician running a lobby in France; but for a native to do so was unthinkable.

Historians Lauren Benton and John Muth describe a situation by which:

> Colonial agents and metropolitan observers responded with particular urgency to unsettling images of subordinate peoples acting in roles that were identified culturally in the West with authority and were assigned the specific, positive cultural associations of dignity, courage, intelligence, and skill. (Benton and Muth 2000: 4)

This observation describes occasions when colonialists evoked special qualities of otherness to explain circumstances when natives functioned like Europeans. For example, when an indigenous army fought well, it was understood in terms of the barbarity or the inherent shrewdness of its soldiers and commanders.[74] Similarly, the 'positive qualities' of local elites were sometimes explained as a result of having become westernised. The use of 'westernisation' was problematic, though, given that the common colonial claim was that the locals could never understand the rationality of (for example) European law, putting westernisation beyond them (Benton and Muth 2000, 5). This line of thought indeed typifies Babin's narrative, insisting that al-Glaoui could not grasp virtues like 'French justice' or 'truth' – and therefore could not become French.

Studies of colonialism often discuss the idea that characterisation of the 'other' by European colonialists effectively enabled definitions of 'the European'. These studies have further demonstrated that these characterisations were often undermined by mimicry, ambivalence, hybridity and the multiplicity of identities, which collectively weakened and resisted colonial authority (Bhabha 1984). Developing these ideas, Benton and Muth propose a differentiation between two main behaviours in these contexts: 'colonial discourse' and 'colonial cultural conduct'. They frame the first as a binary conception focused on two opposing cultures – a hegemonic culture versus a subaltern one. Next to it, they envision what they label 'colonial cultural conduct' – a multi-faceted practice displaying a cultural blend emerging from the colonial encounters. In their view, 'colonial cultural conduct' creates a state of 'in-betweenness', asserting that:

> Cultural in-betweenness was present in the colonial context as both a cultural category, encompassing some social actors and excluding others, and as a widely available resource, a stylistic repertoire, which could be used strategically. The mere presence of cultural blending forced articulation of the most resilient and, therefore, essential aspects of dominant and subordinate cultures. In other words, a discourse of cultural dualism emerged out of the practice of cultural confusion. (Benton and Muth 2000: 2)

Within this theoretical formulation, Babin's texts appear as products and expressions of 'colonial discourse', while al-Glaoui and some parts of the French apparatus, especially field personnel and his lobby in Paris, represented the 'in-betweenness' of the 'colonial cultural conduct'.

Pending Collapse of World Orders

Between 1934 and 1937, relations between the French Protectorate and a large swathe of Moroccan society deteriorated. In 1934, nationalist activists established the Comité d'Action Marocaine (Moroccan Action Committee, CAM), demanding economic, educational and health-care reforms, a reduction of the protectorate's authority, the increase of local rule, and al-Glaoui's dismissal. Ponsot, the French Resident-General, rejected these demands, and large protests ensued. In 1936, a left-wing coalition led by the Front Populaire won France's general elections. The new government was supportive of the working class, raising hopes for social and political change in Morocco as well (Ayache 1982: 139, 149). However, the newly appointed Resident-General, Charles Noguès, stuck to existing policies vis-à-vis the local population. In retaliation, CAM called for further protests, which led to confrontations between the nationalists and the French. In 1937, the authorities dismantled the committee. In response, a few other bodies were established, but the French dismantled these too; the administration prohibited all nationalist activity, arresting or expelling the leaders of the movement (Abun Nasr 1987: 393; Pennell 2000: 232).

Al-Glaoui seemed untouched by these events. He continued to amass wealth, do business and travel abroad. In accordance, his image gained unprecedented proportions, as can be seen in newspaper coverage of his visit to London in July 1937:

> In London now is The Paramount Pasha of Marrakesh
> *This article by Charles Graves, tells you all about this glamorous sultan, a ruler who has been wounded 17 times and has a 10 handicap at golf.*
> The visit to Great Britain of his Excellency El Hadji Fahmi El Glaoui, paramount Pasha of Marrakesh, Hereditary Sultan of the Atlas, is a matter of great significance.
>
> He is not just a picturesque figure with a particularly large Harem and an infatuation for golf. He is the most powerful man in Morocco – the country which, in view of the present world situation, is of intense importance.
> Not even the Pasha himself can really know exactly how many subjects he has. But they run into millions. His suzerainty extends to the deepest south, hundreds of miles beyond the Atlas Mountains. By contrast with the Pasha, the Sultan of Morocco (a very religious young man) is, as a territorial ruler, of minor importance.[75]

Despite this flamboyance – or perhaps due to it – al-Glaoui's financial situation continued to deteriorate. In the late 1930s, he experienced increasing difficulty in repaying his 50-million-franc loan – arrears had accrued, and the interest rate increased the debt exponentially. In 1938, the protectorate's administration became increasingly troubled by this situation. General Fougère, the French commander of the Marrakesh area, wrote to his superiors:

> [W]e already knew that he could only very exceptionally face his deadlines, that his temperament was not well suited to a control which is an attenuated form of guardianship, and that finally the Muslim fatalism will lead him to lose interest in his future and that of his family, and to think only of the present.[76]

Simultaneously, indigenous affairs officer Paul Schoen submitted his wide-ranging dissertation about al-Glaoui (see also Chapter 2). The thesis emphasised three problems, which, in their author's opinion, needed to be solved immediately: a financial problem, a political problem and the urgent need to find a successor for al-Glaoui (Schoen 1938: 203–11). Schoen's opinion was that al-Glaoui should be removed from office, so that the French could build the French Morocco that they wanted.

However, no action was taken. In part, this was due to the sense of an approaching war, with France and Britain on one side and Germany on the other side; other protectorate officers recognised the need for staunch allies like al-Glaoui in such circumstances.[77] Schoen warned of rumours suggesting that the Germans would seek to woo al-Glaoui into an alliance, by promising that in the event of hostilities they would offer independence to Egypt, and arrange in Morocco a territory ruled by 'a prince from the south'. Schoen's guess was that this referred to al-Glaoui (Schoen 1938: 120).[78] Nevertheless, the protectorate's heads decided to restore al-Glaoui, conjuring up another solution for his financial problems. Some of the unpaid debt was written off by realising the real estate assets provided as collateral for the loan: houses and land in Tangier, and the Hotel Tour Hassan and the Jean Amic structure in Rabat.[79]

Hence, on the eve of the Second World War, al-Glaoui's image had reached a magnitude exceeding any previous imaginable scale. His influence extended to France; popular narratives in Britain described him as 'the Sultan of the Atlas'; and rumours from Germany suggested that he was seen there as 'the Prince of the South'.

End of One Story, the Beginning of Another

Narratives about al-Glaoui from the years preceding the period discussed in this chapter continued to evolve in the 1930s, influenced by the practical impact of the legal and political events of the time. New strands included additional takes about the rescue of the French hostages in Marrakesh in 1912, and about al-Glaoui's war medals and who actually awarded them. At the same time, new narratives concerning al-Glaoui emerged. The most influential of these are Babin's texts; as we will see in the next chapters, these have continued to reverberate up to the present day.

New stories were added, but others came to end. On 30 April 1939, the following short note was published in the Parisian *Le Journal des Debats*:

> A piece of news that is painful announces the death of Gustave Babin
>
> ...
>
> In *L'Illustration*, as with us, Gustave Babin gained a reputation of a narrator both precise and colourful. At a particular moment he was tempted by the colonial life and settled in Morocco where he had been called by the princes Murât and d'Essling. A few years ago, he returned to Paris where all his old friends had been happy to find again the warm friend he was. Last year Gustave Babin gave a much-appreciated informal talk at the Historical Society of the 3rd Republic about Aristide Briand whom he knew in his youth at Nantes.
>
> Under the title of a war correspondent, Gustave Babin received the *Légion d'Honneur* and the *Croix de Guerre*. His funeral will be held on Monday, May 1st at 9 am. We shall meet at the chapel of Saint-Joseph hospital, 3 Pierre-Larousse Street.[80]

Notes

1. Registres paroissiaux et d'état civil des paroisses et communes de Loire-Atlantique, Rezé, *Registre de Naissances*, An 1865, No. 89.
2. His first independent article in this newspaper was: Gustave Babin, 'Le canal maritime de la basse Loire', *L'Illustration*, 15 July 1893.
3. 'Gustave Babin', *Le Journal des Debats*, 30 April 1939, p. 2.
4. Ibid.
5. To note some of his titles in *L'Illustration*: 'Le Gaz d'éclairage' (1902); 'La fermeture des écoles libres' (1902); 'Le privilège des bouilleurs de cru' (1903); 'La révolte du "Kniaz-Potemkine" et les émeutes d'Odessa' (1905); 'Comme un oiseau' (1908); 'Impressions de Suède' (1908).
6. 'Gustave Babin', *Le Journal des Debats*, 30 April 1939, p. 2.
7. CADN 1MA/282 95, 'Le pacha et la presse' undated, most probably from 1937.
8. Ibid. A. Massenat Prince d'Essling and Prince Charles Murât invested in a number of companies in Morocco during the interwar period, including La Société des Moulins du Maghreb (available at <http://www.entreprises-coloniales.fr/afrique-du-nord/Moulins_du_Maghreb.pdf> (last accessed 18 August 2023)), and the

perfume company Paris-Flor (available at <http://gallica.bnf.fr/ark:/12148/bpt6k6120200p/f48.textePage> (last accessed 18 August 2023)). Prince Murât was also the director of the Moroccan aero-club (available at <http://bibdigital.rjb.csic.es/Imagenes/P0065_07/P0065_07_257.pdf> (last accessed 13 October 2022)).
9. Gustave Babin, 'Le sac de Marrakech', *L'Ère Française*, 18 July 1927.
10. Gustave Babin, 'Marrakech: Heureuse Nouvelle', *L'Ère Française*, 18 August 1927. Lafont was a left-wing member of the French National Assembly and a member of the League for Human Rights. In 1927 he was part of a group that proposed new French citizenship laws (Irvine 2006: 77; Weil 2008: 202).
11. Gustave Babin, 'Les dernières histoires', *L'Ère Française*, 1 October 1927.
12. For example, 'La discussion du budget des colonies', *Les Annales Coloniales*, 26 December 1924.
13. Gustave Babin, 'Dans la ville empoisonnée: Faux: usage de faux', *L'Ère Française*, 5 November 1927.
14. CADN 1MA/282 97, 'Pour monsieur le directeur général des affaires indigènes', 7 November 1927.
15. The Tijania is a Sufi *tariqa*. Founded in Fes at the end of the eighteenth century, it then spread to other North African countries, as well as to Senegal.
16. To note, twenty first-century Amazigh activists propose different perspectives on the Dahir and its actual consequences. See further elaboration on this topic in Chapter 7.
17. Ministère des affaires étrangères (henceforth MAE), Série 'Maroc-Tunisie', sous-série no. 18–19 'El Glaoui May 1931 – November 1937', 159.
18. The contract was signed on 29 September 1931. Founded in 1816, La Caisse de Dépôts et Consignations is a French public financial institution that carries out activities of general interest on behalf of the state and local authorities.
19. CADN 1MA/200, No. 818, 'Le directeur général des finances, à monsieur le directeur des affaires politiques', 4 March 1938.
20. 'Le Roi du Sud', *Le Cri Marocain*, 4 April 1931; 11 April 1931; 18 April 1931; 9 May 1931; 23 May 1931.
21. CADN 1MA/282 95, 'Le Général Catroux commandant la région de Marrakech, à monsieur le commissaire résident général', 10 December 1932.
22. Subsequently, Georges Catroux was appointed to multiple positions, mainly in the French Overseas Empire – Governor General of Vietnam, Syria-Lebanon, Algeria, and many other roles; 'Georges Catroux', Ordre de la Libération. Available at <https://www.ordredelaliberation.fr/fr/compagnons/georges-catroux> (last accessed 23 August 2023).

23. CADN 1MA/282 95, 'Le Général Catroux commandant la région de Marrakech, à monsieur le commissaire résident général', 10 December 1932.
24. MAE, Série 'Maroc-Tunisie', sous-série no. 18–19 'El Glaoui May 1931 – November 1937', 170.
25. Adrien Fongrave and Georges Grilhé were the signatories to these articles, which appeared between mid-1933 and 1934; CADN 1MA/282 95, 'Copie, article paru dans la Tribune de Paris', 16 August 1933. One article accused al-Glaoui of assassinating people in conflict with him, and unsuccessfully trying to assassinate his own *khalifa*, al-Biaz; CADN 1MA/282 95, 'Les crimes du pacha', *La Tribune de Paris*, 1 October 1933.
26. CADN 1MA/282 95, 'Note de renseignements 12535', 24 August 1933; 'Le contrôleur civil chef de la région de la Chaouia, à monsieur le chef du service du contrôle civil', 29 December 1933.
27. MAE, Série 'Maroc-Tunisie', sous-série no. 18–19 'El Glaoui May 1931 – November 1937', 170, 142–3. CADN 1MA/282 95 'Pièce no. 7. Déclaration de Mr Picard, avocat de Mr Eustache, devant le tribunal de Rabat', undated, probably from January 1934.
28. Left-wing newspapers of the period included *L'Humanité*, *La Guerre Sociale* and *Le Bonnet Rouge*. Among the centre-bloc papers were *L'Homme Libre*, later named *L'Homme Enchaîné*. In addition, there was a large number of right-wing papers, like *Le Matin* and *Le Journal*, and the extreme right-wing *Écho de Paris*, *Action Française* and *L'Ami du Peuple* (Cobban 1965: 86–99, 130–43; Wilson 1968).
29. For example, *Candide*, *Je Suis Partout* and *Gringoire* (Cobban 1965: 154).
30. For pre-colonial newspapers published in Morocco, see Bensoussan 2012: 179–84.
31. 'Global Charter of Ethics for Journalists', International Federation of Journalists. Available at <https://www.ifj.org/who/rules-and-policy/global-charter-of-ethics-for-journalists> (last accessed 24 August 2023).
32. CADN 1MA/282 95, 'Le pacha et la presse', undated, most probably from 1937.
33. CADN 1MA/282 98, 'Le bruit court . . .', 17 December 1937.
34. *Le Petit Marocain*, *La Vigie Marocaine*, *Le Courier du Maroc*, *L'Echo du Maroc*.
35. During this period, the Moroccan nationalist movement also discovered the power of the press (Ihrai-Aouchar 1982; Haji 2003).
36. There was another legal system occasionally used by the administration – martial law, with its accompanying emergency regulations. This system was in use during the Great War and the Rif War (see Perkins 1981).

37. For example, CADN 1MA/282 97, 'Le consul de France à Tanger, à monsieur le Général Lyautey, résident général France au Maroc', 1 May 1913.
38. For example, CADN 1MA/282 97, img 20150331_165950 'Consultation pour monsieur le Pacha Hadj Thami Glaoui', 22 May 1923.
39. MAE, Série 'Maroc-Tunisie', sous-série no. 18–19 'El Glaoui May 1931 – November 1937', 170, 144, 158; CADN 1MA/282 95, 'Le Pacha Si el Hadj Thami el Glaoui au Général Catroux', 30 November 1933.
40. CADN 1MA/282 95, Thami al-Glaoui to 'Monsieur le général commandant la région de Marrakech', 7 December 1933.
41. MAE, Série 'Maroc-Tunisie', sous-série no. 18–19 'El Glaoui May 1931 – November 1937', 140–1; 146–57.
42. CADN 1MA/282 95, Thami al-Glaoui to 'Monsieur l'ambassadeur résident général France au Maroc', not dated.
43. MAE, Série 'Maroc-Tunisie', sous-série no. 18–19 'El Glaoui May 1931 – November 1937', 158.
44. MAE, Série 'Maroc-Tunisie', sous-série no. 18–19 'El Glaoui May 1931 – November 1937', 140–1.
45. CADN 1MA/282 97, 'Général Daugan à monsieur le juge de paix', 27 June 1922. This is a case in which the administration gave al-Glaoui legal support before instigating a large ḥarka that they wanted him to lead.
46. MAE, Série 'Maroc-Tunisie', sous-série no. 18–19 'El Glaoui May 1931 – November 1937', 146–57.
47. MAE, Série 'Maroc-Tunisie', sous-série no. 18–19 'El Glaoui May 1931 – November 1937', 171.
48. MAE, Série 'Maroc-Tunisie', sous-série no. 18–19 'El Glaoui May 1931 – November 1937', 145, 173–4; CADN 1MA/282 95, Thami al-Glaoui to the Sultan, 20 November 1933.
49. MAE, Série 'Maroc-Tunisie', sous-série no. 18–19 'El Glaoui May 1931 – November 1937', 146–57, 175–8.
50. CADN 1MA/282 95, 'P.J./4, P.12.284', 30 December 1933.
51. MAE, Série 'Maroc-Tunisie', sous-série no. 18–19 'El Glaoui May 1931 – November 1937', 134, 139–41, 179–80; CADN 1MA/282 95, 'Le minstre des affaires étrangers à monsieur Ponsot, commisaire résident général de France à Rabat', 17 January 1934.
52. MAE, Série 'Maroc-Tunisie', sous-série no. 18–19 'El Glaoui May 1931 – November 1937', 142–3; CADN 1MA/282 95, 'Général de Brigade de la Baume, chargé de l'expédition des affaires étrangers de la région de Marrakech, à monsieur le commisaire résident général de la République Française au Maroc', 22 December 1933.
53. MAE, Série 'Maroc-Tunisie', sous-série no. 18–19 'El Glaoui May 1931 – November 1937', 159.

54. MAE, Série 'Maroc-Tunisie', sous-série no. 18–19 'El Glaoui May 1931 – November 1937', 140–1.
55. CADN 1MA/282 95, 'Le commissaire résident général de la République Française au Maroc, à son excellence monsieur le minstre des affaires étrangers', 8 January 1934.
56. MAE, Série 'Maroc-Tunisie', sous-série no. 18–19 'El Glaoui May 1931 – November 1937, 183–5.
57. MAE, Série 'Maroc-Tunisie', sous-série no. 18–19 'El Glaoui May 1931 – November 1937', 134–9, 181–2. The letter proves that the senator had full access to information submitted by the general security office to the minister of foreign affairs.
58. CADN 1MA/282 95, 'Monsieur le commissaire résident général de la République Française au Maroc, à son excellence monsieur le minstre des affaires étrangers', January 1934.
59. Ibid. In this update, Ponsot also assessed the possibility that al-Glaoui's lawyers would call witnesses from the very highest echelons of France's political establishment.
60. 'La vérité, rien que la verité!', *La Tribune de Paris*, 16 January 1934.
61. As can be understood from 'Notre procès, avec le pacha de Marrakech', *La Tribune de Paris*, 1 February 1934.
62. 'Le pacha el Glaoui contre ses détracteurs', *La Presse Marocaine*, 2 February 1934.
63. 'Le procès en diffamation du pacha de Marrakech contre M. Grilhé', *La Presse Marocaine*, 26 April 1934.
64. MAE, Série 'Maroc-Tunisie', sous-série no. 18–19 'El Glaoui May 1931 – November 1937', 195.
65. MAE, Série 'Maroc-Tunisie', sous-série no. 18–19 'El Glaoui May 1931 – November 1937', 189–90 and 191–2, correspondingly.
66. MAE, Série 'Maroc-Tunisie', sous-série no. 18–19 'El Glaoui May 1931 – November 1937', 193–5.
67. For example, see MAE, Série 'Maroc-Tunisie', sous-série no. 18–19 'El Glaoui May 1931 – November 1937', 142, 143, 159.
68. For example, MAE, Série 'Maroc-Tunisie', sous-série no. 18–19 'El Glaoui May 1931 – November 1937', 193–5.
69. A sultan of the Saʿadi dynasty (which preceded the ʿAlawi), who ruled Morocco at the end of the sixteenth century. This dynasty also claims Sharifian descent.
70. It should be noted that General Mangin, whom Babin knew personally from 1910s Morocco and Great War fronts in Europe, advocated the recruitment of blacks to the colonial French army. In his opinion, their nervous systems were less developed than those of white soldiers, and they thus lacked imagination and were fearless. As such, he proposed sending them as a strike force leading the most dangerous missions (Mangin 1910: 77–80, 89).

71. MAE, Série 'Maroc-Tunisie', sous-série no. 18–19 'El Glaoui May 1931 – November 1937', 222–3.
72. Actress Simone Berriau, widow of Henri Berriau, protégé of Lyautey and his confident, who had run the training and teaching programme of officers of indigenous affairs in Lyautey's administration, became a personal friend of al-Glaoui during this period (Berriau 1973). Rumours suggested that their relationship was more than an innocent friendship.
73. Oued – a river; hence 'Oued Seine' – River Seine in Paris. Others also shared this term: for example, Carette-Bouvet the editor of *Le Cri Marocain*; for example, in 'Le Roi du Sud', *Le Cri Marocain*, 4 April 1931.
74. For example, General Guillaume described the local forces as 'an extraordinary group ... which its fighters' primordial spirit of freedom and xenophobia brought to insanity' (Guillaume 1946: 372).
75. Charles Graves, 'In London now is The Paramount Pasha of Marrakesh', *Daily Mail*, 29 July 1937.
76. CADN 1MA/200 818, 'Le Général de Division Fougère, chef de la région de Marrakech, à monsieur le général, résident général', 17 June 1938. Later on, during the Vichy period, this general became the head of the right-wing Légion Française de Combattants in Morocco, proving once again his racist attitudes; Archive du Maroc (henceforth AdM) D667, 'Le Général Fougère, président du comité provincial da la legion du Maroc à monsieur le secrétaire général du protectorat', 1 January 1942.
77. CADN 1MA/200 818, 'Le Général de Division Fougère, chef de la région de Marrakech, à monsieur le général, résident général', 17 June 1938.
78. At the height of the Babin–Glaoui affair of 1933–4, someone discovered a copy of a letter, purportedly written in 1913 and indicating that he had had contact with the Germans that year – hinting at a potential betrayal of France. The note of the discovery of this letter appeared in 'Notre procès, avec le pacha de Marrakech', *La Tribune de Paris*, 1 February 1934.
79. CADN 1MA/200 818, 'Le directeur général des finances, à monsieur le directeur des affaires politiques', 30 December 1936.
80. 'Gustave Babin', *Le Journal des Debats*, 30 April 1939, p. 2.

4

The Age of Conspiracies

Following the outbreak of the Second World War in September 1939, Sultan Mohammed V declared Morocco's unconditional support for France (Pennell 2000: 254) – despite growing tensions between the Moroccans and the French. France surrendered to Germany in June 1940; a short while later, a pro-German government headed by Marshal Philippe Pétain was established in Vichy. General Noguès, the Resident-General in Morocco, pledged allegiance to the new regime, and the Sultan chose the same course (Abun-Nasr 1987: 393; Pennell 2000: 254–6).

The humiliation of France's defeat rippled through the Pasha's family, in part because his son Mehdi had witnessed the unfolding events personally. In the early 1930s, the Pasha sent Mehdi to be educated in France. After graduating from his *lycée*, Mehdi enrolled at the French military school at Saint Cyr, becoming an officer shortly before the outbreak of hostilities in 1939. During the war, his Moroccan Spahis unit fought in the 1940 Battle of France, part of the attempts to stop the German offensive. Mehdi was in the thick of the action and was awarded two medals for his bravery in leading his platoon in rescuing another unit that had been surrounded by the enemy.[1] These smaller victories notwithstanding, the larger battle was lost. After the armistice, Mehdi returned to Morocco. Consulting with his father, he decided to quit the army, as there were no promotion opportunities in the French army for Moroccan officers.[2]

Under the new regime, Resident-General Noguès arrested supporters of France Libre, denied a British delegation permission to visit Morocco, and promised the Germans that he would act to defend the Atlantic coast. In return for his actions, the Germans did not station any troops in Morocco, ostensibly preserving Morocco's sovereignty (Abun-Nasr 1987: 393; Pennell 2000: 254–6).

Back in France, one of the main agendas of the collaborationist government was 'to restore French values' – abandoned, according to Marshal Pétain and his followers, by the governments of the Third Republic. This restoration programme, embodied by the so-called *Révolution nationale*, substituted the older Republican motto of *Liberté, Égalité, Fraternité* (Freedom, Equality, Fraternity) with a new one: *Travail, Famille, Patrie* (Work, Family, Homeland). Intended to revive pre-revolutionary Christian ideals of community, this dictum underpinned the Vichy government's reorganisation of social, economic and political life in the territories under its control. A new economic plan, embracing the corporatist idea, was declared (*l'économie dirigée*); new regulations were announced; and punitive laws were promulgated, targeting mainly the sectors deemed responsible for France's pre-war misfortunes – Jews, Freemasons and communists. The outcome of these initiatives was a massive purge, known as *l'épuration*, of these groups from workplaces, many professions, occupations and from the universities (Kammerer 1943: 421; Paxton 1972; Zdatny 1986; Curran 1998: 7; Joly 2006: 71).

The new Vichy rules found their way to Morocco, with the protectorate administration responsible for enacting them (see Chapter 5 for more on this). Economic activity in Morocco, which had accelerated after the beginning of the war, had ceased with the armistice. Despite the new economic programme, the situation deteriorated to the point that the French were obliged to impose food quotas, which in turn created a substantial black market. Simultaneously, the poor maintenance of civic infrastructure led to a deterioration in sanitary conditions; several epidemics broke out, the government lacking the capacity to manage these adequately (Rivet 1992; Pennell 2000: 256–9; Ouaknine-Yekutieli 2015).

Al-Glaoui himself remained largely untouched by the events. He continued to consolidate his position, enlarging his range of activities. Rumours suggested that he was a beneficiary of black-market activities in Marrakesh.[3] Other than that, he expanded his collaboration with French businessman Jean Epinat, the founder of the Moroccan CTM bus company (la Compagnie générale de transports et du tourisme au Maroc), and of the business agglomerate ONA (Omnium Nord-Africain). The two had worked with each other since in the early 1930s, when they established a mining company. Exploiting mines in al-Glaoui's territory, particularly the cobalt mine at Bou 'Azzer, they frequently resorted to manipulating local tribes and the protectorate's regulations, with the tacit consent of the government (Badissi 2016–17: 31–2; Benargane 2020). During the war, activity at Bou 'Azzer intensified; at some point, Epinat and al-Glaoui met with Aouer, the German consul to Morocco, and agreed in principle to provide the Germans with minerals from these mines.[4] One might infer from this agreement that regardless of the outcome of the war, al-Glaoui was preparing himself for every eventuality. But other evidence suggests that Epinat – and therefore al-Glaoui as well – had been forced by the Vichy government to sign up to the deal with the Germans. According to these claims, they were able to deflect the pressure placed on them by delaying deliveries, and only supplying a small proportion of what was required of them (Nataf 1987: 47).

Bolstering the notion that al-Glaoui had resisted the Germans, numerous testimonies report that immediately after the armistice, he hid French weapons and ammunition in his various rural estates, preventing German access to them and in preparation for a future allied invasion (Morsy 1986: 158; Berdugo 1996: 72; Maghraoui 1998: 27; El Glaoui 2004: 36, 53).

During the Vichy years, relations between al-Glaoui and the Sultan improved. A contemporaneous French intelligence report claimed that the Sultan considered replacing his grand vizier and offered the job to al-Glaoui, but that the latter refused.[5] Regardless of the authenticity of this report, it is quite clear that an alliance between the two would have been beneficial for both. Local elites had been a power base of the sultan's court since pre-colonial times, a situation reinforced and adapted to contemporary objectives by the Sultan and the French alike. In addition, facing the rise of a new power – the nationalists – the Sultan had use for another base, allowing for political manoeuvrings when needed. From al-Glaoui's standpoint, the situation was much the same. The rising wave of nationalism was vehemently set against him, due to his collaboration with the French – and because, as a symbol of *qa'idalism*, he was considered evil and corrupt (Bidwell 1973: 125). The survival of his status and fortune hence depended on keeping the nationalists on a tight leash. An alliance with the Sultan would have helped in achieving this goal.

On 8 November 1942, American forces landed on Moroccan shores. General Noguès, loyal to Vichy France, ordered his troops to resist the Americans. However, the troops lacked the manpower and the munitions necessary for the task. The Sultan, for his part, instructed his soldiers that they had no obligation to fight the Americans. After a short battle, the French surrendered; control of the protectorate passed to the forces of Free France (Pennell 2000: 259).

A few months after the landing, the US president Theodore Roosevelt and British prime minister Winston Churchill arrived in Casablanca for an international summit, the Anfa Conference (14–24 January 1943). During this visit, they also met with the Sultan. At the meeting the two expressed the view that Morocco should no longer remain a French protectorate; they would not object to Moroccan independence, and the United States would provide financial support to an independent Moroccan state (Joffé 1985).

Thami al-Glaoui was kept within the circle of these discussions. Acting as the Sultan's special envoy, he was sent to determine whether the British and Americans would support the replacement of the French Protectorate with a joint British, American and French governing structure. In exchange, Mohammed V offered (via another emissary) to declare war on Germany and Italy. The Americans and the British turned down his offer, not wishing to disrupt their fragile relationship with De Gaulle and Free France. Instead, they announced that the colonies would gain independence only when their leaders were in a position to rule effectively (Sangmuah 1992).

Intermediating with the Americans was not the only mission that the Sultan entrusted to al-Glaoui. In September 1943, al-Glaoui travelled to Tangier to express his condolences to the former sultan 'Abd al-'Aziz's family upon his passing. Mohammed V asked al-Glaoui to use the opportunity to invite the family, on his behalf, back to the French zone from exile in Tangier.

In the context of the international manoeuvres unfolding before them, the French became more and more irritated by al-Glaoui's travels, refusing to believe that his frequent visits to Tangier were only to deal with courtesy and personal matters. These concerns dated back a few years. In 1935, the French civil controller of Petitjean (Sidi Kacem) claimed in a secret intelligence report that Thami al-Glaoui had reached an agreement with the ex-sultan 'Abd al-'Aziz to depose the incumbent

Mohammed V; as a token of gratitude for his support, he would be nominated as Grand Vizier in the new administration. The source added that al-Glaoui's accomplices in this plot were a group of young nationalists. Not only that, the same source claimed that during his last visit to Egypt, al-Glaoui had been chauffeured to meetings with secret German and British agents, who had given him large sums of money. It seems that this informant was a treasure trove for paranoid officials, as he returned two weeks later with more spectacular news. This time, he notified them of rumours circulating in Fes of a secret anti-French conspiracy in the southern region of the Souss, organised by al-Glaoui, the Spanish, and German agents of the Third Reich.[6]

As the meticulous French record-keeping attests, no matter how fantastical their stories sounded, storytellers-cum-informants like the one from Sidi Kacem – producers of a kind of speculative fiction – tended to be taken seriously. Under such circumstances, story and history were continuously creating each other.

Drawing from a factory of speculative fiction, by 1943 the French suspected that the attempts to bring 'Abd al-'Aziz's family back to the royal palace at Fes were nothing less than a counter-strategy to a Spanish plot. Allegedly, the intrigue cooked up by the Spanish was for the daughter of 'Abd al-'Aziz to wed the *khalifa* of Tetouan, thus compelling her to stay within their zone. Rumour had it that the princess, who served as her father's secretary and was fluent in several languages, had access to secret family documents – including a German proposal to restore her father to the Moroccan throne. The secret documents, some claimed, were the real motivation for the Moroccan royal invitation to return to Fes, and for the insistence of the Spanish that they keep the princess under their control.[7]

The French also interpreted al-Glaoui's trips to Tangier as an indicator that the Sultan was seeking control of the city as part of a unified Morocco. The final proof for them was the fact that he was turning an attentive ear towards the nationalists and their demands. The French also realised that al-Glaoui was deeply involved in the Sultan's stratagems; but they were not sure if he was aligned with the Germans, or with the Americans (see also Waller 1996: 252; El Glaoui 2004: 184).[8]

People, polities and companies conspiring against each other is a part of their essential nature. It does seem, though, that in the 1930s, and even more so during the Second World War and the immediate post-war period, suspicions escalated to such a level that everyone was in constant fear of everyone else potentially plotting against them. The possible soundness of some of these fears notwithstanding, the period's discourse is overwhelmingly dominated by narratives of intrigue. Tales describing plots against al-Glaoui spearheaded by his servants began to circulate during these years (see Chapter 5); the Sultan suspected that al-Glaoui was seeking to replace him on the throne;[9] the French were sure that the Sultan was conspiring with the Americans and the Germans; the French were scheming against al-Glaoui and the Sultan, according to other narratives; and the Germans, Americans, Russian, British and French repeatedly accused each other of duplicity. Thus, the dominant storytelling genre from the 1930s to the late 1950s, within which al-Glaoui's history and historiography were enmeshed, was the 'tale of a conspiracy'.

There were conspiracies, of course. The point here is that tales of intrigue were readily available as both an explanatory device and as a call for action. By their very nature, conspiracy stories tend to organise authors and readers alike into joining the struggle against an enemy who, more often than not, was operating extremely clandestinely (Earle 2013: 6). The enormous availability of such stories also had a dialectical effect, rendering them more likely to materialise. The interchangeability between telling and acting, and between story and history, was thus emphasised by the sense of intrigue.

Conspiracy theories became a seductive mode of explanation for everything. Not only were such theories proffered more and more readily, but increased energy was invested in 'deciphering' the clues allegedly hinting at these narratives. For instance, French agents were exclusively assigned to compile hour-by-hour reports of al-Glaoui's movements, in order to uncover evidence of the plot of the moment.[10] Such reports read like the excerpt below, taken from a much longer account of a visit by al-Glaoui to Tangier:

Tuesday 14 September 1943
His Majesty the Pasha received a visit of Si Ahmed Bel Bachir ... at 10:30 H.M. the Pasha and Si Ahmed Bel Bachir went together to the mountains to make an official visit to the Khalifa ... the visit took 15 minutes ... at noon

Si Abderahaman Menebhi looked for H.M. the Pasha, and then they went together to the British Legation where they met with the British Military Attaché ... At 16:00 Si Ahmed Bel Bachir returned to accompany H.M. the Pasha to visit the Spanish High Commissioner ... etc.[11]

The French were sure that something was up but could not decipher the 'clues' indicating as much. They were clearly in a bind, since they both needed and feared al-Glaoui at the same time.

Intensifying their concerns, al-Glaoui's recurring health problems put a question mark over his survival; the question of his succession in the event of his death was very much at the forefront of their minds.[12]

Paris Succumbed to Him; Its Leaders Submitted to Him[13]

As time passed, the Vichy-era prohibitions were gradually wound down. Political association in Morocco was permitted once again, and to a more liberal degree than in the pre-war years. The Parti Communiste du Maroc (Communist Party of Morocco; PCM), was established in July 1943; this was soon followed by the founding of the much grander Moroccan nationalist party, the Istiqlal, in December 1943 (Miller 2013: xvi).

In parallel, a grand purge, labelled *la seconde épuration* (also known in later historiography as the legal purge – *l'épuration légale*), took place. Vichyist and right-wing organisations were outlawed; many of the functionaries of the previous era were fired, and some were tried and convicted of various offences.[14] The second purge targeted the full range of former pro-Vichy administrators, from simple workers up to the Resident-General himself, who was removed from office in June 1943. Many high-ranking officials were charged with 'national indignity' (*indignité nationale*), tried and convicted.[15] In addition, the assets of private citizens and political organisations found guilty of collaborating with Vichy or Germany were impounded.[16]

As part of this process, Jean Epinat, al-Glaoui's partner, was accused of selling cobalt to the Germans, and of being in contact with Pierre Laval, prime minister of Vichy France. He was placed under house arrest and his assets were sequestered. Al-Glaoui rushed to the defence of his friend and associate, writing to General de Gaulle, Winston Churchill, the sitting Resident-General Puaux and Catroux, the commander of the Marrakesh region, asking that they intervene. In his view, the allegations against Epinat were untrue, inventions of people jealous of his financial successes. Eventually, and apparently in large part due to al-Glaoui's pressure, Epinat was found not guilty by the military court at Algiers (El Glaoui 2004: 82–3; Badissi 2016–17: 39–47).

In mid-1944, al-Glaoui suffered a severe blow, closer to home and much more serious than the inconveniences related with the purge – but that, nevertheless, contributed to his international prestige, especially among the French. His son Mehdi, who had returned to active military service after the liberation of Morocco by the Allies, was killed in action in 1944, while commanding his Moroccan unit in battle in Italy.[17]

Owing to his father's status, the repatriation of Mehdi's body to Marrakesh for burial was a state-scale event. On the day of the funeral, a large crowd assembled near Zawiya Si Youssef ben Ali in Marrakesh, to where the corpse was brought. Among the huge assembly were the representative of the Sultan, pashas of major Moroccan cities, prominent religious figures, *qa'id*s and *qadi*s of various tribes, leading religious and civil personnel, notables from across Morocco, representatives of urban institutions and political parties, the French Resident-General, the Spanish Consul, several American officers, the British Consul in Casablanca and major functionaries in the French protectorate administration.

At the ceremony, the Resident-General gave a moving speech, in which he highlighted the sacrifice of Mehdi and his family. He spoke about the bravery in battle common to father and son, quoting from the citations for the medals that the two had been awarded. A central theme in his speech was the family's strong links with France. Expanding on this theme, he declared:

> el Mehdi ben Hadj Thami loved France and, in his heart, he did not separate it from Morocco. This loyal attachment ... was in accordance with the tradition of the noble family to which he belonged. The son of the Pasha of Marrakech, by his life and by his death, gave new testimony to the value of his house ... In the name of General de Gaulle, president of the provisional government, I express to His Excellency the Pasha Si el Haj Thami Glaoui the feelings of deep sympathy of France. We understand his pain: we also understand his pride. A great lesson and a magnificent example are given

to us. They will both serve the cause of Franco-Moroccan friendship. The brotherhood of arms will continue in the great works of peace with the same spirit of mutual sympathy, of loyal mutual aid and of faith in the future, under the enlightened reign of His Majesty Sidi Mohammed, who has not ceased to show his confidence in the common destinies of France and the Shereefian Empire.[18]

Alongside the necessary 'toll' of expressing human sympathy and compassion, the speech transmitted a nakedly political message. Its timing marked the speech as a direct response to the Manifesto of Moroccan Independence, published by the Istiqlal six months earlier (January 1944). In the manifesto, the nationalists demanded Morocco's independence as a democratic state under Sultan Mohammed V, and requested that Morocco sign the Atlantic Charter,[19] and take a part in the peace conference planned for the end of the ongoing war (Joffe 1985; Pennell 2000: 265). Ostensibly paying homage to Mehdi and his father, the Resident-General was in fact presenting the outlines of an alliance to resist the nationalists and their demands. Weaved dialectally into a moment of grief was an attempt to harness al-Glaoui and the Sultan to the French cause.

The tragedy of Thami al-Glaoui coping with the death of his son invites comparisons with the story of his older brother, Madani. In 1918, Madani confronted a similar situation when his beloved son was killed in battle (Chapter 2). Madani died a few months later, unable to bear the sorrow, as the story is told. Was Thami al-Glaoui more immune to personal tragedy of such a scale? The answer remains within the domain of the storytellers.

Related or not to this event, the relationship between al-Glaoui and the Sultan improved markedly during this period. Towards the end of 1944, the Sultan asked al-Glaoui to represent him at several formal events.[20] A few months later, a second stab was taken at a very delicate mission – the planned marriage of the ex-sultan Mawlay 'Abd al-'Aziz's daughter to the *khalifa* of Tetouan, to which the Sultan objected. The Sultan entrusted negotiations regarding the issue to al-Glaoui personally.[21]

The French, for their part, continued to be concerned by the alliances evolving before them. They were especially troubled by al-Glaoui's gradually strengthening ties with the Americans. Hoping to gain some control over the situation, they continued their intense and comprehensive monitoring of al-Glaoui's actions.[22] The accumulating body of logs – a distinct literary genre in itself – in addition to giving up names of suspected accomplices and schedules, often included comments about the events being reported upon, in the process revealing much about the informers' preconceptions. For example, a report on a meeting between a group of Americans and two of al-Glaoui's sons, at their father's palace, exposed the informer's biases about Jews.[23] The American delegation was accompanied by Ohana Semtob, a Casablancan Jew holding a British passport.[24] The French informer was stunned by Ohana's behaviour at this meeting, which he described as completely atypical for Jews 'who had been granted an opportunity to sit at the same table with Americans and al-Glaoui's sons'. The informer reported, in astonishment, that Ohana set the tone at the meeting, giving the impression that he was the host at al-Glaoui's house. Worse still, he apparently omitted the honorary prefix 'Si' while translating for Si-Brahim and Si-Ahmed.[25]

A clear indicator of al-Glaoui's contacts with the Americans during this period was his frequent use of planes owned by the Americans for his long-distance trips. He was picked up at Marrakesh and returned there, sometimes received on arrival with the pomp and pageantry usually reserved for heads of state.[26]

In the mid-1940s, having already made several pilgrimages, al-Glaoui decided to embark on another Hajj, and in the process to assist others in performing this religious duty (Mutafakkir 2007: 87–8). On realising his intentions, the French government quickly offered to sponsor a Moroccan pilgrimage party, headed by him, to the holy city.[27] This idea was conceived as a way of rewarding its loyal natives, and to demonstrate France's generosity across the Muslim world.[28] However, al-Glaoui declined the offer. His view was that to head a delegation to Mecca sponsored by France would be demeaning for a person of his stature and would present him as *meskine* – poor and pitiful, unable to afford his own Hajj. He also declined an offer to use Air France for the pilgrimage, saying that he preferred an American plane. Citing the experience of a fellow Moroccan *qa'id*, who had told him that he had felt unsafe flying with Air France, al-Glaoui remarked that the engines of Air France's fleet of planes were weak and prone to failing. The French functionary who reported al-Glaoui's response to his superiors seemed to have taken extreme offence on behalf of his country.[29]

Al-Glaoui indeed performed the Hajj that year. He stopped en route in Egypt, where he was received respectfully. A praise poem was composed for the occasion, welcoming him to Egypt, blessing his Hajj, and praising his courage in overpowering Paris and its leaders (Mutafakkir 2007: 90–1).[30] In Mecca, as a representative of the Sultan of Morocco and on his behalf, he presented King Ibn Saʻud with an embroidered tent that he (al-Glaoui) had purchased in Cairo on his way to Mecca.[31]

Returning to Morocco, al-Glaoui's rapport with the Sultan continued to strengthen. At the request of the Sultan, he began an initiative to establish a charity in Marrakesh. He invited some 400 local leaders to his palace, informed them of how much each was expected to contribute, and registered the more important *qa'id*s as the charity's founders. Al-Glaoui himself donated 1 million francs to the new institution;[32] the important *qa'id*s contributed smaller sums.[33]

With al-Glaoui's prestige on the rise, the Jamaican-American author and historian Joel Augustus Rogers interviewed him for his *World's Great Men of Color* project, published in 1946. At the meeting, Rogers discussed international politics with him, their conversation ranging from the German misconceptions that had brought about their failures in the two World Wars, to al-Glaoui's analytical and critical judgements of American conduct across the world. Rogers was tremendously impressed by al-Glaoui (Rogers 1972 [1946]: 405–12). But despite al-Glaoui's enviable position, a breakup was in the air.

The Seeds of the Split

During the first months of 1946, the Istiqlal boosted its ties with the monarch. This did not auger well for al-Glaoui, given he had now been in head-to-head conflict with the nationalists for some years. Notably, the nationalists had accused him of collaborating with the French. Noting the change in the Sultan's attitude following this rapprochement, al-Glaoui begun to prepare for the new situation. Attempting to effect a reconciliation by meeting with the Sultan's sons,[34] he simultaneously opened a round of meetings with numerous notables, trying to urge them away from the nationalists.[35]

In mid-September 1946, a rumour began to spread in Morocco that al-Glaoui was planning to publicly denounce the Moroccan nationalists during a forthcoming visit to France, and to ask the French to remain in Morocco.[36] Two days later he received an anonymous letter, threatening his life if he did not change his course.[37] Refusing to submit to this intimidation, al-Glaoui intensified his activity. As a first step, he conducted another round of meetings with leaders he had identified as being at odds with the Istiqlal. He met in Tetouan with Khalid al-Raisuni, the pasha of Larache and the head of the Liberal Party;[38] in Casablanca with Hassan al-Wazanni, who had just founded the Party of Democracy and Independence (PDI; Hawas 2018);[39] and in his hometown, Marrakesh, with his fellow *qa'id*, al-'Ayadi.[40]

Visiting France a short time later, al-Glaoui met with Prime Minister Bidault. At the meeting, he declared that if France should abandon Morocco, it would be replaced by another force (hinting at the United States). He was given immediate reassurances concerning France's commitment to Morocco.[41] He went on to state that he regarded the Istiqlal as a group of young men unable to promote anything, and that he was urging the Sultan to act decisively against them. At the same time, his ally and religious leader 'Abdelhay al-Kittani accused the Sultan of leading the country to atheism, by letting his daughter, the princess 'Aisha, to appear in public without a veil.[42]

Al-Glaoui's acts were met by increasing opposition. The Moroccan communist party (PCM) joined the Istiqlal's critique. 'Ali Yatta, its leader, sharply criticised al-Glaoui,[43] as did Fortuné Sultan, the Jewish president of the Union des Femmes Marocaines (Union of Moroccan Women) and widow of the former PCM leader Léon Sultan (Ouaknine-Yekutieli 2019: 237; Heckman 2021: 126). At a union gathering, Mrs Sultan declared: 'He [al-Glaoui] despises his co-religionists and gives himself up to the imperialists.'[44] As if this was not enough, this criticism found its way into al-Glaoui's own household. At the beginning of 1947, Abdessadeq, his son, denounced his father's acts against the nationalists;[45] a short while later, some of his sons dared to raise their voices against him for the first time.[46]

It may that all these gave al-Glaoui cause for pause, and to consider reconciliation once again. When he met with the Sultan and declared loyalty to his dynasty, he nevertheless retained his views about the nationalists. The conversation ranged across several issues, focusing particularly on the nationalists and the French; middle ground could not be found, and the meeting ended in disagreement.[47]

On 10 April 1947, during a visit to Tangier, Sultan Mohammed V gave what was later dubbed the 'Tangier speech', in which he called for Moroccan independence. This speech became a symbolic turning point in the Moroccan struggle for independence (Reich 1990: 342–3; Hajji 1998: 428). It did not change al-Glaoui's views, however – not least because a week earlier he had caught two people spying on him, allegedly on behalf of the Sultan. He sentenced them to 100 lashes each and expressed his outrage to the court's representatives.[48] He continued his attacks on the nationalists, accusing them in harming the country, religion and Moroccan women; he added that independence would arrive in due course, but that in the meanwhile Morocco should continue to be supported by France.[49]

Al-Glaoui was able to gather support for his stand in meetings with *qa'id*s and pashas in the French and the Spanish zones.[50] He made declarations against the Istiqlal at public events, reproaching *qa'id*s who, in his view, were too passive in their resistance to the party.[51]

With the atmosphere heaving with conspiracy theories, and due to the thick cloud of confusion that enveloped the situation, the key parties – al-Glaoui, the nationalists, the court and the French – were all suspicious of each other. A rumour spread that al-Glaoui had met with agents of Franco's administration, and had discussed the wishes of a number of tribes, living on the border between the French and Spanish zones in the south, to join his command and come under his protection.[52] The nationalists were irritated by these rumours, unsure whether the alleged meetings were at al-Glaoui's or the Sultan's initiative, or whether it was just another Spanish–French conspiracy.[53] The French were similarly befuddled. They sent an official representative to join a meeting between al-Glaoui and al-'Ayadi, seeking to obtain information about the Sultan's contacts with other nations. The two senior *qa'id*s replied that although they were loyal to France, the Sultan remained their master and that they therefore were subordinate to him; they were not able to provide any information.[54]

Against this backdrop of tension and mutual suspicion, the final break between the Sultan and al-Glaoui occurred during the Mulud event of 1950.

Rashomon Effect: Narrating the 1950 Mulud

Moroccan custom holds that during the Mulud, also called Eid el Mawlid – the birthday of the Prophet – the Sultan invites Moroccan dignitaries to his palace to celebrate the event. During the event, notables pay homage to the Sultan and offer him a *hediya* – a symbolic present.

The importance of the 1950 Mulud lies in the historiographic assertion that this was the specific event that finally set the Sultan and al-Glaoui apart, triggering a snowball effect that led to the eventual expulsion of the Sultan from Morocco two and a half years later, and the independence of Morocco a further two and a half years on. From a storytelling point of view, this event is pivotal as it provided the starting point for some of the parallel narratives that have developed ever since – their dissemination casting some light on the intricate relationship between story and history.

By pure coincidence, the common literary, cinematic and psychological label denoting the creation of diverse plausible narratives concerning a single event – as was to happen with the 1950 Mulud – came into being at much the same time as the preparations for the event were stepped up at the Sultan's palace. On the opposite side of the globe, Japanese film director Akira Kurosawa was premiering in Tokyo his newest film, *Rashomon*. The film presents four different accounts of a dramatic event, the murder of a notable and the rape of his wife. The different reports leave the viewer unsure as to which version is correct and, more generally, to question the notion of their being only one 'truth'. It is clear in the film that the different accounts are not inventions created to protect their respective narrators, but rather all equally genuine. Hence, the film calls attention to the idea – one that historians had been aware of much earlier – that different truths could exist for different actors with regard to the same experience (Roth and Mehta 2002: 131–2). Describing such a general phenomenon, the film's name has become a label for cases in which a single dramatic event is seen and interpreted significantly differently by diverse witnesses: 'the Rashomon effect' (Davis et al. 2016).

Descriptions of what did happen at the palace on 23 December 1950 were collected by French agents immediately after the event. Written reports arrived at the central protectorate offices, one after the other, from across Morocco. Accordingly, accounts of what had happened date from a couple of days after the event to versions that emerged weeks later. The numerous accounts also testify to the importance given to the occurrence both by Moroccans and French.

The first report, from Rabat, was penned four days after the occasion. French agents were informed that people who had been at the palace claimed that while greetings by the delegations of notables were under way, the Sultan was heard saying suddenly, in a high tone, to the Grand Vizier: 'Take this man and his sons away from here! I don't want to see them anymore at my palace. And let them take back all the presents they have brought for the Hediya, which I will not accept.' Al-Glaoui then left the room, saying: 'This makes the situation much clearer, and personally I am strongly satisfied.'[55]

A day later, another description of the event arrived from Meknes. Local notables returning from the Mulud related that when they arrived in the palace, they saw members of the Istiqlal all over the place. After al-Glaoui had been received by the Sultan, and following the common blessings, the Sultan remarked that he had received a complaint that local sheikhs in al-Glaoui's territory, and under his authority, were harassing nationalists, and that he wanted the matter to be taken care of. Al-Glaoui replied that he was the only one with the authority to determine how to run affairs in his region, and then warned the Sultan of the intentions of nationalists; the only consistently loyal subjects, he said, were the pashas and *qa'ids*. The Sultan replied that he had confidence in al-Glaoui, assuring him that his politics were not affected by the wishes of any political party. Al-Glaoui replied: 'Enough with verbal promises, we want to see action.' The Sultan, offended by al-Glaoui's tone, insisted that he wanted the sheikhs in question to be suspended until an investigation was carried out. Al-Glaoui repeated: 'I am the sole master in my territory, and I will judge what should be done.' The Sultan violently dismissed al-Glaoui from his presence; al-Glaoui took his leave in a dignified manner. The Sultan sent the Grand Vizier after him, ordering that he return to Marrakesh. Al-Glaoui gathered his people, instructing them to return home and not to forget to take their presents back with them. The Pasha of Meknes added that he completely approved of al-Glaoui's position.[56]

Qa'id al-Hajj Mawlay Abderahman of Agadir provided his version of events somewhat later (30 December 1950). He reported that according to the custom, Moroccan notables gathered at the *méchouar* (the inner court), to be received by the Sultan. Al-Glaoui was there too, escorted by his two sons, Si Brahim and Si Mohamed. They were introduced first into the Sultan's reception hall. After twenty minutes, the chiefs heard the Sultan shouting: 'Go out of here!' Al-Glaoui, accordingly, left. The Sultan then searched out Grand Vizier al-Mokri and told him: 'From now on, I forbid Hajj Thami from setting foot in the palace.'

The *qa'id* from Agadir further reported that later that day he met a musician of the Sultan who had been present in the reception hall where the drama took place and was given an eye-witness account of what had happened indoors. Apparently, al-Glaoui entered the room, giving the usual wishes and reciting the *Fatiha* (the first chapter of the Quran). Everyone in the room rose. Hajj Thami asked the permission of the Sultan to speak with him for a few moments. The Sultan agreed. Al-Glaoui said: 'Do you like the work of these troubling kids? They are going to dig a pit under your feet and make you fall, to ruin Morocco. They attack us in their journals, us, the Moroccan chiefs credited with your authority, and you let this happen. You have to crack down on them, and we are at your disposal to help you.' The Sultan answered: 'Did these people insult you in public? In the street? In your face?' Al-Glaoui replied: 'What they do is worse, they make us lose Morocco.' The Sultan, enraged, replied: 'Well, go then and kill them, in the street, wherever you meet them.' Al-Glaoui said: 'You should give the order, and we'll perform it with joy.' The Sultan, even angrier now, said: 'Go out!' Al-Glaoui replied: 'It is impossible to talk with you calmly about the interests of your reign.'[57]

Notables from Tangier delivered their testimony a week later:

On the day of the Hediya, when al-Glaoui entered the méchouar, the Qa'id méchouar stopped him and said that the Sultan forbade him to enter his palace and that the Grand Vizier had received his instructions. Al-Glaoui went to the Grand Vizier and stayed with him for an hour and a half. He then went out and made a gesture to twelve qa'ids of the south who were there. These gathered and followed al-Glaoui. In the meantime, the qa'id méchouar made it known that al-Glaoui and those qa'ids had taken back the presents that they have brought.[58]

Istiqlal members from Tangier, who were present in Rabat on the Mulud, reported on 5 January that they have heard from the chief of the Imperial Cabinet the 'real' explanation of what had happened.

> In order to send the Sultan the traditional gifts for the Hediya of the Mulud, al-Glaoui made a frida [a special tax] in the area under his control. This had prompted opposition from the Istiqlal party, who had told the ones who had to pay that what would be taken from them will be offered to the Sultan in the name of al-Glaoui. Because of this, an eight-person delegation of the Mesfioua arrived to the Sultan to complain about the abuses of al-Glaoui.[59] When they returned to their tribe, they were arrested by orders of their qa'id, Si Brahim, al-Glaoui's son. The Istiqlal brought the affair to [the attention of] the Sultan, who sent an order through the Grand Vizier to release the arrested people. But Si Brahim refused, even after the intervention of the tribe's contrôlleur, who informed him very seriously that the entire Mesfioua tribe was about to rise up. After these events, the Sultan sent a formal letter to al-Glaoui demanding their release, but they remained [under arrest]. On the day of the Mulud, al-Glaoui, duly advised by the French authorities, arrived at the Sultan's, and complained to him with vehemence about the attitude of the nationalists: the articles in their press, the reunions they arranged, and the general character of their conduct. He demanded that the Sultan take a stand against them. The Sultan answered that it was the feast of the Mulud, and that this was not the right moment to talk about these issues. Al-Glaoui nevertheless repeated his grievances two additional times. After his third intervention, the Sultan got angry and asked why al-Glaoui had not carried out his order to release the [arrested] Mesfioua. Al-Glaoui answered that they were exactly the category of people against whom he was complaining. On hearing this response, the Sultan gave him the order to leave [his presence]. When al-Glaoui left, the Sultan summoned the qa'id méchouar, giving him the order to escort al-Glaoui out of his palace and to send back to him his presents.[60]

Reading through these differing reports, all made in close proximity to the event, a few observations can be made – bearing in mind that all had passed through a French 'filter', which might have touched up the testimonies.[61]

There is agreement in all the versions that al-Glaoui annoyed the Sultan, who became enraged and consequently ordered al-Glaoui from his court. All agree that the 'hot issue' was the nationalists – should they be outlawed, as al-Glaoui demanded, or tolerated, as the Sultan thought.

The main discrepancies in the reports relate to the issue of how enraged the two became, and who managed to stay calmer. The pashas' and *qa'ids'* reports were clearly more supportive of al-Glaoui and his conduct; those by Istiqlal members favoured the Sultan. Another impression that can be derived from these tales is that the Sultan was angered mainly because his orders had been ignored by al-Glaoui, and not necessarily out of a desire to protect the nationalists.

Regardless of the exact details, it is clear that the Sultan and the Pasha both felt extremely insulted after the event, and that neither of them was ready to let the matter go. As such, and whether by design or not, it was a French 'success'. Consequently, 'on the ground' events continued to unfold rapidly, as will be discussed in the next section. Simultaneously, the narration of the Mulud gained its own lease of life in the realms of history- and story-telling. It continued to develop across the years, fashioned according to the perspectives and biases of specific authors. For example, in 1966 Gavin Maxwell described the events in the following way:

> The Glaoui had always been the first to be received, and the magnificence of his gifts was legendary . . . On this occasion it was not he but the ten Istiqlal members . . . who were the first to have audience with the Sultan. Moulay Larbi el Aloui was charged with lighting the fuse by saying to the Sultan, 'I want to tell Your Majesty that that nigger Hadj T'hami El Glaoui is going to reproach you' . . . The Glaoui and his son arrived in the *mechouar* or inner court, and waited for seven minutes – an unprecedented delay that was tantamount to a stinging insult . . . [the Glaoui] after having made his obeisance began immediately upon an attack on the Istiqlal and the Sultan's support of it, saying that these hooligans would bring the name of the throne into world disrepute. The Sultan cut him short, saying, 'Listen, Your Excellency, from now on you will have to change your outlook, because we are going to work

for the independence of Morocco.'. . . The conversation went on so long that those who were waiting outside began open speculation as to what could be going on between the Sultan and the Glaoui.

The moment that the French had planned came at last. The Glaoui lost his temper, and, rising to his feet, shouted, 'You are nothing but the shadow of a Sultan! You are not the Sultan of Morocco – you are the Sultan of the Istiqlal!' With that he left, and passed through the astonished courtyard with his face twisted by anger. (Maxwell 1966: 207–8)

Hence, thirteen years after the event, nothing but the skeleton of the original story remained intact. New episodes were added, along with new conversations and a lot of literary décor. The pivotal issue now was the declaration, which might have been said, or not, by al-Glaoui at the palace in 1950:[62] 'You are not the Sultan of Morocco – you are the Sultan of the Istiqlal!'

In 1995, the General Encyclopedia for the History of Morocco and al-Andalus, a prototypical post-colonial Moroccan nationalist text (Chapter 7), described the same event in the following words:

Thami al-Glaoui approached the king to greet him, and said, according to a pre-planned intrigue: 'Leave the Istiqlal party and withdraw your hands from it.' He said this as if he was ordering the king of the land. The king whispered in his ear to postpone the political discussion to another opportunity, and not do it on the Prophet's birthday. The king behaved in the appropriate way, but al-Glaoui turned his face from the king and shouted loudly, telling his royal highness: 'You are not the Sultan of Morocco anymore, you have turned out to be the Sultan of the communist and heretic Istiqlal party.' The king asked al-Glaoui to leave the palace and not return unless he was summoned. (Zebib 1995: 135)

The multiple accounts of the 1950 Mulud bring to the fore a situation of concurrent realities, crafted by storytellers with political and personal stances. A consideration of the spread of the narrative and its multiple versions (for example, Janon 1953: 61–3; El Glaoui 2004: 153–90) reveals a 'ripples and circles' pattern, typical of the Rashomon effect (Davis et al. 2016). As one moves further away, in time and space, from the events of a certain day in Rabat, the tales about it become more diverse and elaborate, differing to an almost exponential degree from the original batch of reports. Expanding Davis et al.'s (2016) metaphor of the 'ripples and circles' of waves, we may characterise the multiple stories as waves interfering with each other. When the waves are 'in phase' – to use the terminology from physics – they reinforce each other, the tales increasing in amplitude and thus lasting, as can be seen from the enduring popularity of al-Glaoui's alleged cry: 'You are not the Sultan of Morocco anymore!' But when not 'in phase', the waves create a 'destructive interference' and die out – until reawakened by some new historical reverberation.

'When a Man Has Two Wives, Which One Should Be Honoured? The Older'[63]

Immediately after being kicked out of the Sultan's palace, al-Glaoui began to amass support among his fellow *qa'id*s and pashas for his stand against the Sultan and the Istiqlal.[64] A mere three weeks after the Mulud, he had managed to convince a large number to sign petitions directed to the Resident-General. The petitioners declared their loyalty to a French–Moroccan partnership and protested the influence of the nationalists and the communists, claiming that under the banner of 'independence', they would lead Morocco to collapse.[65]

Writing retrospectively, Abdessadeq El Glaoui, al-Glaoui's son, believes that the real initiators and promoters of the petitions were the French, particularly Resident-General Juin. The objective was to widen the gap between al-Glaoui and the Sultan, a first step towards the deposition of the latter (El Glaoui 2004: 195–7). Regardless of such later rationalisations (and, of course, they also deprive al-Glaoui of much of his agency), it is clear that by early 1951 al-Glaoui and his son Si Brahim had rallied numerous *qa'id*s and pashas to their cause,[66] and that the French administration was certainly very keen on assisting them.

One of the major events that al-Glaoui harnessed to consolidate his coalition was an annual *fête berbere* (Berber Feast). The celebration was organised in the Middle Atlas town of Khenifra, in the heart of the Amazigh Zaian confederation's territory, towards the end of January 1951. On this occasion many Amazighs, especially those from the Zaian but also from the

Glaoua, gathered to participate in the award of decorations to their *qa'ids* by the Resident-General and by al-Glaoui. During the event – not attended by representatives of the *makhzen* – al-Glaoui conducted numerous talks with tribal leaders. They all subsequently expressed their support for his actions against the nationalists and the Sultan.[67] The nationalists, supported by the *'ulama* of Fes,[68] for their part saw the 'Berber Feast' as an attempt by the French to divide Moroccan society between 'traitors' and the legitimate sovereign of Morocco.[69]

Following the gathering at Khenifra, al-Glaoui prepared a list of ten demands on behalf of his group and sent it to the Resident-General, asking that they be imposed on the Sultan. The first and the most important was a call for the Sultan to publish an edict expressly and specifically condemning the Istiqlal and the Communist parties. The other demands included forbidding 'sons of the Sultan who have no right to claim succession to the throne' (al-Glaoui was referring mainly to Prince Hassan II) from representing their father or speaking on his behalf, and a request for the control and suppression of the Arab press. The list also contained several requests for specific al-Glaoui supporters to be appointed to various posts, and for specific opponents to be removed from their offices.[70]

Resident-General Juin, on receiving the list, issued an ultimatum to the Sultan, that he officially denounce the Istiqlal before a set hour on 26 February 1951, and to make additional concessions. Failure to do so would result in the immediate deposition of Mohammed V.

Close to the deadline, and without any indication of the Sultan's intention to comply, an incident occurred, one which Maxwell described later thus:

> a piece of trickery so gigantic that it must be difficult to find its parallel in the history of any nation . . . T'hami launched the whole might of his southern mounted warriors against Fez and Rabat without giving them an inkling of the true reason. (Maxwell 1966: 209–10)

Maxwell's dramatic description gives the impression of a huge cavalry attack storming the imperial cities. However, Abdessadeq El Glaoui gives a totally different version, describing this event as 'a comedy' staged up by Resident-General Juin (El Glaoui 2004: 196). He quotes from a letter written by the French president Auriol, describing an urgent phone call from Juin during which the latter informed him that even as they were speaking (close to the expiration of the ultimatum), 10,000 members of al-Glaoui's cavalry were marching on him demanding the Sultan's abdication (El Glaoui 2004: 203). Thus, Abdessadeq El Glaoui suggests, Juin staged or even invented 'the attack' in order to put pressure on the French president.

Documents from the period indeed attest to al-Glaoui organising a substantial opposition to the nationalists and the Sultan. But they reveal nothing about a cavalry attack against the palaces, other than General Juin's rather unclear descriptions (for example, Wyrtzen 2015: 264 n. 36). Whether in fact or through Juin's manipulation, the Sultan nevertheless yielded to the pressure; he signed a document that satisfied the Resident-General and escaped being deposed by the French.

On the literary front, however, the somewhat blurred nature of these events mattered much less. A tale relating a huge assault by al-Glaoui's cavalry took root, in part due to the fantastic storytelling skills of authors like Maxwell.

From al-Glaoui's point of view – as well as that of some of his allies[71] – the French decision to accept the Sultan's alleged repentance was a bitter betrayal. Al-Glaoui was astonished by their actions; he had been convinced that having mobilised such a coalition against the Sultan, his revenge was at hand. Given his extensive experience of Moroccan and French politics, al-Glaoui did not have any illusions about the situation that he now found himself in. In a 1951 interview with a high-ranking French officer, he said:

> [L]et me remind you that I have designated myself as the irreducible enemy of the Makhzen, and while I remain certain of the support of the present government of the Protectorate and its local representatives, I know too well the fluctuations of the French politics, and the instability of those who bring it, to know that in the more or less near future I will be left alone to defend myself against the Sultan . . .[72]

As if to validate his prediction, two months later General Juin began to confiscate al-Glaoui's weapons. The French sent trucks to collect a large part of al-Glaoui's arsenal, allegedly for routine checks and maintenance. When they were not returned, al-Glaoui understood that he had been tricked.[73] His rage was

Figure 4.1 Thami al-Glaoui. Source: *Ce soir: grand quotidien d'information indépendant*, 17 January 1951, p. 1. Modifications have been made to the original image.
Courtesy: BnF.

felt all over. Hearing that students at Ben Youssef Islamic University, in his hometown, were striking in support of protests against him at the Qarawiyyin of Fes, he arrived personally at the madrasa. He gathered all the students and asked if anyone still supported the Fassi strike. Eight students raised their hands. Al-Glaoui took them to his residence and ordered that each be given 300 lashes.[74]

Al-Glaoui's decision was to keep moving along the course of action he had set for himself. He continued to augment his coalition, arranging further 'petition attacks' propelled by hundreds of *qa'id*s and pashas. Some of the petitions were directed against the Istiqlal,[75] while others called directly for the removal of Mohammed V.[76]

In parallel, hostilities in Morocco reached an unprecedented peak in December 1952 (Benseddik 1990: 496). The Istiqlal and the trade unions organised large-scale strikes in Morocco, following the assassination in Tunis of trade unionist Ferhat Hached. Hached had previously shown solidarity with the Moroccan struggle for independence. In retaliation, French security forces targeted poor Moroccan urban districts, killing between thirty and 300 Moroccans (the French insisted on the lower number, while the Moroccans reported the greater; Benseddik 1990: 465–73; House 2012: 78–9, 96; 2018: 3). Taking advantage of the situation, the French arrested the entire remaining leadership of the nationalist, syndicalist and communist movements. The Moroccans amongst them were either arrested or expelled to southern Morocco, where they were placed under surveillance; those of other nationalities (mainly Algerian or French, and a few others), were expelled from the country (Benseddik 1990: 471).

Throughout this period, several attempts were made by Moroccan personalities to reconcile the Sultan and al-Glaoui.[77] But nothing came of this – mainly due to French interference, in Abdessadeq El Glaoui's view.

Despite the dramatic events, throughout this period al-Glaoui continued to attend diligently to his financial affairs. Thanks to post-war inflation (Barbe 2016: 92) and the collapse in the value of the French franc, he was finally able to repay his 50-million-franc loan (Chapter 3); he was even able to negotiate new real estate deals with the French. Some of the hot-spots that al-Glaoui offered to the French were tracts of land near Cap Spartel, Tangier – sought after by the French due to their strategic location, right on the shores of the Straits of Gibraltar.[78] In addition, al-Glaoui continued his extensive schedule of trips abroad. One of his more ambitious forays was his participation in Queen Elizabeth's coronation in June 1953. According to Maxwell, this was interpreted as an unsuccessful attempt to present himself as a representative of Morocco, an act blocked by the British (Maxwell 1966: 220). At home, he received far greater recognition. Returning to Casablanca by boat from the coronation, he was met at the harbour by a large audience, the welcome ceremony itself of the magnitude usually reserved for heads of state.[79]

Thus, by the early 1950s several conflicts were simultaneously shaping Moroccan realities. French colonial authorities were fighting Moroccan nationalists; the nationalists were confronting the French and the old regime of *qa'id*s and pashas; the latter, led by al-Glaoui, were grappling with the nationalists; and above all, the Sultan was calculating his next moves.

Events in Morocco were also dialectically linked with overseas processes: political instability in France, the Cold War, the worldwide wave of decolonisation and the subsequent creation of the so-called Third World. The international discourse was defined by themes of struggle, the transformation of the existing world order, and conflict between old and new. Within this turmoil, Moroccans too had to choose sides.

In mid-1951, three *qa'id*s from Had-Kourt, invited to a reception honouring al-Glaoui, were discussing these very complex circumstances. As the conversation progressed, Qa'id Layachi told his friends: 'When a man has two wives, which one should be honoured? Who should rule? To whom should the keys be given?' He then answered his own question: 'To the older one.'[80]

From Top to Bottom

In August 1953 the French authorities, Thami al-Glaoui and Muhammad 'Abdelhay al-Kittani – the last a scholar, popular religious leader and collaborator with the French colonial rule – jointly deposed Sultan Mohammed V and expelled him from the country (Maxwell 1966: 218–30; Berdugo 1996: 125–54; El Glaoui 2004: 211–20).

A half-century-old prophecy was thus fulfilled (Chapter 2): having been involved in the deposition of Sultan 'Abd al-'Aziz in 1908, Thami al-Glaoui had done it again, this time taking a leading part in the deposition of 'Abd al-'Aziz's nephew, Mohammed V. Mawlay Mohammed Ben 'Arafa, 'Abd al-'Aziz's cousin, was proclaimed as the new sultan.

But al-Glaoui's aspirations for supremacy were immediately curtailed by the French. Without delay, the protectorate administration ensured that the block of *qa'id*s and pashas who had facilitated the Sultan's deposition would not gain power. Hand-in-hand with their efforts to limit the nationalists, the capacities of the local elites were limited through the enactment of reform policies favouring French settlers and companies over the former (El Glaoui 2004: 227–34).

The reaction of Moroccan society to the deposition was immediate and severe. The clashes were so intensive and continuous that the French soon realised that they had gone too far and had no other choice but to return Mohammed V to the throne.[81]

Figure 4.2 Thami al-Glaoui and Martinaud-Deplat, French minister of justice in 1952–3, a hard-liner against granting independence to the French North African colonies.
Source: *France-Illustration*, 5 April 1952, p. 313. Modifications have been made to the original image. Courtesy: BnF.

Their decision was influenced by events in other parts of the French Empire. At the beginning of 1954, the French suffered the humiliating defeat of Dien Bien Phu, leading to their withdrawal from French Indochina. In all probability directly inspired by this, the Algerian War of Independence erupted in November 1954. The situation in Algeria deteriorated very rapidly, reaching unprecedented levels of violence during the Philippeville massacre of 20 August 1955 (Stickland 2015). By chance, the day of the Philippeville massacre happened to be the second anniversary of the Moroccan Sultan's removal. As violence broke out in Algeria, demonstrations in Morocco to commemorate the deposition of the Sultan turned into violent clashes. Hundreds of Moroccans and Europeans were killed (Maxwell 1966: 253–4).

In face of the crisis sweeping the Maghreb, Grandval, the sitting French Resident-General in Morocco, resigned. His successor, General Boyer de Latour, engineered the abdication of Mawlay Ben 'Arafa, the Sultan appointed by al-Glaoui and al-Kittani. This decision came as a surprise to al-Glaoui.[82] Simultaneously, a new Moroccan government was established, and Mohammed V was invited to return to France from exile in order to begin negotiations for Morocco's independence.

Under these circumstances, al-Glaoui, whose health had deteriorated very rapidly,[83] decided to change course. He considered retiring from political life and relocating abroad. To this end, he began to liquidate his significant land portfolio, aided by David Mimran, president of the Marrakesh Jewish community and his counsellor on these issues.[84] At much the same time, towards the end of October 1955, he decided to support the Sultan's return to Morocco, releasing a press statement read by his son:[85]

> I feel the joy of the entire Moroccan people at the announcement of the return to France of His Majesty Sidi Mohammed Ben Youssef. I make mine the wish of the Moroccan nation, which is the prompt restoration of Sidi Mohammed Ben Youssef and his return to the throne, return which is the only way to unify the minds and the hearts.
>
> I take this opportunity to express my gratitude, and that of entire Morocco, to France and to the French who have helped the Moroccans to bring the crisis, just experienced in our country, into the phase of its resolution. The friendship of France and Morocco must be safeguarded at all costs, and it is not in anyone's mind to accept that the interests of France and of the French in this country are ignored. My aspiration merges with the aspiration of the entire Moroccan nation: it is the independence of my country in a circle of interdependence between it and France. I address to God the fervent prayer that this sincere union of national aspirations, is the prelude to an era of peace and prosperity for all, and contributes to bringing a definitive end to this period of trouble, where too many were already the victims, both French and Moroccan. (El Glaoui 2004: 323–4)

In November 1955, al-Glaoui travelled to Paris to ask for Mohammed V's forgiveness. This was granted.[86] Two and a half months later, on 23 January 1956, al-Glaoui died in Marrakesh. French intelligence's daily monitoring of the mood on the street reported that the French residents were sad, that the Moroccan Muslims were generally happy and that the local Jews refrained from commenting.[87]

On 2 March 1956, agreement was reached between France and Morocco to cancel the Treaty of Fes, confirming Morocco's independence as a constitutional monarchy. The protectorate was annulled, and the last Resident-General, André Dubois, became the first French ambassador to Morocco (Maxwell 1966: 260–3).

The Collapse

After al-Glaoui's death, acts of vengeance erupted against his former allies in Marrakesh (Maxwell 1966: 266–8). In an interview I conducted in 2005, a Jewish woman of Marrakshi origin told me that the looters rummaged al-Glaoui's house like crows. Albert Berdugo, al-Glaoui's secretary (Chapter 5), describes his narrow escape that day:

> A few days after the death of al-Glaoui, qa'id Si Brahim called me in the middle of the night. At his home he assembled a few intimate friends who shared with him, since it was the Ramadan, the traditional mint tea with Moroccan patisseries. After the invited people had departed, the qa'id asked me to call my wife and tell her to prepare a suitcase, as we had to leave immediately. My driver was instructed to bring her to me, as we were to leave Morocco at 3 am. The general residency had arranged for us an aeroplane that would evacuate us immediately to France. During the whole trip, Si Brahim kept a silence of anxiety. He had a cadaveric paleness and tension, tense as I had never seen him before. It was not until he arrived at the hotel that he regained his usual coolness, no doubt happy to have escaped the tragic destiny that had been promised to him. I still did not know what had motivated this hurried escape, but then the radio announced the terrible news: bloody incidents had just occurred in Morocco, which were immediately called 'Saint Bartholomew of Marrakesh'... A long series of individual executions had taken place in Djemaa el-Fna in the presence of a hysterical crowd. A list had been circulated, it seems; and about forty collaborators and servants of al-Glaoui were victims of these massacres, including two notables and two khalifas. (Berdugo 1996: 229–30)

Berdugo and his wife had a narrow escape; a day later, Si Brahim managed to escape as well. He found refuge in France where, a few days later, he married his long-time love, the French actress Cécile Aubry.[88] Meanwhile, al-Glaoui's other sons and family relatives in Morocco were arrested. They included

Abdessadeq, Mohamed, Hassan, Madani and Abdellah ben Hammou al-Glaoui. In addition, a sweeping confiscation of documents, items and arms stored in his former palace took place.[89] However, this arrest was brief. After a short while the family members were released, and by the end of the year the King had even appointed Abdessadeq – who despite being loyal to his father, had challenged the pasha's political views and embraced Moroccan nationalism – to official posts: first as president of the regional tribunal of Marrakesh, and then to the post of attorney of the king at the Sharifian Tribunal.

Despite this reconciliation between the court and the family, in May 1957 forces of the Moroccan Liberation Army re-arrested three of al-Glaoui's sons – including Abdessadeq – and two of his close relatives, and charged them with treason. Following a direct intervention by the King, government forces managed to gain possession of the captives, transferring them to house arrest under the direct supervision of the minister of interior.

People of the Glaoua tribe reacted very angrily to these arrests. In the protests that ensued, they chanted slogans like 'Morocco is Berber!' and 'the Arabs are invaders!'[90]

Within four months of the initial arrests, the government published a list of 196 people charged with taking part in the 1953 plot to depose the Sultan. The list included Thami al-Glaoui, the ex-grand vizier Hajj Mohamed al-Mokri, and three of al-Glaoui's sons: Brahim (the ex-*qa'id* of the Glaoua), Mohamed (the ex-*qa'id* of the Mesfioua) and Abdessadeq (the magistrate in office). The official announcement stated that although the King had pardoned all those who took part in his expulsion in 1953, his pardon was personal and not in the name of the people. Consequently, the people had the right to demand that the traitors be punished. However, if they were then pardoned again by the King, punishment would be limited to 'national degradation' and fines.

This government decision became the basis for the establishment of a national inquiry committee, in March 1958. It announced its findings five months later. The punishments determined by the committee included various degrees of 'national indignity' (*indignité nationale*), including the confiscation of parts or all of the entire assets of those convicted thus, and the withdrawal of civic rights for set periods of time.[91] With regard to Thami al-Glaoui, the committee decided to convict him, post-mortem, for the offence of national indignity for fifteen years, and to confiscate all of his properties.[92] The committee's decisions terminated the house arrests of the Glaoui family members, who were now punished personally. Mohamed, for example, was convicted of *indignité nationale* and sentenced to *dégradation nationale* – the loss of all civic rights – for six years, and the confiscation of most of his property.[93]

The term *indignité nationale* had been taken from post-war France and its purge (*épuration*) of collaborators with the Nazi regime. Those charged in France were often tried on charges of *indignité nationale* and sentenced to punishments ranging from *dégradation nationale* to death. French newspapers reporting on the developments in Morocco at the time used the term *épuration*.[94] The choice of words equated those who participated in the King's expulsion with the leaders of the Vichy government, who had collaborated with the Nazis.

Abdessadeq resisted the verdicts relating to his immediate family. Well versed in legal matters, he appealed to the King, claiming that the verdict passed on his mother Lalla Zineb, his brother Hassan and himself was unjust. He argued that during his trip to the King in November 1955, al-Glaoui had not asked forgiveness from Mohammed V 'the person' but from Mohammed V 'the symbol' – and thus there was no legal basis for the claim of justice being delivered on behalf of 'the people'. Furthermore, he claimed, the inquiry committee's resolutions only applied to living people. As Thami al-Glaoui had died before the resolution, the parts of the inheritance due to his mother, brother and himself were outside the scope of the confiscation order, as these ought to have passed to them immediately after Thami al-Glaoui's death. He also cited Islamic law to buttress his case.[95]

Reflections

This chapter opened with four powers struggling for supremacy in Morocco: the Sultan and his court, the nationalists, the French protectorate and the Moroccan *ancien régime* led by al-Glaoui. By the end of 1956, only two remained, the Sultan and the nationalists. However, the palace was extremely wary of this potential bipolar power balance. At face value, the court had many reasons to celebrate the fall of al-Glaoui. Historically, the largest threats encountered by Moroccan ruling dynasties came from Amazigh families such as the Glaoua. Long before the intrigues of the mid-twentieth century, Amazigh dynasties from the fringes of the Sahara – the Almoravides (1055–1147) and the Almohads (1130–1269) – had deposed ruling dynasties. In fact, the 'Alawi dynasty itself, an Arab dynasty of Sharifian descent, had come from the oases at the southern slopes of the Atlas (Dunn 1977: 16). Thus, the removal of al-Glaoui, who had accumulated enormous powers, would have been seen as a relief.

The likelihood of the Glaouis attempting to replace the 'Alawi dynasty seemed very plausible at the time. This threat was increased by French discourse and actions, constantly toying with the notion of Amazigh separatism as a plank of their divide-and-rule policy. The notion was also encouraged by Ibn Khaldunian sociological theories, well known in North Africa and spread further by the colonial French academic corpus – namely, that the 'pool' of nomadic tribal organisations on the edge of the desert would from time to time instigate the overthrow of the ruling dynasties in central Morocco (Eickelman 1989: 24–5; Brett and Fentress 1997: 116–19). But in practice, even though they might have had the power, and despite having discords with specific sultans, the Glaoui brothers never attempted to remove the ruling dynasty. This was also true the other way around. To continue functioning, the Moroccan court needed families like the Glaoua, 'Ayadi, Goundafi, Mtougi and others. Historically, the *makhzen* relied on such families; the French colonisers replicated this pattern by nurturing *caïdalisme* (Chapter 2).

With independence, a reshuffle of powers occurred. *Caïdalisme* was abolished, the French were leaving, and the nationalists were pushing to rid the country of the *ancien régime*, which they viewed as despotic and feudal. In this fast-evolving reality, it was clear that the next conflict would be between the nationalists and the King. To survive this, the royal court needed a counter-balance to the nationalists; the most readily available option was the old elites, despite the role they played in the conspiracy that led to the deposition of Mohammed V. The court needed the *ancien régime* as a check on the aspirations of the nationalists – and vice versa. This would explain why the court softened the blow of the Moroccan Liberation Army and the Inquiries Committee on the Glaoui family, while simultaneously enabling a certain degree of public punishment for the conspirators.

The usefulness of the pashas and *qa'ids* was actualised very quickly. For example, King Hassan II relied on them to achieve the desired results in the December 1962 referendum and, later, the April 1963 legislative authority elections (Leveau 1985; 1998).

As regards al-Glaoui, the last five years of his life are the ones that feature the most prominently in assessments of his biography and legacy. For many observers (see Chapters 5, 6 and 7), many of his earlier deeds could be excused, but not his prominent role in the deposition of Sultan Mohammed V in 1953. Consequently, a large part of the post-1950s historiography on al-Glaoui concentrates on these five years (for example, Janon 1953; Berdugo 1996; El Glaoui 2004). But before continuing with the analysis of the development of narratives about al-Glaoui after his death, the next chapter will concentrate on a special aspect of the Pasha's history and tales which cut across all his long career: his special relationships with a particular Moroccan group, the Jews.

Notes

1. 'Les Émouvantes Obesques du lieutenant Si Mehdi Glaoui Fils de S. E. le Pacha de Marrakech', *Le Petit Marocain*, 12 July 1944.
2. CADN 1MA/282 100, 'Le Général Henri Martin, chef de la région de Marrakech, à monsieur le directeur ministre des affaires politiques', 25 August 1941.
3. CADN 1MA/282 98, 'Bulletin de renseignements. No. 35 B.R./C/2.P', 9 May 1942; CADN 1MA/282 98, 'Bulletin de renseignements. Confidentiel', 28 May 1942.
4. CADN 1MA/282 98, 'Bulletin de renseignements. Confidentiel', 28 May 1942.
5. CADN 1MA/282 98, 'Le contrôleur civil chef de la région de Rabat, à monsieur le directeur des affaires politiques', 15 March 1941.
6. CADN 1MA/282 98, 'Note Politique', 18 July 1935; and CADN 1MA/282 98, 'Note Politique', 3 July 1935.
7. CADN 1MA/282 98, 'Monsieur Gabriel Puaux, ambassadeur de France à son excellence, Monsieur René Massigli', September 1945; CADN 1MA/282 98, 'Monsieur Gabriel Puaux, ambassadeur de France à son excellence, Monsieur René Massigli', 23 September 1945.
8. CADN 1MA/282 98, 'Note de renseignements. No. 118 RF/2C', 30 January 1943.
9. NARA RG338 5th Army Box 4–ii, pp. 63–4.
10. CADN 1MA/282 98, 'Sécurité. Note', 11 September 1943.
11. CADN 1MA/282 98, 'Note sur le voyage de S. E. le Pacha de Marrakech', mid-September 1943.

12. CADN 1MA/282 100, a sub-file with information about al-Glaoui's health issues at the beginning of the 1940s and thoughts about who may replace him.
13. The title derives from Ashanqiti Mohamed Ben Ba's poem: 'Tahiyat al-Farah Wasurur ila Maʻali Zaʻim Murakush al-Hamra' bi-Munasabat Hudurihi bi-Masr li-Taʼsiyat al-Haj' (in Mutafakkir 2007: 90–1).
14. CADN, Épuration Administrative Maroc 6, 'Liste des sanctions que l'Administration a déjà prises contre certains fonctionnaires et autres personnes pour participations à des Arrestations, séquestrations arbitraires, violences et voies de fait et complicité'; CADN DI 1MA/10/37, 'Mutations dans le haut personnel de la résidence générale et des administrations du protectorat'.
15. CADN DI 1MA/10/37, 'L'épuration au Maroc', 15 January 1945.
16. CADN DI 1MA/200/439, 'Police Administrative, Casablanca, Note de renseignements', 11 December 1944; CADN DI 1MA/10/37, 'Liquidation des groupements économiques', 30 August 1945.
17. CADN 1MA/282 100, 'Note sur le Lieutenant Mehdi Glaoui', 6 June 1944.
18. 'Les Émouvantes Obesques du lieutenant Si Mehdi Glaoui Fils de S. E. le Pacha de Marrakech', *Le Petit Marocain*, 12 July 1944.
19. The 'Atlantic Charter', signed by Roosevelt and Churchill on 14 August 1941, declared their common goals for the post-war period. Among other things, the two leaders stated their acknowledgement of the right of all people to choose the kind of rule under which they wished to live.
20. CADN 1MA/282 98, 'Région de Rabat. Renseignements', 9 December 1944.
21. CADN 1MA/282 98, 'Bulletin de renseignements', 5 October 1945.
22. CADN 1MA/282 98, 'Renseignements. Origine Police – du 12 Octobre 1944', 19 October 1944.
23. CADN 1MA/282 98, 'Renseignements. Marrakech', 7 June 1945.
24. Ohana Semtob Santiago, an export merchant born on 1889 in Casablanca and described as 'a good friend of al-Glaoui'; CADN 1MA/282 98, 'Renseignements. Marrakech', 10 June 1945.
25. CADN 1MA/282 98, 'Bulletin de renseignements. No. 198 CBR/2ind', 8 June 1945.
26. CADN 1MA/282 98, 'Renseignements. No. 3170 RC/2/C', 31 August 1945; CADN 1MA/282 98, 'Bulletin de renseignements. No. 213 CRMA /2-Ind', 8 September 1945.
27. CADN 1MA/282 98, 'Bulletin de renseignements', 5 October 1945.
28. For a similar idea applied in the French West African Muslim colonies, see Ginio 2017: 127–8.
29. CADN 1MA/282 98, 'Bulletin de renseignements. No. 8 TSRMA /2-Ind', 10 September 1945.

30. Ashanqiti Mohamed Ben Ba, 'Tahiyat al-Farah Wasurur ila Ma'ali Za'im Murakush al-Hamra' bi-Munasabat Hudurihi bi-Masr li-Ta'siyat al-Haj' (in Mutafakkir 2007: 90–1).
31. CADN 1MA/282 98, 'Renseignements. Rabat', 30 November 1945.
32. CADN 1MA/282 98, 'Renseignements. Marrakech', 10 January 1946.
33. CADN 1MA/282 98, 'Renseignements. Marrakech', 15 January 1946.
34. CADN 1MA/282 98, 'Bulletin de renseignements. No. 16 SRMA/2ind', 18 April 1946.
35. CADN 1MA/282 98, 'J. L. Renseignements', 2 February 1946; CADN 1MA/282 98, 'Renseignements. No. 1383 RC/2/C', 27 April 1946.
36. CADN 1MA/282 98, 'Note de renseignements. No. 50', 16 September 1946.
37. CADN 1MA/282 98, 'Source: Bonne', 18 September 1946.
38. CADN 1MA/282 98, 'Cabinet diplomatiques Rabat No. 751, consulat général Tanger No. 478', 25 September 1946.
39. CADN 1MA/282 98, 'Bulletin de renseignements speciaux', 14 November 1946; CADN 1MA/282 98, 'Confidentiel, Marrakech', 15 November 1946.
40. CADN 1MA/282 98, 'Bulletin de renseignements speciaux. No. 13 C.R.M.A/B.S.', 11 November 1946.
41. CADN 1MA/282 98, 'Rabat. Rumeurs', 21 November 1946.
42. CADN 1MA/282 98, 'Traduction d'une note', 6 November 1946.
43. CADN 1MA/282 98, 'Marrakech', 18 November 1946.
44. CADN DI 1MA/200 328, 26 March 1951; CADN DI 1MA/200 328, 'Casablanca, direction de l'intérieur', 13 February 1951.
45. CADN 1MA/282 98, 'Secretariat politique, 1ère section. Note de renseignements', 14 January 1947.
46. CADN 1MA/282 98, 'Le colonel d'Hauteville chef de la région de Marrakech, à monsieur le chef de secretariat politique (1ère section)', 18 August 1947; CADN 1MA/282 98, 'Bulletin d'opinion no. 119', not dated.
47. CADN 1MA/282 98, 'Bulletin spécial de renseignements. No. 47 CRMA/BS', 22 February 1947.
48. CADN 1MA/282 98, 'Marrakech', 4 April 1947.
49. CADN 1MA/282 98, 'Cabinet Civil 698 cc B', 14 May 1947.
50. CADN 1MA/282 98, 'Le Lt. Colonel d'Arcimoles, chef du cercle de Khénifra', 7 May 1947; CADN 1MA/282 98, 'Notes sur un conversation tenu le 28 Mai 1947', 28 May 1947; CADN 1MA/282 98, 'Note sur la situation politique au 7 Juin 1947', 7 June 1947.
51. CADN 1MA/282 98, 'Bulletin de Quinzaine', 13 May 1947.
52. CADN 1MA/282 98, 'Note confidentielle, No. 9255 D.S.P./R.G.', 17 September 1947.

53. CADN 1MA/282 98, 'Consulat général de France de Tanger, No. 671', 11 September 1947.
54. CADN 1MA/282 98, 'Renseignements, 1273 RC/2.C', 11 July 1947.
55. CADN 1MA/282 99, 'Note de renseignements, No. 1600 0/AM', 27 December 1950.
56. CADN 1MA/282 99, 'Bulletin special de renseignements, No. 2001 SMK/2', 28 December 1950.
57. CADN 1MA/282 99, 'Bulletin special de renseignements. No. 1', 30 December 1950.
58. CADN 1MA/282 99, 'Note de renseignements', 5 January 1951.
59. See the Glaoua family point of view concerning the Mesfioua affair as presented by Abdessadeq El Glaoui (El Glaoui 2004: 157–60).
60. CADN 1MA/282 99, 'Note de renseignements', 5 January 1951.
61. Relevant to this observation is a nationalist claim made in Oujda, and reported in a French information report, accusing the French administration of spreading false descriptions of the Mulud event; CADN 1MA/282 99, 'Note de renseignements, No. 84 RO/2', 6 January 1951.
62. Abdessadeq El Glaoui holds the same opinion. He believes that this sentence was invented by people with an interest in defaming al-Glaoui (El Glaoui 2004: 188).
63. Following a conversation between several *qa'id*s against the backdrop of the conflict between al-Glaoui and the Sultan; CADN 1MA/282 99, 'Note No. 54 CL', 30 May 1951.
64. File CADN 1MA/282 98.
65. CADN 1MA/282 99, 'à son excellence le Général de l'Armée Juin', 12 January 1951; CADN 1MA/282 99, 'Fi 3 Rabi' 'Am 1370 Muwafiq 12 Yanayer 1951, Nahnu Aru'asa' al-Maghariba min Bashawat wa-Quwad'.
66. For example, CADN 1MA/282 99, 'Bulletin quotidien d'information, 19–20 Janvier 1951', 20 January 1951.
67. CADN 1MA/282 99, 'Compte Rendu', not dated; CADN 1MA/282 99, 'Meknes', 29 January 1951; CADN 1MA/282 99, 'Bulletin quotidien d'information, 28–29 Janvier 1951', 29 January 1951; CADN 1MA/282 99, 'Bulletin quotidien d'information, 19–20 Janvier 1951', 20 January 1951.
68. CADN 1MA/282 99, 'Bulletin special de renseignements. No. 6', 30 January 1951.
69. CADN 1MA/282 99, 'Meknes', 29 January 1951.
70. CADN 1MA/282 99, 'Liste des conditions dont le Pacha demande qu'elles soient imposées au Sultan', Februray 1951.
71. CADN 1MA/282 99, 'Note de renseignements, . . . R/1', 27 February 1951.

72. CADN 1MA/282 99, 'Le Général d'Hauteville chef de la région de Marrakech, à monsieur le général de l'armée . . .', 28 February 1951.
73. CADN 1MA/282 99, 'Note de renseignements, No. 1689 RO/2', 28 April 1951.
74. CADN 1MA/282, 'Bulletin de renseignements, 75c', 28 April 1951.
75. CADN 1MA/282 99, '3 pétitions en date du 2 juillet 1953, des caïds des tribus El Guich, El Feija, et de la circonscription de Mogador . . .', 6 August 1953; CADN 1MA/282 99, 'Traduction – Région Ouarzazate et Cercle d'Azilal . . . 2 juillet 1953'.
76. CADN 1MA/282 99, 'Louange à Dieu Seul', 20 March 1953; CADN 1MA/282 99, 'Le president de la chambre Marocain de l'agriculture à monsieur le Général de l'Armée Guillaume', 17 April 1953.
77. CADN 1MA/282 99, 'Note de renseignements, No. 1351 C/AM', 28 June 1952; CADN 1MA/282 99, 'Note de renseignements, No. 1122 RR/2.C', 25 March 1952.
78. CADN 1MA/282 97, 'Dahir autorisant la vente de trois immeubles domaniaux (Tanger)', 1949; CADN 1MA/282 97, 'Le directeur du cabinet civil du résident général à monsieur le directeur de l'interior', 5 March 1951.
79. CADN 1MA/282 98, 'Casablanca', 31 July 1953.
80. CADN 1MA/282 99, 'Note. No. 54 CL', 30 May 1951.
81. CADN 1MA/282 97.
82. CADN 1MA/282 98, 'Traduction, lettre du Pacha Glaoui au président de la République', 3 August 1955.
83. CADN 1MA/282 98, Sub-file 'maladie & décès du Pacha de Marrakech el Hadj Thami Glaoui'.
84. CADN 1MA/282 98, 'Renseignements', 15 October 1955.
85. CADN 1MA/282 98, 'Décleration de S. E. El Glaoui', 25 October 1955.
86. CADN 1MA/282 98, Sub-file 'Communiqué du Glaoui en faveur du retour de l'ex-sultan sur le trône', 25 October 1955.
87. CADN 1MA/282 98, 'Note. Commentaires provoqués dans les divers milieux', 25 January 1956.
88. CADN 1MA/282 100, 'Monsieur Roger Lalouette, chargé d'affaires a.i. de la République Française au Maroc', 4 June 1957; CADN 1MA/282 100, 'Note de Renseignements, No. 2.668 /2', 5 December 1956.
89. CADN 1MA/282 100, 'Monsieur Roger Lalouette, chargé d'affaires a.i. de la République Française au Maroc', 4 June 1957; CADN 1MA/282 100, 'Note de Renseignements. B.C.I. No. 514/2', 3 May 1957; Jean Lefèvre, 'L'occupation du palais de l'ancien pacha aurait permis la saisie de documents importants', *Le Monde*, 4 May 1957.

90. CADN 1MA/282 100, 'Service des Liasons. Note de Renseignements', 16 May 1957.
91. CADN 1MA/282 100, 'L'Ambassadeur de France, envoyé exceptionnel de la République Française au Maroc. No. 2725 L', 28 August 1958.
92. CADN 1MA/282 96, 'Supplique addressee à sa majesté le roi par Abdessadek Ben Hadj Thami el Glaoui . . .'.
93. CADN 1MA/282 100, 'M. Jean Le Roy, chargé d'affaires a.i. de la République Française au Maroc. No. 2684 /L', 26 August 1958.
94. CADN 1MA/282 100, 'M. Jean Le Roy, chargé d'affaires a.i. de la République Française au Maroc. No. 2684 /L', 26 August 1958; Jean Lefèvre, 'Des mots d'ordre d'«épuration» sont lancés par l'Istiqlal', *Le Monde*, 8 May 1957.
95. CADN 1MA/282 96, 'Supplique addressee à sa majesté le roi par Abdessadek Ben Hadj Thami el Glaoui . . .'; CADN 1MA/282 96, 'Note sur la situation faite au Maroc à Lalla Zineb . . .'.

5

'He is the Jews' Friend'[1]

But perhaps you are more surprised by the place he occupies near me because he is a Jew? Know, my dear qa'id, he is the only one to hold preciously the key to this iron cassette which contains my medications. Because if I had entrusted it to someone else [implying one of you] I wonder if someone would not have been tempted to poison me a long time ago!

These remarks had been reported to me by the intendant, and I confess to having been touched by the confidence thus displayed in public by the pasha. (Berdugo 1996: 92)

The quote above is taken from Albert Berdugo's (1996) book *Les Dessous d'une Conspiration*. It gives a hint as to how Berdugo – a Moroccan Jew, serving as one of the Pasha's secretaries since 1943 – thought that al-Glaoui regarded him. The explanation that al-Glaoui allegedly gave the *qa'id* harks back to myths of Jewish sages saving the life of the Pasha (see below). As the ultimate author of this text, Berdugo probably did not intend to be equated with a Jewish sage. However, this paragraph reveals how entrenched the literary topos of 'a Jew saving al-Glaoui from being poisoned' had become. Whether the Pasha really said these words, or even if they had merely just related to him, this text effectively becomes a part of the myth about the special links between al-Glaoui and the Jews, creating a situation in which story and plausible reality dissolve into one another.

Albert Simon Berdugo (1906–2001) was born to a Jewish family in the cosmopolitan town of Tangier. His family's recorded history runs back many centuries. It includes expulsion from Spain in 1492; subsequent settlement in Meknes; and then relocation to Tangier at the beginning of the twentieth century, by Albert's father, goldsmith Simon Berdugo (Berdugo 1996: 111).

Due to its geographic location at the mouth of the Straits of Gibraltar, where the Mediterranean meets the Atlantic and Africa meets Europe, Tangier was a regional centre, an international hub where European diplomatic and commercial activity and rivalry had existed amid a Moroccan milieu for centuries. The city's cosmopolitan atmosphere was accentuated by its mixed population of Muslims, Jews and Christians, and by the significant numbers of foreign businessmen, consuls, spies and tourists in the city at any given time (Ben Srhir 2005; Brown 2012; Bensoussan 2012; Miller 2021: 9–13).

Berdugo was born in the year that the European powers and Morocco signed the treaty of Algeciras (1906), which, among other things, reached an accommodation for Tangier and its special character. France had already effectively acknowledged Spain's 'historic claim' to northern Morocco in a secret 1904 agreement. But at Algeciras, it managed to detach Tangier's status from the previous agreement. Tangier's status remained unresolved when Morocco was split between France and Spain in 1912, principally because the British insisted that the city become an international zone with no single dominant foreign power. The question of Tangier was finally settled after the Great War. In 1923, France, Spain and Britain decided to create an international administration for the city, under the symbolic leadership of the Sultan of Morocco. By acknowledging the Sultan's sovereignty, the agreement satisfied France; and by preserving Tangier's international character, it also suited British aspirations (Miller 2013: 88). Under this arrangement, as Mary Vogl writes: 'From 1923, when it was made an international zone until after Morocco's independence in 1956, the city was a haven for foreign artists, writers, spies, smugglers, hippies, [and] eccentric millionaires' (Vogl 2015: 38).

Albert Berdugo, the first of his parents' six children, was born into these realities. He was educated at the Alliance Israélite Universelle school in Tangier, where he excelled in his studies. He continued to the city's Rabbinical Seminary, where he undertook theological studies before embarking upon additional higher education in Spain. Finally, Berdugo enrolled on a one-year study programme at a college in Britain. In these various locales, he also became a polyglot, knowledgeable in Spanish, Haketia, Arabic, Hebrew, French and English.

On his return from Britain, he took up a job at the managing office of Hotel Villa Valentina in Tangier. There, he happened to meet the manager of the Moroccan daily newspaper *La Dépêche Marocaine*. The latter proposed that Berdugo join the newspaper as its production secretary. Berdugo took the job, and in due course was promoted to the editorial board. While working at *La Dépêche Marocaine*, Berdugo expanded his role to three other newspapers, *L'Écho de Tanger*, *Adelante* and *Democracia* (Berdugo 1996: 111–14).

Tangier was the birthplace of Moroccan journalism; very often, as in Berdugo's case, Alliance Israélite graduates were incorporated into this new sector. Schroeter (2018: 232) notes that a characteristic shared by these young journalists was their advocacy of modernity, alongside positive engagement with the idea of a Moroccan Judaism linked to a local Arabo-Hispanic past. The latter concept appears clearly in Berdugo's journalistic writing, in which he comes across as proud of both his Moroccanness and Jewishness. A good example of this is his response to allegations published in the French newspaper *L'Oeuvre* in 1931 by journalist Roland Charmy. *L'Oeuvre* started off to the left of the political spectrum, but during the interwar period turned first anti-Semitic, and then collaborationist during the Vichy era. Charmy, like Babin and his colleagues in the same period (see below), held narrow-minded beliefs about Moroccan Jews. Charmy's article claimed that while Moroccan Jews were in favour of the French occupation, it was risky to rely on their friendship because the Muslims hated them to begin with and were constantly becoming more and more anti-Semitic. He declared that before the French arrived in Morocco, local Jews had in effect been the Muslims' slaves, and that the Muslims hated them but could not do any trade without them. Furthermore, since Moroccan Jews allegedly controlled the moneylending markets, 'the Arabs' could not bear the humiliation, and from time-to-time slaughtered Jews and looted their *mellah*s, to 'recover' their debts and pride. Charmy maintained that the French occupation had made it possible for the Jews to enrich themselves through speculation, and thus the Jews ought to be thankful to France. But rather, he argued, the Jews maintained an insolent pride; they 'deny their miserable and greedy past', and 'were not ashamed of their origins'.

Berdugo's response to these allegations, from which I quote below, reveals just how confident he felt as a Moroccan and a Jew:

> [T]he world knows that the Israelites and the Muslims of Morocco have always lived in the frankest communication and in the most perfect harmony. Admittedly, at the beginning, Jewish religion was rather difficultly tolerated by the Moroccan Empire, which was essentially Muslim, but as civilisation began to do its work with us, this tolerance was reflected in an equal gratification of civil rights as much for the Muslim as for the Israelites ... the Muslim, of the Semitic race, was never anti-Semitic ... the Israelites of Morocco, like their fellow believers in France, were never slaves ... the Israelites of Morocco have always been very esteemed by the Sultans and often occupied the highest offices of the State. Thanks to its scholars, to its brilliant qualities in commerce and the interior, to its peaceful spirit, Moroccan Judaism, composed largely of Sephardi Israelites expelled from Spain, has never had to complain about its conviviality with the Muslims of Morocco ... Where and when did Mr Charmy read ... that there were massacres in Morocco? ... Usury ... Mr Charmy seems unaware that ... [in Tangier] there are still Catholic usuries who number in the thousands ... (Berdugo 1931)

Berdugo turns directly to Charmy at the end of the article, saying:

> Dear sir, nothing like this will happen in Morocco: anti-Semitic demonstrations – oh curious paradox! – are born and developed in certain so-called civilised countries and where criminal people are always ready to prove their animosity against us, provided they see the innocent blood of their victims shed. (Berdugo 1931)

Simultaneously with his counter-attack on external allegations against Moroccan Jews, Berdugo did not spare his critique of occurrences within his own community. He wrote a series of investigative articles for the local Jewish press, signed with the pseudonym 'Shema Israel'. In one, he exposed corruption cases involving leading figures in Tangier's Jewish community, that had almost led to the bankruptcy of the local Benchimol Jewish

Hospital. Berdugo later claimed that his articles saved the hospital from closure (Berdugo 1996: 114).

Berdugo's career as a journalist recalls episodes from the biography of Gustave Babin (Chapter 3). Despite their many differences, the two shared a common preconception, typical of the period's public discourse, about journalism's potential to serve as a restorative social agent. However, Berdugo's journalistic career was much shorter than Babin's. With a large family, and in the knowledge that employment as a journalist in Tangier would not suffice to support them, Berdugo left the profession, taking up a position at the local branch of the British Bank.

As it happens, this specific branch of the bank had maintained the accounts of the ex-sultan Mawlay 'Abd al-'Aziz, who had been in exile in Tangier since his deposition in 1908 (Chapter 2). Realising Berdugo's qualities as a banker, and knowing of his father's expertise as a goldsmith, Mawlay 'Abd al-'Aziz decided to nominate Berdugo to become one of his secretaries. Berdugo held the post until the ex-sultan's death in mid-1943 (Berdugo 1996: 115). In carrying out this job, Berdugo seems to have personally fulfilled many of his beliefs about Muslim–Jewish relationships in Morocco, as described in his article above.

During one of al-Glaoui's frequent visits to his estate near Tangier and to his many relatives in that town,[2] he happened to meet Berdugo at a public event in 1943. Impressed by Berdugo's skills and aware of his good work for the late ex-sultan, al-Glaoui proposed that he join his staff as one of his secretaries, an offer which Berdugo gladly accepted.

Accordingly, Berdugo moved with his family to Marrakesh. He worked at the Pasha's palace, often travelling with his patron in Morocco[3] and abroad, as his translator and secretary.[4] Al-Glaoui, it appears, worked to improve Berdugo's working conditions as time passed. For example, because the job of secretary of a senior civil servant (a pasha of a major town) was defined as a governmental post, al-Glaoui requested that the Director of the Interior improve Berdugo's employment terms, and officially enlist him as an employee of the French Protectorate.[5]

After the deposition of the Sultan in 1953, another task was added to Berdugo's secretarial duties – getting rid of annoying journalists seeking to interrogate al-Glaoui about his political moves (as documented in French journalist René Janon's reports; 1953: 104–5). However, somewhat contradicting the apparently good relationship between the boss and his secretary, a French intelligence note from mid-1954 reported that following a dispute with al-Glaoui, Berdugo allegedly sold the Spaniards a text of the Pasha's memoirs, and was planning to take refuge in Spain.[6] Another note, from around the same time, claimed that al-Glaoui had separated from his secretary Berdugo and that his post was taken by Mimran, president of the Jewish community of Marrakesh – Berdugo's predecessor in the very same position. Nevertheless, the report also made it clear that Berdugo continued to live in Marrakesh and had not departed for Spain.[7] I found no other testimony that supports this information, so it might as well belong within the realm of conspiracy narratives.

Immediately after his boss's death, fearing the likelihood of reprisal attacks on people linked to al-Glaoui (as indeed did happen), Berdugo and his family fled to France (Chapter 4) and settled in Nice. He initiated a few businesses in Monaco[8] and was involved in scholarship, particularly in studying Jewish Andalusian dialects (Manzanera 2001; Verdú and Torres 2001). Berdugo died in Nice in 2001.

Les Dessous d'une Conspiration

In his new homeland of France, forty years after his narrow escape from Marrakesh, the ninety-year-old Berdugo summed up his memories of al-Glaoui's final years in a volume titled *Les Dessous d'une Conspiration* (Berdugo 1996), variously translated into English as 'The Conspiracy's Inside Story' or 'The Story Behind the Conspiracy'. *Les Dessous* takes a completely different approach to the Pasha than that of *Son Excellence* (Chapter 3). In place of Gustave Babin's complete disdain, Berdugo shows admiration and respect to the Pasha – albeit leavened with some criticism. The dissimilarity between the books obviously reflects the authors' different biographies and perspectives. Babin was a colonial storyteller, the role model of the French *mission civilsatrice*; Berdugo, from the indigenous Moroccan Jewish community, had a local perspective on al-Glaoui, combined with an intimacy emanating from his place on the Pasha's staff.

Les Dessous is a 230-page book divided into short chapters. It begins with an introduction in which Berdugo recreates the tension and fear that he, as al-Glaoui's secretary, felt on the day of the Sultan's expulsion, and his retrospective disapproval of his master's actions (Berdugo 1996: 9–13). After a general outline of Moroccan history, a biography of Thami al-Glaoui and a description of his court (Berdugo 1996: 14–102), Berdugo details the history of the break between the Sultan and al-Glaoui. The scenario he paints follows the popular narrative: it begins with the 1950 Mulud event at the royal palace, the notorious meeting at which al-Glaoui accused the Sultan of being in thrall to the young nationalists, to which the latter responded by forbidding al-Glaoui from setting foot ever again in his palace (Berdugo 1996: 103–4). After a literary pause to recount his own biography (Berdugo 1996: 105–24), Berdugo returns to describe his opinion about al-Glaoui's crusade against Mohammed V. This narrative is presented in chronological order, supplemented with reproductions of letters and telegrams (Berdugo 1996: 125–226).

Berdugo's book, as much as it describes the Glaoui conspiracy, is a work of personal introspection. Forty years after the events, Berdugo seems caught in a quandary about his own life, in a way that resembles the practice of 'walking beyond the trauma' that Haviva Pedaya describes as shaping the Jewish collective and the Jewish self (Pedaya 2011). Where should his loyalties lie: with his master al-Glaoui; his former homeland Morocco and its royal dynasty; his new homeland, France; or with his family? Reading his deliberations, it becomes clear that Berdugo envied other people close to al-Glaoui, like the Pasha's sons and his personal aide, Hajj Idder. Situating himself among this rank is clearly a misjudgement – or knowing misstatement – of his status at the Pasha's court, since he was but a senior secretary. Nevertheless, what seems to bother Berdugo most is that after the national condemnation of these people in the first years following al-Glaoui's death, they all – eventually – regained their previous fortunes, while he remained in exile, destitute. To justify his sense of being a forgotten hero, or perhaps to redeem his self-esteem, Berdugo goes as far as to claim that he could have prevented the Sultan's expulsion in 1953, and thus the sad outcomes for Morocco and France. He states that he had planned to warn the French Resident-General of the dire consequences of supporting al-Glaoui's scheme to depose the Sultan. However, Berdugo blames al-Glaoui's personal aide, Hajj Idder, for preventing him from approaching the Resident-General:

[W]hen I was about to do it, I saw – pointed at me – the lightning gaze of Hadj Idder, who suspected very well of my moods, and who understood my intentions. I no longer had the opportunity to alert the person in force, and the execution of the insane project took place, with the results that we know of. (Berdugo 1996: 228)

Berdugo's text reads at times as an apologia, in which he answers a set of questions posed by a fictional prosecutor. Weren't you aware of al-Glaoui's immoral conduct? To whom were you loyal – your boss, your sovereign or your new homeland? Did your Jewishness affect your actions? How is it that after working for a billionaire like al-Glaoui, you did not become rich yourself? And finally, why didn't you leave al-Glaoui when his fortunes were falling?

In a short chapter titled 'A Case of Conscience', Berdugo answers all these questions:

[A]t times, I seemed to be witnessing a kind of regression in the history of Morocco, in view of a society that had suddenly become medieval and, in some ways, irrational. That is why I think I must confess what was my case of conscience during this pitiful confrontation . . . I was caught up between my religious beliefs, which forbid all believing and practising Jews to impair, even indirectly, the authority of a sovereign elect . . . and my fidelity to France as well as to the pasha, who after all was my boss and who had always testified to my esteem and confidence.

There was no question, therefore, of leaving him, let alone of disavowing him, without incurring his contempt and incomprehension. He often paid homage to my righteousness, sincerely regretting in front of third parties and my own cousins, familiar with the palace for their business, that my naïveté, my good faith and my Hispanic training, a bit chimerically, prevented me from making fortunes by his side.

It is quite certain that no one has ever wanted to believe that during my years of service with Glaoui I did not become an opulent person like so many others before, and was content with the payments he wanted to pay me.
Flattered by the place I occupied, honoured to be at his service and in the service of France, I had no other ambition than to conscientiously accomplish my work without thinking of abandoning the ship when it sinks as I had intuitively sensed. (Berdugo 1996: 107–8)

Berdugo and his deliberations, while offering original perspectives on the author's biography and on al-Glaoui, are at the same time significant for the discussion of the relationship between al-Glaoui and the Jews in general. Berdugo's case, despite being an individual occurrence, reflects many of the ponderings of large parts of the Moroccan Jewish community in the twentieth century, struggling then with issues of loyalty, and with the question of whether to stay in Morocco or leave.

Jews of Morocco

Before discussing the relationship between al-Glaoui and the Jewish community, a few words about Moroccan Jewry, in general, are in order. The Jewish community of Morocco has a history spanning back some 2,000 years. Over time, it witnessed the arrival of Islam to the country; the influx of the Maghreb by deported Muslims and Jews from Andalusia; and life under the various dynasties of the Moroccan Empire. The Moroccan Jewish community, treated as *dhimma* (a protected community) under Islamic rule,[9] for centuries constituted an integral part of Moroccan socio-economic life, with communities spread out across the country, from the large urban centres to remote desert oases (Kenbib 1994; Zafrani 2005; Schroeter 2008; Ben-Layashi and Maddy-Weitzman 2010; Boum 2011; Gottreich 2020).

Historically, the commercial elite of the Jewish community had been engaged with Morocco's foreign trade from the eighteenth century, if not earlier; other members of the community worked in a number of professions, ranging from artisanal craftsmanship in the cities to petty commerce and farming in rural areas (Schroeter 1988; 2002; 2021; Abitbol 1998; Gottreich 2020).

A significant change in the relationships between Muslims and Jews occurred with the introduction of the Jewish Alliance Israélite Universelle education system to Morocco in 1862 (Laskier 1983; Rodrigue 2010; Boum 2010). This institution, one aspect of the overall European involvement in the country, afforded access to European education and the French language to many Jews. This form of knowledge, within the fast-evolving sociopolitical conditions of colonial Morocco, enabled many Jews to take up professions requiring contact with Europeans – translators, import–export agents, businessmen, merchants, lawyers and doctors. Hence, in the evolving colonial modern environment, many Jews occupied mediating positions between Muslims and Europeans, and consequently became indispensable across multiple administrative and economic activities. This sudden dependency on a group that had habitually been stigmatised, by Christians and Muslims alike, created complex reactions ranging from reliance to rejection; according to some observers (for example, Laroui 1977: 310), it gradually drove a wedge between Jews and Muslims in the country.

Thami al-Glaoui and the Jews

The presence of Jews within the cultural landscape where Thami al-Glaoui had grown up was even a bit more pronounced compared with the rest of Morocco. According to Nahum Slouschz, who visited al-Glaoui's native village of Telouet in 1912, a third of its population (about 800 people) was Jewish, a similar proportion to that in the neighbouring villages (Slouschz 1927: 464).[10] This pattern followed the common phenomenon of large Jewish communities developing around regional centres of power, protected by the local chiefs (Schroeter 2018: 222). Numerous additional Jewish communities resided in the broad circle around Telouet: from Demnat at the foot of the mountains in the north, through the many High Atlas valleys, to Ouarzazate and the great oases of the Draa south of the Atlas. In addition, there was a significant Jewish population in Marrakesh, the region's largest city (Gottreich 2016: 206–7; El Glaoui 2017: 27–8, 180–6).

Within a day's walking distance from Telouet also stood the oft-frequented holy tombs of three Jewish holy men – Rabbi Aharon Abu-Haseira, Rabbi David Ou Moshe and Rabbi David Lachkar. The last, known also as Mawlay Ighi, according to some traditions, was also venerated by Muslims (Slouschz 1927: 462–6). Popular stories attest to Thami al-Glaoui's special respect for Mawlay Ighi, which he allegedly manifested by visiting the latter's tomb and sending donations for its upkeep. Other sources indicate that he also paid homage to the tomb of Rabbi Hananiah Ha-Cohen, Lachkar's brother, in Marrakesh (Ben-Ami 1998: 145).

Living side by side for generations turned connections between the Glaoua, who ruled from Telouet, and the local Jews into a normative state of affairs. Jews were even incorporated into the family's businesses. Moshe el-Drai, sheikh of the village's Jews, whom Slouschz (1927: 464–5, 468–9) had met in Telouet in 1912, is one example. Likewise, Jewish popular stories relate how various Glaoua family members consulted with local Jewish sages on multiple occasions (Ben-Ami 1984: 175; Bilu 1993: 81).

More concrete evidence about the connections between Jews and the Glaoui family in those years comes from letters kept in the archives of the Corcos family.[11] The Corcoses, a wealthy Jewish merchant family, had branches in several Moroccan cities, including Marrakesh. Members of the family were key players in Morocco's import and export trade, and consequently had close ties with both the Sultan and the Glaoui brothers (Schroeter 2010). Letters from the family archives dating from the late nineteenth to early twentieth century often mention Thami, and his elder brother Madani, as clients of the Corcos family's business network. For example, the following excerpt is from a 1908 letter, part of a longer correspondence in Judeo-Arabic between several Corcos family members:

> Friends of my soul and light of my eyes, Shimon Corcos and Mordechai Corcos ... Al-Haj Thami paid 350 rials which he had to pay, but Alum came to me, and at the end of the day after a lot of talking, we agreed that he will pay 200 rials as well as 22 packages of barley and for the rest I will wait for him.
>
> The green mule was taken to Ouariki by my soul's friend Hadan-Yehuda, who told me that he would give for it only 100 rials and let's hope that God will help, and he will pay and sell it. (And this) I may have sent with a good donkey, and I wrote to you that you will send 900, and from the cash register-box – send 550.[12]

The letter illustrates economic transactions taking place between al-Glaoui and the Corcoses, and at the same time it gives a glimpse into the dynamics of everyday life – the common practice, for instance, of Jewish merchants travelling with their merchandise on mules and donkeys between the remote mountain villages and the large cities. These details also disclose how the following tale, about al-Glaoui and the Jewish sage Rabbi Pinhas Ha-Cohen Azzogh, is rooted in this specific reality:

> Rabbi Pinhas Ha-Cohen Azzogh ... used to ride around to all the villages and cities on his mare to collect alms. He arrived

on his mare in Marrakech with his servant ... and wanted to spend the Sabbath with the rich man Yeshuʻah Corcos ... the pasha's policemen told [the pasha] that a Jew had a beautiful mare which he should take [for himself]. He told them to go and bring the mare. They came to Yeshuʻah and told him the will of the pasha. Yeshuʻah Corcos answered that they can take whatever there is in his stable except for his guest's mare ... [The policeman] told Yeshuʻah: Send men to take the mare! Yeshuʻah replied: You send them! He called Rabbi Pinhas to go and appear before the pasha. The pasha wanted to [buy] his mare. Rabbi Pinhas answered that she was not for sale and [said]: Go and fetch her! The pasha immediately sent his police to fetch the mare. When they opened the stable where the mare was kept, they found that it was full of snakes. They were afraid because the snakes wanted to swallow them. They came back. The pasha asked them: What happened? They told him about the snakes. The pasha went in person ... arrived ... and saw snakes everywhere.

He went back to speak with Rabbi Pinhas. He asked him where was he from. Rabbi Pinhas replied that he was born in the Souss. The pasha invited him to stay and live in Marrakech. The rabbi refused. The pasha told him: Look, I am returning the mare. Go through the city of Marrakech and [choose] whatever house you like: I shall give it to you! On Sunday the rabbi went to look for a house. He went back to the pasha and told him which house he liked best. It was the house he [eventually] lived in until his last day. A rich Arab lived there. The pasha sent messengers to tell the tenant to leave. He left. He gave him [the Arab tenant] a different house instead of this one. That week the rabbi came to live in Marrakech. This was the miracle. (Ben-Ami 1998: 262–3)

With its supernatural inferences, this account belongs to a rich literary corpus that refers to the relationship between the Pasha, Jewish sages and the local Jewish community (see more below). In this story as well as in the rest of this corpus, al-Glaoui appears very powerful, yet full of respect. Authoritative and commanding, but just to Muslims and Jews alike.[13]

The last tale also features Yoshua Corcos, whose archives are home to the letter quoted above. Yoshua (Ichou) Corcos was the leader of the Jewish community of Marrakesh, the largest property owner in the town's *mellah*, and a very well-connected merchant. Realising Corcos's many talents, Madani al-Glaoui, Thami's elder brother, appointed him as his representative in delicate matters such as mediating between rivaling *qa'id*s. Simultaneously, Madani and Thami leveraged Corcos's support in organising the Hafidiyya – Mawlay ʿAbd al-Hafidh's revolt against Mawlay ʿAbd al-ʿAziz, in which the brothers were major collaborators (Katz 2006: 85–6; Schroeter 2010; 2021: 57–8; Gottreich 2016: 233, 237–8; 2020: 125; and see Chapter 2).

After Madani's death in 1918, Thami al-Glaoui's various activities skyrocketed. To maintain control over the dense web of affairs – as well as to boost his status and image – al-Glaoui created a quasi-royal court for himself (Chapter 2). Within it, influenced no doubt by his family's good experiences, he employed a considerable number of Jewish employees, a situation not unlike that at the pre-colonial Sharifian court (Schroeter 2021: 55). The employees occupied various ad hoc or more permanent positions: lawyers, business consultants, secretaries, translators, drivers and more (see also Kenbib 2016: 122).[14] In 1921, for example, al-Glaoui hired a certain Josué Benaïm as translator,[15] to be followed by Ben Rimoge (Berrimoj) from Marrakesh, who also functioned as a secretary.[16] In trips to England in the early 1930s, his interpreter was the twenty-eight-year-old Pinto, a native of Tangier and an employee of the local branch of the Bank of British West Africa.[17] In the next decade, Albert Berdugo took over this position, also becoming the personal secretary of the Pasha.

From the 1920s, the Jewish lawyer Félix Guedj represented al-Glaoui in various commercial lawsuits,[18] including his struggle with Babin (Chapter 3). For business affairs he was assisted, beyond Corcos (who passed away in 1927) by Jewish bankers such as Hassan[19] and Gaston Péres. The latter, a native of the region of Oran, was al-Glaoui's property manager in Casablanca and represented him in many business transactions – including negotiations with the French authorities for his 50-million-franc loan (Chapter 3).[20] Another person who served al-Glaoui throughout his life, albeit with breaks in the middle, was Mimran, a leader of the Marrakesh Jewish community.[21]

In his book about his father, Abdessadeq El Glaoui (2004; see more in Chapter 8) explained that his father's choice to employ many Jews was influenced by the efficiency and absolute dedication of his Jewish employees. Abdessadeq reported that people often asked his father why he paid such large salaries to his Jewish employees. The Pasha's usual answer was: 'They earn money with me, but thanks to their work I also earn it. A lot. If they had no interest in being near me, they wouldn't gain any with me, but neither would I' (El Glaoui 2004: 52).

A rather minor incident, reported in a French intelligence note from March 1939, attests to the special connections between al-Glaoui and the Jews. The report stated that the Jewish community of Marrakesh had approached Jewish leaders in Paris, via connections in the Casablanca community. They asked the latter to use their influence to stop the publication of defamatory statements against al-Glaoui in the French newspaper *La Lumière*.[22]

These various links do not mean that every Jewish demand was accepted by the Pasha. For example, in 1922 al-Glaoui de-authorised a request by the Jewish community of Demnat, who fell under his jurisdiction, to be exempted from paying a specific tax. Authorising such a request would have meant loss of income, as a significant proportion of this tax went into his treasury (Schroeter 2021: 57–8).

Gustave Babin – not a big fan of either al-Glaoui or Jews – also undermined the Jewish discourse of ever-harmonious relationships between the two sides. In *Son Excellence*, for instance, he discusses a conflict between al-Glaoui and one of his Jewish employees, Jacob Attias, which ended with the death of the latter. Attias, described as very much in al-Glaoui's confidence, was allegedly sent by the Pasha to 'get rid of' al-Glaoui's *khalifa* al-Biaz, who had fallen out of favour with his boss. However (Babin writes), Attias failed to successfully carry out his secret mission, planned as a nocturnal shootout at the deserted palace of Madani al-Glaoui; Attias was eventually shot himself (Babin 1934: 253–7), dying of his wounds two days later, on the Jewish New Year's Eve of September 1933.[23]

From a literary point of view, this story, a part of Babin's crusade against al-Glaoui (Chapter 3), is highly steeped in notions of conspiracy, typical of the political and journalistic discourses of the 1930s to 1950s (Chapter 4). As a proficient storyteller, Babin was able to strengthen his claims further by way of literary devices typical of the adventure novel – mysterious figures, shadowy spaces and violent surprising turns of fortune. Loyal to this genre, he leaves it to the reader to guess who was responsible for Attias's death; but his insinuations make his thoughts on the matter very clear. This story does not indicate any anti-Jewish feelings of al-Glaoui, but rather that the Pasha treated all his employees, regardless of their religion, the same, for better or worse.

On the contrary, Babin, like many of his compatriots during this period, was possessed by the anti-Semitic atmosphere of inter-war France. An example of this attitude among the French *colons* in Morocco is well illustrated in George Orwell's impressions from his stay in Marrakesh in 1938:

> You hear the usual dark rumours about the Jews, not only from the Arabs but from the poorer Europeans.
> 'Yes, *mon vieux*, they took my job away from me and gave it to a Jew. The Jews! They're the real rulers of this country, you know. They've got all the money. They control the banks, finance – everything.'
> 'But,' I said, 'isn't it a fact that the average Jew is a labourer working for about a penny an hour?'
> 'Ah, that's only for show! They're all moneylenders really. They're cunning, the Jews.'
> In just the same way, a couple of hundred years ago, poor old women used to be burned for witchcraft when they could not even work enough magic to get themselves a square meal.
> (Orwell 1939; italics in original)

Sharing outlooks with many *colons*, Babin viewed al-Glaoui's reliance on Jewish employees as another of his many moral failings. He recounts that during a visit to France, al-Glaoui met with the famous Marshal Ferdinand Foch; he then 'dared to take, impose, make sit at the table of the illustrious soldier, his Jew Berrimoj' (Babin 1934: 42). Babin (1934: 43) adds that even less respected groups in Morocco would not have allowed such a situation to occur, and complains that the Quai d'Orsay (the French ministry of foreign affairs) did not provide al-Glaoui with a decent translator for the occasion.[24]

French misreading of the Jewish–Muslim relationship within al-Glaoui's circle also occurred in the context of the Babin–al-Glaoui legal struggle (Chapter 3). During the court case in France, a rumour spread that Grilhé, editor of *La Tribune de Paris* and defendant in the case, had considered replacing his Jewish lawyer because he had been told that 'the people of the North African races despise Jews', and that 'under this condition' – viz, employing a Jewish lawyer – 'it will be difficult to bring North Africans to testify against the Pasha.'[25] Locked into this stereotypical conception about 'the North-African races', Grilhé probably didn't realise that Guedj, the lead lawyer representing the very North African al-Glaoui, was himself a North African Jew.[26]

Al-Glaoui's relationship with the Jews was put to test by the Second World War. The collaborationist Vichy government, exercising its authority over the French Protectorate in Morocco, passed a series of anti-Jewish laws, beginning with the 1940 Statut des Juifs.[27] The new regulations were transmitted to Morocco, with the French administration and the Sharifian government responsible for their enactment. Jews were banned from taking up work in a range of professional roles, including bankers, money-changers, peddlers, stock or loan brokers, business investors, editors, directors, journalists, and movie producers, directors and administrators. In addition, the number of Jewish lawyers and doctors was restricted to 2 per cent of the total number of practitioners of these professions. Following these rules, Vichy introduced additional projects, such as a plan to eliminate Jewish influence in the economy by means of its 'Aryanisation' and *déjudisation* (elimination of Jewish participants). Preparations for this plan picked up pace in Morocco in 1941; however, the landing of American forces in 1942 prevented their realisation (Ouaknine-Yekutieli 2022).

In retrospect, even though Vichy regulations were certainly applied in Morocco, their impact was not close to the horrifying outcomes of extreme anti-Semitism witnessed in France (as anticipated by Berdugo 1931). Morocco remained, in theory, a sovereign state under a French Protectorate, within which the local Jews were considered a protected minority within the Sultan's Islamic kingdom. To this was added Resident-General Noguès' subtle non-compliance with the German directives, which also served to block or slow down drastic action against Morocco's Jews (Aron 1967: 99–103; Laskier 1991: 348–54; Pennell 2000: 262; Assaraf 2005: 231, 238; Marrus and Paxton 2005: 3, 152–60; Joly 2006: 71; Mouré 2007: 119–23; Crowe 2014: 149; Boum 2014; Boum and Stein 2018; Schroeter 2018: 25–9, 37–42).

With regard to al-Glaoui, the historian Mohammed Kenbib maintains that despite entrusting Jews with multiple tasks in his court and household, the Pasha accepted and propagated Vichy's anti-Jewish laws. For example, he supported plans to prohibit Jews from employing Muslim housemaids, and accepted proposals that would oblige Jewish notables to wear traditional costumes (Kenbib 2016: 150). Others interpret the same information differently. Daniel Schroeter (2021: 56) comments that the discussions on the subject of the employment of Muslim housemaids by Jews had already begun during the 1934–7 period, pre-dating the Vichy rules; Joseph Tolédano (2017: 99–100, 106) notes that in practice, the ban on housemaids was limited to young girls working within the confines of the Jewish *mellah*. Adult Muslim maids could still work in the neighbourhood, and housekeepers of all ages were allowed to work in Jewish households outside of the confines of the *mellah*. Concerning the requirement for Jewish notables to wear traditional costumes, Tolédano writes that al-Glaoui indeed gave this order, but that this was a one-off issued in a moment of rage. He then cites the French commander of Marrakesh, Colonel De Hauteville, who, in recounting his wartime memories from that city, noted that:

> During the period in which the attitude arriving from Vichy inserted administrative anti-Semitism into Morocco, which was intensive in other cities, the Jews of Marrakesh have enjoyed the patronage of Pasha al-Glaoui who knew in a much-sophisticated way how to protect them, and how to spare them the consequences of the racial laws. In this way the Jewish community in Marrakesh suffered the least throughout the period between the armistice and the American landing, both in regard with its honour, and as concerns its property. (Tolédano 2017: 106)

Abdessadeq, al-Glaoui's son, concurs with this view, asserting that his father followed Sultan's Mohammed V's leadership in thwarting Vichy's anti-Jewish instructions (El Glaoui 2004: 51–2). He backs up this claim by citing letters his father wrote to various French administrators in support of Jews who had worked with him (El Glaoui 2004: 83; see also Schroeter 2021: 57). Yet, revelatory as Abdessadeq's text is about wartime Marrakesh, it nevertheless reflects a twenty-first century discourse proposing a historic Muslim–Jewish allyship in Morocco, led during the Second World War by the Sultan (for example, Cohen 2015; Schroeter 2018: 237). This discourse is much more than 'historiography'; it is a wide-ranging historical event that has unfolded over the last few decades, during which the Kingdom of Morocco has gradually embraced its local Jewish heritage (Ouaknine-Yekutieli 2020). The current stage in the creation of al-Glaoui's stories is influenced by this trend, and reciprocally exerts an influence on them as well (as further elaborated in Chapter 8).

Indications that the lives of Jews in al-Glaoui's city remained 'normal' during the Vichy era can be gleaned from reports by Joseph Tolédano of events during the period. In November 1940, according to his accounts, a quarrel erupted near the Marrakesh *mellah* between Jewish youths and Moroccan soldiers. This very rapidly deteriorated into a major clash between Jews, Muslims and the police, continuing over several days and with casualties on all sides. Just as things seemed to be settling down, some Jewish children threw stones at a Muslim funeral. Clashes resumed anew, the police only regaining control of the situation with difficulty. As punishment for the children's behaviour, al-Glaoui fined the Jewish community of the *mellah* the sum of 50,000 francs – which was then doubled by the French administration. The local Jewish community wanted to appeal to the Sultan about what they deemed an unjust punishment; but a compromise was reached, through which the fine was to be reinvested in improving health conditions in the *mellah* (Tolédano 2017: 98).

I have not been able to determine whether al-Glaoui kept his Jewish staff during the Vichy era. Nevertheless, al-Glaoui was certainly recruiting new Jewish workers a very short time after its end. One was Albert Berdugo, as discussed above.

After the Second World War, a new factor began to influence the life of Moroccan Jews: the establishment of the State of Israel in 1948, and the subsequent wave of emigration from Morocco to Israel. Between 1950 and 1953, circa 20,000 Jews left Morocco for Israel (Hacohen 2003: 267). Al-Glaoui had a very clear opinion on the process. Abdessadeq El Glaoui, informed that after the establishment of the State of Israel, his father had commented:

> What a disservice this event does for the Jews themselves: it will crystallise a hostility against them of all the Arabs who will never agree to the despoil of Palestine for their benefit. If there was a chance that anti-Semitism will disappear in the world, we have just destroyed it by creating the State of Israel. The Jews will lose the enormous capital of solidarity

and pity that they acquired in the world as a result of the Nazi persecutions. Moreover, here in Morocco, as everywhere in the Arab world, the Jews had integrated into our communities and inevitably, sooner or later, they will be forced, if only for religious reasons, to create links with Israel, which one day or another will be politicised to the point of making life difficult in Arab countries. In the end, Morocco will lose a lot of its Jews and that is not good for its economy. (El Glaoui 2004: 52–3)

Notwithstanding the accuracy of his predictions, in the early 1950s the still-significant Jewish community in al-Glaoui's territories continued to show its respect to the Pasha, as apparent in the following *qasida* (poem), which mixes Arabic, Judeo-Arabic and Hebrew. This *qasida* was sung at certain *hillulah*s (Jewish religious festivity at set dates) in synagogues and the tombs of holy men, as part of the *mahia* glass auction ceremony:

> This glass is on the lectern
>> This glass is on the lectern
> And the lectern is full of splendor
>> The splendor of Rabbi 'Amram
> May his merit be with us
>> With us and Israel our brethren
> Praise the Lord for He is good
>> These mountains are the mountains of al-Glaoui
> These mountains are the mountains of al-Glaoui
>> Wherein resides the one who heals and cures
> Whose name is Rabbi Shalom Zawi.
> (Ben-Ami 1998: 111–12)

Jews from the 'mountains of al-Glaoui,' are mentioned by Berdugo, who was sent by the Pasha on various missions into their region. Coming from a Jewish urban background, Berdugo testifies to being totally amazed by meeting these rural Jews for the first time. He describes driving early one morning on an assignment, during the Jewish holiday of Passover, escorted by some of the Pasha's officers. When they drove, he noted four Tuareg men, mounted on camels, on the horizon. As they drew closer, the riders suddenly stopped, discarded their Tuareg *djellaba*s, and donned *tefillin* (phylacteries) for the morning prayer. Berdugo comments that he was stunned at this sight, convinced as he was that these were Muslim 'blue men' from the desert. He stopped to speak with them; it took him some time to convince them that he too was Jewish, and working for the Pasha. When he succeeded in convincing them, they kissed him and begged the group to visit their *mellah*, perched high on a hill. Berdugo sums up the event in the following words: 'It was the first time that I have seen Berber Jewish women, with blond hair and blue eyes, preparing traditional pancakes on a *"tanourt"* (oven) as probably our ancestors did in their exodus from Egypt' (Berdugo 1996: 217).

British novelist Elias Canetti depicts his impressions from meeting urban Jews in Marrakesh in these same years. In his *The Voices of Marrakesh*, he quotes a conversation he had with his friend Elie Dahan, a resident of the city's *mellah*:

> 'The Pasha hates the Arabs', said Elie. 'He loves the Jews. He is the Jews' friend. He does not let anything happen to the Jews.' He was talking more and faster than usual, and what he said sounded very odd, as if he had learned it by heart from an old history book. Not even the Mellah had struck me with so medieval a quality as these words concerning the Glaoui. I stole a glance at his face as he said them again. 'The Arabs are his enemies. He has Jews around him. He talks to Jews. He is the Jews' friend.' He preferred the title 'Pasha' to the surname 'Glaoui'. Every time I said 'Glaoui' he answered with 'Pasha'. He made it sound like the word 'commandant', with which he had been driving me mad shortly before. (Canetti 1978: 66)

Zionist agents, operating in Morocco at the time to boost emigration to Israel, apparently heard similar sentiments in Marrakesh. Reporting back after the abduction of Mohammed V and the coronation of Mohammed Ben 'Arafa, agent Yitzhak Rafael reported that 'for some reason the Jews consider the Pasha of Marrakesh as their friend' (Tsur 2001: 160).

When the situation in Morocco deteriorated in 1955, al-Glaoui decided that his best move would be to support the return of the Sultan (Chapter 4). French intelligence, monitoring the reactions in the streets to the Pasha's surprising turn noted that the Muslim population rejoiced at the news. One informant quoted a sentence he had heard among the workers' milieu: 'Al-Glaoui was a Jew yesterday, he became Muslim again.'[28] Among the Jews, French intelligence differentiated between the 'people of the Mellahs' and the 'more advanced' Jews. The only concern of the former was how the new situation would affect emigration to Israel. The latter, for their part, believed that al-Glaoui's decision was the only sensible option left open to him, after being abandoned by both the French and his Moroccan friends.[29]

Following al-Glaoui's death on 23 January 1956, the daily French intelligence report of the mood on the street stated that the French residents were sad, the Moroccan Muslims were generally happy, and the Jews made no comment.[30]

Jewish Narratives of al-Glaoui

In the Pasha's later years as well as after his death, a large corpus of popular tales focusing on his relationships with Jewish mystics circulated among the Moroccan Jewish community. A most common narrative, one with many versions (see below), is recounted in Georges Joseph Harari's *The History of the Jews of the Maghreb* (1974).

In short, the tale recounts that early one morning, back in the 1920s, a rabbi knocked at the doors to al-Glaoui's palace, insisting on an immediate audience with him. Recognising the visitor as Rabbi Pinhas Ha-Cohen Azzogh, a well-respected personage in Marrakesh (the one mentioned above in the tale of the mare and the snakes), the guards dared to wake the Pasha. The Rabbi apologised for the early hour; the Pasha replied that his admiration for the Rabbi was the factor at play, as otherwise he would have only risen from his bed to welcome His Majesty the King. He asked the Rabbi what had led to the urgent visit; the latter replied that he would only explain in the morning.

When breakfast was served, the Pasha took the milk kettle from the table to fill their glasses. The Rabbi stopped him and asked if it was his habit to drink milk every morning. The Pasha confirmed that it was. The Rabbi then asked al-Glaoui to have his servants bring a cat to the room. Bemused by the strange request, the Pasha nevertheless complied. Following the Rabbi's instructions, he poured some of the milk out for the animal. The cat sipped at the milk eagerly, but then suddenly began to sway like a drunken person. It then ran madly around the room, shortly afterwards dropping stone dead, its limbs distorted grotesquely. Realising what might have happened to him, the Pasha summoned two of his staff, whom the Rabbi had identified by

Figure 5.1 Al-Glaoui at his palace's gallery where he received guests. Source: *7 jours: grand hebdomadaire d'actualités*, 31 May 1942, p. 15. Modifications have been made to the original image.
Courtesy: BnF.

their names. The Pasha aimed a loaded pistol at them; seeing that there was no escape, the two confessed to their part in the deed. The Pasha asked the Rabbi how he had learnt about the plot on his life. The Rabbi answered that his late grandfather had revealed it to him in a dream that very night (Harari 1974: 130–1).

Another story with a very similar outline[31] adds the explanation of who may have wanted to harm al-Glaoui. It explains that the Pasha had been in conflict with the King ever since the latter mocked him on account of his reliance on Jews. Al-Glaoui retaliated and insulted the King, who therefore ordered that he be killed. Rabbi Pinhas, hearing of the plot in time, saved al-Glaoui, who consequently loved the Jews of Marrakesh and protected them.

A different version of this tale explains that the attempts on the Pasha's life rather came from the nationalists who were enraged over his contacts with the French. After the common depiction of how Rabbi Pinhas rescued him, the story ends in the following way, which relates to the 1955 media reportage of al-Glaoui's repentance, where he is seen kneeling in front of the King, asking his forgiveness:

> [O]n Independence Day, the Glaoui appeared before the king and bowed to him, but the king did not stop him, and he remained sitting bent on his knees, with his head on the floor next to the king's shoes ... A short time later, al-Glaoui died of general depression and great grief.[32]

The numerous tales about Pinhas Ha-Cohen Azzogh saving al-Glaoui have prompted some Jewish storytellers to suggest that a mystical link existed between the two; to underscore the point, they claimed that the two had died on the same day (Ben-Ami 1998: 260–1). Others, more attuned to temporal calendars – which indicate that al-Glaoui actually died four years after the Rabbi (January 1956 and January 1952, respectively) – note that on hearing of the Rabbi's death, the Pasha, in France at that time, cut short his visit and returned to Morocco for the Rabbi's funeral. Not only that: it is claimed that he also paid the costs of transportation to Marrakesh for the many Jews who wanted to attend the funeral but lacked the means to do so (Ben-Ami 1998: 136).

Al-Glaoui is depicted in another story[33] as a brave, black-skinned war hero, in a way that echoes his portrayals in 1920s narratives (Chapter 2). He is described as a sheikh, heading the Sahara Desert Amazigh tribes, who was dissatisfied with the Sultan's surrender to the French Resident-General. The Rabbi of Marrakesh, a close friend of al-Glaoui, hung an amulet around his neck which ever since protected him from death. The amulet prevented any bullet from hitting the sheikh or a sword from reaching his flesh. This enabled the Amazigh hero to fight his enemies on the battlefield without receiving a single scratch. However, when the Sultan's war minister realised that he would not defeat the sheikh in battle, he decided to use trickery to hunt him down. The Rabbi found out about the planned ambush and sent his son to warn al-Glaoui, who was thus saved. Thereafter, al-Glaoui loved the Jews and helped them, especially during the years of the Nazi regime, when he removed French officers who wished to harm the Jews of Marrakesh.[34]

Not all the stories refer to Thami. For example, a 1950s story refers to his brother's brother-in-law Hammou al-Glaoui,[35] who ruled some of the family's territory. This tale narrates how Rabbi Aharon Ha-Cohen performed a few miracles that saved Hammou from death in a strange sickness.

Most of the stories above were created between the 1950s and the 1970s in Morocco. After a few decades without any new tales about the Pasha that correspond to the years of the mass Jewish emigration and their resettlement in the diasporas, the production of popular stories about him re-emerged at the beginning of the 2000s. This revival occurred in Israel, the migration destination of most of Morocco's Jewry, and might be connected with the general revival of diasporic Moroccan culture there in those years (Ouaknine-Yekutieli and Nizri 2016). New tales appeared principally within Moroccan religious Orthodox circles, but surprisingly also beyond them, for example in the Romanian-Hungarian origin Halmin Hassidic court, where the following tale about 'The Rabbi who Stopped Hitler' (Natanzon 2004: 1–2) was narrated:

> At the time, Morocco was divided into two parts. A king named al-Hassan ruled its northern part from the city of Fes, while a king called al-Glaoui, whose capital was Marrakesh, ruled southern Morocco and the Sahara. Rabbi Pinhas Ha-Cohen, who lived in Marrakesh, was a welcomed visitor at al-Glaoui's palace.
>
> At some point, agents of Mawlay al-Hassan sought to assassinate the king of the south. Their plan was to attack the southern king's convoy as it passed through the suburbs of Marrakesh. They planned to strike it from the ground, supported by an airplane that would attack from the air. But Rabbi Pinhas had been granted heavenly foresight about the plot. In the middle of the night, he rushed to announce his astonishing revelation to the southern king. As he was well known, the guards let him in despite the hour, and his message was delivered in time. The king decided to send the convoy at the planned hour, but did not join it. Thus prepared, his men were able to capture the conspirators as they began their attack.

The king then asked Rabbi Pinhas how he could reward him. The rabbi answered that according to the Bible, Jews, wherever they are, are obliged to pray for the wellbeing of their kings. Therefore, he could not accept a reward for his actions. The king insisted. The rabbi answered: 'I ask that if sometime someone will want to harm the Jews, you will try to do whatever you can in order to save them.'

Some years later, Hitler sent emissaries to the king requesting that all the Jews of the kingdom be delivered to him. The king answered: 'I am surprised that you come searching for Jews in my country! Everyone knows that I hate the Jews so much that I expelled them a long time ago.' The emissaries accepted the king's answer, and so the Jews were saved. (Natanzon 2004, 1–2)

One can glean from the story the relatively limited knowledge of modern Moroccan history in the Hassidic court where the story was produced. The tale, framed in a standard format that praises ultra-pious rabbis, creates a fantastic melange of periods, personalities, popular tales and ideas. Al-Glaoui appears as the strong man of southern Morocco, ranked as a king. To this is appended the famous story of King Mohammed V saving Moroccan Jews during the Second World War (for example, Schroeter 2018: 237; Gringauz 2019; Chetrit 2021); evocations of the assassination of Ben Barka, supposedly by agents of King Hassan II (Daoud and Monjib 2000); and references to the Israeli army's method of land- and air-strikes on the convoys of whom they suspect as terrorist leaders. However, and most relevant for our discussion within this amalgam of anachronisms, is the fact that al-Glaoui's stories had become so renowned that they had spread beyond the Moroccan Jewish community, creating a continuous flow of literary products.

Over the last decade (as of 2022), a newer trend within this form of Jewish popular stories has emerged, namely attribution of the mystic revelations to Rabbi Makhlouf Abu-Haseira rather than to Rabbi Pinhas Ha-Cohen. (This may well reflect inner politics within contemporary Jewish religious circles.) Abu-Haseira, chief judge of the Jewish rabbinical court of Marrakesh in the 1940s and 1950s, is currently positioned as the one who saved Pasha al-Glaoui's life on several occasions. In these tales, as a token of gratitude, al-Glaoui helped the Rabbi

Figure 5.2 Rabbi Makhlouf Abu-Haseira (on the left) welcomes Pasha al-Glaoui (behind the French officer, on the right).
Source: Miyara 2012: 307. Modifications have been made to the original image.
Courtesy: Shlomo Zalman Miyara.

save Jews not from Hitler, but from inter-community marriages and conversion (Arosh 2010). A more recent narrative in this vein tells that Rabbi Abu-Haseira saw in a dream two assassins, dressed as women, sneaking into the palace to kill al-Glaoui. He was able to inform the Pasha in time, thus saving him. Appropriately, Abu-Haseira became 'the Pasha's friend', who in return protected the Jews (Haskin 2017). Another story narrates that al-Glaoui made his final decision to change course and support the return of Sultan Mohammed V from exile in October 1955 (Chapter 4), only after consultation with the Rabbi, who gave his blessing to the decision (a testimony by Rabbi Makhlouf Abu-Haseira himself, as quoted by Miyara 2012: 305–7).

From the perspective of literary history, the narratives above all fit within a well-established and long-standing Jewish storytelling genre. The basic model is of a Jewish sage rescuing his non-Jewish ruler from death: in gratitude, the latter saves his country's Jews from impending doom. The genre was established as early as the fifth century BC biblical story of Esther, also known as the Esther Scroll. In this story, the Jewish sage Mordechai saved Ahasuerus, King of Persia, from a plot hatched against him by his servants. The King shows his gratitude by saving his kingdom's Jews from persecution at the hands of his grand vizier, Hamman.

Beyond recitation of the Esther Scroll as part of the cyclic reading of the Bible, the story of Esther, Mordechai and Ahasuerus is commemorated every year during the Jewish holiday of Purim. Over time, a Jewish tradition evolved from this model, combining the narration of unique rescues (collective or individual) with annual commemoration. This pattern, which refers to the original Purim, is called Purim Sheni or Purim Katan (Second Purim or Minor Purim; Yerushalmi 1996: 46–8; Nizri 2018: 335). The annual celebration often includes the reading of a specific scroll, borrowing from the concept of the Esther Scroll, and setting out the details and morals of the salvation story in poetic form. Indeed, various cases of Purim Sheni, accompanied by dedicated scrolls, are known to have been produced by Moroccan Jewry from the sixteenth all the way to the twentieth century (Nizri 2018; Guedj 2018).

Even though none of the stories referring to al-Glaoui reached the Purim Sheni stage of commemoration, they all fall within the genre of 'a sage saving a ruler who in return saves the Jews'. In al-Glaoui's case, the direct message of these stories is gratitude for the heaven-ordained rescue. Yet, the stories also propose explanations for the favoured relationship between the Jewish community and their non-Jewish Pasha, and (in the context when the older stories were produced) the hope that such relations will endure. The act of telling stories of this type established morals, created realities and became a part of intercommunal relationships. With regard to al-Glaoui, the stories of being rescued from doom by local rabbis framed the common attitude of Moroccan Jews towards him – a combination of fear, respect, collaboration and gratitude.

Conclusion

The mutually respectful ties between al-Glaoui and the Jews rested on historical links between his family and its region's Jewish Amazigh community. In time, these connections extended to realms encompassing the practical, ontological and storytelling domains, bringing into their orbit other Jewish Moroccan communities and individuals. A recurring theme within these associations is the unique protector-protégé sociopolitical culture that developed between the Jews and the Pasha, broader than resembling link patterns with local strongmen (see examples for these in Brown 1976; Rosen 1984; and Schroeter 1988), and replicating in many ways the community's links with the Moroccan royal court. Jews, especially those under his jurisdiction, feared and respected the Pasha, and saw him as their ruler and protector. Al-Glaoui, for his part – and like the historical practice of the 'Alawi dynasty's relationship with the Jews – found the community instrumental in running many of his court affairs, as well as in facilitating various other activities (see a global perspective on such processes in Zenner 1990). At first these were mainly trading operations at various scales, but with time expanded to other endeavours: from translation and secretarial services to legal, business, and financial consultation and representation. In their actuality, and in the ways that these connections came to be told and celebrated in time, they endowed al-Glaoui with the aura of a monarch.

As in the other cases discussed above, these connections were expressed concomitantly in deeds and storytelling, which supported each other. Within the latter domain, the Jewish perspective on al-Glaoui contributes literary styles not encountered in previous chapters, most notably tropes linking the Pasha with venerated Jewish rabbis with prophetic and mystic powers. These stories added a mythical component to the unique relationship between the ruler and the distinct group he ruled, while attempting to explain this relationship and wishing for its endurance. This kind of tale has experienced a revival of sorts in the last decades, many years after al-Glaoui's death. In their earlier forms, and more so in the new ones, they retrospectively construct an imagined past. Testifying to the broad spread of al-Glaoui's repute within some Jewish milieus, a half-century after he died, a non-Moroccan Jewish Orthodox circle in Israel chose to present him as a sympathetic non-Jewish ruler.

The first part of this chapter focused on the specific biography of Albert Berdugo, and on the text that he produced in his dotage about his relationship with al-Glaoui. Berdugo's narrative is a complete departure from the mythical genre above, inter-textual links notwithstanding – such as the anecdote in which he portrays himself as a Jew saving the Pasha from being poisoned by his rivals. Even though it was written in the 1990s, Berdugo's text shares the 1930s–1950s discourse of conspiracies, as described in the previous chapter. The fact that the book, which is effectively Berdugo's autobiography, focuses so much on Mohammed V's deposition – al-Glaoui's Big Conspiracy – signals that Berdugo also saw it as the fatal turn for him, with everything since being under a cloud, so to speak. Writing in his dotage, from the diaspora, Berdugo's text reverberates with his longing for bygone times, and for a lost homeland and community. He expresses misgivings about previous life-changing decisions and reflects on the conflict of loyalties foisted on him, as a Jew in a Morocco, torn apart due to the colonial situation.

Having made this detour to survey the inter-relationship between al-Glaoui and the Jewish community, which included unique storytelling productions that bolster the Pasha's image as a protective ruler, the narrative now returns to where the previous chapter ended – the second half of the 1950s. By then, a major phase in the narration of al-Glaoui had ended, with many actors leaving the scene: al-Glaoui himself; the French, who left the by now independent Morocco; and the Jews, who had emigrated en masse, mainly to Israel but also elsewhere. However, despite the change of stage settings and the entrance of new actors, the tellings of al-Glaoui's life did not end. It merely changed formats. Among the new actors was another storyteller, whose personal story is intertwined with the story of al-Glaoui: the British author Gavin Maxwell, whom the next chapter concentrates on.

Notes

1. The chapter's title is an epigram referring to Thami al-Glaoui, told to British novelist Elias Canetti during a visit he made to Marrakesh in the 1950s by a Jewish resident of that city (Canetti 1978: 66).
2. It is noteworthy that many of al-Glaoui's international connections were conducted in Tangier – either during his numerous visits, or via messengers. He had family contacts there – Menhbi, 'Abd al-'Aziz's former minister of war, and a British protégé, lived there, and al-Glaoui married his daughter.
3. CADN 1MA/282 98, 'L'inspecteur-chef chef de la brigade de sûreté', 16 June 1952; CADN 1MA/282 98, 'Résidence général de France au Maroc, cabinet diplomatique', 21 January 1952.
4. CADN 1MA/282 98, 'Monsieur le directeur de cabinet civil résidence générale', 17 August 1951.
5. CADN 1MA/282 95, 'à Monsieur Vallat – directeur de l'interieur', 31 January 1953.

6. CADN 1MA/282 100, 'Note de Renseignements', 29 June 1954.
7. CADN 1MA/282 98, 'Le contrôleur civil Hardy. No. 1804 CRMA/2', 7 July 1954.
8. 'Cession De Bail Commercial', *Journal of Monaco*, 22 July 1957, pp. 761–2.
9. In Islam, *dhimma* are peoples with (revealed) books (*ahl al-kitab*), referring mainly to Jews and Christians – to be protected in return for payment.
10. In my current fieldwork in the region, interviewees referred to some of the more important Jewish hubs in the region under al-Glaoui's authority, which beyond Telouet also included Anmiter, Tizgui, Asaka, Tiguert, Tikirt and Imini.
11. Correspondence Corcos-Glaoui, Collection Dahan-Hirsch, Centre de la Culture Judéo-Marocaine, Brussels.
12. Correspondence Corcos-Glaoui, Collection Dahan-Hirsch, CC77, '16 Kheshvan 669', 10 November 1908.
13. Similar imagery emerged in testimonies I heard during my fieldwork. For example, a Muslim informer, whose grandmother had been a cook in one of al-Glaoui's kasbahs not far from Telouet, indicated that his father told him that 'under El Glaoui everyone got a sense of justice. It didn't matter whether you were a Jew or a Muslim, El Glaoui treated people fairly.'
14. For example, driver Meyer Lévy, CADN 1MA/282 97, 'Le secrétaire général du protectorat de la République Française au Maroc. B/MB', 10 November 1928; and on a more domestic level, music teacher Yehuda Sebag (Silver 2021).
15. CADN 1MA/282 96, 'Le receveur de l'enregistrement et du timbre à Marrakech', 14 September 1921.
16. CADN 1MA/282 100, 'Mon Colonel', 12 Februry n.d.; CADN 1MA/282 96, 'Le commissaire chef de la sûreté régionale', 16 March 1929.
17. CADN 1MA/282 98, 'Le commissaire divisionnaire chief de la sûreté régionale', 17 October 1938; CADN 1MA/282 100, 'Note. Objet: Pinto', 22 November 1932; CADN 1MA/282 100, 'Le Capitaine Lebrun', 10 February 1933; CADN 1MA/282 100, 'No. 184/C', 10 February 1933; CADN 1MA/282 100, 'M/S Marrakech. No. 395/C', 31 October 1932.
18. CADN 1MA/282 97, 'Consultation pour monsieur le Pacha Hadj Thami Glaoui', 22 May 1923.
19. CADN 1MA/282 96, 'Le Capitaine de Seroux', 27 March 1928.
20. CADN 1MA/200 818, 'Note pour le monsieur le délégué', 9 May 1934; CADN 1MA/200 818, 'Le pacha de Marrakech, à monsieur le directeur des affaires politiques, Rabat', 1 April 1938; CADN 1MA/282 98, 'Contrôle des autorités Chérifiennes, No. 833/17', 3 August 1938.

21. CADN 1MA/282 98, 'Contrôle des autorités Chérifiennes, No. 833/17', 3 August 1938; CADN 1MA/282 97, 'Société immobilière de Settat', 23 November 1938.
22. CADN 1MA/282 95, 'Bulletin de Renseignements', 1 March 1939.
23. Dadia (2011) mentions that the merchant Jacob Attias, who was on friendly terms with the Pasha, passed away on 15 September 1933, New Year's Day.
24. Babin also complains, in an article he published in his newspaper *L'Ère Française*, that al-Glaoui created a situation in which Marshal Foch had to shake hands with Berrimoj; he equates the relationships between al-Glaoui and Berrimoj to that between Charles Dickens' characters Mr Pickwick and his servant Sam Weller. Gustave Babin, 'Marrakech', *L'Ère Française*, 18 August 1927.
25. MAE, Série 'Maroc-Tunisie', sous-série no. 18–19, 'El Glaoui May 1931 – November 1937', 134–9.
26. In 1941, during the Second World War, Guedj was sentenced to five years' imprisonment by the French authorities in Morocco for assisting a young French man to escape to London. Guedj committed suicide in prison a few weeks before the American landing in Morocco (Tolédano 2017: 223–4).
27. The law was issued on 17 July 1940. It became applicable in Morocco by a *dahir* dated 29 August 1940, published in the *Bulletin Officielle* of 30 August 1940. Its application in Morocco was delayed until 31 October 1940. It was circulated through the *circulaires résidentielles* of 27 September 1940 and 5 November 1940. CADN DI 1MA/10/37, 'Note pour monsieur le délégué à la résidence générale a/s de l'épuration en 1940', 9 September 1943; CADN DI 2MA/100/2, File 'Épuration Administrative au Maroc'.
28. CADN 1MA/282 98, 'Note de Renseignements, No. 1543 RG/2', 26 October 1955.
29. This information is taken from a more expansive letter. CADN 1MA/282 98, 'Note, No. 2 077/RG Réactions parmi population locale . . .', 26 October 1955; CADN 1MA/282 98, 'Note, No. 2 077/RG Réactions en milieu israëlite . . .', 26 October 1955.
30. CADN 1MA/282 98, 'Note. Commentaires provoqués dans les divers milieux', 25 January 1956.
31. 'A Tale about the Late Rabbi Pinchas HaCohen'. Registered by: Shlomo Alfasi. Narrator: Yitzhak Moyal, Morocco. The Dov Noy Popular Story Archive in Israel (henceforth: PSAI), story no. 12908.
32. 'The Glaoui and the Rabbi'. Registered by: Moshe Bort. Narrator: Aharon Atiya, Morocco. PSAI 7212.
33. 'The Berber Sheikh and the Rabbi of Marrakesh'. Registered by: Zalman Beharev. Narrator: Avraham Shukron of Spanish Morocco. PSAI 3818.

34. Another story narrates how Rabbi Hanania Ha-Cohen had a dream that al-Glaoui was going to be hurt. He warned him in time and saved him. 'Rabbi Hanania Ha-Cohen Saves al-Glaoui'. Registered by: Issachar Ben-Ami in 1959. Narrator: Yosef Moreno, Morocco. PSAI 1095.
35. 'Rabbi Aharon Ha-Cohen Heals a Minister'. Registered by Yaakov Lasri, Morocco. From his memory. PSAI 13635.

6

Erasure and Revelation: Telling al-Glaoui from the 1960s to the Late 1990s

One of the greatest storytellers of al-Glaoui's tale was Gavin Maxwell. His book about the Pasha became a must-read for generations of anglophone readers and travellers who came to visit Morocco, and its wide distribution affected later narrations of al-Glaoui. This chapter analyses the book as well as its intertextualities with earlier tales, with sociopolitical processes, and with Maxwell's biography.

Gavin Maxwell was born in 1914, at Elrig, a large estate house built by his parents next to their family's residence in Monreith, Scotland. His father, Colonel Aymer Maxwell, heir presumptive of the Baron of Monreith, fought in the Boer War, planted rubber plantations in Malaya, and raised short-legged Labrador dogs in Scotland. His mother, Lady Mary Percy was the fifth daughter of the seventh Duke of Northumberland, her family accustomed to travelling between their palaces accompanied by the pomp and pageantry of a servants' entourage (Botting 2000).

A decade before Maxwell's birth, Britain was a prosperous nation, heart of the largest empire that the world had ever known (More 2014: 2). But many sectors of British society were seething with discontent. From the late 1880s on, a series of strikes swept across the country, indicators of a dramatic change in the sociopolitical power balance of the country. This change was clear by 1906, when the left-wing Liberal David Lloyd George was appointed Chancellor of the Exchequer, setting the stage for a transition of power from the hereditary aristocrats to the middle class (McCord and Purdue 2007: 406–38).

The rise of the middle class and the decline of aristocracy was linked to the worldwide collapse of agricultural prices: estate rentals fell dramatically, and land values dropped correspondingly (Cannadine 1999: 27; Rajamäe 2020). This situation caused broad resentment in the upper class, described by David Cannadine thus: '[M]any patricians disliked Jews, disliked capitalism, disliked the middle classes, disliked modernity, disliked the twentieth century. Many were bitter, many were resentful, some were self-destructive' (Cannadine 1999: 705). As members of the aristocracy, the Maxwells were certainly affected by the dynamics of the age.

However, a more severe blow hit the family as the Great War broke out. Maxwell's father, sent to the front in Belgium, was killed in battle and Gavin, a few months old, grew up without a father. Nevertheless, his early years with his mother, brothers, sister and a few servants were rather happy. As his biographer Douglas Botting notes, his frequent wanderings in the wilds surrounding the family estate created strong and enduring impressions in Maxwell, infused with a constant longing for his childhood's magnificent house and pride in his aristocratic descent (Botting 2000: 3–8).

Maxwell suffered from ill health as a child, but recovered with time and was sent to the prestigious Stowe School in Buckinghamshire. After Stowe, he went up to Oxford, studying Agriculture and Estate Management at Hertford College.[1] During college holidays, he went on trips to Norway and France and acquired some experience of freelance journalism. When the Second World War broke out, Maxwell joined the British Army's Special Operations Executive (SOE), which he later described rather sarcastically as 'the organization responsible for the Resistance Movement in occupied countries, and for training and arming agents to be parachuted – often to their death under torture – into enemy territory' (Maxwell 1968: 36). Due to periodical recurrences of his medical problems, he was posted to serve as an instructor stationed in England.[2]

Routine evaluations by military commanders describe his personality during those years as: 'Quite a cheerful person but rather self-centred. An excellent instructor in Weapon Training and Fieldcraft. Not so interested in demolitions and other branches. Very fit and can take part in any of our training despite his low category.'[3] In retrospect, it seems that these characteristics endured; a couple of decades later, he was similarly described as: 'a manic-depressive minor aristocrat, both talented and charming, but selfish' (Reid and Osborne 1997: 67).

After the war, keeping a family tradition, Maxwell took up a career in writing (his grandfather, Sir Herbert Maxwell, was also a writer). His first book, *Harpoon at a Venture* (Maxwell 1952), described a failed project, commercial shark hunting, that he had initiated in Scotland. His next book, *God Protect Me from My Friends* (Maxwell 1957a), took a different trajectory. Adopting a documentary novel format, it described the life and death of the Sicilian bandit Giuliano Salvatore (1922–50). Maxwell's approach to describing his protagonist almost seems like a rehearsal for the grander and later project on which this chapter focuses – the recounting of Thami al-Glaoui's life story. About Salvatore, Maxwell wrote:

> [H]e had become the most famous outlaw of his century. According to the tinge of political thought colouring the onlooker's vision, he appeared as a brigand or as an idealistic rebel leader, as a vicious criminal killer or as a just but ruthless Robin Hood, but his name and the rumours of his spectacular exploits in Sicily reached every part of the civilised world. The newspapers claimed him; he became a legend, and because few facts about Giuliano were of sober colour they became inextricably interwoven with the garish fantasies of press and propaganda, of worship and of hatred. His image became as a tree smothered by gaudy and luxuriant creepers, the true form of the trunk and limb no longer discernible, many of the parasitic leaves so nearly identical with those of the tree as to make distinction impossible. (Maxwell 1957a: vii)

This description of Salvatore's life and its global reverberations recalls al-Glaoui's intricate tale in many respects. In retrospect, one can reasonably speculate that Maxwell had a special attraction to writing about 'negative–positive' personalities – men operating on the borders of legality and criminality, loyalty and betrayal.

Alongside this theme, Maxwell remained loyal to his childhood fascinations with travel and nature. In 1957, he published *A Reed Shaken by the Wind* (Maxwell 1957b), describing an expedition with the British explorer, writer, and ex-military officer Wilfred Thesiger among the 'marsh Arabs' of Iraq. Three years later, he published *Ring of Bright Water* (Maxwell 1960), which brought him his greatest literary success in Britain. This volume describes his life in an isolated house on a small bay opening on to the Sea of the Hebrides, set within the enchanting landscape and wildlife of Scotland. His 1966 book about al-Glaoui,

The Lords of the Atlas, which I discuss in detail below, became a worldwide bestseller.

Maxwell died of cancer in 1969. The British author and researcher Louis Stott wrote about him: 'He conveyed an eye for nature and a determination to live life in his own way, in elegant, readable prose, close to poetry' (Stott 2007). Maxwell's life story makes him sound like a Buchanian hero of sorts (referring to the novels of the Scottish writer John Buchan (1875–1940)). Like Buchan's heroes, Maxwell keenly felt the decline of the British aristocracy, and set out on quests intended to somehow compensate for this loss, often retreating to the wild of nature to cope with his existential crises (Rajamäe 2020: 541).

The Quest for al-Glaoui's Story

Maxwell does not explain what triggered his decision to write a documentary novel about al-Glaoui; with little knowledge about Morocco, this endeavour necessitated intensive research. Maxwell arrived in Morocco in the early 1960s, eager to begin his work. However, to his great disappointment, he soon discovered that the country was not ready for inquiries into its sensitive political affairs – especially by a foreigner.

During this period, King Mohammed V was held up as the unmistakable hero of independence, consolidating his role of Amir al-Mu'minin (Commander of the Faithful). Buoyed by his successful resistance to French colonialism, he garnered unprecedented public support. Facing him was the Istiqlal, who aspired to eradicate the monarchy and to rule Morocco as a single, urban, middle-class-based party, following contemporaneous trajectories in Egypt, Iraq, Tunisia and Yemen. Tackling the threat immediately after independence, King Mohammed's court dismantled all of the ominous armed forces scattered across Morocco, including the Liberation Army,[4] various gangs, the militias of political parties and remnants of the local units that had operated within the colonial apparatus. The King established a national police force, and a military headed by Crown Prince Hassan. Most of these forces' high-ranking officers came from families of rural notables; many were of Amazigh origin and had previously served in the French colonial army. This body, closely controlled by the palace, was very different from the urban middle-class make-up of the core of the Istiqlal – and were thus easily able to resist the latter (Hammoudi 1997: 16–17, 25–6; Leveau 1998; Pennell 2000: 300–1).

The power struggle that unfolded after independence was often violent; it was not uncommon for opponents of the Istiqlal to be harassed or even killed (Eickelman 1992: 160). This situation led to considerable hostility towards the party, especially in rural Amazigh areas. In these places, former commanders of the Liberation Army founded their own party, the Harakat al-Shaabiya (in Tamazight: Amussu aүerfan; in French: Mouvement populaire). Trying to suppress it, Istiqlal officials used legal procrastination to block its registration for the 1958 general elections, a fact that further amplified hostility towards them in Amazigh areas. The discontent, especially in the Rif, was further aggravated by challenging economic circumstances, an agricultural crisis, and anger over the Istiqlal's tendency to nominate people from other areas to local posts. Turmoil in the region rapidly deteriorated into a general rebellion against the government. The insurrection was suppressed by a military force commanded by Prince Hassan. Hassan's success in supressing this revolt, and other smaller insurgencies, further strengthened the palace and weakened the Istiqlal, particularly in rural areas (Maddy-Weitzman 2001: 29; 2011: 85–6)

Simultaneously, the court succeeded in instigating disagreements within the Istiqlal, which led to the party disintegrating in 1959. In addition to this, it implemented a complex policy with regard to old elites and rural nobility: on the one hand supporting a purge of the people who had collaborated with the French, on the other strengthening tribal networks. This two-pronged approach helped the court in taking precedence over the political parties in rural areas, and to entrench its reliance on the successors of previous tribal elites as a significant power base (Ouardighi 1975: 147–53; Daoud and Munjib 2000: 193–4; Hammoudi 1997: 19; Maghraoui 2001: 76).

Maxwell arrived in Morocco during this tense period. As if designed to worsen the situation, a devastating earthquake struck Agadir in February 1960, just as he began his quest. Many of the officials whom he wished to interview were occupied with dealing with the earthquake's disastrous consequences (Maxwell 1963: 3–18). Compounding the situation, a year later, King Mohammed V died during a routine surgical procedure. The political system, occupied with the transition of power to

Mohammed's son, Hassan II, avoided contested issues (Pennell 2000: 317–18). Hence, Maxwell had little success in securing access to state officials for interview.

Given these limitations, the writing of a documentary novel about al-Glaoui extended over a much longer period than Maxwell had anticipated. It was only after a lot of work that Maxwell succeeded in arranging a series of interviews, and to be granted access to a few unpublished documents held by informants (who, uniformly, asked to remain anonymous). With regard to published material, Maxwell indicated that data about the Glaoua was spread across a large number of difficult-to-find books and documents in French. As an outsider largely unaware of Moroccan and French publications, it took him some time to discover that there was actually already a printed book about the Pasha – Gustave Babin's *Son Excellence*. However, he describes obtaining a copy of this book only after a 'year-long exhaustive search'. In his view, the difficulties he encountered in tracking down a copy of the book were because al-Glaoui had arranged for most copies of it to be destroyed immediately after publication (Maxwell 1966: 11, 176, 292–302).

Maxwell's biographer, Douglas Botting, comments about the writing of *The Lords of the Atlas* that it was one thing for Maxwell to formulate the idea, but quite another for him to find the way through 'the labyrinth of secrets that had surrounded it' (Botting 2000: 264–71, 467–9). He cites a letter, in which Maxwell describes his feelings on arriving in Rabat for the first time:

> Life here is rather hell. I live between interviews with ministers of that and this and the palace and my empty hotel bedroom. Dinner with the Minister of Bubble-blowing, drinks with the Minister of Crossword Puzzles, endless research in the national library; but this empty room seems the core of my life and I am VERY LONELY. I've given several broadcasts on Radio Morocco but apart from these one is terribly lonely and only one man in ten speaks anything but Arabic. I spend part of my time wandering about the Medina (old Arab walled town), where one is back again in the seventeenth century, but one is a stranger and remains LONELY . . . (Botting 2000: 266)

After finding little success in Rabat, Maxwell decided to move to al-Glaoui's capital, Marrakesh, hoping to glean information there. And indeed, Marrakesh proved to be different. Writing another letter to his friend, Maxwell now reports:

> I'm so relieved to have left Rabat that this seems like paradise even though I am alone. This is really one of the most fabulous cities left in the world, and hasn't changed much since I last saw it five years ago – in fact so far as one can tell it hasn't really changed since it was built in the year 1200. (Botting 2000: 267)

Exhilarated, Maxwell set out to investigate the main sites of al-Glaoui's life story, assisted by a young Amazigh translator. His visit to Telouet reignited his enthusiasm; the place, and the story behind it, appeared mysterious, magnetic, hypnotic, as if haunted by ghosts (Botting 2000: 269). The sight of the decaying fortress might have also touched Maxwell in another way. A few commentators have suggested that Maxwell's special interest in the ex-noble family, whose crumbling forts dotted the landscape of the Atlas Mountains, had been triggered by himself being part of the disintegrating British aristocracy, and by his feelings towards the ruined castles of the Scottish Highlands (Gellner 1970: 227; Rogerson 1995).

Concurrently with his travelling around al-Glaoui's territory, Maxwell tried to get the court's permission to interview several informants. The permits, however, were continuously delayed. After many disappointments, he eventually succeeded in meeting a woman whom he described as 'ex-princess Madani Glaoui'. Maxwell writes that the ex-princess told him that she was a personal witness to Thami al-Glaoui's bouts of rage, and his poisoning of his opponents. She explained that seeing these, her life was under threat from both the Glaoua and the French. She agreed to talk with Maxwell only if he could provide an official permit for the interview, signed by the King or by the minister of the protocol – a request that he eventually managed to fulfil.

Returning to England after his first visit, Maxwell wrote to his publishers:

> It is impossible to complete this work without a further visit. I think the whole subject has greater possibilities than any I have yet tackled or indeed thought of. But time is needed, and in estimating the length of a visit full consideration must be

given to the infinite procrastination of Moors. (Botting 2000: 271)

On 24 October 1966, *The Lords of the Atlas* was finally published. Because Maxwell made a number of allegations in the text against France and various French personalities, the publishers were wary of libel suits in that country: consequently, the book was not distributed there until 1968 (Maxwell 1968). In Morocco, in accordance with the policy of the period – avoiding unnecessary political turmoil – distribution of the book was completely prohibited, deemed as antagonistic to the public interest (Botting 2000: 468).

Summing up the project, Maxwell noted that it was 'like collecting and assembling widely dispersed pieces of a jigsaw puzzle' (Botting 2000: 467). Botting added his own Orientalist interpretation to the endeavour, commenting that 'delving into such an arcane and secret history in such a closed, medieval and culturally alien society proved even more difficult and time-consuming than primary research does at the best of times' (Botting 2000: 468). Accordingly, he believed that the fact that Maxwell eventually reached his goal was proof of his unique talents of persuasion, diplomatic skills, stamina and professionalism.

The Lords of the Atlas – the Book and its Reception

Maxwell's *The Lords of the Atlas* is a comprehensive, semi-academic study describing the rise of the Glaoua family from the end of the nineteenth century to the death of Thami al-Glaoui. The book is divided into three parts: the first part is dedicated to Madani al-Glaoui, the second to Thami al-Glaoui. The third is made up of a few appendices: a short description of the looting of al-Glaoui's house in Marrakesh after his death, several quotes regarding Mawlay al-Hafidh and a critique of Babin's *Son Excellence*.

Written in fluent prose, the book combines investigative work, poetic descriptions, anecdotes and pieces taken from other sources. The last is especially evident in the first part of Maxwell's book, where more than a third (circa forty-five pages) has been copied from Walter Harris's *Morocco That Was*. This fact is acknowledged by Maxwell (1966: 11), who thanked Harris's agent (Harris died in 1933) for permission to do this.

Ernest Gellner, who reviewed the book in 1970, writes about it:

> The story goes like a bomb, thanks both to its heroes and to the storyteller. Mr Maxwell's wizardry lies not in his prose, but in a masterly handling of scissors and paste. This need not be read in a pejorative sense. Mr Maxwell achieves a kind of collage (as in effect he admits) which really conveys a very powerful picture of the Moroccan politics of the period ... The author of this book evidently aimed at writing a shocker, providing the reader with a maximum of frissons by dwelling lovingly on violence, brutality, treachery, sex and perversions, and he succeeds brilliantly. In the course of doing so, he also provides something which, in general outline, presents a remarkably good picture. On details, he is far less trustworthy, and his comments are not profound. (Gellner 1970: 224)

Gellner further observes that 'Maxwell's stories are often amusing rather than plausible', and that a number of his ethnographic accounts are neither correct nor coherent, while others 'are a curious mixture of error and valid perception' (Gellner 1970: 225). He notes that in many places Maxwell is wrong with dates, that he offers implausible interpretations, and that he copies ideas from French scholars like Robert Montagne without acknowledging them and without understanding them. Gellner's review ends with the comment: 'But if the details are suspect and the comments lack depth, nevertheless the many readers who will obtain their picture of the period from this book will be given, in outline, a correct picture' (Gellner 1970: 227).

In the long run, Maxwell's book has enjoyed remarkable success, having been printed in ten editions (the most recent in 2012). It raised awareness of al-Glaoui's figure at a time when it had been silenced in Morocco (1960s–1980s) and provided important context of Moroccan history for the anglophone world. It also became an essential part of travellers' baggage when visiting Morocco. One prominent travel website recommended in 2014: 'If you only have time to read one book before you go to Morocco, then Gavin Maxwell's *Lords of the Atlas*' (Kilkelly 2014).

Dictated Amnesia

The atmosphere of silencing that Maxwell had witnessed while researching his book was not unique to his pursuit, but rather typified Moroccan historiography of the period. After independence, local historiography became engaged with a decolonising project, based on the premise that the liberation of Moroccan soil should be accompanied by the liberation of its history. Accordingly, the new historiography that emerged aspired to draw principally on Arabic sources, and challenged colonial notions such as the purported distinction between Arabs and Amazighs, or the idea that there was no sentiment of Moroccan unity in pre-colonial times (for example, Benabdellah 1958; 'Ayash 1959). Vermeren writes (2011: 11) that the political powers became deeply involved in the production of historical knowledge, transferring the writing of official history 'from the hands of historians to those of ideologues'. In these circumstances, many academic historians were obliged to confirm and execute the decolonising project – even if they conceived it as no more than sloganeering (Rachik and Bourqia 2011: 9) or found themselves caught in a struggle between political necessity and historical findings. As a result of this indoctrination, the main part of Moroccan historiography of the era 'forgot' certain topics, instead focusing mainly on the history of the monarchy and on revered patriotic personalities (Peyron 2010: 157; Vermeren 2011: 8–10).

Forgetting – as well as its obverse, remembering – are essential elements in constructing a national identity (Gillis 1994; Najmabadi 1998). Affected by the situation, the story of Thami al-Glaoui underwent a dictated historiographic amnesia in the post-colonial struggle over the narration of Moroccan national history. Under these circumstances, Maxwell's attempts to interview officials about the Pasha were, in most cases, futile.

On the making of history, Michel-Rolph Trouillot has observed that it consists of inherent silencing, which occurs all along the historiographic procedure: in the gathering of facts, the filing in archives, the retrieval from these, and finally in the creation of the historic tale. Accordingly, he emphasised that when reading historic narratives, it is as important to pay as much attention to what is not said as to what is said. The absences are not coincidental or a result of simple forgetting: they are active actions (Trouillot 1995: 48).

Al-Glaoui's memory was witnessing such a historiographic erasure. This manifested many forms, one being the non-collaboration that Maxwell encountered in the 1960s. But the erasure had begun even earlier, immediately after the Pasha's death. On that occasion, governmental agents confiscated all the documents from his palace and blocked public access to them.[5] Refusal to talk with Maxwell about al-Glaoui came next; and finally, when Maxwell's book was published, distribution in Morocco was forbidden. Thus, the official telling of al-Glaoui was minimised.

Yet, away from official sites of history production, narratives about al-Glaoui continued to thrive during those years, their echo rippling as side stories within other tales. For example, American researcher Elizabeth Fernea describes her experience of living in Marrakesh for a year during this period in her book *A Street in Marrakech*. Among her many stories, she relates the following conversation between her neighbours:

> 'The Glaoui who lives next door to me gives herself airs', said Aisha, 'just because she's a member of the pasha's tribe. But we don't pay much attention. After all, she's from the country, not from Marrakech. And the pasha doesn't run Marrakech anymore.' (Fernea 1975: 109)

Later on, Aisha, Fernea's host, gets into a fight with her Glaoui neighbour:

> The voice of Glaoui was heard, screaming, 'What do you mean, to talk to me, a Glaoui, a relative of the pasha, like that? You work as a servant for foreigners! You are nothing, nothing, nothing!'
>
> Aisha interrupted, and I scarcely recognized my friend's voice, heightened, raucous. 'Nothing!' screamed Aisha. 'If it's nothing to work and support your family and keep them decent so they don't have to beg, then I'd rather be nothing. And who was the great Glaoui Pasha? Nothing but a butcher!'
>
> 'Shhhh!' Someone was trying to stop the words, but Aisha pressed on.
>
> 'A butcher!' she repeated. 'His dead hands and the hands of his descendants are covered with innocent blood!' (Fernea 1975: 338)

After the quarrel ended, Fernea discusses the incident with her friend Lateefa:

> 'It's no fun. Glaoui has a mean tongue.' She smiled. 'But Aisha doesn't do too badly either. Butcher!' She nodded. 'She got Glaoui there. For all her airs, it's true that the pasha was a cruel man.'
> 'But powerful.'
> Lateefa nodded. 'Powerful because he had the French behind him,' she said scornfully.
> I was surprised at her tone. Was Lateefa, usually so sweet and yielding, really that concerned about the politics of the past, the days of Thami Glaoui, or was her feeling due to loyalty to Aisha? (Fernea 1975: 340)

Hence, and official forgetting aside, vivid and complex feelings towards al-Glaoui and his family still existed in the streets of Marrakesh long after he was gone. The Glaoua girl still considered herself an elite; the hushing of Aisha by the people around her suggests that there was still a fear of the Glaoua family. Simultaneously, the conversations expose the continuing influence of the rhetoric of al-Glaoui as a traitor and collaborator with the French. This reduction was emphasised further by comments that the Glaoua's origin is in the country – a common urban discourse, expressing the superiority of city folk over tribal migrants from the rural areas.

The Spirit of the Thing

The Lords of the Atlas, and letters he wrote to friends (Botting 2000: 267) testify that Maxwell was no less enchanted by the city of Marrakesh than by al-Glaoui. This enchantment percolated into his writing, transmitting a sense of likeness between the Pasha and his city. The attraction of being in this unusual place intertwines with the magnetism of the eccentric figure who made it cosmopolitan in the twentieth century. Maxwell's fascination with the city was not unique. In the 1960s, Marrakesh became a chic station on the so-called 'Hippie Trail' running from America and Europe to the Orient (Moretta 2017: 1; Billock 2019).

Other international icons lived in the city for short periods at the same time as Maxwell, who was already a recognised author by the 1960s. They included celebrities such as the Rolling Stones' guitarist Brian Jones; writer and musician Brion Gysin; fashion designer Yves Saint Laurent with his partner, fashion businessman Pierre Bergé; John Paul Getty and his actress wife Thalita Pol-Getty (Freud 1993; Fenwick 1998; Bergé and Mynott 2010; Cochrane 2016: 38–9). This contingent of expatriates also included several authors who wrote about the city. George Orwell wrote critical thoughts about European imperialism in Morocco and elsewhere, titled 'Marrakech', after living for a few months in the city (Orwell 1939). Bulgarian-British Elias Canetti visited the city in the mid-1950s, publishing his experiences in *The Voices of Marrakesh* (Canetti 1978). British writer Peter Mayne lived there for a year, publishing his experiences in *The Alleys of Marrakesh* (Mayne 1957) – later editions renamed *A Year in Marrakesh* (Mayne 1982). American Elizabeth Fernea wrote *A Street in Marrakech* (Fernea 1975); Estonian Leonora Peets, who lived in the city for about forty years between the 1930s and 1970s, described this period in her *Women of Marrakech* (Peets 1988).

Besides a keen interest in the story of al-Glaoui, Maxwell's choice to spend time in Marrakesh was a part of a global trendy bohemian zeitgeist. This emerged from the city's publicity as an Oriental wonder which, besides traditional crafts and nice *riads*, also included the availability of good quality hashish (Moretta 2017: 1) and prostitutes. This vibe was created during al-Glaoui's time, having enabled these norms while he was the city's pasha. Furthermore, al-Glaoui had certainly invested in constructing his and the city's representations as Oriental marvels, qualities that were reciprocally sought in him and in Marrakesh by many foreigners (for example, Barthou 1919: 79–81; West 1932: 215).

The production of these iconic representations included the physical construction of attractions in Marrakesh, like his palace, which Babin described in the following words:

[T]he Palace of the Thousand and One Nights, this beautiful garden where so many distinguished guests, men of letters, artists or politicians have paraded their dreams of silk and gold, to the rhythm of the dances of the Bathylles chleuhs, with the shrill tinkling of their rattlesnakes, an enchanting stay, a perfect setting for heroic novels. (Babin 1934: 243–4)

Al-Glaoui's palace in Marrakesh turned into an attraction for the European elite,[6] and al-Glaoui in his lifetime became 'a myth in

Europe, an image of oriental splendor and romance unrivaled even by the most gorgeous of the Indian maharajahs' (Maxwell 1966: 154). Maxwell further described the formation of al-Glaoui as a cultural phenomenon in the following words:

> In the 1920s T'hami had become, among many Europeans, a fashion, like American jazz, or the Charleston dance, or the new art form of cubism. To be aware of 'The Glaoui', and to be able to speak of him with familiarity, was equivalent to what was known forty years later as being 'with it'. It was fashionable to quote his *bons mots*, as, for example, his comment upon M. Daladier, at that time the French minister of war: 'He is like a dog without a tail – there's no way of telling what he is thinking.' (Maxwell 1966: 161)

Hence, even if al-Glaoui, the person, was gradually disappearing from official historiographies in the 1960s, his memory remained engraved into the cityscape and vibe of Marrakesh, a fact intertwined in subsequent writing about him. Nevertheless, the character al-Glaoui gave to his city, much liked by foreign visitors, was not necessarily considered positively by everyone. Fifty years after Maxwell's visit, and thus in a different historiographic setting, Moroccan researcher, critic and translator Abdeljalil ben Muhamed al-Azidi al-Murakushi, wrote about those times:

> Al-Hajj Al-Tohamy worked to transform the city of Marrakesh ... from the city of saints, righteousness, honorable people, scholars, ascetics, mystics, jurists, philosophers, and doctors, into a khan or a tavern that serves delicious alcohol, in which males and females have fun and people forget what might happen in it. (al-Murakushi in Benhadar 2010: 11–15)

This perspective will be elaborated on further in Chapter 8, which also discusses the turning of al-Glaoui's palaces into touristic–economic resources in the twenty-first century.

Borrowing and Objecting – Maxwell, Harris and Babin

A major source for Gavin Maxwell's book was British writer Walter Harris's *Morocco That Was* (Harris 1921), its ideas adopted wholesale and uncritically in *The Lords of the Atlas*. About half of the text between pages 23 and 124 of Maxwell's book, as well as its second appendix, are derived wholesale (with permission) from *Morocco That Was*. Justifying his action, Maxwell explained that 'to use his [Harris] information while changing his words would be unthinkable; for his style, both moving and hilariously satirical, must have been unique in his epoch' (Maxwell 1966: 11). Even though Maxwell marked all citations with quotation marks, it would have been difficult for the casual reader to notice these and to determine who wrote each section of *The Lords of the Atlas* – Maxwell or Harris.

The confusion between the two texts corresponds with a marked resemblance between the two authors: both Brits of aristocratic descent, exceedingly self-centred personalities, openly gay men, and enthusiastic about travel and adventures in 'the Orient'. Walter Burton Harris was born in 1866 in London, about fifty years before Maxwell. His father was a well-off English shipping and insurance broker, his mother a descendant of a wealthy Scottish family. In adulthood, Harris was briefly married to a daughter of another aristocratic family, but the marriage collapsed swiftly. At the age of nineteen, Harris travelled to Tangier and decided to settle there. He became the permanent correspondent of *The Times* in Morocco in 1906, a post he held until his death in 1933. Harris was deeply involved in British politics in Morocco and maintained contact with many Moroccan figures – including al-Glaoui – and French Protectorate personnel (Schoen 1938: 115; Best and Fisher 2011; Hamilton 2019). A gifted writer, Harris wrote several books about Morocco (Harris 1889; 1895; 1921; 1927). One of his best-known volumes is *Morocco That Was* (1921), a book that won a lot of praise – but also criticism: 'It is hard to distinguish [in it] the truth from the legend'; and claims that Harris 'loved to tell stories, especially about himself . . . a hymn about his own cleverness, cunning, bravery, popularity, and importance' (Zur Mühlen 2010: 209).

Maxwell's writing style was very similar to that of Harris. Both relied heavily on anecdotes, tended to the satirical, and often shared similar picturesque perspectives on people and events. These parallels, multiplied by their similar origins and upbringing, and the fact that Harris had thirty to forty years of 'Moroccan experience' ahead of Maxwell, probably led the latter to accept Harris's text as authoritative, and thus readily transferable.

A second author who also strongly influenced Maxwell's *The Lords of the Atlas* – but in much the opposite way to Harris – was Gustave Babin (Chapter 3). Maxwell was exceptionally critical of Babin's book, quite the radical contrast to his very high confidence in Harris's narrative. His critique – quite possibly reflecting some of the age-old animosity between the British and the French – is evident already in the tones of the names the two authors chose for their corresponding volumes: Maxwell's admiring *The Lords of the Atlas* versus Babin's judgemental *His Excellency – Morocco without a Mask*.

It is not that Maxwell ignores al-Glaoui's numerous misdeeds, which are at the core of Babin's text. But he prefers to interpret them differently: in his view, these were not proactive acts of the Pasha, but an inevitable result of the circumstances created by France (Maxwell 1966: 155–6). In *The Lords of the Atlas*, Maxwell harshly criticises French conduct in Morocco from the beginning of the protectorate (a single exception aside – Resident-General Grandval, who was in office for three months in 1955), and blames it for creating the more spiteful face of al-Glaoui.

Maxwell's anti-French and very British predispositions might explain his total acceptance of Harris's inaccuracies, and his critique of Babin, whose volume he describes in the following words:

> A considerable proportion of it [Babin's book] is factually inaccurate, but it is not so much the falsehoods as the misconceptions that demand attention. He displayed a complete absence of knowledge of the traditional customs of the country; it was as if a Muslim attacking a particular Christian made major issue of the fact that he ate pork, urinated standing up, slept in the same bed as his wife, and did not shave his body; as if an Englishman attacking a particular Frenchman were to scream that this monster of depravity (a favourite epithet of Gustave Babin's) ate frogs and snails and gave his infant children wine to drink. For this reason his book is childish even where it is interesting . . . Babin was a Frenchman, and he never brought himself to say that the true blame lay with France.
>
> Much of the stupidity of this book is plain to any reader acquainted with Moroccan custom. To give but a few

examples, Babin ... praises the Goundafi's personal generosity in giving soup to the poor, as if unaware that the giving of alms is one of the five fundamentals of the Islamic faith; he accuses T'hami of having been, in his boyhood, the M'touggi's lover, as if unaware that this form of homosexuality was an established custom; he accuses T'hami of 'stealing' his dead brother's women, without reference to the long and quite respectable establishment of this practice; he cites the loans made by France to T'hami as evidence of profligacy, without noting that all the Great *Caids* had made it plain that in default of customary pomp they would lack authority. (Maxwell 1966: 175)

As Babin was no longer among the living by 1966, he could not respond to Maxwell's allegations. However, another French author, Jacques Le Prévost, took upon himself the task of answering on behalf of Babin and France. In 1968, two years after the publication of *The Lords of the Atlas*, Le Prévost published *El Glaoui*, a book that like Maxwell's, presents a journey across the Glaoua family's history from the late nineteenth century until al-Glaoui's death in 1956.

Le Prévost begins his book by stating that despite the consensus that the feudal regime ended in Morocco with the death of al-Glaoui, he questions the validity of this statement beyond the country's urban sphere. This observation echoes an a priori and condescending approach towards Morocco, setting the stage for his next argument, namely that in the 'general anarchy of a people who used to let off steam on every occasion, most of the time at the instigation of their traditional chiefs', France had had no other choice but to count on a person like al-Glaoui (Le Prévost 2013: 7).

Le Prévost admits that ruling through the grand *qa'ids*, and especially through al-Glaoui, represented the opposite of the values of the French's civilising mission; yet, he admits that this approach made it possible for France to rule Morocco in the most convenient and the least expensive way. The failure, in his opinion, was that only people on the scale of Lyautey were capable of utilising *caïdalisme* correctly, while those who followed him were not.

Often, it seems that Le Prévost took upon himself the task of being the representative of the French government, at times lapsing into writing in first person plural, as though speaking in the name of France – as, for example, when he explains that al-Glaoui's power was increased 'by our weaknesses' (Le Prévost 1968: 8–9). He goes on to clarify that his reason for writing his book is that general perceptions of al-Glaoui were distorted: on the one side, he identifies 'lovers of the picturesque' – most probably relating to Maxwell – who refer mostly to the Pasha's pomp and fantasy, while on the other hand spotting the profoundly biased authors who were either advocates or detractors of the Pasha. In order to show 'the greater complexity of al-Glaoui', Le Prévost declares that he had set out to write an 'intellectually honest' book about him and about his family. He also asserts that 'with an anachronism of which he was not aware, the Glaoui embodied a Morocco that France could not or did not want to destroy. As such, he unleashed passions that eventually overwhelmed him and caused his loss' (Le Prévost 1968: 8–9).

With such views about al-Glaoui, the Moroccans and the French, Le Prévost's book, in patronisingly avowing to reveal 'the truth', in fact regurgitates a Babin-like colonialist discourse.

The Two Decades after *The Lords of the Atlas*

With its reconsolidation as an independent state, Morocco experienced a series of turbulent events, climaxing in the early 1970s with two failed coup attempts against King Hassan II. The failures of the coups, and the ensuing detention of their instigators, emphasised the court's triumph over its various contestants, particularly the Istiqlal Party that had sought to turn the King into a representational figure. Recuperating from the coups, Hassan II strongly suppressed dissent and restricted public freedom throughout a period that was later known as 'the Years of Lead' (Leveau 1998; Oufkir and Fitoussi 2000; Maghraoui 2001). Simultaneously, the King initiated a project of rebuilding Moroccan society; its most noticeable act was the Green March of 1975, designed to promote Moroccan claims over Western Sahara (Pennell 2000: 339). In this period and context, al-Glaoui's story was far from the main concern in Morocco. The country's mainstream historiography of the period evaded conflictual issues, focusing instead on the consolidation of society and the ongoing effort to decolonise the existing historical narrative (for example, Lahbabi 1975; Laroui 1977; Abun Nasr 1987).

In the non-Moroccan historiography of Morocco written during the first decades after Maxwell and Le Prévost's publications, no full volumes about al-Glaoui were published. Nevertheless, short references to him continued to appear, such as, for example, in British historian Robin Bidwell's *Morocco under Colonial Rule* (Bidwell 1973). This book offers a pro-French and introspective account of the protectorate's years. The absence of Moroccan sources from this treatise stands out in contrast to the extensive use of French research literature, documents and interviews with ex-colonial officials. Accordingly, it is no surprise that Bidwell, while occasionally mentioning al-Glaoui, constructs his image as it appears in French historiography; that is, his main concern is not the interrelationships between al-Glaoui, Morocco and Moroccan society, but whether France should be blamed for the Pasha's behaviour. Bidwell writes:

> For the nationalists, Hadj Thami was a coward, a traitor and a felon. One of their first demands in the Plan de Reformes of 1934 was for his dismissal. In propagandist writings both Allal al Fassi and Balafrej regarded the Great Caids as created from nothing by the French to 'serve as a threat against the central power, specifically against the Sultan, whenever he might refuse to surrender the prerogatives of national sovereignty'. We have seen that this is untrue. (Bidwell 1973: 125)

Bidwell continues to elaborate on the circumstances in which the pre-colonial *qa'idal* system was adopted by the French administration. Returning to the case of al-Glaoui, he comments:

> The crimes and the extortions of the Glaoui were a disgrace to the French flag which covered them. Many officials, particularly the officers of AI [Service des affaires indigènes], felt this acutely, but they were powerless. Behind the Pacha, tacitly supporting his every misdeed, stood all the highest authorities of Morocco and of France itself. Many officers felt that they prevented things from being worse in his area simply by being there, but they could not fight the abuses on their own. To their credit many officers risked their careers trying to do so. They took many chances trying to alleviate oppression and to see justice done in individual cases. The air of triumph with which even today former AI officers speak of some minor victory over a Glaoui khalifa is the measure of their struggle and their weakness. (Bidwell 1973: 125)

In the quotes above, Bidwell mentions two groups who had criticised al-Glaoui's actions – the Moroccan nationalists and the French affaires indigènes officers. From his vantage point, the nationalists' critique is conceived as incorrect propaganda, while the colonial officers' criticism is framed as a sign of dignity, courage and intelligence. In the same vein, Bidwell constructs al-Glaoui's figure as one part of a long-lasting evil (the *qa'idal* system) that, in combination with corrupt top-ranking Moroccan and French administrators (as opposed to the junior French officers who behaved appropriately), brought miserable but inevitable results. The Moroccan part within these circumstances – the *qa'idal* system – is considered an inherent cultural problem; the improper behaviour of the French is deemed the result of particular and corrupt personalities. All these conceptions layer his narrative with a thick colonial historiographic veneer.

In the 1970s and 1980s, al-Glaoui's story was buried away somewhat in mainstream historiographies. On the fringe, however, it evolved in surprising new avenues. One of these is Ahmed Rami's narrative.

Ahmed Rami, an ex-junior officer in the Moroccan army, was one of the participants in the coup attempts against Hassan II in the early 1970s. When the royal security service began to round up the coup's instigators, he managed to escape to Sweden. Settling in his new homeland, he created a small broadcast initiative, called Radio Islam.[7] From that station and elsewhere, Rami broadcasted a political manifesto, which targeted all that he deemed as 'global illnesses'. Taking the lead in his list of evil-doers were the Moroccan royal family and especially King Hassan II. Next were the court's alleged collaborators: Jews, Zionists, Americans and several figures whom Rami named as those who actually ran Morocco and the imperialist world.

Al-Glaoui appeared as part of this list in a somewhat indirect way. During an interview published in the Spanish *Playboy*-style magazine *Interviú* in June 1983, Ahmed Rami made a fantastic claim:

> In actual fact Hassan II is Glaoui's son, the man who was Pasha in Marrakesh and collaborator with the French at the time of the Protectorate. At the end of 1925 Glaoui offered to Mohammed V, who was Sultan, a beautiful slave but he

didn't tell him she was already pregnant. Six months later that woman gave birth to a child who Mohammed V decided to adopt as if he were his own. It was Hassan II. The secret was always jealously guarded within the Court, in spite of the fact that Hassan is the image of Glaoui, something one realizes by merely comparing their two photographs. (Rami 1983)

According to Rami, Hassan II decided to kill Mohammed V because the latter refused to declare him the hereditary prince and heir to the throne. Rami claimed that King Hassan shared his plot with the officers who eventually initiated the coup against him, Generals Gharbaoui, Madbouh, Oufkir and Dilmmi, and that he had learned about the plot from Dilmmi. According to Rami's story, Hassan II seized on an opportunity created by his father's need for an operation. When Mohammed V entered the operating room, Hassan II gathered his officers:

'When the moment comes,' he told them, 'I will make sure that nobody enters the operating chamber and I myself shall disconnect the oxygen tubes. But don't believe I murder my own father. I am not Mohammed V's son. My true father is Glaoui. If I act thus, it is for love of the Army and only you will know the secret. If this should ever leak out, I shall know with certainty that one of you has spoken.' (Rami 1983)

Putting the fantastic plot aside, Rami's story reveals the extreme track that al-Glaoui's story had entered. In this narrative, not only was the Pasha evil, but he was indeed a genetic source of vice, passing this on to future generations. In Rami's scenario, Hassan II was immoral not only due to his actions, but also because he allegedly had al-Glaoui's blood in him.

Short takes on al-Glaoui's tale began to reappear in mainstream Moroccan historiography in the late 1980s, mostly as reference points in deeper analyses examining other issues. For example, historian Jamil Abun Nasr pondered whether the actions that King Mohammed V performed in coordination with the French should be considered as collaboration. His decisive opinion was that this was not collaboration; the French held the Sultan as their hostage and had used him against his will. The real collaborators, Abun Nasr asserts, were those who cooperated with the French of their own free will. These included, in his view, the heads of the Taybiyya, Kitaniyya and Tijjaniyya

Sufi orders,[8] and above all, the greatest collaborator – al-Glaoui (Abun Nasr 1987: 382).

The issue of whom among the Moroccans serving in the state administration during the colonial period should be considered collaborators troubled other people at the turn of the 1990s. In these deliberations, al-Glaoui's image was often brought up. Anthropologist Dale Eickelman cites a conversation he had with his informant, ʿAbd ar-Rahman, *qadi* of the village of Bzu during the protectorate years. The *qadi* told him:

> To justify their increasing pressure against the king, the French encouraged Hajj Thami al-Glawi to circulate a petition denouncing Sidi Muhammad bin Yusif for, among other matters, his disregard of Islamic values. ʿAbd ar-Rahman claimed that even Hajj Thami al-Glawi was against the wording of the petition and 'raised his hand' against it, although in the end he yielded to the French. (Eickelman 1992: 151)

The issue behind this conversation was whether the *qadi* and his peers, who may have been signatories to al-Glaoui's petitions (Chapter 4), should be considered collaborators with the French or not. The *qadi*'s argument is that reality under colonialism forced people in official positions – such as the pasha (al-Glaoui) or *qadi* (himself) – to compromise. They obviously did not like the French and their orders, but in order to run their communities, they had no choice but to act according to these dictates, which eventually included the signing of the anti-Mohammed V petition that the French had formulated. The rhetorical question constructed thus is this: if powerful al-Glaoui could not resist them, then how could minor officials like the *qadi*?

As the 1990s progressed, references to al-Glaoui became more frequent in the official Moroccan historiography, and these were much less forgiving than ʿAbd ar-Rahman's commentary. Their formulations reveal additional hot topics of the period, addressed indirectly while narrating al-Glaoui's image. Most discernible among these is the question of Amazigh-ness, which fully manifested in the sociopolitical context of the mid 1990s (see more on this topic in Chapter 7). At that time, Amazigh activists increased their struggle against the Moroccan state's disregard for Amazigh languages and culture, an allegation that the official functionaries tried to refute.

Al-Mawsuʿa al-ʿAmma li-Taʾrikh al-Maghrib wa-al-Andalus – the General Encyclopedia for the History of Morocco and al-Andalus (Zebib 1995) – represents the court's perspective on Moroccan history (as indicated by the introduction, written by King Hassan II's consultant Ahmed Ibn Suda). References to Thami al-Glaoui appear mainly in the encyclopedia's fifth volume. While describing the consolidation of the Glaoua tribe from 1908 onwards, the author, Najib Zebib, writes that 'al-Glaoui amassed a huge property in a value of milliards, by means of robbery.' After describing the exploitation of the population of the south by the Pasha, Zebib adds: 'There are those who claim that al-Glaoui was an Amazigh, but this is a false claim, because his skin was black as charcoal, while the original Amazigh people are white' (Zebib 1995: 180–3).

In the political climate of the mid 1990s, claims against al-Glaoui, who considered himself an Amazigh (see Chapter 7), could have been understood as reflecting an anti-Amazigh policy. It seems that in order to avoid such an allegation, the encyclopedia's author attempted to invalidate any link between al-Glaoui and Amazighness. Quite interestingly, the demeaning presumptions about blacks inherent in the claim did not seem to trouble the encyclopedia's editors at the time.[9]

The Amazigh issue pops up again in the discussion about al-Glaoui's 1953 petitions against Mohammed V. The author describes these appeals, then contrasts them with petitions written by the pashas and the *ʿulama* of the large cities, who condemned al-Glaoui's disloyalty to the throne. The entry then refers to a French newspaper article of the period, which claimed that the signatories to al-Glaoui's petition did not represent the Amazigh population, given that most of them were officials appointed by the French administration, and that their minority belonged to 'a small tribe of robbers and land-owners from the south' – referring to the Glaoua (Zebib 1995: 186). The effort to dissociate al-Glaoui from his claimed Amazighness is reasserted.

Descriptions of other episodes in al-Glaoui's life give Zebib a pretext for referring to other matters. A most notorious event in the Pasha's history was the Mulud of 1950, often cited as the trigger for the split between the Sultan and al-Glaoui (see Chapter 4). According to the encyclopedia's version, al-Glaoui arrived in the palace that day with a pre-planned intrigue to humiliate the King. Then, in contrast with the King's respectable behaviour, al-Glaoui's aggressive conduct embarrassed Mohammed V and disgraced the event. Events culminated with al-Glaoui allegedly shouting at the King: 'You are not the Sultan of Morocco anymore; you have turned out to be the Sultan of the communist and heretic Istiqlal Party' (Zebib 1995: 135. As noted in Chapter 4, this sentence might have been a 1960s literary creation).

As with the previous examples, where the text about al-Glaoui could also be seen as a means of addressing Amazigh activists, here too relating al-Glaoui's behaviour at the Mulud might bear another message. As the text makes clear, Mohammed V was not offended by al-Glaoui's 'allegation'. Thus, by accepting the link with the Istiqlal ('you . . . turned out to be the Sultan of the . . . Istiqlal') who had previously been critical of him, the King emerges majestic and benevolent, transcending petty party politics.

Al-Glaoui's repentance at the end of 1955 is also recounted in the encyclopedia. It states that the Pasha admitted that his claim – that the Sultan's deposition was based on a spontaneous call from the people – was a lie that he had made up with the French (Zebib 1995: 280–1). Finally, the meeting between the King and al-Glaoui in Paris is presented in the following words:

> Tens of photographers and journalists looked into the big hall to observe the historic meeting between the King and al-Glaoui . . . he [al-Glaoui] was allowed to enter only after an hour when he crawls on his feet and hands, his head leaned towards the floor, while he kisses the King's grey robe. Then he kissed his legs, bowed four times in front of him, and said: 'I am a slave at the feet of your highness, I hope that you would forgive me, Sidi Mohammed Ben Youssef.' The magnanimous king answered him: 'Don't talk with me about the past, the future is the important thing. You will be judged according to what you'll do in the future.' (Zebib 1995: 290)

The encyclopedia's depictions of al-Glaoui, beyond straightforward statements, use various rhetorical devices like contrasts, allusions and metaphors to hint at other matters. Presenting al-Glaoui in his meetings with the King as quick-tempered, extroverted, greedy, conspiratorial, treacherous, and finally yielding, effectively emphasises the opposite virtues of Mohammed V: calm, discreet, noble, spiritual and solid. Thus, al-Glaoui provides a canvas for presenting the character of the King.

Similarly, by way of subtle allusions, the author can send messages to various audiences. Amazigh readers are informed that since al-Glaoui 'is not an Amazigh', disapproving him is not an anti-Amazigh act, and the Istiqlal are reassured through the reference to al-Gloaui's alleged call, that the King is not repelling them. Hence, for the encyclopedia, telling al-Glaoui is not just an aim but also a means to an end.

The encyclopedia's message, that the King transcended the Istiqlal, was not necessarily accepted by pro-party historiographies, which claimed that the party's share in the struggle for independence was far greater than his. Yet, not unlike the encyclopedia's narrative, they also used al-Glaoui's image as a means of delineating and elevating their heroes. This is clearly apparent in historian and anthropologist Abdellah Hammoudi's *Master and Disciple* (Hammoudi 1997). Hammoudi repeatedly criticises the actions of the court (for example, 1997: 22–3), and applauds Moroccan Istiqlal leader Allal al-Fassi. When he comes to describe al-Fassi, Hammoudi writes:

> If one went in search of the two most radically antithetical personages, one could not find a better pair than Allal al Fassi and Thami al Glaoui. Everything Ihaj Thami stood for was transcended by Allal al Fassi or was foreign to his experience. Allal al Fassi exemplified a new Islamic universalism; Ihaj Thami exemplified localism. The former was a man of culture who fought with the pen, the latter a political animal who imposed his will by sword, ruse, and cash. One exuded urbanity, the other the austere condition of a mountaineer upbringing. Whereas al Fassi was reserved and studious, Ihaj Thami was known for his taste for the good life and the pleasures of the flesh. One man reflected on Islam and European values in order to draw a specific lesson for the future; the other believed in Western might with blind faith. In the one we see a readiness to sacrifice, in the other a passion for opulence and the power pushed to sacrifice. I could go on with these antinomies, but they do not tell the whole story. (Hammoudi 1997: 129–30)

Towards the end of the 1990s, al-Glaoui's story was turned into a tool of sorts, his persona becoming a means of addressing other topics or to emphasise the nobleness of others. To express someone's greatness was to describe his dissimilarity with al-Glaoui. This representation was as 'anti-al-Glaoui' as Babin's colonialist stand, but different in its goals. While Babin objected to al-Glaoui's transgressions due to their effects on Frenchness, post-colonial discourses embraced his misbehaviours as a tool for acclaiming their heroes through a set of literary contrasts. To wit, while he was a 'political animal', 'nervous', 'a relic of an old period', 'corrupt' and 'black', their heroes were 'men of culture', 'calm', 'modern', 'honest' and 'white'. Post-colonialist discourses on al-Glaoui, like their colonial predecessors, are markedly binary. Politically motivated in their nature, they required a clear-cut definition of the 'front line', where one needs to easily differentiate between 'an enemy' and 'a friend'.

Vis-à-vis these narrations, Gavin Maxwell's tale, which opened this chapter, was rare in its attentiveness to the complexity of the Pasha and to his multi-dimensionality. It presented a very different strand from the dichotomising colonial and post-colonial approaches. But as time passed after the publication of *The Lords of the Atlas*, al-Glaoui's new tales seemed to be variations of a one-dimensional perspective. Yet, a change was to come towards the turn of the century.

Notes

1. National Archives (United Kingdom), HS 9 1010 2.
2. National Archives (UK), HS 9 1010 2 033.
3. National Archives (UK), HS 9 1010 2 021.
4. The 'Armée de la libération du Maghreb Arabe' was established in 1955, with the aim of driving the French out of Morocco and securing Mohammed V as the leader of the independent country. This body was not connected with the Istiqlal, and it had a large Amazigh component (Pennell 2000: 289–90).
5. Personal communication by witnesses.
6. Winston Churchill, for example, became a good friend, a returning visitor and a partner for games of golf (Maxwell 1966: 161).
7. Ahmed Rami; available at <https://rami.tv/eng/biog.htm> (last accessed 31 August 2023).
8. Various Sufi *tariqa*s are called by the founders' names. Al-Glaoui was a member of the Tijjaniyya.
9. In southern Morocco lives a large population of blacks – the Harratin – who are descendants of slaves originally brought from sub-Saharan Africa to serve the local tribes, and who are partly mixed within the Amazighs. In the past these groups lived under the patronage of local tribal organisations, including many Amazigh

tribes, and were considered by those tribes as inferior, a concept which was strengthened during the colonial period (Hoffman 1967: 13; Hart 1972: 53–5; and see Babin's and other French functionaries' views concerning the blacks in Chapter 3, above).

7

'I am a Moroccan and a Berber': al-Glaoui and Amazighness

Before moving to discuss the late 1990s and onward digression of narratives about al-Glaoui from the post-colonial nationalist discourse described in the previous chapter, I shall make a pause to elaborate on the issue of Amazighness (*Amazighité*), which is one of the sociopolitical processes which is exceedingly relevant to the current state of stories about the Pasha. The identity politics of Amazighs, the indigenous population of North Africa, and the awakening of Amazighness in the last decades has had a major bearing on the twenty-first-century telling, and a parallel phenomenon of 'non-telling', of al-Glaoui. In order to fully analyse this process, I will first present a very brief overview of the history of Amazigh activism in Morocco, then connect this to al-Glaoui and the ways in which he is told today.

A focal landmark in the discussion of Amazighness in Morocco was the French Protectorate's so-called 'Berber Dahir' of 1930 which launched various new legal procedures to be implemented in Amazigh regions (discussed in detail in Chapter 3). From its publication onwards, nationalist Moroccan historiography viewed this Dahir as the most blatant French attempt at dividing Moroccan society, and as a turning point in the practice of Moroccan nationalism and its subsequent broad reception (Azaoui 2018).

When, twenty-six years later, Moroccan independence was finally achieved, the hegemonic state worked to reverse the boost colonialism gave to Amazigh distinctiveness (Peyron 2010: 157–8). The course of action taken, as in contemporaneous post-colonial situations in other countries, was to consolidate a uniform national culture, one that could hopefully erase former divides, especially the Arab–Amazigh split. In the Moroccan case, the choice was to forge an exclusive Arab identity for all the citizens of the re-emerging nation state.[1] Nevertheless, a large portion of Moroccan society, numbering from between a quarter to more than a half of the country's population (the estimate usually corresponds with the political position of the source of the information) continued to define itself as Amazigh, possessing a unique language and culture, and not as Arab. In this situation, the inevitable consequence of the move towards Arabisation was that many Amazighs felt that they were being fenced away from sensitive positions, that their language was being rejected, their culture degraded, and that they were being exploited. Furthermore, many felt that their patriotism was constantly being questioned, and their contribution to the struggle for independence diminished. This created a state of affairs that the Amazigh researcher Brahim el Guabli described thus: 'Folklorized, disempowered, and forgotten about in the refashioned collective memory of the post-independence states, Imazighen's glorious history of cultural and literary prowess was de facto banned from circulation in the public arena' (El Guabli 2021).

Resisting the Arabisation policy, associations for the preservation of Amazigh culture, language and heritage were founded in the 1960s and 1970s, part of the Amazigh Cultural Movement (ACM; El Guabli 2022; El Ibrahimi 2022: 6). This trend was nourished by the rise of a nationalist Amazigh wave in Algeria, and by the activism of overseas Amazigh diasporas, mainly in France and the United States. Yet, within the tense political atmosphere that defined the Morocco of the time, separationist ideas were suppressed until the end of the 1980s, and the issue of Amazighness very much concealed.

This political situation is reflected in the historiography of Morocco of the period. While decolonising the past, and resisting all aspects of imperialism and colonialism, authors have claimed that the distinction between Arabs and Amazighs was an invention of French colonialism. Accordingly, works from that period tended to emphasise the similarities, and not the differences, between Arabs and Amazighs (for example, Gellner and Micaud 1972; Norris 1982: 1; Nelson 1985: 110–1; Abun-Nasr 1987: 3).

However, at the beginning of the 1990s, the gradual easing of political restrictions in Morocco led to the resurfacing of Amazighness. In 1991, six Amazigh associations from Agadir published a bill of rights, the Agadir Charter (*mithaq Agadir*).

The document objected to the state's disregard for Amazigh language and culture, calling for the acceptance of Tamazight as an official language alongside Arabic, and for the inclusion of Amazigh cultural studies in educational programmes (Budahan 2013: 125–9).

In 1994, Amazigh activists wrote a protest letter to the then prime minister, demanding recognition of Tamazight as an official language. Some of the activists were arrested; however, following a wave of protests, they were released a short time later. Two months after their release, King Hassan II expressed, in his traditional throne day speech to the nation, his positive attitude towards Tamazight, announcing that he was considering including it in the school curriculum. This was not immediately implemented; still, the mere fact that the issue had been raised by the King marked a change in government policies (Maddy-Weitzman 2001: 31–2).

The debate about Amazigh rights erupted again after the death of Hassan II. A few months after the accession to the throne of Mohammed VI, the so-called 'Berber Manifesto' was published, and signed by 229 university lecturers, writers, poets, artists and industrialists (Maddy-Weitzman 2022: 130). A large part of the manifesto is dedicated to a detailed historical survey emphasising prominent Amazigh leaders (see more below), and their strict loyalty to Morocco and to Islam. Amazighness, according to the manifesto, is expressed mainly through language and culture; therefore, most of the demands – phrased as nine requests, submitted to the new king – were within these realms.

The government's initial reaction to the manifesto was rejection, but this eased into a restrained acceptance. Soon thereafter, the government inaugurated radio, television and educational programmes in Tamazight; a national institute for Amazigh culture, the Institut Royal de la Culture Amazighe (IRCAM), was established in 2001 (Al-Hahi 2013: 220; Khakee 2017: 243). However, between 2007 and 2009, Amazigh activists protesting their systematic exclusion were still harassed, and in several cases imprisoned (Al-Hahi 2013: 152). It took a few more years for Tamazight to be recognised as the second official language of Morocco, as part of the constitutional reform undertaken after the 2011 protests (Maddy-Weitzman 2012: 141). In 2019, a specific law spelled out the meaning of this officialisation. Since then, there has been a noticeable awakening (*tankra*) of the Amazigh language and culture in Morocco (El Guabli 2021).

As part of the relegitimisation of Moroccan Amazighness, critical thoughts about the historiography of Arab–Amazigh relationships in the country began to be published as well. For example, Amazigh historians and activists proposed a different perspective on the politics surrounding the colonial 'Berber Dahir'. Historian Mustapha El Qadéry asserts that despite the historiographic prominence of the Dahir, its impact was rather small, except in one area: its materialisation into the founding myth of the Moroccan nationalist movement. In that realm, he claims, it became the basis for the movement's legitimacy, and a pretext for its existence (El Qadéry 2007: 7, 27). Activist Rashid al-Hahi states the issue more radically. For him, the Dahir is the biggest political lie in contemporary Morocco, exploited by members of the urban elite and the nationalist movement for their political needs, utilised to perpetuate the superiority of Arabism over Amazighness. He adds that this myth became the frame of reference that governed the exclusion of Amazighs for nearly eighty years, setting them on the outer margins of Moroccan national politics and culture (Al-Hahi 2013: 112–14; also Hima 2019: 76).

Another major issue brought up by Moroccan Amazigh activists in the debate over Amazighness, is the erasure of Amazigh heroes from the national historiography (El Guabli 2021; Al-Hahi 2013: 119). El Qadéry proposes some explanations for this 'collective amnesia'. He claims that popular Moroccan historiographies are dominated by the attitudes of two influential Moroccan politicians, Mehdi Ben Barka and Allal al-Fassi. Each of the two had singled out a specific historical aspect as the most important in the development of the Moroccan state: the impact of Abbasid scholars for the first, and Andalusian civilisation for the second. Thus, both ignored the earlier Amazigh origins of the Moroccan state. This concept was perpetuated in the historiographies of their followers (El Qadéry 2007: 12).

A second cause for the 'forgetting' of the Amazigh past, in El Qadéry's view, is the severe criticism of the *qa'idal* system implemented by French colonisers, and especially of its central representation – Thami al-Glaoui. The post-independence repelling of *qa'idalism* involved the elimination of its symbols. As al-Glaoui was often seen as 'the lord of the Berbers', it became essential to wipe out his remembrance, together with the notion of Amazighs as a legal and historic entity (El Qadéry 2007: 12).

Al-Hahi proposes another reason for the 'collective amnesia': that Amazigh history, until very recently, was only written by non-Amazighs (Al-Hahi 2013: 101). In his view, this created a situation in which:

> Morocco in the twentieth century witnessed several major events that are still not covered in national history and curricula ... concealing some facts and covering up the historical hotbeds of tension ... Although some of these events are of great importance at the level of the history of the contemporary state, and the construction of the political system and its transformations, they are still outside the narrative of national history ... these include ... local history, whose facts were taking place outside the sphere of influence of the central state, and other manifestations of acts of resistance and political developments, especially in the countryside ... as well as ... distortion of some facts and the dissemination of ideological fallacies in a way that allowed some urban elites to control the situation and exercise exclusion. (Al-Hahi 2013: 111–12)

In light of these statements, it is interesting to look at how al-Glaoui – most certainly a major Moroccan Amazigh leader operating outside the core of the central state, yet very influential on political processes in Morocco – appears in Amazigh demands for the retelling of their history. To do this, I will first describe how al-Glaoui and his close circles related to his Amazighness, and then to how current Amazigh activists engage with his story.

Al-Glaoui and Amazighness

In September 1943, reacting to an accusation that he liked Anglo-Saxons too much, Thami al-Glaoui told his sons that he indeed had good connections with the Americans, but the reason for this was that they were in a position to save France – who held the keys to saving Morocco. He then added: 'I am neither an American nor British. I am a Moroccan and a Berber.'[2]

Information from additional sources shows that his personal identity politics were even more complex, as in other places he is purported to have claimed that his family has Arab origins (El Glaoui 2004: 9). The latter claim was refuted by critics such as Gustave Babin who asserted that al-Glaoui was definitely not an Arab, but an Amazigh, adding racialistically that even as an Amazigh, he was of a lesser status, given that his racial background was mixed with that of the black population (Babin 1934: 16–19).

Regardless of his infrequent references to this facet of identity politics, the issue of al-Glaoui's Amazighness was expressed by others during his lifetime. Poet Othman al-Mahmudi, for example, opened his address of al-Glaoui, in a poem he wrote in the latter's honour, with the following words: 'My heart chanted its loyalty in Berber / Our race remained united and Amazigh' (al-Mahmudi in Mutafakkir 2007: 191).

Another occasion occurred in the wake of the clash between the Pasha and the Sultan during the 1950 Mulud event at the palace (Chapter 4). Many people in al-Glaoui's hometown supported his position in this conflict. French intelligence reports on 'the mood in the streets' indicated that people in Marrakesh were saying that if al-Glaoui had been younger, he should have taken the throne. In their view, this was legitimate; there were precedents of Amazigh dynasties originating in the south, and particularly in Marrakesh, taking over the rule of the country.[3]

Similar voices were heard among Amazigh *qa'id*s, who complained (on 3 January 1951) that despite constituting the greater part of Moroccan society, Amazighs were not represented in Moroccan higher state offices.[4] In this context, French officials noted that the rallying of *qa'id*s and pashas to al-Glaoui's side in 1951 awakened issues of 'Berber identity'.[5] Concurrently, the nationalists, for their part, suspected that the French were trying to impose, through al-Glaoui, a 'Berber policy'.[6]

As tensions between al-Glaoui and the court intensified, a French information sheet reported that at a meeting between al-Glaoui and his supporters, some of the *qa'id*s referred to the Sultan in demeaning terms; one *qa'id* declared that they were Amazighs, and that they would never allow Arabs to rule them. The French author of this document drily observed that he thought this very *qa'id* to be of Arab descent.[7]

After al-Glaoui's death, and the first arrest of his sons and close relatives – and their re-arrest in May 1957 (Chapter 4) – the people of the Glaoua reacted angrily. In the protests that erupted, they shouted slogans like: 'Morocco is Amazigh!', and 'the Arabs are invaders!'[8]

Hence even if al-Glaoui did not bother too much about his Amazighness, he was regarded as an Amazigh leader by those around him, by the large population of his region, and by many others. In light of these declarations during his lifetime, it is interesting to look at how Amazigh proclamations of the last twenty-five years have referred to him, especially in view of the claim that Amazigh heroes have been erased from Moroccan historiography.

Telling and Non-telling al-Glaoui in New Amazigh Historiography

A good starting point for discussing al-Gloaui's place in recent Amazigh historiography is the manifesto of 2000. The manifesto protested the omission of important Amazigh personalities on Moroccan official sites, naming figures like al-Jazuli, Ibn Muti', Ajerrum, al-Hasan al-Yusi and Mohamed Ben Abdelkrim al-Khattabi. Thami al-Glaoui is absent from the list. Accordingly, in subsequent reconstructions of Amazigh history in Morocco over the last decades, iconic Amazigh figures were often brought up for consideration. Some, like Yogurta, al-Kahina and Tariq bin Ziad,[9] were mythological or ancient; others, like Mohamed Ben Abdelkrim al-Khattabi, were more contemporary (Maddy-Weitzman 2001: 25; 2012: 141). Thami al-Glaoui is conspicuously absent from the new lists as well. Al-Glaoui's absence is also noticeable in the writings of Moroccan Amazigh activists such as, for example, Muhamad Budahan (2013) and Rashid Al-Hahi (2013), who are otherwise very critical of Moroccan state narratives and policies which omit Amazigh history.

Thami al-Glaoui's non-appearance in these contexts is most probably not due to his Amazighness but because of his debatable conduct, which is also potentially destructive for the Amazigh cause in Morocco. He and his apparatus committed serious abuses against several Amazigh tribes and individuals, collaborated with the colonisers, acted against the nationalists and, most seriously, he personally conspired against King Mohammed V.

Al-Glaoui is not the only powerful Amazigh leader overlooked in this accounting. A second name pointedly omitted is that of General Oufkir, one of the heads of the coup against King Hassan II. Bruce Maddy-Weitzman explains that for many Amazigh activists, Oufkir, like al-Glaoui, was a 'prototypical Berbére de service, doing the bidding of the king in order to advance his own interests, without reference to the Berber community's needs' (Maddy-Weitzman 2011: 94). Yet Maddy-Weitzman adds that '[i]n private, though, some Amazigh activists speak more favourably of Oufkir' (Maddy-Weitzman 2011: 94).

An Amazigh researcher-activist who does refer to al-Glaoui, however, is Mustapha El Qadéry. One of his studies (El Qadéry 2007) surveys the ways in which the French established their 'Berber policies' – which ultimately endowed al-Glaoui with a command of a huge zone and population in southern Morocco. El Qadéry notes that interestingly, no Franco-Berber school was ever created in al-Glaoui's area; and that, even though he only had Amazigh tribes under his jurisdiction, none were subject to the procedures decreed on the basis of the Berber Dahir. Rather, jurisdiction in his territories continued to be practised as in pre-Berber Dahir times (El Qadéry 2007: 26, 41). Thus, even if he did not position al-Glaoui as a national hero, El Qadéry certainly took note of the Pasha's resilience and his refusal to implement certain colonial measures in his territory.

More blatant views on al-Glaoui's assertiveness in facing colonial rule, contradicting his automatic designation as an ultimate collaborator, can, however, be found in the Amazigh diaspora.[10] Such a perspective was articulated, for example by Helene Hagan, an Amazigh activist who lives in the United States. Hagan is the founder (in 1993) and President of the Tazzla Institute for Cultural Diversity, whose mission is to safeguard, support and disseminate Amazigh cultural heritage, in the United States and abroad. Hagan is also the executive director of the LA Amazigh Film Festival (LAAFF).[11]

In a review of Michael Brett and Elizabeth Fentress's volume *The Berbers* (1997), Hagan specifically criticised their portrayal of al-Glaoui, writing:

> The depiction of the role of Thami El Glaoui, the Pasha of Marrakesh, in this process, seems far too thin, and his hasty dismissal from the historical scene plainly arrogant. The Berber leader was a very controversial figure of the era, and yielded great power indeed. He was directly instrumental to the return [sic] of Sultan Mohammed V from his exile in Madagascar, where he had been banished by French politicians with The Glaoui's assent. The text reads, page 191: 'Thami El Glaoui . . . was exposed as a man of straw, his empire

in the south a hollow mockery of his power in the past,' a quotation said to arise from the reading of 'Maroc' authored by Julien. Such an extrapolation and cavalier evaluation is, in the face of ample documentation on the Glaoui family, a distortion of history. Berber historians will no doubt review the complex role and personality of this towering figure of the twentieth century. He was no man of straw, by any standard, before, after, or during his planned and public submission to the throne. His powerful alliances and astute politics need to be weighed far more subtly in the context of the French colonisation period. This formidable Berber warrior, politician, and leader, who steered the politics of Morocco for over half a century, consciously made a decision for the benefit of all Moroccans as a very old man on the brink of death. Morocco and its freedom from the yoke of Europe was his goal. He knew that by asking the French allies to return the Sultan from exile, this Sultan would follow age-old practices of eliminating him, the Glaoui, and his family from positions of power in Morocco, and that his vast holdings would be confiscated. Thami El Glaoui may have been a controversial figure, but he was not the fool the authors of this book present to the readers without any explanatory detail to demonstrate why he is called 'a man of straw'. Such a travesty of history is not permissible in a scholarly work. (Hagan 2013: 196–7)

Hagan also refers to al-Glaoui in another place where she describes him as 'shrewd, glamorous, fabulously wealthy ... more powerful than the sultan himself ... steered the politics of Morocco in international matters for decades. He was instrumental to the return of Sultan Mohammed V from forced exile in Madagascar' (Hagan 2011: 51). Thus, for her al-Glaoui was certainly a figure who should be placed on the list of the most prominent Amazigh leaders in Moroccan history.

Another diasporic Amazigh-affiliated project that engages with al-Glaoui as an important Amazigh leader is the *Encyclopédie Berbère*. This long-evolving project was started in France in 1984 under Gabriel Camps, an Algerian-born French historian of Amazigh culture. After he passed away in 2002, Camps was replaced as project director by Salem Chaker, a researcher of Amazigh languages of Algerian Kabyle origin. The encyclopedia treats Thami al-Glaoui as an Amazigh whose significance warranted a unique entry, which was authored by the historian

Michael Peyron (Peyron 1999). Yet, quite naturally, a diversity of views also exists among diasporic Amazighs. The 2006 *Historical Dictionary of the Berbers (Imazighen)*, written by the US-based Amazigh researcher Hsain Ilahiane, does not list al-Glaoui separately, rather discussing him within the entry dedicated to the Glawa tribe (Ilahiane 2006: 51–3).

This broad range of perspectives about al-Glaoui in the Amazigh diaspora reflects various aspects: a greater distance from the sociopolitical contexts and discourses in Morocco, the intricate work of memory and nostalgia, and teleological interpretations of Amazigh past. It might also forecast a situation in which he will be added to the list of acknowledged historical Amazigh leaders in Morocco. Such change seems unlikely at the present time; it should be remembered, though, that the Moroccan state once opposed Abdelkrim al-Khattabi, only to subsequently adopt his memory, most particularly under King Mohammed VI (Maddy-Weitzman 2012: 145; Pennell 2017: 809).

We may wonder what al-Glaoui would have commented on the discourses of Amazighness in Morocco and its diasporas taking place in the last few decades. His actions and their narrations as surveyed in this volume suggest that he defied rigid labelling and rather used multiple identities to run his politics. He sometimes portrayed himself as 'Berber', at other times as 'Arab', and occasionally even as 'French' – upsetting, perhaps deliberately, some of his severe critics such as Babin. Yet most common for him was the encompassing designation of 'Moroccan'.

The next chapter returns to the storyline which examines the ongoing production of narratives about al-Glaoui from the late 1990s to the present. Unlike his absence from historiographies penned by certain Moroccan Amazigh activists, it reveals that his tale did not disappear in twenty-first-century Morocco. Rather, precisely the opposite happens – narrations of his story only intensify and expand into multiple new channels.

Notes

1. This approach links to a pan-Arabic ideology that called for the assimilation of minorities – as done, for example, with the Kurds in Iraq, and with other minorities in other Arab states.
2. CADN 1MA/282 98, 'Bulletin de renseignements. Confidentiel'. R.F/B.R., 11 September 1943. The sentence continues: 'Remember

always – we owe a lot to the French, and Morocco will march with France to the future.'
3. CADN 1MA/282 99, 'Bulletin quotidien d'informations, 29 Décembre 1950', 29 December 1950.
4. CADN 1MA/282 99, 'Le Général de Brigade Leblanc, chef de la région de Meknes à monsieur le directeur de l'intérieur (section politique)', 2 January 1951.
5. CADN 1MA/282 100, 'Bulletin special de renseignements, No. 0339 C.MK/2', 19 February 1951; CADN 1MA/282 99, 'Note de renseignements, No. 116 /C1', 27 February 1951.
6. CADN 1MA/282 98, 'Fes, Le Pacha Glaoui est arrivé', 25 January 1951.
7. CADN 1MA/282 98, 'Le contrôleur civil, chef de circonscription d'El Hajeb', 10 January 1953.
8. CADN 1MA/282 100, 'Service des Liasons. Note de Renseignements', 16 May 1957.
9. Yogurta was an Amazigh leader who fought the Romans in the second century BC (Brett and Fentress 1997: 41–3); this reference to him thus establishes Amazigh antiquity and priority in North Africa, long before the Arabs. Kahina was a mythologic female Amazigh leader who fought against the Arab Islamic forces that invaded North Africa in the seventh century AD (Roth 1982; Hannoum 2001). Bringing up her name expresses the idea of Amazigh resistance to the Arabs. Tariq bin Ziad was the Amazigh leader of the Islamic forces that crossed the straits of Gibraltar (thus named after him) and conquered Andalusia at the beginning of the eighth century AD (Brett and Fentress 1997: 85–6). His figure represents the significant contribution of the Amazighs to the spread of Islam in its first century.
10. In the Amazigh diaspora exists a large array of organisations and individuals that promote cultural activities and convey diverse political perspectives and demands (Maddy-Weitzman 2011: 131–152; Jay 2015: 331).
11. Amazigh Film Festival U.S.A.; available at <https://www.laaff.org/aboutus> (last accessed 31 August 2023).

8

Reconciliations

Mahi Binebine, a Moroccan writer and painter, was born in Marrakesh in 1959. He emigrated in his early twenties to Paris, moved to New York in 1994, and returned to live in Marrakesh in 2002.[1] While still in the diaspora, Binebine wrote his first two books, both relating to his early life in Morocco. *Les Funérailles du lait* (The Milk Funerals, 1994), is constructed around the image of his mother, who single-handedly raised seven children in the medina of Marrakesh. The main theme of the book is her constant anxiety about whether her son was alive or not. That son was Mahi's brother, Aziz, an army officer who participated in the failed coup against King Hassan II in the early 1970s, and was subsequently imprisoned at Tazmamart for eighteen years, his family denied any information about his fate (Jay 2015: 99; Salon maghrébin du livre 2018: 52–3).[2]

The plot of Binbine's second book, *L'Ombre du poète* (The Shadow of the Poet, 1997), is also set in Marrakesh and its environs but a few decades earlier, during the last twenty years of the French Protectorate. The book describes a conflict between two childhood friends who, on growing up, find themselves in opposition to one another. One is a protesting poet who joins an underground nationalist cell, the other became a man of power – al-Glaoui's secretary – who ends up killing the poet (Binebine 1997). One key insight of the novel is that the character who ends up working for al-Glaoui is not necessarily a villain and that the one who joined the nationalist movement is not automatically a hero. Both were driven by their aspirations, emotions, constraints, and by coincidences, all unfolding within very complex situations.

This perspective, presented in *The Shadow of the Poet*, signalled the advent of a new and more complex approach to narrating al-Glaoui, starting towards the end of the 1990s. It was visible first in the Moroccan diaspora, where at that time freedom of expression was less restricted than in Morocco itself. Yet even there, Binbine was cautious. As he later explained, what he actually wanted to do was to criticise the court's policies; but wary of doing so directly, he decided to take a different route by way of indirect, insinuating stories. In the first book, he criticises the cruelty of the Tazmamart prison by narrating a tale about his mother's grief; al-Glaoui's court in the second book was in fact intended as a metaphor for the royal court (Binebine 2002; Salon maghrébin du livre 2018: 52–3). Binebine could use al-Glaoui's court as a convenient setting for his tale because he was familiar with its intricacies by way of his father, who had been a court entertainer there (Binebine 2017; see below). Therefore, even though his intent was to express his disapproval of certain aspects of the royal palace, the actual narrative that the reader encounters is about al-Glaoui's court, revealing its better and worse actualities. As such, Binebine's book indicated the beginning of a new path for discussing the conflict of values that surrounded al-Glaoui's rule.

The restrictive situation in Morocco began to change in the last years of King Hassan II, more so after the accession of King Mohammed VI to the throne in 1999. The transfer of rule from father to son was accompanied by various steps towards democratisation, internationalisation and modernisation. These included improvements in the personal status code (*mudawwanat al-ahwal al-shakhsiyyah*), with amendments to women's rights; greater recognition of the *Amazighité* (Chapter 7); and major changes in the realm of human rights. Concerning the latter, political opponents expelled from the country were allowed to return to Morocco; the profession of journalism was granted greater freedom; and human rights infringements under Hassan II were acknowledged, with steps taken towards reparation through the establishment of a Committee for Equity and Reconciliation (L'Instance equité et réconciliations; IER; *Hay'at al-insaf wa-l-musalaha*), the last recommending a series of amendments to the existing human rights domains.

All these steps were encouraged by international bodies like the International Monetary Fund, the World Bank and governments of the West. These all provided support for change in Morocco, conditioned on the liberalisation of the financial sector, greater efficiency and transparency in the management of the state and large corporations, guarantees of the independence of the judicial system, steps to address poverty and literacy levels, and increased flexibility in the labour market (Cohen 2003; Khayr Allah 2007; Ramzi 2015; Pennell 2017: 809). All these conditions, besides indicating desired practical measures, are at the same time part of the typically neo-liberal and neo-colonial discourses that have prevailed globally since the last decades of the twentieth century.

An event that significantly affected life in Morocco at the beginning of the twenty-first century was the May 2003 terror attacks in Casablanca. Two weeks after the attacks, a new law was passed. This legislation enabled large-scale arrests and the repression of anyone suspected of supporting terrorism. Simultaneously, Morocco launched a programme titled the National Initiative for Human Development (L'Initiative nationale pour le dévelopement humain; INDH), based on the premise that a general socio-economic reconstruction will also act to curtail the activities of terrorist groups. The programme, which had a huge budget, defined multiple goals. It dealt with infrastructure improvement, specifically roads, electricity and water supply; and the state reasserted its monopoly in the domain of religion by encouraging moderate Islam, controlling its proliferation through the training of clergy, the broadcast of religious programmes on national radio and television, and the closure of Salafi and Wahhabi Quranic schools – a few of which had served as recruitment bases for terrorist cells. The INDH was partly funded by Morocco but also secured support from bodies including the UNDP, the World Bank, the European Union, the United States, various Western states and NGOs (M'Jid 2010; Kalpakian 2011: 2–5; Khakee 2017: 243, 245).

All these processes created a greater openness for historical research, which was allowed to expand its gaze. As the Moroccan historian Driss Maghraoui phrased it, in 2007 historical research in Morocco began to enable contestation and competition between contradictory memories (Jay 2012). In addition, the IER's recommendation for the opening of a Moroccan national archive, granting free access to documents relating to the history of Morocco, was accepted; the National Archives were opened in 2011.

As these processes were set in motion, a wave of demonstrations linked to the broader 'Arab Spring' began to spread across the kingdom in 2011, with protesters making demands in the social, economic and political domains. Tackling the situation, the court formulated a new constitution, which transmitted a message of positive response to the protesters' demands. However, in retrospect, this seems to have merely fortified the status of the court (Khakee 2017: 244; Dayani and Waterbury 2018).

Although the government managed to re-establish control and suppress these expressions of dissent, a second wave of protests erupted in 2016–17. Restricted to the Rif area, these protests broke out after a fish seller was crushed to death while trying to rescue fish confiscated from him by police because they had been caught illegally. The protests developed into a series of demonstrations against the economic failings of the region in the realms of employment, communications, education and health (Pennell 2017: 810). The channelling of police forces on the one hand, and extra investments in infrastructure on the other, brought the protests under control.

In sync with these changes, the narrations of al-Glaoui also took on new forms. Mahi Binebine's novels indicated the beginning of the transformation, but more was to come.

Abdessadeq El Glaoui and the Telling of al-Glaoui in Morocco Since the Turn of the Century

In 1999, an Arabic translation of Babin's *Son Excellence* was published in Morocco, under the title *Al-Basha al-Glawi: al-ustora wa-l-haqiqa fi hayat basha Murrakush* (Al-Pasha al-Glaoui: The Myth and Truth in the Life of the Pasha of Marrakesh; Babin 1999). The translated book proved a success, with a second edition announced in 2002. In the foreword to the book, 'Abderrahim Hazal, the book's translator, acclaimed Babin's work, citing a few sources that had praised it and adding that 'the translation of this book is a duty towards [our] national history, and reading it is a necessity in order to reshape our awareness of this history' (Hazal in Babin 1999: 9).

The success of the book might have hinted at a return of the Glaoui story to the one-dimensional track framing him as total evil – all the more so given that, unlike the situation in 1932 when Babin's original book was published (Chapter 3), in 1999 al-Glaoui was no longer around to defend himself. But then, a turn in the narrative occurred: Abdessadeq, Thami's son, came to his father's defence.

Abdessadeq El Glaoui was born in 1924.³ He was one of the sons of Thami al-Glaoui and Lalla Zineb, widow of Madani al-Glaoui, whom Thami had married after his brother's death in 1918. Abdessadeq was raised in al-Glaoui's palace, a unique experience that he was later to describe in detail (El Glaoui 2004: 99–124). Abdessadeq testifies that as a young man, he was quite remote from his father, but that he developed a close relationship with him after 1954 when he started to accompany the Pasha on various missions, representing him at official functions from time to time.

After studying law, Abdessadeq took up a position as a judiciary *khalifa* of his father (El Glaoui 2004: 37, and Annexe 17). From an early age, Abdessadeq's views on Moroccan national issues differed from his father's; consequently, during the 1950 crisis between the Sultan and al-Glaoui, Abdessadeq was torn between his loyalty to both personalities, not to mention his commitment to the nationalist cause.⁴ As described above (Chapter 4), immediately after al-Glaoui's death, Abdessadeq and his brothers (except for Brahim, who managed to escape to France) were arrested (Lefévre 1957).⁵ On his release, he was appointed by the King to the post of president of the regional tribunal of Marrakesh, and then promoted to the role of attorney of the King at the Sharifian Tribunal (*procureur du Roi près le Tribunal Chérifiene*). These nominations did not prevent the by then almost independent Moroccan Liberation Army from re-arresting Abdessadeq and some of his brothers and relatives in May 1957, on the charge that they had participated in Thami al-Glaoui's conspiracy against the King. Four months later, the government published a list of persons accused of taking part in the plot to depose the Sultan. The list included Abdessadeq. Abdessadeq appealed directly to the King, claiming that at least with regard to his mother Lalla Zineb, his brother Hassan and himself, this accusation was untrue. He requested their immediate release, and that their share of their father's inheritance be restored to them. The arrests of the Glaoui family members ended towards the end of 1958; indeed, Abdessadeq was not punished.

During the rule of Hassan II, Abdessadeq was nominated to various prestigious appointments. In 1970 he was appointed Morocco's ambassador to France;⁶ a year later, he was promoted to the role of the Moroccan ambassador to the United States. A *New York Times* report describing the celebration of Morocco's fifteenth Independence Day at the ambassador's residence presents Abdessadeq and his family in the following words:

> At tonight's party at the Moroccan Embassy, olive skinned Ambassador Adessadeq el-Glaoui was marvelous to behold in his native desert white djellaba, but the most opulent sight at the party had to be the Ambassador's wife. Mrs el-Glaoui's crimson lined, gold encrusted, flowered caftan trailed in traditional fashion several yards across the floor; around her neck was what appeared to be at least two king's ransoms in the form of an ancient Berber necklace of beaten gold set with cabochon emeralds the size of the proverbial pigeon's eggs. The necklace, an heirloom of her husband's family, was complemented by earrings set with diamonds, emeralds and long lozenge-shaped rubies and an emerald-encrusted girdle that fastened her caftan at the waist. Mrs el-Glaoui, born in Normandy, France, met her husband 11 years ago in Marrakech, and thought he was 'the handsomest man she'd ever met'. (Bonihi 1971)

Thus, it seems that Abdessadeq and his close family had not been significantly impacted by the political and financial sanctions enforced against Thami al-Glaoui's close kin – and indeed succeeded in retrieving their inheritance.

In the mid-1970s, Abdessadeq returned to Morocco to take up the post of president of the Court of Accounts (La Cour des comptes is a Moroccan financial institution mainly responsible for monitoring the integrity of public accounts of the state, public companies, municipalities and Moroccan political parties), a post he held up to his retirement in 2003. The commitment of the Glaoui family to foreign service continued through his son, Thami, who was appointed Morocco's ambassador to South Africa (Rees 2015). In retirement, Abdessadeq published a book about his father (below). He died in 2017; his family received the sincere condolences of King Mohammed VI.

Le ralliement. Le Glaoui, mon père.

Following the publication of the Arabic translation of Babin's *Son Excellence* (Babin 1999; with a second edition in 2002), regurgitating the historical negative image of Thami al-Glaoui, Abdessadeq published *Le ralliement. Le Glaoui, mon père* (The

Rallying: Glaoui, My Father), a book dedicated to his father's memory. The volume was published simultaneously in Arabic (al-Glawi 2004) and French (El Glaoui 2004). Organised into multiple short chapters, it begins with a historical introduction to the family (El Glaoui 2004: 9–17) before moving to other issues, which can be grouped into two main sections. The first includes testimonials to the magnitude and splendour of Thami al-Glaoui's public image, reviewing topics such as his contacts with various European leaders, descriptions of his palace, and his renowned hospitality alongside less-known sides to him, such as his love of music, theatre and cinema (El Glaoui 2004: 19–124). The second and main section of the book is the author's version of the history of al-Glaoui's conspiracy against the Sultan. Noteworthy is the fact that beyond the reference to the general history of the family at the beginning of the volume, Abdessadeq ignores the early history of his father and goes directly to the 1940s and beyond.

The second part of the book is arranged chronologically, describing step by step what Abdessadeq presents as the major events in his father's life between the Second World War and his death (El Glaoui 2004: 125–346). The book ends with an acknowledgement to one of Thami al-Glaoui's secretaries, who gave Abdessadeq many of the documents that he refers to in the text (El Glaoui 2004: 347), and with appendices presenting images of many of the key documents named in the text (El Glaoui 2004: 347–83). In addition to the appendices, the book is replete with transcriptions of letters that al-Glaoui received throughout the years, and with many quotes taken from texts, written mainly by French personalities, commenting on key events in the final years of the protectorate.

The overall impression of the book is that of a legal manifesto. Its organisation, as well as the numerous documents cited, distinctly resemble the presentation of the case for the defence. The author's goal, it would seem, was to rehabilitate his father's image from the allegation that he was a traitor.[7] The main claims the book makes are that Thami al-Glaoui was always profoundly loyal to the 'Alawi dynasty; that he was led into the conspiracy to depose the King by the French and by some rivals; and that his grandest deed, outstripping all his other actions, is his final and courageous expression of regret. This regret, which came into public view in the press statement released by al-Glaoui in October 1955 (Chapter 4), is presented by Abdessadeq as a key factor enabling the King's return to Morocco. Al-Glaoui's rallying by the King – further magnified by its use as the title of the book – is portrayed by Abdessadeq as the pivotal act enabling the swift return of Mohammed V. This, purportedly, curtailed additional French manipulations, and prevented the violence and bloodshed that would have otherwise occurred. The inevitable conclusion – as the book rests its case – is that the correct verdict of the 'treason trial' of Thami al-Glaoui should be: 'not guilty'.

The book's combining a wealth of documents with a literary narrative bolstering the hero's image is a legal defence technique with a long history (for example, Zemon-Davis 1987; Fraher 1988). In the practice of law, where the main goal is to persuade people to accept a specific claim, storytelling is highly valued. As the legal researchers Robert Weisberg and Michael Hanne state: '[M]any legal theorists argue that narrative is the primary device by which persuasion occurs in the courtroom. In the words of Chris Rideout, one of the scholars who has written most comprehensively on the topic: "lawyers persuade by telling stories".' (Weisberg and Hanne 2019: 57–60).

Aside from defending his father, Abdessadeq takes personal credit for changing the Pasha's views in 1955, which (in his opinion) led to the extremely significant event for the entire Moroccan nation – the return of the Sultan. The ability to change long-held opinions and act for the benefit of the country makes Thami al-Glaoui, in his son's opinion, a national hero.

Abdellatif Jebrou, a journalist and a commentator on Abdessadeq's book (see below), testifies that Abdessadeq held the view that his father should be considered a hero for a long time, but only felt safe enough to say as much publicly in the 2000s. Jebrou explains that the political situation up until the late 1990s was too restrictive; a book making such claims about al-Glaoui would not have been permitted. As he states, the 1970s and the 1980s were too close to the events to allow one to speak freely about them (Jebrou 2005: 8).

The publication of Babin's translation and Abdessadeq's reaction to it (although he never acknowledged that it was indeed a response) triggered further publications. The first was journalist Abdellatif Jebrou's commentary on *Le ralliement*, titled *Qira'ton fi kitab al-Ustadh 'Abdessadeq al-Glawi 'an walidihi al-Basha Tuhami al-Glawi* (Reading in the Book of Mr Abdessadeq El Glaoui about his Father the Pasha al-Thami al-Glaoui; Jebrou 2005).

Jebrou explains in the preface to his volume that 'Moroccan society is heading towards maturity, and has the desire to obtain the necessary information about past events' (Jebrou 2005: 3). This statement creates a dialogue with Hazal's declaration (in Babin 1999: 9) that the information in Babin's book is a necessary prerequisite for the process of reshaping Moroccans' awareness of their history. Thus, both Hazal and Jebrou share a post-2000 historiographic discourse, proposing that a national maturity enabling re-evaluation of the past had been reached in Morocco. The difference is that Jebrou claims that any assessment of al-Glaoui's history requires more than a mere rereading of Babin.

Commenting on Thami al-Glaoui's biography, Jebrou proposes a division into two phases. The first covered the period during which he was one of the feudal lords set up by the colonial powers to oppose the nationalists; the second is condensed to the last three months of his life, his reversion to the nationalist line, the surprising announcement supporting the King's return to his throne, and his aspirations for Moroccan independence (Jebrou 2005: 13). Jebrou hence accepts and supports Abdessadeq's version. The acceptance is evident too in the very lengthy passages that he copies almost verbatim from *Le ralliement* (for example, Jebrou 2005: 24 is a copy of El Glaoui 2004: 14–15; the detailed description of al-Glaoui's household in Jebrou 2005: 32–57, is a replica of El Glaoui 2004: 99–118; and more). In certain places, Jebrou adds information from other sources. For example, he comments that Abdessadeq did not write about his father's history in the years before his (Abdessadeq's) birth. Therefore he (Jebrou) decided to consult books about those years, such as Babin's *Son Excellence* (Jebrou 2005: 21). Jebrou uses the Arabic translation of Babin's book (Babin 1999), from where he picks various stories, such as Babin's accusation that al-Glaoui was responsible for a murder and the silencing of its subsequent investigation in 1920 (Jebrou 2005: 19–22).

Jebrou's book was followed by other publications about Thami al-Glaoui. In 2007, Ahmad Mutafakkir published his *Nuzum al-qawafi fi al-Basha al-Glawi: ibbana wala'ihi lil-'arsh al-'Alawi* (Arranged Poems for al-Pasha al-Glaoui: During his Loyalty to the 'Alawi Throne), a compilation of poems written between the 1920s and the 1950s by numerous poets, all in honour of Thami al-Glaoui. Mutafakkir focuses on Thami al-Glaoui's affection for poetry, revealing that he supported poets from the Maghreb and beyond, and collected their manuscripts in his extremely rich library.

Beyond poems, which present a previously unexplored perspective on al-Glaoui's life and his relationships with others, Mutafakkir's book also includes an informative preface. He begins by emphasising al-Glaoui's support of the Sultan's return – citing a welcome letter that al-Glaoui wrote to Mohammed V upon his arrival, and the latter's reply (Mutafakkir 2007: 6). The fact that the collection begins this way, combined with the book's subtitle – 'during his loyalty to the 'Alawi throne'– hints that these steps were taken by the author to forestall criticism objecting to the publishing of poems honouring a person that some considered a traitor. Mutaffakir's cautiousness was not limited to the ruling dynasty and the nationalists. Given that al-Glaoui had exploited and ravaged many tribes and groups in southern Morocco, Mutaffakir pre-emptively responded to the likely complaints from the descendants of these tribes, writing:

> Before I edited this collection, the reader is reminded that I wrote it with a neutral pen without political or tribal backgrounds; or prejudice against it; or a victory for him or not. This is a subjective compilation that highlights the most important stations in the life of Tuhami bin Mohammed bin Hamm al-Glaoui Mzouari. (Mutafakkir 2007: 7)

Abdessadeq, Jebrou and Mutafakkir's books are not the only publications about al-Glaoui that have appeared in recent years. Besides these more popular texts, the resurgence in writing about al-Glaoui in the last two decades has also extended to academic texts relating to specific aspects of his life and his rule (for example, Yasin 2003; al-Buzidi 2010; El Adnani 2010; Azawi 2022). In addition, old books about al-Glaoui have been republished in Morocco, in their French versions (Le Prévost 2013; Maxwell 2016).

A Qa'idal *Revival*

The intensification of writing since 2000 about Thami al-Glaoui – the Pasha of Marrakesh and a grand *qa'id* during the protectorate period – is part of a wider biographical turn, in which the descendants of southern Moroccan *qa'id*s have published books about their forebears' histories (for example, Maa' al-'Aynayn

2005; Goundafi 2013; El Glaoui 2017). As these *qa'id*s were contemporaries of Thami al-Glaoui, and because the current repositioning of al-Gloui's tale also occurs within this historiographic process, I shall briefly discuss some of these publications.

In 2013, Omar Goundafi published a volume about his grandfather, Taïeb Goundafi – Thami al-Glaoui's rival at the beginning of his career. He writes that Taïeb Goundafi was a high-ranking *makhzheni* personality, and an actor in events related to Moroccan history during the late nineteenth century and the beginning of the twentieth century. Goundafi states that his main motivation for writing the book was to respond 'to the misinformation that continues to afflict his [the grandfather's] memory', further explaining: '[W]ith the exception of university researchers and historians, the opinion in general about Moroccan personalities who occupied important functions in the Makhzen before and under the protectorate, is mixed, often contradictory and superficial, denoting a limited vision.' He testifies that his work, which is based on family archives, interviews and additional research, 'allowed [the reader] to form a somewhat objective opinion of this personality [his grandfather]' (Goundafi 2013: 7).

Likewise, Abderrahman El Mezouari El Glaoui published a volume, titled *Le Grand Vizir Madani El Mezouari El Glaoui, une vie au service du Makhzen* (The Grand Vizier Madani El Mezouari El Glaoui, a Life in the Service of the Makhzen), about his grandfather Madani al-Glaoui (Thami's elder brother). He explains that he was motivated by the desire to know his grandfather better, and his hope that his work would 'shed a new light on the extraordinary destiny of this statesman, who was a powerful supporter of four monarchs that he had served, and a true patriot'. He also explains, replicating Goundafi's discourse, that he tried to demonstrate it 'with the greatest possible objectivity' (El Glaoui 2017: 13), adding:

> Finally, I hope I can erase the mistaken attitude which attributes to Pasha Haj Thami everything about our family and vice versa, to accuse our family (including ancestors!), of all that the pasha could have done ...
> I will return later to this heartbreaking bias because, if we understand the emotion aroused even today among all Moroccans by the attitude of Haj Thami vis-à-vis Sidi Mohammed Ben Youssef, nothing would allow this amalgam that some have against an entire family who played a role of

real service to their country. A family whose most members, some even among his sons, were opposed to the actions of the pasha throughout his entire life or parts of it. (El Glaoui 2017: 14)

Le Grand Vizir Madani El Mezouari El Glaoui was critically reviewed in *Asinag*, journal of the IRCAM (The Royal Institute for Amazigh Culture) and thus representing the establishment's response to it (Bentaleb 2019). The reviewer, Ali Bentaleb, comments that Abderrahman El Glaoui ignored all the negative sides of the grand *qa'ids*' conduct, including that of his grandfather. These included imprisonment, murder, slavery, exploitation, appropriation of other people's money, fiscal pressure and various forms of forced labour (Bentaleb 2019: 88). He thinks that Abderrahman El Glaoui sought to get his readers to sympathise with his grandfather, whom he presents as a patriotic statesman, jealous for his country, defender of the public interest, and loyal servant of the *makhzen*. However, Bentaleb comments, other studies give a completely opposite impression. He thus expressed his strong disapproval of El Glaoui's attempts to seek out only positive testimonies about Madani al-Glaoui, and his avoidance of anything that would have cast a shadow over his character and reputation (Bentaleb 2019: 94).

Reading these texts, and additional ones such as articles referring to grand *qa'id* al-Ayadi (Ayt al-Ketawi 2013; Iburki 2013), reveals the magnitude of the current debate on the question of whether the grand *qai'ds* should be considered traitors or patriots (see more about broader perspectives of this discussion in Chapter 9). These texts, invariably written by descendants of the *qa'ids*, usually highlight their forebears' contributions to Moroccan unity, their overall loyalty to the ruling dynasty, and their resistance to colonialism. Opposing them are the numerous views that choose to emphasise the cruel face of the *qa'idal* system. Within the broad-range historiographic reassessment currently taking place, the leading figure is certainly Thami al-Glaoui, the grandest of all *qa'ids*. As such, the debate over his legacy, which began earlier than the current wave of writing about other *qa'ids*, is much more extensive and is continuing to expand into new domains.

In Constant Creation – Ever New Horizons

Over the last two decades, historiography about al-Glaoui has continued to evolve, and on a much grander scale than that concerning other grand *qa'id*s of the colonial period. Its main novelty is in its expansion to new venues, including theatre, the art scene, social media and cultural resource management. In the following section, I describe and discuss these locations for reassessments of al-Glaoui's legacy.

Theatre and the Art Scene

The interpretational challenge created by the varied twenty-first-century perspectives about al-Glaoui has prompted a public debate on whether he was a patriot or a traitor. Abdelilah Benhadar, a screenwriter of television dramas and a playwright (*Al-Quds al-Arabi* 2012), found a special way to deal with the dispute about the Pasha. He wrote and staged a satirical play, titled *Qayd al-Qyyad: al-Basha al-Glawi* (The Commander: The Pasha al-Glaoui; Benhadar 2010).

The play features imagined scenarios from al-Glaoui's life, relating to disturbing and controversial aspects from his biography gathered from earlier narrations. These include the taxation of prostitutes (pp. 31–2); the arrival of General Mangin to Marrakesh in 1912 and the rescue of the French prisoners held in the city (pp. 54–60); dubious business collaborations with French entrepreneurs (pp. 61–2, 71–2); the benefits reaped from the death of his brother Madani (pp. 64–71); the Bousta murder (pp. 79–96; about the murder, see 'Afalfal 2021); and more.

The fact that all of these events are mentioned in Babin's book about al-Glaoui (Chapter 3), together with the observation that the chosen scenes encompass only the years covered in Babin's book (that is, no later than 1930), indicates that *Son Excellence* was the principal source for Benhadar's script. However, Benhadar develops the situations beyond Babin's narrative. For example, he sometimes 'lets' al-Glaoui reply to Babin's accusations (a method that I have employed too, in Chapter 3, where I create an imagined dialogue between the two). This is most apparent in a scene in the play, in which a French journalist named Henri interviews al-Glaoui and questions him about some matters that annoyed Babin – for example the Pasha's alleged claim that he is of Sharifian origin and that he is a friend of France (pp. 73–6). In his answers to the journalist, the Pasha succeeds in remaining vague, and avoids giving a definite answer to anything:

The journalist Henri: You have declared to a newspaper that you are a descendant of a Sharifian family?
Pasha Glawi: I was born in the Tafilalet region, and Sultan Mawlay Rashid comes from this region, and Mawlay Ismail was the father of this big family.
The journalist Henri: Regarding you, Sir?
Pasha Glaoui: My grandfather is Abdessadeq al-Mezouari, and this is my name al-Hajj Thami al-Mezouari. As you see, we are a big family and we have always been descendants of qa'ids and princes.
The journalist Henri: To my knowledge, there is no black prince!
Pasha Glaoui: This is nonsense!
The journalist Henri: There is no Berber shurafa either!
Pasha Glaoui: This is also nonsense! (Benhadar 2011: 73)

The play *Qayd al-Qyyad* was performed on stage in Marrakesh in November 2010, before a capacity audience. The theatre critic of the *Bayan al Yawm* newspaper praised Benhadar for daring to present a 'problematic' and 'controversial' figure, one who had occupied a key position in a critical historical, cultural and social climate of Morocco's past. The critic further noted that Benhadar made a process of 'an extremely cautious theatrical autopsy, focusing on the dramatic and aesthetic aspects of positions selected from historical rubble'. He further praised Benhadar for discovering 'a dramatic field that constitutes a real addition to the repertoire of Moroccan theatre in general and the Marrakchi in particular' (*Bayan al Yawm* 2010).

The play was also published as a printed volume, including a dedication, introductions by three different authors and a preface by Benhadar. The decision to publish this relatively large number of introductions was probably intended as a way of presenting the existing range of views about the Pasha, and to reflect the wish of the playwright to raise ethical questions rather than to solve them.

The first introduction, by writer and theatre director Abdelwahed Uzri, makes the point that the play is an imagined biography – imaginary 'like everything linked with the Pasha'.

In Uzri's view, the play depicts al-Glaoui's multiple faces: an arrogant man and a lawless ruler – yet with a human face. A person serving colonialism, admiring it – but defending the population from it and loving the poor. He then asks, rhetorically: 'Was al-Glaoui a patriot or a traitor? Did he become a patriot later? Did he have a patriotic tendency to distract him from his ... relationship with the French?' The play does not give an answer to these questions, Uzri continues, and perhaps there is no definite answer to them at all. He then adds that al-Glaoui and his fellow men, despite their betrayal and cooperation with French colonialism, *did* love Morocco (Uzri in Benhadar 2011: 7–9).

The second introduction was penned by the lawyer, intellectual and writer of biographies Ibrahim Saduq, general secretary of the Marrakesh branch of the Union of Moroccan Writers during the period that the play was staged.[8] Saduq explains that the play is concerned with a national character who also drew widespread attention beyond Moroccan borders. The play's importance, in his view, lies in the fact that it focuses on the relationships of al-Glaoui with the French, the *makhzen*, grand *qa'id*s al-Ayadi, al-Goundafi and al-Mtougi, and the citizens of southern Morocco (Saduq in Benhadar 2011: 10).

The third introduction, written by the researcher, critic and translator Abdeljalil ben Muhamed al-Azidi al-Murakushi, is much less forgiving. Al-Murakushi asserts that al-Glaoui was an agent of the French intervention in Morocco, that he engaged in debatable trading relations with the coloniser, and assisted many high French officials who had material interests in Morocco. In al-Murakushi's opinion, al-Glaoui was 'a tyrant, a murderer, scattering poetry and messing with women', who ruled Marrakesh and southern Morocco 'with iron and fire'. He might have been 'patriotic in a sense, as he did not flee – and it was never proven that he took abroad even one dirham from the Muslim treasury'. However, the Pasha also had a long list of misconducts: he was involved in a fierce struggle with the Bousta family and assassinated its head with the complicity of his *khalifa*, al-Biaz. Also, after the death of his brother, Madani al-Glaoui, Thami took possession of his property, his women and his maidservants, displacing his brother's children, an act which was 'a clear cowardly stabbing in the back'. Finally, the Pasha had scarred his city for generations. In al-Murakushi's words:

> Al-Hajj al-Thami worked to transform the city of Marrakesh
> ... from the city of saints, righteousness, honourable people,
> scholars, ascetics, mystics, jurists, philosophers, and doctors,
> into a khan or a tavern that serves delicious alcohol, in which
> males and females have fun and people forget what might
> happen in it ... In this sense, what Marrakesh is experiencing in our time ... [has] its roots in the past. (al-Murakushi in
> Benhadar 2011: 11–15)

Following these introductions, drawing together a range of views about al-Glaoui, Benhadar explains his motivations for writing the play at that specific time. He says that despite changes in people's practices since the arrival of French colonialism to Marrakesh, a lot of 'residues' from that period remain. He believes that the decadent values that prevailed in the time of the Pasha – corruption, favouritism, exploitation, prostitution, pimping, bribery and more – were the results of education and ideas practised and planted by colonial agencies. He explains that he was not interested in al-Glaoui specifically, but rather in practices and actions, since 'names change, while ideas, values, principles, and practices do not'. To change them, he further writes,

> requires a lot of courage and sacrifice, and not being ashamed of a history that is ours and we are part of it. Raising our voices denouncing the brutal and oppressive tribal regimes, without counting what this might cost on a personal level. Our only goal according to Frantz Fanon is: 'the creation of new souls'. (Benhadar 2011: 17–19)

These clarifications indicate that *Qayd al-Qyyad*, in addition to proposing an original way to discuss the narrative about al-Glaoui, is also a part of the reality and zeitgeist of a 'national maturity' mentioned above. This discourse supplies the justification and legitimisation for public reflection on problematic past events and personalities and concomitantly assists in further shaping their telling. It also relates to other sociopolitical discourses: the narrative of Moroccan cultural pluralism, and the notion of a so-called 'Moroccan exceptionalism' (Hashas 2013).

Similar discourses are also apparent in a performing arts event that took place at the 2014 Marrakesh Biennale, facilitating further debate over Thami al-Glaoui's legacy. The biennale's curator, Hisham Khalidi, a Moroccan artist living in the diaspora, described the way by which he developed the theme of the event:

> What if we looked at Morocco itself as a work of art? Would it be possible to view national identity as something plural and multiple, something that can be experienced and altered by the 'other'? . . . What can we learn from the fact that everyone views things differently? (Khalidi 2018: 53)

Accordingly, he defined the biennale's theme as 'Where Are We Now?' Participating artists were encouraged to reflect upon this.

One of the respondents to the biennale's call, the Nigerian-born contemporary-art performer Atiku Jelili, decided to anchor his project around Thami al-Glaoui. Jelili, who uses drawing, installation sculpture, photography, video and live art performance, usually focuses on protests against violence, war, poverty, corruption and climate change.[9] In Marrakesh, he set up a street-art performance titled 'I Will Not Stroll With Thami El Glaoui'.[10] Using Amazigh fabrics and design, he organised a procession leading to Djemaa el-Fna, himself standing in a horse-drawn carriage dressed like a king with Amazigh fabrics, followed by fifty sheep similarly decorated.[11]

On his Facebook page,[12] Jelili indicated that the inspiration for his performance came from his appreciation of the economic, political and social reforms and the modernisation drive led by King Mohammed VI, adding:

> The theme of the Marrakech Biennial 5, 'Where Are We Now', was a window through which I was able to reflect and review the 'presence' and cornucopia experiences, especially Islamisation and Arabisation of Amazigh – the indigenous people of Morocco. Therefore, the performance *I Will Not Stroll with Thami El Glaoui* draws attention to a subtly nuanced contemporary and ancient Moroccan history in which the tenuous line between present and the past; reality and fiction is blurred. Thami El Glaoui who is popularly known as T'hami El Glaoui or Lord of the Atlas and Feudal Warlord is used as a metaphor of tangible historical monument to bring the reality of social, political, economic and religious experiences of

Moroccans ... 50 clothed rams walk behind were to create a narrative and characteristic of followership and leadership. (Jelili 2014)

Presenting an African rather than a Moroccan view, Jeilili relinked al-Glaoui with his African Amazighness (Chapter 7), and perhaps with blackness as well. His performance opens up several options for interpreting al-Glaoui, depending on the observer's judgement. These vary from viewing the Pasha as a trustworthy leader to be respected, to the complete opposite – a leader obeyed only by short-sighted followers.

Social Media and Cultural Resource Management

Over the last two and a half decades, social media has become a critical venue for social, cultural, business and political activity in Morocco, a process accelerated by the COVID-19 pandemic (Amsidder et al. 2012; Sedrati 2017; El Marhoum et al. 2020; Ferrati 2021). The telling of Thami al-Glaoui through social media has made the production and consumption of tales about him more accessible to larger sectors of the general public and Moroccan society. The creation of new narrations is especially prominent on YouTube, where many videos about Thami al-Glaoui have been uploaded. Their production rate exhibits a distinct pattern, with an average of one new video about him uploaded every year between 2015 and 2019. But thereafter, the number rose dramatically: ten new videos in 2020, thirteen in 2021 and five in the first half of 2022, altogether gathering a little more than eight and a half million views since 2015 (Table 8.1).

The tremendous rise in the production and distribution since 2020 of YouTube videos retelling al-Glaoui's story/history is certainly multi-causal, and it follows the growing freedom of speech with respect to Morocco's history over the last two decades. However, what is probably the most crucial factor in this rise is the COVID-19-period-imposed confinements, with the subsequent development of online learning, and its consumption by people of all ages.

The YouTube videos are made by private individuals, usually operating small-scale, single-person channels, and vary greatly in quality. On the one side, there are high-quality productions like those by Marouane Lamharzi Alaoui. Alaoui, a media expert

Table 8.1 YouTube videos about Thami al-Glaoui, the date of their first appearance and number of views until mid-August 2022[13]

Link	First published	Number of views as of 21-8-22
https://www.youtube.com/watch?v=wec3y-qEjgk	20-01-2015	2,212
https://www.youtube.com/watch?v=Cr50W4f8gWA&t=14s	12-11-2016	2,783,556
https://www.youtube.com/watch?v=oRnpZBDlJSo	24-12-2017	1,774,627
https://www.youtube.com/watch?v=zm5-EwdWNvs&t=680s	25-11-2018	1,241,705
https://www.youtube.com/watch?v=sC_QAEPZNpM	28-08-2019	844,083
https://www.youtube.com/watch?v=d6gzpY-xsjM	13-01-2020	37,200
https://www.youtube.com/watch?v=7FU2RhiMDQE	27-01-2020	5,364
https://www.youtube.com/watch?v=mdPNoqk1OdU&t=16s	01-02-2020	9,920
https://www.youtube.com/watch?v=M67SKNWWkyk	12-02-2020	965,262
https://www.youtube.com/watch?v=wUTrGdmONXg	14-02-2020	19,234
https://www.youtube.com/watch?v=nrMWy0yHaUg	16-02-2020	952
https://www.youtube.com/watch?v=m114fkZt6iQ&t=71s	27-04-2020	17,547
https://www.youtube.com/watch?v=u_xO8IuZYJk	15-07-2020	290,150
https://www.youtube.com/watch?v=4CtJ8ske9lM	07-08-2020	18,332
https://www.youtube.com/watch?v=MRA2EJKGrNo&t=88s	01-10-2020	1,445
https://www.youtube.com/watch?v=TwnQIiu-Phw	15-02-2021	537
https://www.youtube.com/watch?v=tIh9ELt4jaQ	28-02-2021	1,140
https://www.youtube.com/watch?v=7gZ0jHly1wM	25-03-2021	8,608
https://www.youtube.com/watch?v=yj544F9FLEg	21-04-2021	4,606
https://www.youtube.com/watch?v=Nw7Op0d0qv4	25-05-2021	1,692
https://www.youtube.com/watch?v=tRnAJLp-8lU	23-06-2021	8,116
https://www.youtube.com/watch?v=mAfpDH2l4DY	04-07-2021	2,625
https://www.youtube.com/watch?v=IMCaxFp_Ii4	22-11-2021	1,721
https://www.youtube.com/watch?v=f_ibp-l-O-I	24-11-2021	69,200
https://www.youtube.com/watch?v=r3ORVUc1a9w	25-11-2021	317,668
https://www.youtube.com/watch?v=4deFRB5Xw7E	12-12-2021	9,129
https://www.youtube.com/watch?v=ngXlrvun1So	13-12-2021	856
https://www.youtube.com/watch?v=aE6C8X_Ccg4	14-12-2021	5,453
https://www.youtube.com/watch?v=L13pw5ecpn	07-01-2022	28,365
https://www.youtube.com/watch?v=Zl4eD_aF-m4	23-04-2022	68,308
https://www.youtube.com/watch?v=pWo-PxaXmVw	01-05-2022	8,205
https://www.youtube.com/watch?v=r7LRWF8jdeU	10-05-2022	17,286
https://www.youtube.com/watch?v=7PSzpTL5Wzc	19-07-2022	96,743
	Total	**8,661,847**

and entrepreneur, produced a YouTube series about Moroccan history titled *Atarikh li-Maqrawnash* ('The history that we were not taught' or 'The untaught history'). The eighth episode in the series is a twenty-three-minute-long documentary about Thami al-Glaoui. The production of the series in general, and of this episode in particular, is technically and academically highly invested, with this episode based on a close reading of major publications about al-Glaoui up to that date. The episode was first published in 2016 and has since then gained 2.8 million views and many comments.[14]

Then there are many lower-quality videos, usually featuring a speaker explaining aspects of al-Glaoui and his life, sometimes with relevant images running in the background. One such example is an episode of *Qanat dar l-khabar* (The News Channel), titled 'How did Pasha Glaoui become richer than the Sultan of Morocco?' with about one million views.[15]

Among the many videos, there is a plurality of presenters and goals: a video by people seeking to reclaim lands that al-Glaoui stole from their families in the protectorate years;[16] an audiovisual presentation discussing the rumour that al-Glaoui was the father of King Hassan II;[17] the Nour Bladi channel, which focuses on the African, 'black', history of Morocco, and considers al-Glaoui from that point of view;[18] women speakers guiding tours of Dar al-Basha (al-Glaoui's palace, which was turned into a museum; see below);[19] and more.

An integral part of these web pages are the short comments contributed by viewers. Most of the commentators tend to view al-Glaoui negatively, but here and there are comments that value aspects of his conduct. For example: 'Al-Thami al-Glaoui is the one who restored prestige to the people of the south-east'; 'Pasha Glaoui was a just ruler', and so on.[20]

The flourishing of social media perspectives about Thami al-Glaoui has also extended to other platforms such as Facebook, home to the 'El Glaoui Legacy' group,[21] and Instagram, where the leading account on the topic, active since 2017, is curated by Samia al-Glaoui.[22] Samia al-Glaoui is the granddaughter of Lalla Zineb and Madani al-Glaoui (thus, Thami al-Glaoui is her father's uncle and step-father, and Abdessadeq El Glaoui is her uncle). Her posts share an invaluable collection of historic photographs of the family members, including a presentation of a previously almost undiscussed aspect of the Glaoui story – that of the female members of the family. Alongside the photographs she contributes short introductory notes, followed by comments by her numerous followers, who include many representatives of the current generation of the Glaoui family and friends.

Finally, in recent years the memory of Thami al-Glaoui has also emerged in the cultural resource management domain. The principal manifestation of this particular trend is the restoration of his palace in Marrakesh, and its inauguration as a traditional art museum.[23] The new museum, called Dar El Basha (The House of the Pasha) and run by the Moroccan National Museum Foundation, was opened to the public in 2017.[24] The museum presents the marvels of the structure itself, as well as permanent and temporary exhibitions dedicated 'to the exceptional character of Morocco, the wealth and the diversity of the components of the Moroccan identity',[25] thus officially showcasing the narrative of 'Moroccan exceptionalism'. However, al-Glaoui the person is hardly mentioned in the museum – making him, ironically, conspicuous by his absence from his own palace. In other words, even though the memory of al-Glaoui has also become officially inscribed into the cityscape of Marrakesh through Dar El Basha, full reconciliation with the man who he was is yet to be achieved.

Reconciliation

Since the turn of the twenty-first century, al-Glaoui's tale has undergone a dramatic change. From being presented through restrictive state-controlled and one-dimensional avenues in the last decades of the twentieth century, the story has been opened up to multiple interpretations and forms of expression. These offer many new readings, complex perspectives, and the never-ending development of multiple unexplored avenues.

The millions of views on social media, and the numerous new iterations of the Glaoui story indicate huge curiosity about the Pasha and other Moroccan *qa'id*s of the colonial period. Within this flow of new narrations, there has been an attempt by descendants of the *qa'id*s to reclaim the good names of their forebears – albeit with parallel attempts by the descendants of families victimised by the Pasha and other *qa'id*s to claim back what had been taken from their ancestors. The publicly pronounced perspectives still seem restricted, but the limits are much broader than previously. The general framework of the current discussion is shaping and being shaped by the banner of pluralism and reconciliation with the past – even with its unpleasant aspects.

In 2017, Mahi Binebine, with whom this chapter had opened, published a new book, *Le Fou du roi* (The King's Fool; Binebine 2017), anchored by the theme of reconciliation with the past. The book focuses on his father, Mohamed ben Mohamed, known also as Mohamed Binebine. Young Mohamed ben Mohamed had accompanied his father, a servant at al-Glaoui's court, on occasion to the palace's servants' quarter. On one such visit, he happened to meet Ben Brahim, the so-called 'Red Poet', also in the service of al-Glaoui. In part, because Mohamed Binebine had a unique talent for memorising texts and stories, he became Ben Brahim's assistant. Due to these same talents, he eventually became an entertainer at al-Glaoui's court.[26] After the death of al-Glaoui and following several coincidences, Mohamed Binebine entered the service of Hassan II, whom he entertained with good words, anecdotes and stories.

The dramatic arc of Mohamed Binebine's biography reached its zenith at the royal court. Aziz Binebine, a young army officer and Mohamed's eldest son, took part in the coup against Hassan II. The son was imprisoned in the notorious Tazmamart prison, and for years no one knew if he was alive or not. This notwithstanding, Mohamed Binebine remained loyal to the King and denounced his son's actions, and consequently was perpetually condemned by his wife and children.

In this new book, Mahi Binebine forgives his father. Mahi Binebine does not try to vindicate his father's actions, but he is nevertheless able to reveal some understanding of the complex situation that his father found himself in and the reasons for his behaviour. This book, politically permissible in the Morocco of 2017, further explicates Mahi's earlier books (presented at the beginning of this chapter: Binebine 1994; 1997), written at a time when he could only insinuate criticism of the court and his father's role in it.

Mahi Binebine's path to reconciliation with his father and his past captures in a nutshell the process by which public narratives of Thami al-Glaoui are currently evolving. This observation, together with others, will be further elaborated on in the next chapter, which analyses insights gained from the route that the story has taken between the end of the nineteenth century and the present day, in its entirety.

Notes

1. Mahi en quelques mots'. Available at <https://www.mahibinebine.com/biographie> (last accessed 1 September 2023).
2. The life story of Aziz Binebine was also the basis for Tahar Ben Jelloun's 2001 *Cette aveuglante absence de lumière,* translated into English as *This Blinding Absence of Light* (Fernandes-Dias 2007: 187–91).
3. CADN 1MA/282 95, 'Tableau généalogiques des Glaoua', November 1948(?).
4. CADN 1MA/282 97, 'Dissensions dand la famille du Glaoui', 8 June 1955. In this document, Abdessadeq is reported as having said that if no solution could be found for the crisis in Morocco, he would resign of his post in the Marrakesh Tribunal. Other information indicated that Abdessadeq expressed his loyalty to Mohammed V.
5. CADN 1MA/282 100, 'Note de Renseignements. B.C.I. No. 514/2', 3 May 1957; CADN 1MA/282 100, 'Monsieur Roger Lalouette, chargé d'affaires a.i. de la République Française au Maroc', 4 June 1957.
6. 'Morocco's New Ambassador in Paris, Abdessadek El Glaoui, Son of the Late Pacha de Marrakech, Presents his Credentials to President Pompidou' (Credit Image: Keystone Pictures USA/ ZUMAPRESS). *Almay.com,* 14 January 1970. Available at <https://www.alamy.com/jan-14-1970-moroccos-new-ambassador-in-paris-abdessadek-al-Glaoui-image69461121.html> (last accessed 3 September 2023).
7. Abdessadeq acknowledges this. See an interview with him about his book (Chifaâ n.d.).
8. Available at <https://www.marrakechalyaoum.com/44451/>, <https://anfaspress.com/news/voir/69540-2020-08-31-08-19-26> (last accessed 3 September 2023).
9. Jelili Atiku, 'Manifesta'. Available at <http://m12.manifesta.org/artists-jelili-atiku/> (last accessed 3 September 2023).
10. Jelili Atiku, 'I will Not Stroll with Thami El Glaoui', *Vimeo,* n.d. Available at <https://vimeo.com/91068242> (last accessed 3 September 2023).
11. Jelili Atiku, 'I Will Not Stroll with Thamy el Glaoui', *Marrakech Biennale* 5, 2014, Photo Tour, photo 35. Available at <https://universes.art/en/nafas/articles/2013/marrakech-biennale-5/photo-tour/bank-al-maghrib/jelili-atiku-2> (last accessed 3 September 2023).
12. 'I Will Not Stroll with Thamo El Glaoui'. Available at <https://www.facebook.com/groups/296497947169486> (last accessed 3 September 2023).

13. All websites last accessed on 1 September 2023.
14. Available at <https://www.youtube.com/watch?v=Cr50W4f8gWA> (last accessed 3 September 2023).
15. Available at <https://www.youtube.com/watch?v=zm5-EwdWNvs> (last accessed 3 September 2023).
16. Available at <https://www.youtube.com/watch?v=wec3y-qEjgk> (last accessed 3 September 2023).
17. Available at <https://www.youtube.com/watch?v=rGegMM24raU> (last accessed 3 September 2023).
18. Available at <https://www.youtube.com/watch?v=tIh9ELt4jaQ> (last accessed 3 September 2023).
19. Available at <https://www.youtube.com/watch?v=ngXlrvun1So> (last accessed 3 September 2023).
20. To preserve the anonymity of the individuals who pronounced these views, I have not identified them here.
21. 'The El Glaoui's Legacy'. Available at <https://www.facebook.com/ElGlaouiLegacy> (last accessed 3 September 2023).
22. 'Samiaelglaoui'. Available at <https://www.instagram.com/samiaelglaoui/> (last accessed 3 September 2023).
23. Of Thami al-Glaoui's other palaces, the most renowned are those in Fes – Dar el Glaoui, which is pending restoration (Kurzac-Souali 2010: 99), and his deserted kasbah at Telouet.
24. Musée des Confluences Dar El Bacha. Available at <https://fnm.ma/musees-ouverts/musee-des-confluences-dar-el-bacha/> (last accessed 3 September 2023).
25. Available at <https://visitmarrakech.com/discover-marrakech/tourist-attractions/confluences-museum-dar-el-bacha> (last accessed 12 December 2020).
26. On several occasions al-Glaoui took with him on his trips musicians and other entertainers. Si Mohamed Bin Bin, also called 'el Marrakchi' was often among them. CADN 1MA/282 98, 'Le commissaire chef de la brigade spéciale', 24 May 1938.

9

A Never-ending Story

The prompt for this book was the fascinating public presence of Thami al-Glaoui; the constant references to him in various media and literature over the course of more than a century; realisation of the sheer number of people impacted by him in some way; the thrill, and the accompanying Pavlovian conditioning of uneasiness, that seems to manifest whenever his name is mentioned.

Regardless of the ways in which al-Glaoui has been judged by various people and discourses, his mode of living, his engagement in power relations and webs of loyalty, his actions with respect to the court, the various French agents, the tribal populations of southern Morocco, the local Jewish community, and various international actors: all these contribute to a full engagement with the complex fabric of modern Morocco, its history and its historiographies.

All this notwithstanding, much of the narrations of al-Glaoui's biography are shrouded in fog and uncertainty. This book is an attempt to clear some of these historiographic and historic mysteries and to retrieve his story from the simplistic and reductionist interpretations that certain historiographies have proffered. I have attempted to provide fresh data and perspectives about the individual, simultaneously reflecting on his story and the various ways in which it has been told, how it continues to evolve, and how the story has influenced processes within Moroccan history and has reciprocally been shaped by them.

By merging al-Glaoui's biography with the many different narratives about his tale and with the life stories of the authors who wrote about him, this book has also sought to offer perspectives on major processes of twentieth- and twenty-first-century Morocco, and of the colonial empires that were a part of these processes. These include the effects of colonial modernity, and the traumatic shifts from an imperial world order into nation-state configurations and subsequent global post-national formulations.

This research underpins the claim that the history of the creation and continual evolution of the story of Thami al-Glaoui is no less intriguing than the history of the person himself, and that the two intermingle. The analysis of the evolution, more than a century long, of narratives about al-Glaoui illustrated the interconnectivity between history, historiography and historical storytelling. The story of 'the evolution of the story', its passage through a host of authors of various stands and nationalities, its links with multiple literary genres and devices, and finally its recent expansion into new media, all prove that 'the Story' is as fascinating as 'the Person'. It is not simply because 'events vanish and literature endures' (Acosta 1993: 66), but furthermore because stories continue to live and to thrive, giving history an ever-changing dimension.

This book analysed the origins and contextual manifestations of the multiple narratives about al-Glaoui as historical events, equal in importance to his 'history'. It departed from the common model utilised in many projects, which present past treatises of their main subject by earlier authors merely as 'previous research'. For me, these are not just 'background' material, but rather components of the foreground – a part of the main topic and the history. This goal was emphasised by anchoring each chapter with at least one unique text about al-Glaoui, and analysing the part that each played in the construction of his evolving tale. The importance granted to these narratives made it possible to highlight the elements that shaped them, which in turn assist in understanding the construction of al-Glaoui's image.

The heroes of the book are, thus, al-Glaoui and the authors who wrote about him, together with the numerous stories that have been continuously generated and shaped in a process of ceaseless creation. These perspectives complement each other, their combined and forceful outcome calling attention to a protagonist whose legacy as a central pillar of Moroccan history has often been underrated.

As the book's chapters elaborate, al-Glaoui's story entered the public domain in the first decade of the twentieth century. It was bolstered by French colonial writing, and by his own public relations activity in the following decades. In the 1920s, narratives casting al-Glaoui in a negative light began to appear. In the next decade, stories about him spread far beyond the borders of Morocco, the range of available opinions about him becoming richer and broader – from the extremely negative to the flattering and adulatory. This continued until his demise in 1956. In the first decade after his death, stories about him were generated primarily beyond Moroccan borders (Maxwell's and Le Prévost's volumes). In Morocco, until the 1980s, al-Glaoui's story remained in hibernation, peripheral perspectives like Ahmed Rami's conspiracy narrative aside. But from the late 1980s on, al-Glaoui's story has become a tool of sorts, his persona being used as a way to obliquely address other topics or to emphasise the nobleness (or otherwise) of others. His story was shaped by restrictive state-controlled and one-dimensional outlooks. A new and more complex approach to narrating al-Glaoui began to emerge towards the end of the 1990s, primarily in relation to the conflict of values surrounding his rule. Since the turn of the twenty-first century, al-Glaoui's tale has been opened up to multiple interpretations and ways of expression. These offer many new readings, complex perspectives and a seemingly unending extension into multiple new avenues.

By following this succession of texts referring to a single personality, this book was able to explore how new texts imitate and transform older ones, how previous texts are harnessed in the development of new meanings, and how all these relate to other sociopolitical and cultural processes – in this case including decolonisation, the struggle between the Moroccan court and the major parties, the change of kings and the transformations that accompanied this, the rise of *Amazighité*, the social effects of the COVID-19 pandemic, and the spread and reach of social media.

The links between history and story, between the actions and the storytelling mechanisms that translate a past into a narrative, were considered across the book. It explored how deeds are told, and probed the extent to which actions and tales become intrinsically intertwined, continually producing and reproducing each other and in the process creating an ongoing multi-track historical narrative.

This examination of al-Glaoui's tales, not only as a narration mechanism but as history in their own right, further emphasised a situation in which stories become historicising mechanisms, themselves triggering further histories. For example, the case of the legal struggle between al-Glaoui and Babin (Chapter 3) demonstrated how constructed narratives became points of reference for future demarcations of the boundaries between colonial and metropolitan entities. In a similar vein, it emerged that the talent of a storyteller could well support the eager reception of his stories as 'history'. One's expressive ability, dialectic skills and choice in retouching episodes so that they make narrative 'sense' all lend these events greater historic credibility. Such was the case with the tale concerning the (alleged) fierce assault by al-Glaoui's cavalry – a tale that, at least in part, might be the product of Maxwell's undoubted talent for storytelling (Chapter 4). One consequence of this situation is that personalities whose stories are told and retold intensively, such as al-Glaoui, become the product of tales about them as much as the outcome of their past actions and manifestations.

Researching the texts about al-Glaoui involved the posing of multiple questions: what new information and opinions do they bring in relation to older tales? Which previous information was used? What was ignored? Why was it selected? What was changed? Which events and actors are selected as the 'leading' characters in various tales, and why? What literary devices do the authors use to make their point? What metaphors are used, by whom, and to what end? How are the stories structured? And how do they belong in broader discourses or historiographies?

This methodology facilitated multiple observations regarding the effects of historiographies and discourses, the identification of principal formats of stories, and the detection of common literary topoi and motifs. All of these enabled a clearer view of the forces at play in the creation of various perspectives about the Pasha, and who he actually was.

Many of the texts about al-Glaoui reflect the major historiographies about Morocco, which aggregate around three themes: the colonial, the nationalist and the postcolonial.

Colonial and nationalist historiographies, as the names suggest generally serve to promote distinct political agendas, while postcolonial historiography evolves from a stand that criticises the colonial discourse. Despite being different from and critical of one other, colonial and nationalist historiographies about al-Glaoui share many common characteristics. The basic assumption of the former is that French colonialism was just and benevolent, deploying a series of binaries in defence of this point of view. The latter, to the contrary, depicted how harmful and exploitative French colonialism had been, employing its own binary formulations to prop up its claims. Both schools, in their different ways, oversimplify historical processes – including the case of al-Glaoui – by dichotomising them. For example, while colonial historiography hails the European and constructs European identity as the opposite of the backward local incumbent, the nationalist's mirror image praises the Moroccan and construes the local as counter to the condescending European. Accordingly, al-Glaoui, as a collaborator with the French, was seen by the authors of colonial historiography as a cherished supporter of their stance (for as long as he was under their control, mind), but was depicted almost unanimously by the nationalist discourse as a traitor.

Postcolonial theory takes the gaze beyond these opposing constructions, critiquing colonial dichotomies. This school highlights, with regard to the colonial encounter, the importance of previously voiceless actors, hybridisation, resistance, multiple causalities, the abundance of agents and the occasional internalisation of repressive patterns by the colonised. By opposing the colonial, postcolonial texts often give precedence to the colonised and their voice, and frequently disregard narratives based on colonial voices. As such, in the case of French colonialism in Morocco, postcolonial narratives sometimes fail to respect the colossal colonial ethnographic project and the wealth of the colonial archives – which, despite the a priori oppressive nature of colonialism, are priceless in the study of Moroccan history.

In the case of al-Glaoui, it appears that many Moroccan postcolonial[1] texts present a mix of nationalist and postcolonial historiographies. Loyal to the postcolonial theory, they reject colonial constructions and seek previously voiceless agents; but with regard to al-Glaoui they adopt the nationalist perspective, which compresses his figure into the narrow tropes of 'traitor' and 'collaborator' (for example, Abun Nasr 1987: 382; Hammoudi 1997: 129–30). Complex acts by al-Glaoui, including manipulations directed at various agents, French and Moroccan alike, are often airbrushed out of the wider narrative by these depictions. For example, accounts of the alternative political channel that al-Glaoui proposed to the Sultan – namely, to rely on the established elites rather than the young nationalists, and to prolong the French presence in Morocco so that they may attain independence in a state of better preparedness – was smothered by the might of the nationalist discourse adopted by post-colonial Moroccan historiography.

Beyond the effect of the major historiographies about Morocco, accounts of al-Glaoui reflect several highly discernible periodic discourses which have shaped narration trajectories. These created easily accessible frameworks for describing the Pasha, which reciprocally bolstered further the corresponding discourses. In the colonial period, the 'rescue' and 'warrior' discourses stood out, while in independent Morocco the common discourses were initially 'loyalty and treason', and later 'maturity for self-reflection' and 'cultural pluralism'. A few words are warranted about each of these.

The 'rescue' discourse in colonial Morocco was a major factor in narrations of the French Protectorate's actions. This discourse was used for legitimising the French *mission civilisatrice*. The French claimed that their conquests around the globe were a generous and selfless gesture, intended to save millions of Africans and Asians from barbarism, decadence, tyranny and disease (Conklin 1997: 1–10). Thus, beyond its political and economic frames, the *mission civilisatrice* also became a way of narrating a story. It was a plot, a discursive pattern and a type of narration that focused on rescue and salvation. Stories of that time that refer to al-Glaoui, intentionally or not, concomitantly focus on the matter of rescue. The Glaoui brothers are described as having saved Mawlay Hassan I on the Atlas Mountain pass; the Pasha rescued French hostages in Marrakesh, according to other tales; and the two brothers rescued Lyautey, by enabling his evacuation of forces from Morocco to help metropolitan France during the Great War (Chapter 2). This discourse also displays a common literary topos: the loyal servant coming to his master's rescue in moments of peril. In later occasions, this topos continued to cut across different contexts and times, constituting a basic motif in tales sympathetic to al-Glaoui – and, likewise, as a preferable point for his antagonists to refute.

The warrior discourse appeared in relation to the Great War raging in Europe, and to continuing 'pacification' skirmishes in Morocco. It comes into view in newspaper reports, battle chronicles, citations accompanying the award of medals, and in praise poems referring to al-Glaoui's bravery in combat. One outcome of this discourse was Thami al-Glaoui's increasing value to the French, and the consolidation of his image, on both sides of the Mediterranean, as a mythical warrior of unrivalled qualities.

The wide distribution of such stories praising his bravery in battle, which circulated globally in relation to the Great War, served as a canvas, atop which the topos of the 'brave warrior' was added to the already existing one of the 'rescuer'.

After independence, the main discourse regarding al-Glaoui was a totalising outlook that labelled him a traitor. Al-Glaoui 'earned' this title 'honestly' by being one of the leaders whose actions contributed to the expulsion of Mohammed V. But the effect of this discourse was so immense that for decades afterwards virtually no other aspect of his conduct was considered in the discourse. The discourse was further strengthened after the attempted coups against King Hassan II, when new groups of traitors were identified and penalised. Thus, a discourse informed by the notion of treason and punishment hung in the air in Morocco for several decades.

Following the accession of King Mohammed VI to the throne, two other discourses began to influence the telling of al-Glaoui – Morocco's pluralism and the collective maturity enabling self-reflection. From the beginning of the twenty-first century, and the establishment of the Equity and Reconciliation committees, a repeatedly voiced claim has opened the way to new treatments of al-Glaoui's legacy: that the time has arrived to learn Morocco's 'real' history – including the history of difficult periods. Productions such as the translation of Babin's book to Arabic, books by Jebrou, Mutaffakir and Benhadar about al-Glaoui (Chapter 8) and other avenues have all relied on this concept. This recurring notion is propped against another Moroccan sociopolitical discourse, particularly popular since the publication of the 2011 Constitution – the discourse of Moroccan cultural pluralism, acknowledging the country's social and ethnic groups, languages and religions.

Surveying the texts about al-Glaoui revealed that many of them carried additional goals beyond writing about the Pasha. Identifying these goals enabled micro-historical observations that lent substance to many historical moments. These goals are sometimes very clear, at other times more subtle. They might be recognised – borrowing Stoler's (2009) terminology originally directed at archival documents – by reading the texts both *along* and *against* the grain. For example, reading Paul Schoen's *mémoire* about al-Glaoui (Chapter 2) *against* the grain reveals the objective of colonial control; but reading it *along* the grain displays Schoen's creeping fear that al-Glaoui could develop into a great danger for France. Other books expose additional feelings. Babin (Chapter 3) appears to be mourning an unfulfilled colonial dream, on whose behalf he seeks revenge; Maxwell's text (Chapter 6) seems to indirectly lament the decline of the British aristocracy, of which the Maxwells were a part; Berdugo (Chapter 5) cries out the frustrations of his life course, claiming to be a major but forgotten player in the drama that is contemporary Moroccan history; and Abdessadeq El Glaoui (Chapter 8), in redeeming his father's prestige also seeks to aggrandise himself.

Sometimes, such claims manifest more subtly. Binebine (Chapter 8), for example, wrote initially about al-Glaoui's court; but as he explained later, this was actually a subtle way of criticising the actions of the royal court. In another approach, Zebib, author of the Moroccan encyclopedia of 1995 (Chapter 6) in his references to al-Glaoui utilises rhetorical devices such as contrasts, allusions and metaphors to make various claims. By presenting al-Glaoui in his meetings with the King as quick-tempered, extroverted, greedy, conspiratorial, treacherous, and finally yielding, Zebib effectively emphasises the opposite virtues of Mohammed V: calm, discreet, noble, spiritual, solid. Similarly, by way of subtle allusions the Amazigh readers are reassured that since al-Glaoui 'is not an Amazigh', disapproving of him would not be an anti-Amazigh act; the Istiqlal are reassured, through the reference to al-Gloaui's alleged call 'You are the Sultan of the Istiqlal', that the King was not repelling them. Hence, for the encyclopedia, telling al-Glaoui was not merely an end in itself but also a means to an end. All these exhibit the degree to which these historical narrations are infused with claims and goals of the present – while being based on telling of the past, or on 'Pastness' (Wallerstein 1991: 78).

The claims made by the various authors analysed throughout this research were often supported by the unique literary formats and genres that they co-opted to bolster their claims. Babin, for example, in order to establish his claims of criminality against al-Glaoui's, made use of the *adventure-novel* format in some of his chapters. This set-up often produces up mysterious figures, shadowy spaces, and violent and surprising turns of fortune (Chapter 3). A more romantic take on the adventure novel manifests in the *nostalgic-Orientalist* genre adopted by Maxwell, who expressed admiration for Thami al-Glaoui as a magnificent relic of a glorious past – a past that Maxwell himself still longed for (Chapter 6). Following the dictum that 'lawyers persuade by telling stories' (Rideout in Weisberg and Hanne 2019: 60), Abdessadeq El Glaoui (Chapter 8) arranged his book in the form of a *judicial defence* manifesto, combining documents and accounts, and here and there also employing tropes borrowed from the *thriller* genre of creative writing (such as, for example, in telling how al-Glaoui's rallying behind the King was consolidated; El Glaoui 2004: 305–25). Finally, a novel format of telling al-Glaoui has appeared in the last decade in various *social media* narratives, using the popular communication platforms of YouTube, Facebook and Instagram.

A broader look at these multiple texts collectively indicates that many of them share 'Freytag's pyramid' organisation (Devine 2011: xi). This presents a dramatic arc: a life-long build-up of a conflict, reaching its climax with the deposition of the Sultan. The conflict is finally resolved with al-Glaoui's transformation – his rallying behind the Sultan – which, like a Greek tragedy, is but a precursor of his demise. This death is identified by some as a final punishment (for example, Zebib 1995); by others as noble self-sacrifice in order to save his nation (El Glaoui 2004; Jebrou 2005).

Many of these narratives also make use of the building blocks of iconic and mythological stories: a hero's rise from nowhere to the top; exciting rescue scenes; evidence of treachery and loyalty; and conflicts between a provincial hero and a supreme sovereign (be this al-Glaoui versus the Sultan and the French Resident-General, or Morocco confronting France), all before a final resolution. The judicious use of themes makes al-Glaoui's tales very accessible and catchy.

The pivotal point in al-Glaoui's life story, according to many of his storytellers, was the 1950 Mulud celebration at Mohammed V's palace (Chapter 4). That specific event was what finally set the Sultan and al-Glaoui apart, triggering a snowball effect that led first to the expulsion of the Sultan from Morocco two and a half years later, and then to Morocco's independence another two and a half years on. From a storytelling point of view, the event is significant because it provides the starting point for some of the parallel narratives that have developed in the decades since. The multiple accounts of the 1950 Mulud brought to the fore a situation of concurrent realities, typically described as a Rashomon effect (Davis et al. 2016), crafted by storytellers with varying political and personal stances. This pivotal point led to al-Glaoui's ultimate action, which many storytellers and laypersons have been unable to forgive – taking an active role in the expulsion of the King. This was the main act that positioned him, in the eyes of many, as a traitor.

For the nationalists, al-Glaoui was certainly a traitor. Aside from participating in the deposition of Mohammed V, he actively and vehemently opposed the nationalist movement; he collaborated with the French, who had outlawed them; and he ran roughshod over many Moroccan populations.

Yet, such actions were not a unique exception during his lifetime. Pre-colonial and colonial historiographies portray the full spectrum of actions taken by local Moroccan leaders and tribes, ranging from collaboration to resistance. Tribes were one day on the Sultan's side and the next against him, and some even attempted to seize the throne (such as the struggles related to al-Hiba, Chapter 2). Tribes switched allegiances frequently, sometimes even in a middle of battle (as in the battle of El Herri, Chapter 2). Moreover, many Moroccans served in French armed units, and thus were deployed to fight against their co-patriots. Al-Glaoui was a part of this conduct, shaped by these 'rules of the game', and shaping them.

Many years ago, commenting on these realities, Ernest Gellner wrote:

> Treason, if so harsh a word must be used, is natural in a society which suffers not merely from endemic violence, but also from what may be called a plethora of legitimacy. There were always too many, not too few, legitimate claimants to authority. It was not legitimation, but permanently reliable sanctions, which were lacking. Under such conditions, one hedges one's bets, as many observers have noted. (Gellner 1970: 226)

Al-Glaoui indeed collaborated with the French on many issues. But concomitantly, he maintained a sense of independence, disobeying certain French instructions regarding running his territory, meeting with certain Moroccan and foreign personalities despite French opposition to this (for example, with the ex-sultans), defying financial directives, and more besides. Not only that: while doing so, he consistently blurred the borders that had been laboriously erected by the coloniser – an act which Frenchmen such as Gustave Babin considered his biggest transgression. Babin's volume (Chapter 3) is full of accusations of al-Glaoui crossing the line: presenting himself as French on occasion, using the French legal system to his own gain, buying off French functionaries, sending his sons to be educated in France, and even 'tempting' French women. His acts, as far as Babin was concerned, obscured where 'Moroccan' ended and 'French' began, and allowed Moroccanness to invade the very heart of France.

Most troubling for Babin was the fact that al-Glaoui had set up a political lobby in Paris to promote his interests – 'the Glaoua tribe on Oued Seine'. Its very existence symbolised the colony's incursion into the metropole – a fusion that, from Babin's viewpoint, threatened to destabilise the metropole. Postcolonial research notes that colonial encounters often blurred the borders separating the coloniser and the colonised. The case of al-Glaoui demonstrates this, and particularly emphasises how this process 'spilled over' into the metropole. Not unlike how colonisers arrived in the colony and manipulated the colonised, colonised subjects like al-Glaoui manipulated the coloniser, and with time found their way to its metropolitan centres of power.

Al-Glaoui also dismantled the colonial discourse's dichotomy of modern versus traditional. Arriving from the pre-colonial *qa'idal* apparatus, he called upon 'modern' and 'authentic' representations alternately, and very skilfully: one moment presenting his observers with the image of the noble savage that they expected; the next proficiently deploying attributes of French modernity, such as its legal system and journalism; and in a third moment, presenting as the cruel *qa'id* of a mountainous Amazigh tribe of the High Atlas, attacking and looting neighbouring tribes. He was an actor continuously updating his toolkit and adding new abilities to his existing skills.

In a review of Pennell's *Morocco Since 1830* (1999), Victor Vyssotsky, an amateur historian with first-hand knowledge of Morocco, having served there as an American soldier after the Second World War, wrote:

> El Glaoui was one of the most complex and enigmatic characters of the 20th Century. Pennell portrays El Glaoui basically as a supporter of the French, and of conservative forces. I believe this is somewhat of a misinterpretation. El Glaoui used the French, and was used by the French, for most of El Glaoui's years in power; however, El Glaoui's primary

motive was neither radical nor conservative, neither pro-European nor anti-European, neither a modernizer nor a foot-dragger. El Glaoui's overriding motive was to keep the Berber tribes of Central and Southern Morocco united enough, under his control, to prevent them from being completely subjugated by the French, the Arabs, or anybody else. To do that, he would have made a pact with the Devil, and several times more or less did. (Vyssotsky 2001)

Broadening the view to other Muslim Middle Eastern and North African regions while they were under imperial rule can provide additional insights into examining al-Glaoui's biography. For example, the case of Çerkes Mehmed Bey, a figure from eighteenth-century Egypt. Somewhat reminiscent of al-Glaoui, Mehmed Bey established himself as a local leader, constantly fighting with other local grandees over power and forming treaties with various tribes to consolidate his position. However, he was declared a traitor by the Ottoman Empire when, in pursuit of his goals, he established contact with foreign powers that were not just foreign but also Christian (Hathaway 1998). Local notables within existing imperial realities, such as Mehmed Bey and later Thami al-Glaoui, were accustomed to forging alliances as a way of maintaining their local power base. But, seeking the support of foreigners – especially when these were Christians – led to their subsequent designation, at least by certain agents, as traitors.

A figure closer in time to al-Glaoui was the Jordanian sheikh Mithqal al-Fayiz.

Like al-Glaoui, al-Fayiz was born in the late 1870s, into a family that led the Bani Sakhr tribal confederation for a long time. His father formed an alliance with the Ottomans; the family consequently acquired a large fortune and controlled vast territories. During the Great War, al-Fayiz presented as a skilful warrior, leading raids against other tribes. Calculating the odds in the ensuing clash between the British and the Ottomans, he placed his bet on the latter. In 1917 his elder brother, who was leading the confederation at the time, died. Al-Fayiz attempted to secure the role of leader of the tribal confederation, but lost out to his nephew. However, thanks to his support of the Ottomans, Cemal Pasha – the top official in Syria – granted him the unprecedented title (in the Transjordanian context) of Pasha. This secured al-Fayiz's loyalty to the Ottomans, at least for the time being.

But, when the British and Hashemite armies conquered the country, he switched his allegiances (Alon 2011: 99–100). When the Emirate of Transjordan was established in 1921, al-Fayiz became the paramount sheikh of the confederacy, remaining so until his death in 1967. Yoav Alon, who has studied this character, stated that his 'wheeling and dealing extended far beyond the borders of Transjordan' (Alon 2011: 98), and that he 'had a great impact on the course of events that led to the creation of the Emirate and to its consolidation as a new polity' when 'tribes and their leaders were often in opposition to the emerging state and even to the founder, Emir (later King) Abdullah' (Alon 2011: 91, 97).

The similar reference points in the biographies of al-Glaoui, al-Fayiz and the earlier Çerkes Mehmed Bey illustrate the existence of common practices and trajectories in the Middle East and North Africa during the imperial era, from the Ottoman Empire in the east to the French Empire in the west. Most apparent is the fact that under comparable political conditions and global discourses, empires governing this region chose to co-opt local grand sheikhs or *qa'ids* for their own ends. This is referred to in the Ottoman context as the 'politics of notables' (notwithstanding the debate about the term; Gelvin 2006; Toledano, in press),[2] and in the French imperial context as *caïdalisme*. This resemblance might also provide fresh perspectives for the debate raging within Ottoman historiography over the validity and nature of the term 'politics of notables'. The term, coined first by Albert Hourani (1981), was later appropriated by Middle Eastern Arab nationalist historiographies to denote emerging forms of local nationalism allegedly led by these notables. Current critiques of these historiographies maintain that the notables were neither creators nor products of local nationalisms or the colonial powers, but of local Ottoman-Arab elites who matured in the Ottoman apparatus (Toledano, in press). The case of al-Glaoui, although belonging to another geopolitical context – the intricate dynamics between the Sharifian Empire, the French Empire and Moroccan nationalism – supports the critiques' view. It shows that al-Glaoui, who arose in the Sharifian apparatus was certainly not an invention of the colonial powers, and was also not a Moroccan nationalist-movement leader.

All this notwithstanding, during the first half of the twentieth century, all of these systems became redundant due to immense global changes when, in Dickinson's words, 'the entire world exploded in a series of massive, immensely destructive revolutions and wars that determined, more or less, who would be in charge of this new world, and the societies it comprised' (Dickinson 2018: 5).

Al-Glaoui's life coincided with these global-scale clashes. During the era between the beginning of the Great War and the aftermath of the Second World War, the French, British, German and Ottoman empires all collapsed, with the United States and the Soviet Union emerging as the new superpowers. With the collapse of the old imperial order, features related to it collapsed too. One of them was the old aristocracies that lost their power and influence; first in Europe, and then with decolonisation, in the former colonies where previous power structures had become outdated – including al-Glaoui's rule in Morocco.

From a global history perspective, then, al-Glaoui's story is not a unique occurrence, but a case among resembling processes in an interconnected world, in which modes of operation were in constant flux. Recognising him as part of global phenomenon is also strengthened by the fact that many of the narratives about him and their authors are international – primarily Moroccan, French and British, but lately also Moroccan diasporic authors residing anywhere from the United States in the west to Israel in the east. All of these facilitate a visualisation of the long global process of transition from imperial to post-imperial, decolonised, and national world orders, and then into post-national and diasporic formations.

In the last five years, millions of views on social media, together with an aggregate of the new narrations, indicate that even though many years have passed since Thami al-Glaoui's death, curiosity concerning him is still on the increase. In this study, which adds another story to the Glaoui bookshelf, I have attempted to present an interconnected web of historical moments and processes, storytelling genres, techniques, and topoi, its focus being Thami al-Glaoui. This intricate composition reflects al-Glaoui's constant evolution: not just as an individual, but also as a story made and told by other people, themselves reciprocally steered in the process by the very act of telling him.

Finally, this book did not attempt to answer the question, prominent for many authors and readers alike: was Thami al-Glaoui a traitor or not? It is maintained that the absence of a tidy resolution to this question is what lends a special vitality to al-Glaoui's tale. In other words, his tale is never-ending because no narrative can propose a resolution to the story's conflicts.

I have reserved the honour of the last words of this book to Pasha al-Glaoui himself. However, these are not words uttered by the real Pasha, but rather by the imagined character ingeniously recreated by the playwright Benhadar in his *Qayd al-Qyyad*. I feel comfortable using this speech, fabricated yet based on al-Glaoui narratives as analysed by Benhadar, since – as claimed across this book – al-Glaoui is a constant co-production of the 'real' and the 'imagined'.

Concluding *Qayd al-Qyyad*'s last scene, Benhadar brings the Pasha to stand up in front of many guests he invited to his palace. Al-Glaoui looks around. He waits for the audience to hush. Then his voice rises:

> Welcome and six thousand welcomes. I gathered you today oh brothers, friends, and family in this festivity in order to learn the truth from you. During the years in which I governed Marrakesh and the inhabitants of Marrakesh, have you ever seen something you did not like? Have you ever seen or heard that I oppressed someone in this city? Has anyone ever complained about me? Or was annoyed at me? Please speak. Speak and have no fear. You have nothing to fear. Speak all that goes in your hearts and minds, with no fear or requisition. So, as our masters, the fuqaha say: silence is the sign of approval. Thank God. No one complains. No one is annoyed at me. Thank God. Now I have peace of mind and a light heart. Eat, drink, and celebrate. You are welcome! Enjoy your evening in this palace. Make yourselves at home. Celebrate and have fun, no one will bother you. (Benhadar 2011: 111)

Notes

1. By post-colonial, I mean after the colonial period, that is, from independence onwards. By postcolonial, I am referring to the sociopolitical academic approach known as Postcolonial Theory.
2. I wish to thank Ehud Toledano for generously discussing the topic with me.

Bibliography

Abitbol, Michel. 1998. *Les commerçants du roi Tujjār al-Sulṭān: une élite économique judéo-marocaine au XIXe siècle (lettres du Makhzen, traduites et annotées)*. Paris: Maisonneuve et Larose.

Abun-Nasr, Jamil. 1965. *The Tijaniyya, a Sufi Order in the Modern World*. London: Oxford University Press.

Abun-Nasr, Jamil. 1987. *A History of the Maghrib in the Islamic Period*. Cambridge: Cambridge University Press.

Acosta, Marta. 1993. 'Borges and Bertolucci: Two Conceptions of the Traitor and the Hero'. *Lucero* 4 (1): 55–69.

El Adnani, Jillali. 2010. 'Le Caïd el-Glaoui et la Tijâniyya sous l'ordre colonial français'. In *Pouvoir Central et Caïdalité au Sud du Maroc, Série Colloques et séminaires 164*, edited by Ahmed Ammalek, Abeederrahmane el Moudden and Abdelaziz Belfaïda, 7–20. Rabat: Université Mohammed V.

Afa, 'Omar. 1983. 'Mushkilat a-Nuqud wa-Muhawalat al-Islah fi Maghrib al-Qarn a-Tasi' 'Ashar'. In *Al-Islah wa-al-Mujtama' al-Maghribi fi al-Qarn a-Tasi' 'Ashar*, 73–90. Rabat: Kulliyat al-Adab.

'Afalfal, Said. 2021. "Abbas ben Bustta Sha'er al-Malhun min Murrakush'. *Murrakush al-Yawm*. 28 November.

Alon, Yoav. 2011. 'Silent Voices within the Elite: The Social Biography of a Modern Shaykh'. In *Untold Histories of the Middle East Recovering Voices from the 19th and 20th Centuries*, edited by Amy Singer, Christoph K. Neumann and Selçuk Aksin Somel, 91–105. London: Routledge.

Amenzou, Najib Mohammed. 2000. 'Un héritier du patrimoine du melhûn à Marrakech Entretien'. *Horizons Maghrébins – Le droit à la mémoire* 43: 59–64.

Amsidder, Abderrahmane, Fathallah Daghmi and Farid Toumi. 2012. 'La mobilisation sociale à l'ère des réseaux sociaux. Cas du Maroc'. *ESSACHESS. Journal for Communication Studies* 5, 1 (9): 151–61.

Andrew, Christopher M. 1968. *Théophile Delcassé and the Making of the Entente Cordiale: A Reappraisal of French Foreign Policy 1898–1905*. New York: St Martin's Press.

Annuaire des fonctionnaires et de l'armée: tout le Protectorat de la République. 1937. Casablanca: Les publications Marocaines.

Anuzul, Ali. 2005. 'Hiwar ma'a Mu'nis al-Malik al-Hassan Athani'. *Ilaf al-Maghrib*. 21 October, <https://elaph.com/Web/News Papers/2005/10/99651.html> (last accessed 7 September 2023).

al-'Arabi, Muhammad Ma'rish. 1989. *Al-Maghrib al-Aqsa fi 'Ahd a-Sultan al-Hasan al-Awwal: 1873–1894 M/1290–1311 H*. Beirut: Dar al-Gharb al-Islami.

Arendt, Hannah and Susannah Young-ah Gottlieb. 2007. *Reflections on Literature and Culture*. Stanford: Stanford University Press.

Arnaud, Louis. 1952. *Au temps des 'mehallas', ou Le Maroc de 1860 à 1912*. Casablanca: Éditions Atlantides.

Aron, Robert. 1967. *Histoire de l'épuration*. Paris: Fayard.

Arosh, Shalom, 2010. 'Harav Hakadosh, Makhlouf Abu-Haseira'. *Khut Shel Khesed* 155: 4, 23 January, <https://www.breslev.co.il/parshas_week/bo5770.pdf> (last accessed 7 September 2023).

al-Ashraf, Hassan. 2013. 'Al-Filali, al-Mu'arikh Sahib Qanun "Min Ayn Laka Hada" fi Dhimmat Allah'. *Hespress*, 1 October, <https://www.hespress.com/societe/90241.html> (last accessed 14 September 2023).

Assaraf, Robert. 2005. *Une certaine histoire des juifs du Maroc, 1860–1999*. Paris. J.-C. Gawsewitch.

al-'Atri, 'Abderrahim. 2018. 'Balaghat al-'Ayta, a-Rahamina al-Qabila bayn al-Makhzan wa-Zawiya'. *Alantologia*, 3 March, <http://alantologia.com/blogs/7391/> (last accessed 7 September 2023).

Ayache, Albert. 1982. *Le mouvement syndical au Maroc. Vol. 1. 1919–1942*. Paris: L'Harmattan.

'Ayash, Germain. 1959. *Jawanib min al-Azma al-Maliya bi-al-Maghrib ba'd al-Ghazw al-Isbani Sanat 1860*. Rabat: Royal Print.

'Ayash, Germain. 1986. *Dirasat fi Ta'rikh al-Maghrib*. Rabat: Asharika al-Maghribiyya li-Nashirin al-Mutahidin.

'Ayash, Germain. 1992. *Usul Harb Rif*. Translated by Mohamed Amine Al-Bazaz and Abdelaziz Tamsamani Khaluq. Rabat: Asharika al-Maghribiyya al-Mutahida.

Ayt al-Ketawi, Majda. 2013. '"Takhwin" al-Qaid al-'Ayadi wa "Qadhf" Hafidatihi Yajurru Ustadhan li-Tahqiq'. *Hespress*, 22 May, <https://www.hespress.com/societe/79788.html> (last accessed 7 September 2023).

Azaoui, Hamza, 2018. 'The Politics of Moroccan Identity between Colonial Intervention and Local Struggles. The Berber Crisis as a Case Study'. *SSRN*, 18 December, <https://ssrn.com/abstract=3303432> or <http://dx.doi.org/10.2139/ssrn.3303432> (last accessed 7 September 2023).

Azawi, Mulay Abdelhakim. 2022. 'Anidham al-Qa'idi wa-Tadbir al-Ma' fi Hazw Murakush'. *Lixus* 43: 118–27.

Babin, Gustave. 1902. *Après faillite: souvenirs de l'Exposition de 1900*, Paris: Dujarrie & Cie.

Babin, Gustave. 1912. *Au Maroc, par les camps et par les villes*. Paris: Grasset.

Babin, Gustave. 1916. *La Bataille de la Marne: 6–12 septembre 1915*, Paris: Plon-Nourrit et cie.

Babin, Gustave. 1919. 'The Partition of Kamerun'. *Current History* 5: 496.

Babin, Gustave. 1923. *La mysterieuse Ouaouizert, chronique d'une colonne au Maroc*. Casablanca: Librairie Faraire.

Babin, Gustave. 1932. *Son Excellence: Le Maroc sans Masque I*. First edition. Paris: Éditions G. Ficker.

Babin, Gustave. 1934. *Son Excellence: Le Maroc sans Masque I*. Second edition. Paris: Éditions G. Ficker.

Babin, Gostav. 1999. *Al-Basha al-Glawi: al-ustora wa-l-haqiqa fi hayat basha Murrakush*. Translated to Arabic by 'Abderrahim Hazal. [Morocco]: Afriqya a-Sharq.

Badissi, Riwan Alami. 2016–7. 'Essai de biographie historique de Jean Epinat, fondateur de la Compagnie des Transports et Tourisme marocain (C.T.M.) et de l'Omnium Nord-africain (O.N.A): itinéraire d'un «homme nouveau» au Protectorat français au Maroc, 1919–1956'. MA diss., University of Paris 1, Panthéon Sorbonne.

Baïda, Jamaâ. 1992. 'Situation de la Presse au Maroc sous le "Proconsulat" de Lyautey (1912-1925)'. *Hespéris-Tamuda* 30 (1): 67–92.

Baïda, Jamaâ. 1996. *La presse marocaine d'expression française: des origines à 1956*. Casablanca: Najah El-Jadida.

Baker, Steve. 1993. *Picturing the Beast: Animals, Identity and Representation*. Manchester: Manchester University Press.

Balafrej, Ahmed. 1933. 'Le Maroc sans Masque'. *Maghreb* 8: 3–6.

Baran, Paul. 1957. *The Political Economy of Growth*. New York: Monthly Review Press.

Barbe, Adam. 2016. 'Public Debt and European Expansionism in Morocco from 1860 to 1956'. MA diss., Paris School of Economics.

Barlow, Tani. 1993. *Colonial Modernity*. Durham, NC: Duke University Press.

Barlow, Tani. 1997. *Formations of Colonial Modernity in East Asia*. Durham, NC: Duke University Press.

Barthes, Roland. 1967. 'The Death of the Author'. *Aspen* nos 5–6.

Barthou, Louis. 1919. *La Bataille du Maroc*. Paris: Librairie ancienne honoré Champion.

Bayan al-Yawm. 2010. '"Qayd al-Qyyad" Masrahiyya Tarsido 'Alaqat al-Basha al-Glawi bi-Atharwa wa-Sulta al-Isti'mariyya wa-al-Mar'a'. *Bayan al-Yawm*. 13 December.

al-Bazaz, Mohamed Amine. 1992. *Ta'rikh al-Awbi'a wa-al-Maja'at bi-al-Maghrib fi-al-Qarnayn 18 wa 19*. Casablanca: Annajah al-Jadida.

Bazzaz, Sahar. 2008. 'Reading Reform Beyond the State: Salwat al-Anfas, Islamic Revival and Moroccan National History'. *The Journal of North African Studies* 13 (1): 1–13.

Bazzaz, Sahar. 2010. *Forgotten Saints: History, Power, and Politics in the Making of Modern Morocco*. Cambridge, MA: Harvard University Press.

Beckert, Sven. 2015. *Empire of Cotton: A Global History*. New York: Vintage.

Bédoucha, Geneviève. 2000. 'L'irréductible rural'. *Études rurales* 155–6: 11–24, <http://journals.openedition.org/etudesrurales/13> (last accessed 7 September 2023).

Bekraoui, Mohammed. 1980. 'La révolte de Bou Hmara (L'homme à l'ânesse), contribution à l'histoire du Maroc precolonial'. PhD diss., University of Poitiers.

Bel, Alfred. 1938. *La Religion musulmane en Berbérie, Vol. I*. Paris: Librairie orientaliste Paul Geuthner.

Benabdellah, Abdelaziz, 1958. *Les grands courants de la civilisation du Maghreb*. Casablanca: Impr. du Midi.

Ben-Ami, Isaschar. 1984. *Ha'aratzat Kdoshim Bekerev Yehudei Maroko*. Jerusalem: Magness.

Ben-Ami, Issachar. 1998. *Saint Veneration Among the Jews in Morocco*. Detroit: Wayne State University Press.

Benargane, Yassine, 2020. 'Histoire: Jean Épinat, l'ami de Thami El Glaoui, fondateur de la CTM et de l'ONA'. *Yabiladi*.

com, 3 January, <https://www.yabiladi.com/articles/details/87441/histoire-jean-epinat-l-ami-thami.html> (last accessed 7 September 2023).
Benhadar, Abdelilah. 2010. *Qayd al-Qyyad: al-Basha al-Glawi*. Rabat: Saʿad al-Warzazi.
Ben-Layashi, Samir and Bruce Maddy-Weitzman. 2010. 'Myth, History and *Realpolitik*: Morocco and its Jewish Community'. *Journal of Modern Jewish Studies* 9 (1): 89–106.
Benseddik, Fouad. 1990. *Syndicalisme et politique au Maroc. Vol. 1. 1930–1956*. Paris: Ed. L'Harmattan.
Bensoussan, David. 2012. *Il était une fois le Maroc témoignages du passé judéo-marocain*. Bloomington: iUniverse Inc.
Ben Srhir, Khalid. 2005. *Britain and Morocco During the Embassy of John Drummond Hay, 1845–1886*. London and New York: Routledge Curzon.
Bentaleb, Ali. 2004. 'Athar a-Dart al-Jibaʾi fi Tatawur al-ʿAlaqat bayn al-Makhzen wa-al-Qabaʾil 1894–1912'. PhD diss., Rabat: Faculty of Humanities and Social Sciences.
Bentaleb, Ali. 2019. 'Qiraʾa fi-Kitab Le grand vizir Madani el Mezouari el Glaoui: Une vie au service du Makhzen'. *Asenaf* 14: 81–94.
Benton, Lauren and John Muth. 2000. 'On Cultural Hybridity: Interpreting Colonial Authority and Performance'. *Journal of Colonialism and Colonial History* 1: 1–53.
Berdugo, Albert Simon. 1931. 'Notre réponse à l'Oeuvre'. *Adelante*, 1 November 1931.
Berdugo, Albert Simon. 1996. *Les Dessous d'une Conspiration*. Privately published by the author.
Bergé, Pierre and Lawrence Mynott. 2010. *Yves Saint Laurent: une passion marocaine*. Paris: La Martinière
Bernard, Augustin. 1917. 'La France au Maroc'. *Annales de Géographie*, 26 (142): 42–58.
Bernard, Augustin. 1921. *Enquête sur l'habitat rural des indigenes de l'Algérie*. Algiers: Imprimerie orientale Fontana frères.
Berque, Jacques and Paul Pascon. 1978. *Structures sociales du Haut-Atlas*. Paris: P.U.F.
Berriau, Simone. 1973. *Simone est comme ça*. Paris: R. Laffont.
Best, Antony and John Fisher. 2011. *On the Fringes of Diplomacy: Influences on British Foreign Policy, 1800–1945*. Burlington: Routledge.
Beylié, Léon de. 1909. *La Kalaa des Beni-Hammad*. Paris: Ernest Leroux.

Bhabha, Homi. 1984. 'Of Mimicry and Men: The Ambivalence of Colonial Discourse'. *October* 28: 125–33.

Bidwell, Robin. 1973. *Morocco under Colonial Rule*. London: F. Cass.

Billock, Jennifer, 2019. 'Morocco's "Hippie Trail" Still Pulses with Bohemian Counterculture'. *smithsonian.com*, 5 February, <https://www.smithsonianmag.com/travel/moroccos-hippie-trail-still-pulses-with-bohemian-culture-180968887/> (last accessed 7 September 2023).

Bilu, Yoram. 1993. *Without Bounds: The Life and Death of Rabbi Yáacov Wazana*. Jerusalem: Magness Press.

Binebine, Mahi. 1994. *Les Funérailles du lait*. Paris: Stock.

Binebine, Mahi. 1997. *L'Ombre du poète*. Paris: Stock.

Binebine, Mahi. 2002. 'An Interview on the Occasion of the International Book Fair Organized by the French Institute of Tangier from January 22 to 28, 2002', <https://data.over-blog-kiwi.com/0/62/31/30/201305/ob_898a05_entretien-avec-le-peintre-et-ecrivain-mahi-binebi.pdf> (last accessed 7 September 2023).

Binebine, Mahi. 2017. *Le Fou du roi: Roman*. Paris: Stock.

Bischoff, Eva. 2017. 'Experiences, Actors, Spaces: Dimensions of Settler Colonialism in Transnational Perspective'. *Settler Colonial Studies* 7(2): 135–40.

Bonihi, Rosemary. 1971. 'Opulence Marks Moroccan Envoy's Fete'. *The New York Times*, 4 March.

Botting, Douglas. 2000. *The Saga of Ring of Bright Water: The Enigma of Gavin Maxwell*. Glasgow: Neil Wilson Publishing.

Boujrouf, Said. 2005. 'Innovation et recomposition territoriale au Maroc. Une mise en perspective géo-historique'. In *Le territoire est mort: vive les territoires!: une refabrication au nom du développement*, edited by Antheaume Benoît and Frédéric Giraut, 133–56. Paris: IRD.

Boum, Aomar. 2010. 'Schooling in the *Bled*: Jewish Education and the Alliance Israélite Universelle in Southern Rural Morocco, 1830–1962'. *Journal of Jewish Identities* 3 (1): 1–24.

Boum, Aomar. 2011. 'Saharan Jewry: History, Memory and Imagined Identity'. *The Journal of North African Studies* 16 (3): 325–41.

Boum, Aomar. 2013. *Memories of Absence: How Muslims Remember Jews in Morocco*. Stanford: Stanford University Press.

Boum, Aomar. 2014. 'Partners against Anti-Semitism: Muslims and Jews Respond to Nazism in French North African

Colonies, 1936–1940'. *The Journal of North African Studies* 19 (4): 554–70.

Boum, Aomar and Sarah Abrevaya Stein. 2018. *The Holocaust and North Africa*. Stanford: Stanford University Press.

Boum, Aomar and Thomas Park. 2016. *Historical Dictionary of Morocco*. Lanham: Rowman and Littlefield.

Boutabqalt, Tayyeb. 1997. *Abdelkarim al-Khattabi: Harb Rif wa-Ra'y al-'Am al-'Alami*. Silsilat Shira'. Tangier: The Shira' Agency for Media and Communication Services.

Brett, Michael and Elizabeth Fentress. 1997. *The Berbers*, Oxford: Blackwell.

Brown, James. 2012. *Crossing the Strait: Morocco, Gibralter and Great Britain in the 18th and 19th Centuries*. Leiden: Brill.

Brown, Kenneth. 1976. *People of Salé: Tradition and Change in a Moroccan City 1830–1930*, Manchester: Manchester University Press.

Brown, Roger Glenn. 1970. *Fashoda Reconsidered: The Impact of Domestic Politics on French Policy in Africa, 1893–1898*. Baltimore: Johns Hopkins University Press.

Brown Spencer, Elaine. 2006. 'Spiritual Politics: Politicizing the Black Church Tradition in Anti-Colonial Praxis'. In *Anticolonialism and Education: The Politics of Resistance*, edited by George Dei and Arlo Kempf, 107–27. Rotterdam: Sense Publishers.

Budahan, Muhamad. 2013. *Fi al-Huwiyya al-Amazighiya lil-Maghrib*. Tawiza 5. Private publication.

Burke, Edmund III. 1972. 'The Image of the Moroccan State in French Ethnological Literature: A New Look at the Origin of Lyautey's Berber Policy'. In *Arabs and Berbers*, edited by Ernest Gellner and Charles Micaud, 175–99. London: Duckworth.

Burke, Edmund III. 1998. 'Theorizing the Histories of Colonialism and Nationalism in the Arab Maghrib'. *Arab Studies Quarterly* 20 (2): 5–20.

Burke, Edmund III. 2007. 'The Creation of the Moroccan Colonial Archive, 1880–1930'. *History and Anthropology*, 18 (1): 1–9.

Burke, Edmund III. 2014. *The Ethnographic State: France and the Invention of Moroccan Islam*. Berkeley: University of California Press.

al-Buzidi, Ahmad. 2007. "Alaqat al-Glawi bi-l-Usar al-Qa'diyya bi-Wadi Dar'a'. *Al-Ta'rikh al-'Arabi: Majla 'Ilmyya bi-l-Ta'rikh al-'Arabi wa-l Ifkar al-Islami* 41: 95–136.

al-Buzidi, Ahmad 2010. "Alafihat Fiyadat Tamtukalet Yaklawa

min al-Moʻarada ila al-Mowajaha'. In *a-Sulta al-Markaziya wa-Zaʻamat al-Mahaliyya bi-al-Janub al-Maghribi*, edited by Ahmed ʻAmalek, ʻAbderrahmane al-Mudden and ʻAbdelʻaziz bel al-Fayda, 87–99. Casablanca: Matab'at a-Najah al-Jadida.

Cahm, Eric. 2016. *Dreyfus Affair in French Society and Politics*. Hoboken: Taylor and Francis.

Campbell, Caroline. 2018. 'Experiencing Colonial Violence from Below: French and Amazigh Entanglement during the Conquest of Morocco'. *French History* 32 (4): 532–53.

Canetti, Elias. 1978. *The Voices of Marrakesh*. New York: Seabury Press.

Cannadine, David. 1999. *The Decline and Fall of the British Aristocracy*. London: Papermac.

Cannadine, David. 2001. *Ornamentalism*. London: Allen Lane.

de Certeau, Michel. 1988. *The Writing of History*. Translated by Tom Conley. New York: Columbia University Press.

Chafik, Mohamed. 2000. 'Le vécu individuel d'une appartenance identitaire pluridimensionnelle'. *Tawiza* 44, <http://membres.lycos.fr/tawiza/Tawiza44> (last accessed 7 September 2023).

Chamberlain, Muriel Evelyn. 2013. *The Scramble for Africa*. London and New York: Routledge.

Chartier, Roger. 2011. 'History, Time, and Space'. *Republics of Letters: A Journal for the Study of Knowledge, Politics, and the Arts* 2 (2), June, <http://rofl.stanford.edu/node/100> (last accessed 7 September 2023).

Chekblog, n.d. 'Tighdouine au temps du glaoui', <http://chekblog.over-blog.com/article-tighdouine-au-temps-du-glaoui-78416233.html> (last accessed 7 September 2023).

Cherkaoui, Mouna. 2000. 'Institutional Reform and Efficiency of the Budget Process: A Case Study of Morocco'. *Topics in Middle Eastern and North African Economies* 2, <http://www.luc.edu/publications/academic/> (last accessed 7 September 2023).

Chetrit, Joseph. 2021. 'Sultan Sidi Mohammed ben Youssef and the Jews of Morocco during the Second World War: New Discoveries'. In *Jews and Muslims in Morocco*, edited by Joseph Chetrit, Jane S. Gerber and Drora Arussy, 73–104. Lanham: Lexington Books.

Chifaâ, Nassir. n.d. 'Entretien avec Abdessadeq El Glaoui, auteur du livre Le Ralliement'. *Maroc Hebdo*, <http://www.ouarzazate.com/fr2/glaoui_fils.html> (last accessed 7 September 2023).

Christelow, Allan. 1985. *Muslim Law Courts and the French Colonial State in Algeria*. Princeton: Princeton University Press.

Clancy-Smith, Julia Ann and Frances Gouda. 1998. *Domesticating the Empire: Race, Gender, and Family Life in French and Dutch Colonialism*. Charolettesville: University Press of Virginia.

Clark, Elizabeth. 2009. *History, Theory, Text: Historians and the Linguistic Turn*. Cambridge, MA: Harvard University Press,

Cobban, Alfred. 1965. *A History of Modern France*. Harmondsworth: Penguin.

Cochrane, Lauren. 2016. *50 Women's Fashion Icons that Changed the World*. London: Conran Octopus.

Cohen, Anne. 2015. 'Honoring the Moroccan King who Saved the Jews'. *International March of the Living*, 24 December, <https://www.motl.org/honoring-the-moroccan-king-who-saved-the-jews/> (last accessed 7 September 2023).

Cohen, Shana. 2003. 'Alienation and Globalization in Morocco: Addressing the Social and Political Impact of Market Integration'. *Comparative Studies in Society and History* 45 (1): 168–89.

Cooke, James J. 1973. *New French Imperialism: 1880–1910: The Third Republic and Colonial Expansion*. Hamden: Archon Books.

Conklin, Alice. 1997. *A Mission to Civilize: The Republican Idea of Empire in France and West Africa, 1895–1930*. Stanford: Stanford University Press.

Conklin, Alice. 2000. 'Boundaries Unbound: Teaching French History as Colonial History and Colonial History as French History'. *French Historical Studies* 23 (2): 215–38.

Conrad, Sebastian. 2016. *What is Global History?* Princeton: Princeton University Press.

Cooper, Frederick and Ann Laura Stoler. 1997. *Tensions of Empire: Colonial Cultures in a Bourgeois World*. Berkeley: University of California Press.

Cooper, Nicola. 2001. *France in Indochina: Colonial Encounters*. Oxford and New York: Bloomsbury.

Cornet, Charel Joseph Alexandre. 1914. *A la conquête du Maroc sud*. Paris: Plon.

Crowe, David. 2014. *War Crimes, Genocide, and Justice: A Global History*. New York: Palgrave Macmillan.

Curran, Vivian Grosswald. 1998. 'The Legalization of Racism in a Constitutional State: Democracy's Suicide in Vichy France'. *Hastings Law Journal* 50: 1–96.

Daoud, Zakya. 1996. *Féminisme et politique au Maghreb: sept décennies de lute.* Casablanca: Eddif.
Daoud, Zakya and Maaati Monjib. 2000. *Ben Barka: Une vie, une mort.* Paris: Michalon.
Davis, Blair, Robert Anderson and Jan Walls, eds. 2016. *Rashomon Effects: Kurosawa, Rashomon and their Legacies.* Abingdon: Routledge.
Davison, Roderic H. 2016. *Reform in the Ottoman Empire, 1856–1876.* Princeton: Princeton University Press.
Dayani, Murad and John Waterbury. 2018. *20 Fibrayer wa-Ma'alat a-Tahawul a-Dimuqrati fi al-Maghrib.* Beirut: Al-Markaz al-'Arabi li-l-Abhath wa-Dirasat a-Siyasat.
Derrida, Jacques. 1996. *Archive Fever.* Chicago and London: University of Chicago Press.
Devine, Christine 2011. 'Introduction'. In *Turning Points and Transformations: Essays on Language, Literature and Culture,* edited by Christine Marie Hendry and Christine Devine, xi–xvi. Newcastle upon Tyne: Cambridge Scholars Publishers.
Dickinson, Edward Ross. 2018. *The World in the Long Twentieth Century: An Interpretive History.* Oakland: University of California Press.
Dunn, Ross. 1977. *Resistance in the Desert.* London: Routledge.
Dwyer, Daisy Hilse. 1978. *Images and Self-Images: Male and Female in Morocco,* New York: Columbia University Press.
Earle, Jason W. 2013. 'Conspiracies and Secret Societies in Interwar French Literature'. PhD diss., Columbia University.
Eickelman, Dale. 1989. *The Middle East: An Anthropological Approach.* Englewood Cliffs: Prentice Hall.
Eickelman, Dale. 1992. *Knowledge and Power in Morocco: The Education of a Twentieth-Century Moroccan Notable.* Princeton: Princeton University Press.
Enayat, Hadi. 2013. *Law, State, and Society in Modern Iran: Constitutionalism, Autocracy, and Legal Reform, 1906–1941.* New York: Palgrave Macmillan.
Ennaji, Mohammed and Ernest Gellner. 1994. *Soldats, domestiques et concubines: L'esclavage au Maroc au XIXe siècle.* Casablanca: Eddif.
Faivre, Maurice. 2002. 'Le colonel Paul Schoen du SLNA au comité Parodi'. *Guerres mondiales et conflits contemporains* 208 (4): 69–89.
Fenwick, Gillian. 1998. *George Orwell – A Bibliography.* Winchester, New Castle, DE: St Paul's Bibliographies.

Fernandes-Dias, Maria-Suzette 2007. 'Ode to Human Resilience: Bearing Witness to Surviving Tazmamart'. In *The Camp: Narratives of Internment and Exclusion*, edited by Marta Marin Domine and Colman Hogan, 172–95. Newcastle: Cambridge Scholars.

Fernandez, Juan. 2018. 'Story Makes History, Theory Makes Story: Developing Rüsen's Historik in Logical and Semiotic Directions'. *History and Theory* 57 (1): 75–103.

Fernea, Elizabeth Warnock. 1975. *A Street in Marrakech*, New York: Anchor Press.

Ferrati, Abdesselam. 2021. 'Global Media and Cultural Identity: Opportunities and Challenges for Morocco in the Digital Era'. *International Journal of Language and Literary Studies* 3 (3): 109–20.

Filali, ʿAbdelkarim. 2006. *Al-Tarikh al-Siyasi li-l-Maghrib al-ʿArabi al-Kabir*, vol. 11. [Egypt]: Sharikat Nas li-Tebaʿa wa-Nashr.

Filali, Rachid. 2014. 'El Glaoui: Portrait d'un collabo'. *Tinjdad24.com*, <http://tinjdad24.com/?p=12664> (last accessed 7 September 2023).

Fish, Stanley Eugene. 1980. *Is there a Text in this Class? The Authority of Interpretive Communities*. Cambridge, MA: Harvard University Press.

Forsdick, Charles, 2004. 'Colonial and Postcolonial Experience'. In *Encyclopedia of Modern French Thought*, edited by Christopher John Murray, 146–51. New York: Fitzroy Dearborn.

Forster, E. M. 1928. *A Passage to India*. London: Arnold.

Foucault, Michel. 1972. *The Archaeology of Knowledge and The Discourse on Language*. Translated by Alan Mark Sheridan Smith. New York: Pantheon Books.

Fraher, Richard M. 1988. 'Criminal Defense as Narrative: Storytelling and Royal Pardons in Renaissance France (a review of *Fiction in the Archives: Pardon Tales and Their Tellers in Sixteenth Century France* by Natalie Zemon Davis)'. *The University of Chicago Law Review* 55 (3): 1010–15.

Freud, Esther. 1993. *Hideous Kinky*. New York: Penguin Books.

Galland, Gabriel. 1913. *Le Maroc: un empire qui se réveille*. Paris: Librairie National.

Geertz, Clifford. 1968. *Islam Observed*. New Haven: Yale University Press.

Geertz, Hildred, Clifford Geertz and Lawrence Rosen. 1979. *Meaning and Order in Moroccan Society: Three Essays in Cultural Analysis*. Cambridge: Cambridge University Press.

Gellner, Ernest. 1969. *Saints of the Atlas*. Chicago: University of Chicago Press.
Gellner, Ernest. 1970. 'Review of "Lords of the Atlas. The Rise and Fall of the House of Glaoua 1893–1956", by Gavin Maxwell'. *Middle Eastern Studies*, 6 (2): 224–7.
Gellner, Ernest and Charles Antoine Micaud. 1972. *Arabs and Berbers*. London: Duckworth.
Gelvin, James, L. 2006. 'The "Politics of Notables" Forty Years After'. *Middle East Studies Association Bulletin* 40 (1): 19–29.
Genette, Gérard. 1982. *Palimpsestes: la littérature au second degré*. Paris: Seuil.
Gershovich, Moshe, 1992. 'A Moroccan Saint-Cyr'. *Middle Eastern Studies*, 28 (2): 231–57.
Gershovich, Moshe. 2000. *French Military Rule in Morocco: Colonialism and its Consequences*. London and Portland: Frank Cass Publishers.
Ghosh, B. N. 2017. *Dependency Theory Revisited*. London: Routledge.
Gildea, Robert. 1996. *France 1870–1914*. London and New York: Routledge.
Gillis, John R. 1994. 'Memory and Identity: The History of a Relationship'. In *Commemorations: The Politics of National Identity*, edited by John R. Gillis, 3–22. Princeton: Princeton University Press
Ginio, Ruth. 2017. *The French Army and its African Soldiers: The Years of Decolonization*. Lincoln, NE and London: University of Nebraska Press.
Ginzburg, Carlo. 1980. *The Cheese and the Worms: The Cosmos of a Sixteenth-century Miller*. Translated by John Tedeschi and Anne C. Tedeschi. London: Routledge.
al-Glaoui, Thami. 1933. *Son Excellence. En réponse à une campagne infâme: quelques documents*, Marrakesh: Imprimerie de l'Atlas.
El Glaoui, Abderrahman El Mezouari. 2017. *Le Grand Vizir Madani el-Mezouari el-Glaoui, une vie au service du Makhzen*. Casablanca: Éditions la Croisée des Chemins.
El Glaoui, Abdessadeq. 2004. *Le ralliement. Le Glaoui, mon père*. Rabat: Marsam.
al-Glawi, ʿAbd al-Sadiq al-Mazwari. 2004. *Abi al-Haj al-Tuhami al-Glawi al-Awba*. Rabat: Manshurat Marsam.
Gottreich, Emily. 2016. *Le Mellah de Marrakech*. Rabat: Faculté des Lettres et des Sciences Humaines de Rabat.

Gottreich, Emily. 2020. *Jewish Morocco: A History from Pre-Islamic to Postcolonial Times*. London: I. B. Tauris.

Goundafi, Omar. 2013. *Un Caïd du Maroc d'Antan; Taïb Goundafi (1855–1928)*. Rabat: Marsam.

Grangaud, Isabelle and M'hamed Oualdi. 2016. 'Tout est-il colonial dans le Maghreb? Ce que les travaux des historiens modernistes peuvent apporter'. *Revue d'histoire moderne & contemporaine* 63–2 (2): 133–56.

Grant, Jonathan. 2007. *Rulers, Guns and Money*. Cambridge, MA and London: Harvard University Press.

Gringauz, Lev, 2019. 'Morocco Conference Reveals Thorny Debate on Holocaust,' *Times of Israel*, 2 July, <https://jewishweek.timesofisrael.com/morocco-conference-reveals-thorny-debate-on-holocaust/> (last accessed 7 September 2023).

El Guabli, Brahim. 2021. 'Tankra Tamazight: The Revival of Amazigh Indigeneity in Literature and Art'. *Maghreb*, 1 November, <https://www.jadaliyya.com/Details/43440> (last accessed 7 September 2023).

El Guabli, Brahim. 2022. My 'Amazighitude: On the Indigenous Identity of North Africa'. *Maghreb*, 14 June, <https://www.jadaliyya.com/Details/44207> (last accessed 7 September 2023).

Guedj, David. 2018. 'Post-Second World War Praise Poetry, Lament and a Utopian Treatise in Morocco: Historical Literature on the Theme of the Second World War'. *Journal of Modern Jewish Studies* 17: 1–17.

Guerin, Adam. 2011. 'Racial Myth, Colonial Reform, and the Invention of Customary Law in Morocco, 1912–1930'. *The Journal of North African Studies* 16 (3): 361–80.

Guillaume, Alfred. 1946. *Les Berbères marocains et la pacification de l'Atlas Central 1912–1933*. Paris: R. Julliard.

Hacohen, Dvora, 2003. *Immigrants in Turmoil: Mass Immigration to Israel and Its Repercussions in the 1950s and After*. Syracuse: Syracuse University Press.

Hagan, Helen. 2011. *Tazz'Unt: Ecology, Social Order and Ritual in the Tessawt Valley of the High Atlas of Morocco*. Xlibris Corporation.

Hagan, Helen. 2013. *Fifty Years in America*. Xlibris Corporation.

Al-Hahi, Rashid. 2013. *Al-Amazighia wa al-Maghrib al-Mahdur*. Rabat: Ashabaka al-Amazighia min Ajl al-Muwatana.

Hai, Ambreen. 1997. 'On Truth and Lie in a Colonial Sense:

Kipling's Tales of Tale-telling'. *English Literary History* 64 (2): 599–625.

Haine, Scott. 2000. *The History of France*. Westport: Greenwood Publishing Group.

Hajji, Muhammad. 1998. *Mutanawaʿat Muhammad Hajji*. Beirut: Dar al-Gharb al-Islami.

Hall, Ian. 2017. 'The History of International Thought and International Relations Theory: From Context to Interpretation'. *International Relations* 31 (3): 241–60.

al-Hamamsi, Mohammed. 2012. 'Badiʿ Khayri . . . Turath Shiʿri wa-Masrahi'. *Middle East Online*, 5 August (last accessed 7 September 2023).

Hamilton, Carolyn, Verne Harris, Jane Taylor, Michele Pickover, Graeme Reid and Razia Saleh. 2002. *Refiguring the Archive*. Dordrecht: Springer Science and Business Media.

Hamilton, Richard. 2019. *Tangier: From the Romans to the Rolling Stones*. London: Tauris Parke.

Hammoudi, Abdellah. 1993. *The Victim and Its Masks: An Essay on Sacrifice and Masquerade in the Maghreb*. Chicago: University of Chicago Press.

Hammoudi, Abdellah. 1997. *Master and Disciple: The Cultural Foundations of Moroccan Authoritarianism*. Chicago: University of Chicago Press.

Hannoum, Abdelmajid. 2001. *Colonial Histories, Postcolonial Memories: The Legend of the Kahina, a North African Heroine*. Westport: Heinemann.

Harakat, Ibrahim. 1994. *Atayarat Asiyasiyya wa-al-Fikriyya bi-al-Maghrib Khilal al-Qarnayn wa-Nisf Qabl al-Himaya*. Casablanca: Dar Rashad al-Haditha.

Harari, Joseph, George. 1974. *Toldot Yehudei el-Magreb*. Holon: Greenberg Press.

Harries, Alexander. 2016. 'Faire le bordel: The Regulation of Urban Prostitution in Morocco'. MA diss., University of Oxford.

Harris, Walter Burton. 1889. *The Land of the African Sultan*. London: Sampson Low, Marston, Searle & Rivington.

Harris, Walter Burton. 1895. *Tafilet: The Narrative of a Journey of Exploration in the Atlas Mountains and the Oases of the North-West Sahara*. Edinburgh and London: Blackwood and Sons.

Harris, Walter Burton. 1921. *Morocco That Was*. Edinburgh and London: William Blackwood and Sons.

Harris, Walter Burton. 1927. *France, Spain and the Rif*. London: Longmans, Green.

Hart, David. 1972. 'The Tribe in Modern Morocco: Two Case Studies'. In *Arabs and Berbers*, edited by Ernest Gellner and Antoine Micaud, 25–58. London: Duckworth.

Hashas, Mohammed. 2013. 'Moroccan Exceptionalism Examined: Constitutional Insights pre- and post-2011'. *IAI Working Papers* 13 (34).

Haskin, Gili. 2017. 'Yehudei Maroko – Pulkhan Hakdoshim', <https://www.gilihaskin.com/25779-2/> (last accessed 7 September 2023).

Hathaway, Jane. 1998. 'Çerkes Mehmed Bey: Rebel, Traitor, Hero?' *Turkish Studies Association Bulletin* 22 (1): 108–15.

Hawwas, Muhammad. 2018. 'Hizb a-Shura wa-l-Istiqlal fi al-Maghrib al-Aqsa 1946–1956: Namudhaj li-Dawr a-Tahriri li-Nukhba fi al-Maghrib al-'Arabi'. *Majalat a-Dirasat a-Ta'rikh-iyya* 21(1): 162–94.

Heckman, Alma Rachel. 2021. *The Sultan's Communists*. Stanford: Stanford University Press.

Heine, Heinrich. 1908. *Almansor*. Berlin, Leipzig, Wien and Stuttgart: Deutsches Verlagshaus Bong & Co., <http://www.gutenberg.org/files/45600/45600-h/45600-h.htm> (last accessed 7 September 2023).

Heurtebise, Damien. 2007. *Secrétariat Général du Protectorat: Commissions d'Épurations 1940–1945*. Unpublished Internal Report. Nantes: Centre des Archives diplomatiques de Nantes.

Hima, Hamid. 2019. 'A-Dhakira Bayna Ta'rikh al-Akademi wa-Ta'lif al-Mudaras'. *Asinag* 14: 71–80.

Hoffman, Bernard. 1967. *The Structure of Traditional Moroccan Rural Society*. The Hague, Paris: Mouton.

Hoffman, Katherine. 2010. 'Berber Law by French Means: Customary Courts in the Moroccan Hinterlands, 1930–1956'. *Comparative Studies in Society and History* 52 (4): 851–80.

Holland, Eugene. 2003. 'Representation and Misrepresentation in Postcolonial Literature and Theory'. *Research in African Literature* 34 (1): 159–73.

Hourani, Albert. 1982. 'Ottoman Reform and the Politics of Notables'. In *The Emergence of the Modern Middle East*, edited by Albert Hourani, 36–66. Berkeley and Los Angeles: University of California Press.

House, Jim. 2012. 'L'impossible Contrôle d'une Ville Coloniale? Casablanca, Décembre 1952'. *Genèses* 1: 78–103.

House, Jim. 2018. 'Colonial Containment? Repression of Pro-Independence Street Demonstrations in Algiers, Casablanca and Paris, 1945–1962'. *War in History* 25 (2): 172–201.

Humann, Heather Duerre. 2018. *Another Me: The Doppelganger in 21st Century Fiction, Television and Film*. Jefferson, NC: McFarland and Company, Inc., Publishers.

El Ibrahimi, Abdennacer. 2022. *Amazighité et contestations au Maroc*. Leiden and Boston: Brill.

Iburki, Omar. 2000. *Azahira al-Qa'idiyya: al-Qa'id al-'Ayadi a-Rahmani Namudhajan: Musahamat fi Dirasat al-Mujtama' al-Maghribi*. Morocco: publisher not identified.

Iburki, Omar, 2013. 'Hal Kana al-Qa'id al-'Iyadi Kha'inan lil-Watan am Wafiyyan li-Sultan?' *Hespress*, 29 May <https://www.hespress.com/orbites/80327.html> (last accessed 7 September 2023).

Ihrai-Aouchar, Amina. 1978. 'Décoloniser L'Histoire'. *Lamalif* 96: 38–43.

Ihrai-Aouchar, Amina. 1982. 'La presse nationaliste et le régime de Protectorat au Maroc dans l'entre-deux-guerre'. *Revue de l'Occident musulman et de la Méditerranée* 34: 91–104.

Ilahiane, Hsain. 2006. *Historical Dictionary of the Berbers (Imazighen)*. Lanham, MD: Scarecrow Press.

İnalcik, Halil. 1976. *Application of the Tanzimat and Its Social Effects*. Lisse: De Ridder Press.

Irvine, William. 2006. *Between Justice and Politics: The Ligue Des Droits De L'Homme, 1898–1945*. Stanford: Stanford University Press.

Janon, René. 1953. *Sultans Glaoui and Co*. Algiers: Dominique.

Jay, Cleo, 2015. 'A Berber Spring: The Breakthrough of Amazigh Minorities in the Uprisings' Aftermath'. In *Contentious Politics in the Middle East. Middle East Today*, edited by Fawaz A. Gerges, 331–47. New York: Palgrave Macmillan.

Jay, Salim. 2005. *Dictionnaire des écrivains marocains*. Paris: Eddif.

Jay, Salim. 2012. 'Des universitaires interpellés par le temps présent et les fonctions de l'historien'. *Le Soir Echos*, 18 June <https://www.maghress.com/fr/lesoir/53110> (last accessed 7 September 2023).

Jebrou, 'Abdellatif. 2005. *Qira'ton fi kitab al-Ustadh 'Abdessadeq al-Glawi 'an walidihi al-Basha Tuhami al-Glawi*. Mohammedia: Fedala Press.

Jelili, Atiku. 2014. 'I Will Not Stroll with Thami El Glaoui', <https://vimeo.com/91068242> (last accessed 3 September 2023).
Joffe, E. George. 1985. 'The Moroccan Nationalist Movement: Istiqlal, the Sultan, and the Country'. *The Journal of African History* 26 (4): 289–307.
Joll, James and Gordon Martel. 2013. *The Origins of the First World War*. Abingdon: Routledge.
Joly, Laurent. 2006. *Vichy dans la 'solution finale': Histoire du Commissariat Général aux Questions Juives, 1941–1944*. Paris: Le grand libre du mois, D.L.
Jones, Joseph. 1984. *The Politics of Transport in Twentieth-century France*. Kingston and Montreal: McGill – Queen's University Press.
Kafadar, Cemal. 1997-8. 'The Question of Ottoman Decline'. *Harvard Middle Eastern and Islamic Review* 4 (1–2): 30–75.
Kalpakian, Jack. 2011. 'Current Moroccan Anti-Terrorism Policy'. *ARI*, <http://biblioteca.ribei.org/2197/1/ARI-89-2011.pdf> (last accessed 7 September 2023).
Kammerer, Gladys. 1943. 'The Political Theory of Vichy'. *The Journal of Politics* 5 (4): 407–34.
Kaplan, Samuel. 2002. 'Documenting History, Historicizing Documentation: French Military Officials' Ethnological Reports on Cilicia'. *Comparative Studies in Society and History* 44 (2): 344–69.
al-Karuri, Mahmud Salih and Ahmad Hamid Sadeq. 2016. 'Mu'tamar al-Jazira al-Khadra' 'Am 1906 wa-Tada'iyatihi 'ala al-Maghrib'. *Majalat Surra Man Raa* 13 (47): 1–20.
Katz, Jonathan Glustrom. 2006. *Murder in Marrakesh: Émile Mauchamp and the French Colonial Adventure*. Bloomington: Indiana University Press.
Kenbib, Mohammed. 1994. *Juifs et Musulmans au Maroc, 1859–1948*. Rabat: Université Mohammed V.
Kenbib, Mohammed. 2016. *Juifs et Musulmans au Maroc*. Paris: Tallandier.
al-Khadimi, Alal. 1986. 'Majlis al-A'yan wa-Mashru' al-Islahat al-Faransiyya bi-al-Maghrib sanat 1905'. In *Al-Islah wa-al-Mujtama' al-Maghribi fi al-Qarn a-Tasi' 'Ashar*, 259–92. Rabat: Kulliyat al-Adab.
al-Khadimi, Alal. 2009. *Al-Haraka al-Hafidiyya aw al-Maghrib Qubayla Fard al-Himaya al-Faransiyya, al-Wad'iyya a-Dakhiliyya*

wa-Tahdidat al-'Alakat al-Kharijiyya 1894–1912. Rabat: Dar Abiraqraq.

Khakee, Anna. 2017. 'Democracy Aid or Autocracy Aid? Unintended Effects of Democracy Assistance in Morocco'. *The Journal of North African Studies* 22 (2): 238–58.

Khalidi, Hicham. 2018. 'Where Are We Now? To Whom Do We Ascribe 'Moroccanness'?' /re/framing the international 2: 52–4.

Khalufi, Mohammed Saghir. 1993. *Bu-Hamara, Min al-Jihad ila at'amur: al-Maghrib a-Sharqi wa-Rif min 1900 ila 1909: Dirassa wa-Wataqe'*. Rabat: Dar Nashr al-Ma'rifa.

Khayr Allah, Khayr Allah. 2007. *Al-Maghrib fi 'Ahd Muhamed Sades: Madha Taghayyar*. Beirut: Dar Saqi.

Kilkelly, Colin. 2014. 'Books about Morocco to Inspire You Before You Go'. *AFKTravel*, 24 December, <https://afktravel.com/62895/books-about-morocco/> (last accessed 7 September 2023).

Kurzac-Souali, Anne-Claire. 2010. 'Intentions, Representations et Patrimonialisation Plurielle des Medinas Marocaines'. *Hesperis-Tamuda* 45: 89–117.

Labadie-Lagrave, H. 1925. *Le mensonge marocain: contribution à l'histoire «vraie» du Maroc*. Casablanca: Impr. ouvrière.

Lahbabi, Mohamed. 1975. *Le Gouvernement marocain à l'aube du vingtième siècle*. Casablanca: Éditions Maghrébines.

Lahnite, Abraham. 2011. *L'application du Traité de Fès dans la région du Souss*. Tome 3. Paris: L'Harmattan.

Larkin, Maurice. 2014. *Church and State after the Dreyfus Affair: The Separation Issue in France*. London: Palgrave Macmillan.

Laroui, Abdallah. 1977. *The History of the Maghrib: An Interpretive Essay*. Princeton: Princeton University Press.

Laskier, Michael. 1983. *The Alliance Israelite Universelle and the Jewish Communities of Morocco: 1862–1962*. Albany: State University of New York.

Laskier, Michael. 1991. 'Between Vichy Antisemitism and German Harassment: The Jews of North Africa during the Early 1940s'. *Modern Judaism* 11: 343–69.

Lebovics, Herman. 1992. *True France: The Wars Over Cultural Identity, 1900–1945*. Ithaca: Cornell University Press.

Lefévre, Jean, 1957. 'L'occupation du palais de l'ancien pacha aurait permis la saisie de documents importants'. *Le Monde*, 4 May 1957.

Le Glay, Maurice. 1923. *Itto: Récit marocain d'amour et de bataille*. Paris: Librairie Plon.

Lepp, Ignace. 1954. *Midi sonne au Maroc*. Paris: Aubier.

Le Prévost, Jacques. 1968. *El Glaoui*. Paris: Éditions du dialogue société d'éditions internationales.
Le Prévost, Jacques. 2013. *El Glaoui*. Rabat: Dar al Aman.
Leveau, Rémy. 1985. *Le fellah marocain, defenseur du trone*. Paris: Presses de Sciences Po.
Leveau, Rémy. 1998. 'A Democratic Transition in Morocco?' *Le Monde Diplomatique*, December, <https://mondediplo.com/1998/12/06maroc> (last accessed 7 September 2023).
Levi, Giovanni. 1989. 'Les usages de la biographie'. *Annales. Economies, sociétés, civilisations* 44 (6): 1325–36.
Lorcin, Patricia. 1995. *Imperial Identities: Stereotyping, Prejudice and Race in Colonial Algeria*. New York: I. B. Tauris.
Ma' al-'Aynayn, Muhammad a-Shaykh a-Talib Akhyar a-Shaykh. 2005. *A-Shaykh Ma' al-'Aynayn: 'Ulama' wa-Umara' fi Muwajahat al-Isti'mar al-Urubbi*. Rabat: Mu'assasat a-Shaykh Murabbihi Rabbuhu li-Ihya' al-Turath wa-a-Tabadul a-Thaqafi.
Maddy-Weitzman, Bruce. 2001. 'Contested Identities: Berbers, "Berberism" and State in North Africa'. *Journal of North African Studies* 6 (3): 23–47.
Maddy-Weitzman, Bruce. 2011. *The Berber Identity Movement and the Challenge to North African States*. Austin: University of Texas Press.
Maddy-Weitzman, Bruce. 2012. 'Abdelkrim: Whose Hero Is He? The Politics of Contested Memory in Today's Morocco'. *The Brown Journal of World Affairs* 18 (2): 141–9.
Maddy-Weitzman, Bruce. 2022. *Amazigh Politics in the Wake of the Arab Spring*. Austin: University of Texas Press.
Maghraoui, Abdeslam M. 2001. 'Monarchy and Political Reform in Morocco'. *Journal of Democracy* 12 (1): 73–86.
Maghraoui, Driss. 1998. 'Moroccan Colonial Soldiers: Between Selective Memory and Collective Memory'. *Arab Studies Quarterly* 20: 21–41.
Maghraoui, Driss. 2009. 'The Moroccan Colonial Soldiers: Between Selective Memory and Collective Memory'. In *Beyond Colonialism and Nationalism in the Maghrib: History, Culture and Politics*, edited by Ahmida Ali Abdullatif, 49–72. New York: Palgrave Macmillan.
Magnússon, Sigurður Gylfi. 2017. 'Far-Reaching Microhistory: The Use of Microhistorical Perspective in a Globalized World'. *Rethinking History* 21 (3): 312–41.
Maher, Vanessa. 1974. *Women and Property in Morocco*. Cambridge: Cambridge University Press.

Mangin, Charles. 1910. *La Force noir*. Paris: Hachette.
El Mansour, Mohamed. 1997. 'Moroccan Historiography Since Independence'. In *The Maghrib in Question: Essays in History and Historiography*, edited by Michel Le Gall and Kenneth Perkins, 109–21. Austin: University of Texas Press.
El Mansour, Mohamed. 1996. 'Salafis and Modernists in the Moroccan Nationalist Movement'. In *Islamism and Secularism in North Africa*, edited by John Ruedy, 53–71. New York: St Martin's.
Manzanera, Ángel Luis Riquelme. 2001. 'En Memoria de D. Alberto S. Berdugo Toledano'. *Revista Cangilón* 22: 79–85.
Marçais, Georges. 1946. *La Berbérie Musulmane et l'Orient au Moyen Age*. Paris: Aubier.
Margadant, Jo Burr. 1996. 'Introduction: The New Biography in Historical Practice'. *French Historical Studies* 19 (4): 1045–58.
Marglin, Jessica. 2016. *Across Legal Lines: Jews and Muslims in Modern Morocco*. New Haven: Yale University Press.
El Marhoum, Adil, Elhadj Ezzahid and Lahboub Zouiri. 2020. 'L'enseignement à distance au Maroc: perceptions des étudiants en période du confinement Covid-19 à partir d'une enquête nationale', <https://www.researchgate.net/profile/Elhadj-Ezzahid/publication/343404368_L'enseignement_a_distance_au_Maroc_perceptions_des_etudiants_en_periode_du_confinement_Covid-19_a_partir_d'une_enquete_nationale_1/links/5f28a1b3458515b7290064c8/Lenseignement-a-distance-au-Maroc-perceptions-des-etudiants-en-periode-du-confinement-Covid-19-a-partir-dune-enquete-nationale-1.pdf> (last accessed 7 September 2023).
Marrus, Michael and Robert Paxton. 2005. *Vichy France and the Jews*. Stanford: Stanford University Press.
Maxwell Gavin. 1952. *Harpoon at a Venture*. London: Rupert Hart-Davis.
Maxwell, Gavin. 1957a. *God Protect Me from My Friends*. London: Readers Union Longmans Green.
Maxwell, Gavin. 1957b. *A Reed Shaken by the Wind*. London: Longman, Green & Co.
Maxwell, Gavin. 1960. *Ring of Bright Water*. London: Longmans.
Maxwell, Gavin. 1963. *The Rocks Remain*, London: Longmans.
Maxwell, Gavin. 1966. *The Lords of the Atlas*, New York: E. P. Dutton & Co.

Maxwell, Gavin. 1968. *El-Glaoui, dernier seigneur de l'Atlas: (1893-1956)*. Paris: Arthème Fayard.
Maxwell, Gavin. 2016. *El-Glaoui, dernier seigneur de l'Atlas*. Translated by Jacques Papy. Rabat: Dar Al Aman.
Mayeur, Jean-Marie and Madeleine Rebirioux. 1994. *The Third Republic from Its Origins to the Great War, 1871-1914*. Cambridge: Cambridge University Press.
Mayne, Peter. 1957. *The Alleys of Marrakesh*. London: Travel Book Club.
Mayne, P, 1982. *A Year in Marrakesh*, London: Eland Books.
McCord, Norman and Bill Purdue. 2007. *British History 1815-1914*. Oxford: Oxford University Press.
McDougall, James. 2018. 'Sovereignty, Governance, and Political Community in the Ottoman Empire and North Africa'. In *Reimagining Democracy in the Mediterranean, 1780-1860*, edited by Joanna Innes and Mark Philp, 127-52. Oxford: Oxford University Press.
Meister, Daniel. 2018. 'The Biographical Turn and the Case for Historical Biography'. *History Compass* 16 (1) n. pag.
Mernissi, Fatima. 1987. *Beyond the Veil, Male-Female Dynamics in Modern Muslim Society*. Bloomington: Indiana University Press.
Merry, Sally. 1991. 'Law and Colonialism'. *Law & Society Review* 25 (4): 889-922.
Miège, Jean-Louis, Zaki M'barek and Tayeb Habi. 1992. *Le Maroc et la mer*. Rabat: Editions la porte.
Miller, Susan Gilson. 2006. *Disorienting Encounters: Travels of a Moroccan Scholar in France in 1845-1846: The Voyage of Muhammad as-Saffar*. Berkeley: University of California Press.
Miller, Susan Gilson. 2013. *A History of Modern Morocco*. New York: Cambridge University Press.
Miller, Susan Gilson. 2021. *Years of Glory: Nelly Benatar and the Pursuit of Justice in Wartime North Africa*. Stanford: Stanford University Press.
Mitchell, Timothy. 1989. 'The World as Exhibition'. *Comparative Studies in Society and History* 31 (2): 217-36.
Miyara, Shlomo Zalman. 2012. *Geniuses of the Avihatzeira Family: Their History, Biographies and Legacy for Generations from the Sixteenth to the Twentieth Century*. Volume 3. Haifa: Maor Yitzhak Institute (in Hebrew).

M'Jid, Najat Maalla. 2010. 'L'Initiative nationale pour le développement humain: une initiative novatrice et ambitieuse pour lutter contre la pauvreté et l'exclusion au Maroc'. In *Interventions sociales et rôle de l'État: Regards croisés*, edited by Daniel Verba, 41–6. Rennes: Presses de l'EHESP.

Montagne, Robert. 1924. 'Coutumes et légends de la cote berbère du Maroc'. *Hespéris* 4: 357–403.

Montagne, Robert. 1930. *Les Berbères et le makhzen dans le sud du Maroc*, Paris: Librairie Félix Alcan.

Moore, Niamh, Andrea Salter, Liz Stanley and Maria Tamboukou. 2017. *The Archive Project: Archival Research in the Social Sciences*. Abingdon: Routledge.

More, Charles. 2014. *Britain in the Twentieth Century*. Abingdon: Routledge.

Moretta, John Anthony. 2017. *The Hippies: A 1960s History*. Jefferson, NC: McFarland & Company, Inc., Publishers.

Morsy, Magali. 1986. 'La part des troupes maghrébines dans les combats de la Libération suivi d'une discussion'. *Provence Historique* 144: 155–81.

El Moudden, Abderrahmane. 1997. 'The Eighteenth Century: A Poor Relation in the Historiography of Morocco'. In *The Maghrib in Question: Essays in History and Historiography*, edited by Michel Le Gall and Kenneth Perkins, 201–11. Austin: University of Texas Press.

Mouré, Kenneth. 2007. 'Economic Choice in Dark Times: The Vichy Economy'. *French Politics, Culture & Society* 25 (1): 108–30.

Munslow, Alun. 2019. *Narrative and History*. London: Red Globe Press.

Mutafakkir, Ahmad. 2007. *Nuzum al-qawafi fi al-Basha al-Glawi: ibbana wala'ihi lil-'arsh al-'Alawi*. Marrakesh.

Najmabadi, Afsaneh. 1998. *The Story of the Daughters of Quchan: Gender and National Memory in Iranian History*. Syracuse: Syracuse University Press.

Nasaw, David. 2009. 'Historians and Biography: Introduction'. *The American Historical Review* 114 (3): 573–8.

al-Nasiri, Ahmad ben Khaled. 1954. *Kitab al-Istisqa li-Akhbar Duwal al-Maghrib al-Aqsa*. Casablanca: Dar al-Kutub.

Nataf, Félix. 1987. *Jean Épinat, Un homme, une aventure au Maroc*. Paris: Souffles.

Natanzon, S. 2004. 'Harav she'atzar et Hitler'. *Or Hazohar* 389, <http://www.ha-zohar.info/wp-content/uploads/2013/09/%D7%90%D7%95%D7%A8-%D7%94%D7%96%D7%95%D7%94

%D7%A8-389-%D7%9E%D7%A8%D7%95%D7%A7%D7%95-21.pdf?x5633> (last accessed 7 September 2023).

Nelson, Harold. 1985. *Morocco: A Country Study*. Washington DC: American University.

Nizri Yigal. 2018. 'Judeo-Moroccan Traditions and the Age of European Expansionism in North Africa'. In *The Sephardic Atlantic*, edited by Sina Rauschenbach and Jonathan Schorsch, 333–60. Basingstoke: Palgrave Macmillan.

Nora, Pierre. 1987. *Essais d'ego-histoire: Maurice Agulhon, Pierre Chaunu, Georges Duby, Raoul Girardet, Jacques Le Goff, Michelle Perrot, René Remond*. Paris: Gallimard.

Nordman, Daniel. 1980–1. 'Les Expéditions de Moulay Hassan: Essai statistique'. *Hespéris-Tamuda* 19: 123–52.

Norris, Irvine H. T. 1982. *The Berbers in Arabic Literature*. London and Beirut: Longman and Librairie du Liban.

Orwell, George, 1939. 'Marrakech'. *New Writing*, New Series No. 3, Christmas 1939.

Otero-Pailos, Jorge. 1998. 'Casablanca's Régime: The Shifting Aesthetics of Political Technologies (1907–1943)', *Postmodern Culture* 8 (2), n. pag.

Ouaknine-Yekutieli, Orit. 2003. 'Hasipur she'eino Nigmar: Thami al-Glaoui vehaHistoria shel Maroko haModernit'. MA diss., Ben-Gurion University of the Negev.

Ouaknine-Yekutieli, Orit. 2015. 'Corporatism as a Contested Sphere – Trade Organization in Morocco under the Vichy Regime'. *Journal of the Economic and Social History of the Orient* 58 (4): 453–89.

Ouaknine-Yekutieli, Orit. 2017. 'Khitukhim Le'oreck velerokhav Sivei Ha'Arkhiyon'. *Jama'a* 23: 131–40.

Ouaknine-Yekutieli, Orit. 2019. 'Jewish Women in Intercommunal Political Movements in Colonial Morocco'. *Journal of Modern Jewish Studies* 18 (2): 227–44.

Ouaknine-Yekutieli, Orit. 2020. 'Bled ma-fihash Yahud ma-fihash Ta'arikh – Kheker 'HaYehudim shelano' beMaroko'. *Jama'a* 25: 111–32.

Ouaknine-Yekutieli, Orit, 2022. 'The Purification (l'épuration) of the French Protectorate in Morocco under the Vichy Regime'. *Perspectives, Revue de l'Université Hébraïque de Jérusalem* 26: 76–99.

Ouaknine-Yekutieli, Orit and Yigal S. Nizri. 2016 '"My Heart is in the Maghrib": Aspects of Cultural Revival of the Moroccan Diaspora in Israel'. *Hespéris Tamuda* 51 (3): 165–94.

Ouardighi, Abderrahim. 1975. *La Grande crise franco-marocaine: 1952–1956, toute l'épopée de la résistance armée marocaine*. Rabat: L'Imprimerie nouvelle.

Oufkir, Malika and Michèle Fitoussi. 2000. *La prisonniere*. New York: Doubleday.

Pandolfo, Stefania. 1997. *The Impasse of the Angels*. Chicago: University of Chicago Press.

Pascon, Paul. 1981. 'Al-Fitrat al-Kubra li-l-Qa'idfiya'. *Al-Majalat al-Mar'ribiya li-al-Iqtis'adiya wa-al-Ijtima*, 5–6: 67–149.

Pascon, Paul. 1986. *Capitalism and Agriculture in the Haouz of Marrakesh*. London: Kegan Paul International.

Paxton, Robert. 1972. *La France de Vichy: 1940–1944*. Paris: Editions du Seuil.

Pedaya, Haviva. 2011. *Walking Beyond the Trauma*. Tel Aviv: Resling (in Hebrew).

Peets, Leonora. 1988. *Women of Marrakech, 1930–1970*. Durham, NC: Duke University Press.

Pennell, Richard. 2017. 'How and Why to Remember the Rif War (1921–2021)'. *The Journal of North African Studies* 22 (5): 798–820.

Pennell, Richard. 1999. *Morocco Since 1830: A History*. New York: New York University Press.

Pennell, Richard. 2000. *Morocco Since 1830: A History*. New York: New York University Press.

Perkins, Kenneth. 1981. *Qaids, Captains and Colons*. New York: Africana Pub. Co.

Perrier, Antoine. 2017. 'Le makhzen introuvable: les sources Marocaines de l'histoire de l'état à l'époque contemporaine'. *Hypotheses*, 30 May, <https://cjb.hypotheses.org/225> (last accessed 17 August 2003).

Peyron, Michael. 1999. 'Glaoui/Glaoua'. *Encyclopédie Berbère* 21: 3151–60, <http://encyclopedieberbere.revues.org/1736> (last accessed 7 September 2023).

Peyron, Michael. 2010. 'Recent Cases of Incomplete Academic Research on Morocco's Berbers'. *The Journal of North African Studies* 15 (2): 157–71.

Popkin, Jeremy. 2013. *A History of Modern France*. London and New York: Routledge.

Porch, Douglas. 2005. *The Conquest of Morocco*. New York: Farrar, Strauss and Giroux.

Puyo, Jean-Yves. 2012. 'Une application du «rôle social de l'officier» (Lyautey): les services du contrôle politique dans le

Protectorat français au Maroc (1912–1926)'. *Les Études Sociales* 2, 156: 85–100.
El Qadéry, Mustapha. 2007. 'La justice coloniale des «berbères» et l'État national au Maroc'. *L'Année du Maghreb* 3: 17–37.
El Qadéry, Mustapha. 2010. 'L'Afrique a-t-elle perdu le Nord?' *Cahiers d'études africaines* 198-199-200: 731–54, <http://journals.openedition.org/etudesafricaines/16336> (last accessed 7 September 2023).
Al-Quds al-Arabi. 2012. "Indama Tusbihu as-Shakhsiyya al-Ta'rikhiyya Muharikan li-l-fi'l al-Drami fi al-Masrah'. *Al-Quds al-Arabi*, 1 June.
Rabinow, Paul. 1989. *French Modern Norms and Forms of the Social Environment*. Cambridge, MA and London: MIT Press.
Rachik, Hassan and Rahma Bourqia. 2011. 'La sociologie au Maroc'. *SociologieS*, <http://journals.openedition.org/sociologies/3719> (last accessed 7 September 2023).
Rajamäe, Pilvi. 2020. 'The Call of the Wild: John Buchan's Heroes and the Decline of British Aristocracy'. *Interlitteraria* 24 (2): 540–55.
Ram, Haggai. 2020. *Intoxicating Zion: A Social History of Hashish in Mandatory Palestine and Israel*. Stanford: Stanford University Press.
Rami, Ahmed. 1983. 'Corruption and Crime in Hassan's Court'. *Interviú*, 1–7 June, <https://rami.tv/eng/biog.htm> (last accessed 31 August 2023).
Ramzi, Sofia. 2015. *Muhamed Sades, Malik al-Islah wa-Taghyeer*. Beirut: Dar al-'Arabiya li-l-'Ulum Nashirun.
Raz-Krakotzkin, Amnon. 2005. *Censorship, Editing and the Text: Catholic Censorship and Hebrew Literature in the Sixteenth Century*. Jerusalem: Magnes Press (in Hebrew).
Rees, Phil and Al Jazeera Investigative Unit. 2015. 'The Carjacking and the Friendly Moroccan Ambassador'. *Aljazeera.com*, 24 February, <https://www.aljazeera.com/blogs/middleeast/2015/02/car-jacking-friendly-moroccan-ambassador-spy-cables-guardian-150224160248529.html> (last accessed 7 September 2023).
Reich, Bernard. 1990. *Political Leaders of the Contemporary Middle East and North Africa: A Biographical Dictionary*. New York: Greenwood Press.
Reid, Alan and Brian Osborne. 1997. *Discovering Scottish Writers*. Edinburgh: Scottish Cultural Press.

Richards, Thomas. 1993. *The Imperial Archive: Knowledge and the Fantasy of Empire*. London and New York: Verso.

Rivet, Daniel. 1992. 'La recrudescence des epidémies au Maroc durant la deuxième guerre mondiale: essai de mésure et d'interprétation'. *Hésperis-Tamuda* 30 (1): 93–109.

Rivet, Daniel. 1996. *Lyautey et l'institution du protectorat français au Maroc: 1912–1925*. Paris: L'Harmattan.

Rivet, Daniel. 2012. *Histoire du Maroc*. Paris: Fayard.

Robisheaux, Thomas. 2017. 'Microhistory and the Historical Imagination: New Frontiers'. *Journal of Medieval and Early Modern Studies* 47 (1): 1–6.

Rodrigue, Aron. 2010. 'Alliance Israélite Universelle Network'. In *Encyclopedia of Jews in the Islamic World Online*, edited by Norman A. Stillman, <https://referenceworks.brillonline.com/entries/encyclopedia-of-jews-in-the-islamic-world/alliance-israelite-universelle-network-COM_0001600> (last accessed 7 September 2023).

Rogers, Joel Augustus. 1972 [1946]. *World's Great Men of Color*. New York: Macmaillan Publishing.

Rogerson, Barnaby. 1995. 'Through a Glass Darkly: North Africa as Seen through English Travel Writing'. *Art Quarterly*, <http://www.barnabyrogerson.com/articles/63.html> (last accessed 7 September 2023).

Rollinde, Marguerite. 2002. *Le mouvement marocain des droits de l'homme: entre consensus national et engagement citoyen*. Paris: Karthala.

Rosen, Lawrence. 1980–1. 'Equity and Discretion in a Modern Islamic Legal System'. *Law and Society Review* 15: 217–45.

Rosen, Lawrence. 1984. *Bargaining for Reality: The Construction of Social Relations in a Muslim Community*. Chicago: University of Chicago Press.

Rosen, Lawrence. 1989. *The Anthropology of Justice: Law as Culture in Islamic Society*. Cambridge: Cambridge University Press.

Rosen, Lawrence. 1999. 'Legal Pluralism and Cultural Unity in Morocco'. In *Legal Pluralism in the Arab World*, edited by Baudouin Dupret, Maurits Berger and Laila Al-Zwaini, 89–95. The Hague: Kluwer Law International.

Roth, Norman. 1982. 'The Kahina: Legendary Material in the Accounts'. *Maghreb Review* 7: 122–5.

Roth, Wendy and Jal Mehta. 2002. 'The Rashomon Effect: Combining Positivist and Interpretivist Approaches in the

Analysis of Contested Events'. *Sociological Methods Research* 31 (2): 131–73.

Rowe, David M. 1999. 'World Economic Expansion and National Security in Pre–World War I Europe'. *International Organization* 53 (2): 195–231.

Rubin, Avi. 2017. 'Was there a Rule of Law in the Late Ottoman Empire?' *British Journal of Middle Eastern Studies* 46 (1): 1–16.

Ruxton, Ian. 2018. *The Diaries of Sir Ernest Mason Satow, 1889–1895: Uruguay and Morocco*. Ian Ruxton via Lulu.com.

Said, Edward. 1978. *Orientalism*. New York: Pantheon.

Said, Edward. 1993. *Culture and Imperialism*. New York: Knopf.

Salon maghrébin du livre. 2018. *Lettres du Maghreb*. Agence de l'Oriental, <https://orientalmarocain.com/wp-content/uploads/2020/12/File_1_816.pdf> (last accessed 23 August 2022).

Samama, Yvonne. 2006. 'Thami al-Glaoui ou l'émergence d'un pouvoir parallèle fort au Maroc (fin XIXe – milieu XXe siècle)'. In *Être notable au Maghreb*, edited by Abdelhamid Hénia, 248–60. Tunis: Institut de recherche sur le Magheb contemporain.

Sangmuah, Egya. 1992. 'Sultan Mohammed ben Youssef's American Strategy and the Diplomacy of North African Liberation, 1943–61'. *Journal of Contemporary History* 27 (1): 129–48.

Saunier, Pierre-Yves and Akira Iriye. 2009. 'Introduction: The Professor and the Madman'. In *The Palgrave Dictionary of Transnational History from the Mid-19th Century to the Present Day*, edited by Akira Iriye and Pierre-Yves Saunier, xviii. New York: Palgrave.

Sauvy, Alfred. 1969. 'The Economic Crisis of the 1930s in France'. *Journal of Contemporary History* 4 (4): 21–35.

Schayegh, Cyrus. 2017. *The Middle East and the Making of the Modern World*. Cambridge, MA: Harvard University Press.

Schoen, Paul. 1938. *Le Pacha de Marrakech*. Unpublished report. Nantes: Centre des Archives diplomatiques de Nantes, file 1MA/282 95.

Schroeter, Daniel. 1988. *Merchants of Essaouira*. Cambridge: Cambridge University Press.

Schroeter, Daniel. 2002. *The Sultan's Jew: Morocco and the Sephardi World*. Stanford: Stanford University Press.

Schroeter, Daniel. 2008. 'The Shifting Boundaries of Moroccan Jewish Identities'. *Jewish Social Studies* 15 (1): 145–64.

Schroeter, Daniel. 2010. 'Corcos Family'. In *Encyclopedia of Jews in the Islamic World*, edited by Norman A. Stillman, <https://referenceworks.brillonline.com/entries/encyclopedia-of-jews-in-the-islamic-world/corcos-family-COM_0005780> (last accessed 7 September 2023).

Schroeter, Daniel. 2018. 'Between Metropole and French North Africa: Vichy's Anti-Semitic Legislation and Colonialism's Racial Hierarchies'. In *The Holocaust and North Africa*, edited by Aomar Boum and Sarah Abrevaya Stein, 218–39. Stanford: Stanford University Press.

Schroeter, Daniel 2021. 'Jews and the Moroccan Monarchy in the Age of Imperialism'. In *Jews and Muslims in Morocco*, edited by Joseph Chetrit, Jane S. Gerber and Drora Arussy, 39–72. Lanham: Lexington Books.

Scott, Otto. 1978. 'Revolution and the Press'. *Imprimis* 7 (6): 1–6.

Sebti, Abdelahad. 2013. 'Colonial Experience and Territorial Practices'. In *Revisiting the Colonial Past in Morocco*, edited by Driss Maghraoui, 38–56. London and New York: Routledge.

Sedrati, Anass. 2017. 'The Use of YouTube in Morocco as an Instrument of Social Critique and Opposition: Three Cases: Richard Azzouz, Hamid El Mahdaouy, Najib El Mokhtari'. BA diss., Stockholm University.

Shahar, Ido. 2012. 'Legal Pluralism Incarnate: An Institutional Perspective on Courts of Law in Colonial and Postcolonial Settings'. *Journal of Legal Pluralism* 65: 133–63.

Shaw, Stanford and Ezel Kural Shaw. 1977. *History of the Ottoman Empire and Modern Turkey: The Rise of Modern Turkey, 1808–1975, Volume 2*. Cambridge: Cambridge University Press.

Silver, Chris. 2021. 'Judah Sebag – Elmella and Adon Olam [Sides 1-2], Disques Tam Tam, c. 1955', 22 April, <https://gharamophone.com/author/cbsilver071017/> (last accessed 7 September 2023).

Singer, Barnett. 1998. 'Lyautey: An Interpretation of the Man and French Imperialism'. *Journal of Contemporary History* 26 (1): 131–57.

Slavin, David. 1998. 'French Colonial Film Before and After *Itto*: From Berber Myth to Race War'. *French Historical Studies* 21: 125–55.

Slouschz, Nahum. 1927. *Travels in North Africa*. Philadelphia: Jewish Publication Society of America.

Stanzel, Franz. 1992. 'Consonant and Dissonant Closure in *Death in Venice* and *The Dead*'. In *Neverending Stories: Toward a Critical*

Narratology, edited by Ann Fehn, Ingeborg Hoesterey and Maria Tatar, 112–23. Princeton: Princeton University Press.

Staszak, Jean-François. 2015. 'Colonial Tourism and Prostitution: The Visit to Bousbir in Casablanca (1924–1955)'. *Via,* 8, <http://journals.openedition.org/viatourism/431> (last accessed 7 September 2023).

Stearn, Roger. 2006. 'Maclean, Sir Harry Aubrey de Vere (1848–1920)'. In *Oxford Dictionary of National Biography,* online edition, <http://www.oxforddnb.com/view/article/34781> (last accessed 7 September 2023).

Stewart, Ian. 2018. 'Number Symbolism'. *Encyclopedia Britannica,* <https://www.britannica.com/topic/number-symbolism> (last accessed 7 September 2023).

Stickland, Graham. 2015. *The Philippeville Massacres (1955) as Part of the Algerian War (1954–1962) and Their Enduring Legacy.* Leeds: University of Leeds.

Stoler, Ann Laura. 2002. 'Colonial Archives and the Arts of Governance on the Content in the Form'. In *Refiguring the Archive,* edited by Carolyn Hamilton, Verne Harris, Jane Taylor, Michele Pickover, Graeme Reid and Razia Saleh, 83–102. Dordrecht: Springer Science and Business Media.

Stoler, Ann Laura. 2009. *Along the Archival Grain: Epistemic Anxieties and Colonial Common Sense.* Princeton: Princeton University Press.

Stone-Mediatore, Shari. 2003. *Reading Across Borders: Storytelling and Knowledges of Resistance.* New York: Palgrave Macmillan.

Stott, L. 2007 (January 2004). 'Maxwell, Gavin (1914–1969), Writer and Naturalist'. *Oxford Dictionary of National Biography,* <https://www-oxforddnb-com.ezproxy.bgu.ac.il/view/10.1093/ref:odnb/9780198614128.001.0001/odnb-9780198614128-e-34959> (last accessed 30 September 2023).

Sussi, Muhammad al-Mukhtar. 2014. *Al-Ma'sul fi al-Ilghiyyin wa-Asatidhatihim wa-Talamidhihim wa-Asdiqa'ihim a-Susiyin.* Dar al-Kitab al-'Ilmiyya.

Terem, Etty. 2014. *Old Texts, New Practices: Islamic Reform in Modern Morocco.* Stanford: Stanford University Press.

Tolédano, Joseph. 2017. *Redifa veHatzala: Yehudei Maroko Takhat Shilton Vichy.* Lod: Orot Yahadut Hamagreb and the Claim Conference.

Toledano, Ehud. In press. 'The Study of Elites in the Arabic-speaking Area in the Late Ottoman Period: The Rise and Fall of the "Politics of Notables Paradigm"?' (in Hebrew).

Touzani, Naʿima Harraj, 1979. *Li-Umana' bi-al-Maghrib fiʿahd a-Sultan Mulay al-Hassan 1290–1311, 1873–1894: Musahama fi Dirasat a-Nizam al-Mali bi-al-Maghrib*. Rabat: Faculty of Letters and Human Sciences.

Trouillot, Michel-Rolph. 1995. *Silencing the Past: Power and the Production of History*. Boston: Beacon Press.

Tsur, Yaron. 2001. *Kehila Kru'a: Yehudei Maroko vehale'umiut: 1943–1954*. Tel Aviv: Am Oved.

Vaffier, Ernest. 1917. 'Une Grande Famille Marocaine: Les Glaoua'. *France-Maroc: revue mensuelle illustrée* 15 December, 22–31.

Verdú, Antonio Sánchez and Francisco Martínez Torres. 2001. 'Alberto Berdugo Toledano Nos Dijo Adioós'. *Revista Cangilón* 22: 77–9.

Vermeren, Pierre, 2011. 'L'historiographie des deux côtés de la Méditerranée'. *Revue histoire politique* 15 (3): 147–66.

Veyne, Paul. 1984. *Writing History: Essay on Epistemology*. Translated by Mina Moore-Rinvolucri. Middletown: Wesleyan University Press.

Vogl, Mary. 2015. 'Closed Encounters: Tangier, the Arts, and the North–South Divide'. In *Mediterranean Encounters in the City*, edited by Michela Ardizzoni and Valerio Ferme, 37–56. London: Lexington Books.

Vyssotsky, Victor A. 2001. 'Review of Pennell, C. R. (1999) *Morocco Since 1830: A History*'. Amazon Customer Review, <http://www.amazon.com/exec/obidos/tg/detail/-/0814766773/qid=1039778025/sr=1-2/ref=sr_1_2/104-3765413-2073535?v=glance&s=books> (last accessed 7 September 2023).

Waller, John. 1996. *The Unseen War in Europe: Espionage and Conspiracy in the Second World War*. New York: Random House.

Wallerstein, Immanuel. 1991. 'The Construction of Peoplehood: Raciscm, Nationalism, Ethnicity'. In *Race, Nation, Class*, edited by Etienne Balibar and Immanuel Maurice Wallerstein, 71–85. London: Verso.

Waterbury, John. 1970. *The Commander of the Faithful*. New York: Columbia University Press.

Weil, Patrick. 2008. *How to Be French: Nationality in the Making since 1789*. Durham, NC: Duke University Press.

Weisberg, Robert and Michael Hanne. 2019. *Narrative and Metaphor in the Law*. Cambridge: Cambridge University Press.

West, Gordon. 1932. *By Bus to the Sahara*. London: Black Swan.

White, Hayden. 1973. *Metahistory: The Historical Imagination in Nineteenth-century Europe*. Baltimore: Johns Hopkins University Press.

White, Hayden. 1978. *Tropics of Discourse: Essays in Cultural Criticism*. Baltimore: Johns Hopkins University Press.

Willis, Michael. 2008. 'The Politics of Berber (Amazigh) Identity: Algeria and Morocco Compared'. In *North Africa: Politics, Religion, and the Limits of Transformation*, edited by Yahia Zoubir and Haizam Amirah-Fernández, 227–42. London: Routledge.

Wilson, Stephen. 1968. 'History and Traditionalism: Maurras and the Action Française'. *Journal of the History of Ideas* 29 (3): 365–80.

Wyrtzen, Jonathan. 2015. *Making Morocco: Colonial Intervention and the Politics of Identity*. Ithaca and London: Cornell University Press.

Yasin, Ibrahim. 2003. *Janub Atlas Murrakush Tahta Hukm al-Faransiyyin wa-al-Qadah al-Glawiyyin: Athar al-Ihtilal al-Faransi li-Bilad Ayt wa-Uzgit*. Rabat: Dar Abi Raqraq.

Yerushalmi, Yosef Hayim. 1996. *Zakhor: Jewish History and Jewish Memory*. Seattle: University of Washington Press.

Zafrani, Haim. 2005. *Two Thousand Years of Jewish Life in Morocco*. Jersey City, NJ: Ktav.

Zdatny, Steven. 1986. 'The Corporatist Word and the Modernist Deed: Artisans and Political Economy in Vichy France'. *European History Quarterly* 16: 155–79.

Zebib, Najib. 1995. *Al-Mawsu'a al-'Amma li-Ta'rikh al-Maghrib wa-al-Andalus*. Beirut: Dar al-Amir li-Taqafa wa-al-'Ulum.

Zemon Davis, Natalie. 1983. *The Return of Martin Guerre*. Cambridge, MA: Harvard University Press.

Zemon Davis, Natalie. 1987. *Fiction in the Archives: Pardon Tales and Their Tellers in Sixteenth Century France*. Stanford: Stanford University Press.

Zenner, Walter P. 1990. 'Jewish Retainers as Power Brokers'. *The Jewish Quarterly Review* 81 (1/2): 127–49.

Zimmermann, Maurice. 1905. 'Mission du comité du Maroc. Explorations de MM. de Segonzac, Gentil, de Flotte de Roquevaire'. *Annales de géographie* 75: 285–6.

Zisenwine, Daniel. 2010. *The Emergence of Nationalist Politics in Morocco*. London and New York: I. B. Tauris.

Zur Mühlen, Hermynia. 2010. *The End and the Beginning: The Book of My Life, Volume 1*. Open Book Publishers.

Index

Note: *f* indicates a figure

'Abd al-'Aziz (Sultan of Morocco), 26–9, 100–1, 138
'Abd al-Hafidh (Sultan of Morocco), 28, 30–1
Abu-Haseira, Makhlouf, 158–9*f*
Abun Nasr, Jamil, 186–7
affaires indigènes officers, 37
Agadir Charter (*mithaq Agadir*), 194–5
Alaoui, Marouane Lamharzi, 221–3
   Atarikh li-Maqrawnash ('The history that we were not taught'), 223
'Alawi dynasty, 21, 48, 127
Algeciras treaty, 135
Algeria, 38
Algerian War of Independence, 122
Alleys of Marrakesh, The (Mayne, Peter), 178
Almansor (Heine, Heinrich), 12
Amazigh, the, 10, 34–5, 36–7, 64–5, 85, 126–7, 170, 187
   historiography, 199–202
   history, erasing/forgetting, 196–7
Amazighness, 193–7
America, 100, 106

anti-Semitism, 58, 106, 136, 137, 148–50
Après faillite, souvenirs de l'Exposition de 1900 (After Failure, Memories of the 1900 Exhibition (Babin, Gustave), 58
Arabisation, 193–4
Arabs, the, 64–5, 85, 196
archives, 12, 14–17, 206
L'Association des anciens des affaires Algériennes (The Algerian Affairs Section Alumni Association), 38
Atarikh li-Maqrawnash ('The history that we were not taught') (Alaoui, Marouane Lamharzi), 223
L'Atlas, 73
Attias, Jacob, 147
Au Maroc, par les camps et par les villes (In Morocco, through the Camps and through the Cities) (Babin, Gustave), 59
al-'Ayadi, Milud Ben al-Hachemi, 33, 68–9

Baïda, Jamaâ, 63
Babin, Gustave, 7, 9, 11, 44–5, 57–63, 138

INDEX

adventure-novel format, 235
anti-Semitism, 148
Après faillite, souvenirs de l'Exposition de 1900 (After Failure, Memories of the 1900 Exhibition, 58
Au Maroc, par les camps et par les villes (In Morocco, through the Camps and through the Cities), 59
Bataille de la Marne, La (The Battle of the Marne), 59
Chronique du Sud (Chronicle of the South), 62
colonial discourse, 88
colonialism, 81
critical writing style, 72
death, 91
defamation lawsuit, 76–80
al-Glaoui, Thami, criticism of, 32, 45, 60, 62–3, 68–70, 73, 80–7, 147–8, 182, 198, 238
al-Glaoui's courts, 75
identity politics, 84
journalism, views on, 72–3
Maroc sans Masque, Le (Morocco without a Mask), 80
Marrakesh rescue, 32, 81
Maxwell, Gavin, 181–2
mysterieuse Ouaouizert, chronique d'une colonne au Maroc, La (Mysterious Ouaouizert, Chronicle of a Column in Morocco), 60
racial hierarchies, 85
Son Excellence: le Maroc sans Masque (His Excellency: Morocco without a Mask), 12, 69–70, 71–2, 82, 147, 171, 181, 207, 235
truth or loyalty debate, 80–4
Balafrej, Ahmed, 70
Barthou, Louis, 46–7

Bataille de la Marne, La (The Battle of the Marne) (Babin, Gustave), 59
Baume, General de la, 78
Ben ʿArafa (Sultan of Morocco), 121, 122
Ben Barka, Mehdi, 158, 196
Ben Rimoge *see* Berrimoj
ben Mohamed, Mohamed, 225
Ben Musa, Ba-Ahmed, 26
Benhadar, Abdelilah, 7, 216–19, 242
  Qayd al-Qyyad: al-Basha al-Glawi (The Commander: The Pasha al-Glaoui), 216–19, 242
Bentaleb, Ali, 215
Benton, Lauren and Muth, John, 87–8
Berdugo, Albert Simon, 11, 124, 134–6, 137–8, 140, 235
  Dessous d'une Conspiration, Les (The Conspiracy's Inside Story), 134, 139–42, 161–2
  al-Glaoui, Thami, secretary to, 138–9, 152–3
  Jews, meeting rural, 152–3
  Mohammed V, deposition of, 140–1
Berriau, Simone, 96n
Berrimoj (Ben Rimoge), 146, 148
Barthes, Roland
  Death of the Author, The, 9
Berber Edict, 64–5, 193, 196, 200
Berber Feast, 116–17
Berber law, 35
Berber Manifesto, 195, 199
Berber policy, 37
Berbers, The (Brett, Michael and Fentress, Elizabeth), 200–1
Bidwell, Robin, 184–5
  Morocco under Colonial Rule, 184–5
bin Ziad, Tariq, 199

Binebine, Aziz, 204, 225
Binebine, Mahi, 204–5, 235
    Fou du roi, Le (The King's Fool), 225
    Funérailles du lait, Les (The Milk Funerals), 204, 205
    L'Ombre du poète (The Shadow of the Poet), 204–5
Binebine, Mohamed, 225
biographies, 13–14, 213–15
bled makhzen, 34, 54n, 64
bled, siba, 34, 54n, 64
Botting, Douglas, 171, 173
Bouhmara Revolt, 27
Boyer de Latour, Pierre, 122
Brett, Michael and Fentress, Elizabeth
    Berbers, The, 200–1
Bureau d'aide aux Musulmans Français (Office of Aid to French Muslims), 38

caïdalisme, 3, 39–40, 127, 240; see also *qa'idal* system
CAM (Comité d'Action Marocaine [Moroccan Action Committee]), 88
Canetti, Elias, 153, 178
    Voices of Marrakesh, The, 153, 178
Carette-Bouvet, Pierre, 68
Casablanca terror attacks, 206
Catroux, Georges, 68–9, 76
censorship, 12–13
Chamberlaim, Neville, 47
Charmy, Roland, 136–7
Chronique du Sud (Chronicle of the South), 62
Churchill, Winston, 100, 191n
collaboration
    French Second World War, 103, 126
    Moroccan colonial period, 186–7, 237
colonial historiographies, 231–2

colonialism, 8, 13, 27, 40, 58–9, 84
    archives, 15
    Babin, Gustave, 81
    colonial cultural conduct, 87–8
    colonial discourse, 87–8
    decolonising project, 175
    European, 58–9
    French, 8, 27, 29, 34, 36–7, 40, 58, 61–2, 81, 84, 233
    justification for, 29, 34, 36
    mission civilisatrice, 34, 36, 61, 81, 233
    in Morocco, 8, 27, 29, 34, 36, 40, 81, 233
    otherness, 87
    westernisation, 87
    see also imperialism
Comité d'Action Marocaine (Moroccan Action Committee [CAM]), 88
Comité d'études Berbères (Committee of Berber studies), 36–7
Comité national pour les Musulmans Français (National Committee for French Muslims), 38
conspiracy theories, 100–2, 185–6
Cooper, Nicola, 61–2
Corcos, Yoshua, 145–6
Corcos family, 144–6
Cri Marocain, Le, 68, 73
cultural pluralism discourse, 219, 234

Dahan, Elie, 153
Dahir Berbere (Berber Edict), 64–5
Dar El Basha (The House of the Pasha museum), 224
Death of the Author, The (Barthes, Roland), 9

demonstrations, 206–7
Dessous d'une Conspiration, Les (The Conspiracy's Inside Story) (Berdugo, Albert), 134, 139–42, 161–2
doppelgänger, 33
Dreyfus Affair, 58

education, 142
Egypt, 239
Eickelman, Dale, 65
  Power and Knowledge in Morocco, 65
Encyclopédie Berbère, 201–2
Epinat, Jean, 98–9, 103–4
L'Ère Française, 60, 70
Esther Scroll, 159–60
Europe, 31, 58–9
  education system, 142
  imperialism, 27, 58–9
  military training, 25

al-Fassi, Allal, 190, 196
Fatma, Lalla, 47
al-Fayiz, Mithqal, 239–40
Fernandez, Juan
  Story Makes History, Theory Makes Story, 6
Fernea, Elizabeth, 176–7
  Street in Marrakech, A, 176–7, 178
Fes, 31, 34
fête berbere (Berber Feast), 117
Filali, 'Abdelkarim, 23, 30
Fou du roi, Le (The King's Fool) (Binebine, Mah), 225
France, 8, 16, 27, 29, 31, 57–8, 88–9
  anti-Semitism, 149–50
  Bidwell, Robin, 184
  caïdalisme, 3, 39–40, 127, 240
  coalition, 116
  collaboration, 103, 126
  Colonial Exposition (1931), 84

colonialism, 8, 27, 29, 34, 36–7, 40, 58, 61–2, 81, 84, 233
conspiracy theories, 100–3
debt creation, 67
Dreyfus Affair, 58
economy, 60
French Indochina, 122
al-Glaoui, Thami,
  relationship with, 41, 42f–4, 47, 49–53, 62–3, 65, 77, 78, 86, 104–6, 108, 109, 118, 123, 187
identity politics, 84
journalism, 70–1
Le Prévost, Jacques, 182–3
Marrakesh rescue, 32–4
mission civilisatrice, 34, 36, 61, 81, 233
Mohammed V, deposition of, 117–18, 121
national indignity (*indignité nationale*), 103, 126
Rif War, 51
second épuration, la, 103
Second World War, 97–8
Third Republic, 57
Vichy government, 98, 103, 149–51
violence, 120
'Freytag's pyramid' organisation, 236
Funérailles du lait, Les (The Milk Funerals) (Binebine, Mahi), 204, 205

Galland, Gabriel
  Maroc: un empire qui se réveille, Le, 29
Gellner, Ernest, 174, 237
Germany, 90–1
al-Ghezouli, Bashir, 68, 69
'Glaoua tribe on Oued Seine', 86–7, 238
El Glaoui (Le Prévost, Jacques), 182

El Glaoui, Abderrahman El Mezouari
  Grand Vizir Madani El Mezouari El Glaoui, une vie au service du Makhzen, Le (The Grand Vizier Madani El Mezouari El Glaoui, a Life in the Service of the Makhzen), 214–15
al-Glaoui, Abdessadeq, 108, 116, 125, 126, 207–9, 235
  Jews, the, 146–7, 150
  Juin, Alphonse, 117–18
  ralliement. Le Glaoui, mon père, Le (The Rallying: Glaoui, My Father), 209–12, 236
al-Glaoui, Brahim, 125
al-Glaoui, Hammou, 30, 40, 157
al-Glaoui, Hassan, 125, 126, 208
al-Glaoui, Madani, 20, 21, 23–5, 27, 30, 46, 105
  biography, 214–15
  Corcos, Yoshua, 146
  death, 42, 105
  France, support for, 40, 41
  Lyautey, Hubert, 35
  Marrakesh rescue, 35
  marriage, 30
  military campaigns, 27, 39–41
  power, 20, 24, 27, 30, 31
al-Glaoui, Mehdi, 97, 104–5
al-Glaoui, Mohamed, 112, 125, 126
al-Glaoui, Mohamed al-Mézouari, 21
al-Glaoui, Samia, 223–4
al-Glaoui, Si Brahim, 112, 113, 116, 124
al-Glaoui, Thami, 3
  CAREER: 23; ʿAbd al-ʿAziz, deposition of, 26, 29, 121; allies, vengeance against, 124–6; anti-Semitism, 149–50; as businessman, 48, 67–8, 74, 98–9, 120, 123, 144, 146; Berber Feast, 116–17; Berdugo, Albert Simon, 138–42; charity, 107; correspondence, alterations to, 43–4, 79–80; court of, 48, 49, 146; doppelgänger, 33; Israel, opinion on, 151–2; as judge, 75; military campaigns, 27, 39–47, 117–18, 156; Mohammed V, deposition of, 117–18, 121, 125, 189; Mohammed V, restoration of, 123, 153–4, 210–11; Mulud (1950), 110, 111–16, 188–9, 198; nationalism, 107–9, 111, 113–15, 184; opposition, 49, 108, 118–19, 172, 184–5, 238 ; Parisian political support, 86–7, 238; as Pasha of Marrakesh, 30, 33, 74; politics, 100–1, 105–6, 107–8; power, 3–4, 7, 13, 20, 29, 30, 31; as Qaʾid, 42; travel, 89, 100, 106, 120
  CRITICISM: Babin, Gustave, 32, 45, 60, 62–3, 68–70, 73, 80–7, 147–8, 182, 198, 238; Schoen, Paul, 90
  IMAGE: 33, 45–50, 53, 74, 89, 90, 145, 178–9, 200–1, 210; as conspirator, 27; Frenchness, 85–6, 87; identity, 84–5, 197–8, 202; as (loyal) patriot, 21, 32, 33, 83, 214, 216 , 218; newspapers, 74; palace, 178, 224; photographs of, 28*f*, 41*f*, 42*f*, 45*f*, 52*f*, 76*f*, 119*f*, 122*f*, 155*f*, 159*f*; as rescuer, 21, 32–3, 35, 81, 233; as traitor, 177, 184, 210, 216, 218, 234; as warrior, 39–47, 233–4
  LEGACY: 7, 176, 184–91, 216–24; memory, erasure of, 176, 196, 199, 224; museum, 224

LEGAL CASES: Babin, Gustave, defamation lawsuit, 76–80; defamation, 12–13, 62, 74, 76–80, 147; legal status, 44, 79–80; lawsuits, 44, 63, 74, 75–80, 148–9

LIFE AND FAMILY: Amazighness, 187–8, 190, 197–9; character, 50, 89, 145; death, 4, 7, 18–19, 123, 154, 156, 176; family, 47, 97, 104–5, 108, 124–6; financial affairs, 49, 66–8, 73, 86, 89–90, 120, 146; genealogy, 84–5, 197–8; Hajj, 106–7; Hassan II, as father of, 185–6; health, 103, 122; poisoning of, 134, 154–5; scholarship, 48–9, 212–13; truth or loyalty debate, 80–4

MARRAKESH: 67, 178–9; as Pasha, 30, 33, 74; prostitution zone, 67; rescue, 32–3, 35, 81

RELATIONSHIPS: Abu-Haseira, Makhlouf, 158–9f; 'Alawi dynasty, 48; America, 105–6; Corcos family, 144–6; Epinat, Jean, 98–9, 103–4; Europe, 47; France, 41, 42f–4, 47, 49–53, 62–3, 65, 77, 78, 86, 104–6, 108, 109, 116, 118, 123, 187; Germany, 90, 99; Jews, 134, 143–61; Lyautey, Hubert, 35–6; Mimran, David, 123; Mohammed V, 99–100, 105, 107, 108–10, 111–16, 123, 126, 189; Spain, 109

WORKS: *Son Excellence. En réponse à une campagne infâme: quelques documents* (In Response to a Scandalous Campaign), 74, 82–3

see also al-Glaoui, Thami, stories of
al-Glaoui, Thami, stories of, 1, 2, 4, 5, 7–14, 17–18
Abun Nasr, Jamil, 186–7
al-Glaoui, Abdessadeq, 209–12, 235, 236
al-Glaoui, Samia, 223–4
al-Mahmudi, Othman, 198
al-Mawsu'a al-'Amma li-Ta'rikh al-Maghrib wa-al-Andalus (General Encyclopedia for the History of Morocco and al-Andalus), 188–90
al-Murakushi, Muhamed al-Azidi, 218–19
Alaoui, Maouane Lamharzi, 223
Amazigh diaspora, 199–202
Amazigh historiography, 199–202
archives, 12, 14–17
as tools, 190–1
Barthou, Louis, 46–7
Benhadar, Abdelilah, 7, 216–19, 242
Bidwell, Robin, 184–5
Binebine, Mahi, 204–5, 235
Brett, Michael and Fentress, Elizabeth, 200–1
conspiracy theories, 100–3, 185–6
cultural pluralism discourse, 219, 234
cultural resource management, 224
death plots, 134, 154–5, 156–7
Encyclopédie Berbère, 201–2
evolution of, 229
Fernea, Elizabeth, 176–7
goals of, 234–5
Hagan, Helene, 200–1
Hammoudi, Abdellah, 190
Harris, Walter Burton, 173, 179–80

al-Glaoui, Thami, stories of (*cont.*)
   Historical Dictionary of the Berbers (Imazighen), 202
   Jebrou, Abdellatif, 211–12
   Jelili, Atiku, 220–1
   Jewish narratives, 154–60
   Juin, Alphonse, 117–18
   Le Prévost, Jacques, 182–3
   maturity for self-reflection discourse, 234
   memory, erasure of, 176
   metaphors, 30, 205
   Mutafakkir, Ahmad, 212–13
   Pinhas Ha-Cohen Azzogh, 144–5, 154–6, 157–8
   post-colonial, 183–91
   prophecy discourse, 29, 121
   El Qadéry, Mustapha, 200
   Qanat dar l-khabar (The News Channel), 223
   Rami, Ahmed, 185–6
   recurring narratives, 21
   rescue discourse, 21, 32–3, 35, 81, 233
   Saduq, Ibrahim, 218
   Schoen, Paul, 16, 37–9, 90, 234–5
   social media, 221–4
   theatre and the art scene, 216–21
   traitor discourse, 177, 184, 210, 216, 218, 234
   Uzri, Abdelwahed, 217–18
   Vyssotsky, Victor, 238–9
   warrior discourse, 39–47, 233–4
   Zebib, Najib, 188–9, 235
   see also Babin, Gustave; Berdugo, Albert Simon; Maxwell, Gavin
Glaoui tribe, 21, 23–4, 126–7, 176–7
   biography, 214–15
   Bouhmara Revolt, 27
   Jews, relationships with, 143–4

global history, 240–1
God Protect Me from My Friends (Maxwell, Gavin), 168
Goundafi, Omar, 214
Goundafi, Taïeb, 214
Grand Vizir Madani El Mezouari El Glaoui, une vie au service du Makhzen, Le (The Grand Vizier Madani El Mezouari El Glaoui, a Life in the Service of the Makhzen) (El Glaoui, Abderrahman El Mezouari), 214–15
grands caïds, 3
Great Britain, 25, 82, 100, 135, 166–7
Great War, the, 40
Green March, 183
Grilhé, Georges, 78–9, 149–50
Guedj, Felix, 146, 149
Guêpe Marocaine, Le, 72

Hached, Ferhat, 120
hagadah, 5
Hagan, Helene, 200–1
al-Hahi, Rashid, 196, 197
Hai, Ambreen, 61
al-Hakim, ʿAbd, 63
Hammoudi, Abdellah
   Master and Disciple, 190
Harakat al-Shaabiya, 170
Harari, Georges Joseph
   History of the Jews of the Maghreb, The, 154–5
Haratin/Harratin, the, 24, 191n
Harpoon at a Venture (Maxwell, Gavin), 168
Harris, Walter Burton, 47, 180
   Morocco That Was, 173, 179–80
Hassan I (Sultan of Morocco), 22–3, 24–6
Hassan II (King of Morocco, formerly Crown Prince), 128, 169, 170, 205
   coup attempts, 183

al-Glaoui, Thami, as son of, 185–6
Rami, Ahmed, 185–6
Tamazight, 195
Heine, Heinrich
Almansor, 12
al-Hiba, Ahmed, 31–2, 33, 39
histoire, 5
Historical Dictionary of the Berbers (Imazighen), 202
history
biographies, 13–14
erasing/forgetting, 175–7, 196–7
global, 13, 240–1
micro, 13
Trouillot, Michel-Rolph, 175
truth in, 80–1
see also history–story link
History of the Jews of the Maghreb, The (Harari, Georges Joseph), 154–5
history–story link, 5–6, 230–1

'I Will Not Stroll With Thami El Glaoui' (Jelili, Atiku), 220–1
Idder, Hajj, 140
identity politics, 84, 193
imperial storytellers, 61–2
imperialism, 27, 58–9, 61–2, 240, 241; *see also* colonialism
independence, 100, 105, 109, 123, 169–70; *see also* Istiqlal
INDH (National Initiative for Human Development [L'Initiative nationale pour le dévelopement humain]), 206
Instagram, 223–4
Institut des hautes études Marocains (Institute of Higher Moroccan Studies), 37
Islam, 64–5, 142, 206; *see also* Muslims, the

Israel, 151–2
Istiqlal, 107, 108, 119–20, 169, 170, 190
founding, 103
Mohammed V (Sultan of Morocco), 189
Mulud (1950), 113, 114, 115

Jebrou, Abdellatif, 211–12
Qira'ton fi kitab al-Ustadh 'Abdessadeq al-Glawi 'an walidihi al-Basha Tuhami al-Glawi (Reading in the Book of Mr Abdessadeq El Glaoui about his Father the Pasha al-Thami al-Glaou), 211–12
Jelili, Atiku, 220–1
'I Will Not Stroll With Thami El Glaoui', 220–1
Jewish Alliance Israélite Universelle education system, 142
Jews, the, 136–8, 142–3
clothing rules, 150
employing Muslims, 150
Esther Scroll, 159–60
al-Glaoui, Thami, 134, 143–54
al-Glaoui, Thami, narratives of, 154–60
Jewish narratives, 154–60
Muslim–Jewish allyship, 150–1
Purim Katan/ Purim Sheni, 160
rural, 152–3
urban, 153
see also anti-Semitism
Jordan, 239–40
Jourdan, 72
journalism, 70–4, 136, 138, 205
Juin, Alphonse, 116, 117–18
justice, 81

al-Kahina, 199
Kenbib, Mohammed, 149–50
Khalidi, Hisham, 220

al-Khattabi, Abdelkrim, 50–1
Khayri, Badiʻ, 48–9
al-Kittani, Muhmmad ʻAbdelhay, 108, 121
Krupp cannon, 24–5, 26
Kurosawa, Akira
   Rashomon, 110

Labadie-Lagrave, Henri
   mensonge marocain: contribution à l'histoire «vraie» du Maroc, Le (The Moroccan Lie: Contribution to the 'True' History of Morocco), 72
Lachkar, David *see* Moulay Ighi
Lafont, Ernest, 62
Le Prévost, Jacques, 182, 183
   El Glaoui, 182–3
legal system, 74–5, 170
Lords of the Atlas (Maxwell, Gavin), 20, 169, 173, 191, 235
   Babin, Gustave, 181–2
   Harris, Walter Burton, 173, 179–80
   influences, sources, 173, 179–81
   publication and distribution, 9, 173
   reception, 173–4
   research, 3, 169–73
loyalty or truth debate, 80–4
Lyautey, Hubert, 34–7, 40, 51, 59, 71–2

Maclean, Harry Aubrey de Vere, 25–6
Maddy-Weitzman, Bruce, 199–200
al-Mahmudi, Othman, 198
Mangin, Charles, 32, 33, 39, 95n
Maroc sans Masque, Le (Morocco without a Mask) (Babin, Gustave), 80

Maroc: un empire qui se réveille, Le (Galland, Gabriel), 29
Marrakesh, 177–9
   celebrity inhabitants, 178
   decadence, 219
   Jewish community in, 143, 147, 148, 150–1, 153
   rescue affair, 32–4, 35, 81
'Marrakesh' (Orwell, George), 178
Marrakesh Biennale (2014), 219–21
Martinière, Henri de la, 86
Master and Disciple (Hammoudi, Abdellah), 190
maturity for self-reflection discourse, 234
al-Mawsuʻa al-ʻAmma li-Taʼrikh al-Maghrib wa-al-Andalus (General Encyclopedia for the History of Morocco and al-Andalus), 115, 188–90
Maxwell, Aymer, 166, 167
Maxwell, Gavin, 3, 7, 9, 11, 118, 166–9
   censorship, 12
   al-Glaoui's courts, 75
   God Protect Me from My Friends, 168
   Harpoon at a Venture, 168
   invention, 18–19
   Marrakesh, 177, 178
   metaphors, 30
   Mulud (1950), 113–14
   nostalgic-Orientalist genre, 235–6
   Reed Shaken by the Wind, A, 168
   Ring of Bright Water, 168
   writing style, 180
   see also Lords of the Atlas
Mayne, Peter
   Alleys of Marrakesh, The, 178
   Year in Marrakesh, A, 178
Mehmed Bey, Çerkes, 239
mensonge marocain: contribution à l'histoire «vraie» du

INDEX

Maroc, Le (The Moroccan Lie: Contribution to the 'True' History of Morocco) (Labadie-Lagrave, Henri), 72
Mesfioua affair, 113
Middle East and North Africa, 240
military, the, 25–6
Mimran, David, 123
mission civilisatrice, 34, 36, 61, 81, 233
Mission scientifique du Maroc (Scientific Mission of Morocco), 36
Mohammed Ben 'Arafa (Sultan of Morocco), 121, 122
Mohammed V (Sultan of Morocco), 3–4, 97, 99–100, 105, 107, 108
  death, 170
  deposition of, 117–18, 121, 125, 186, 189
  al-Glaoui, Thami, relationship with, 99–100, 105, 107, 108–10, 111–16, 123, 126, 189
  independence, 109, 169
  Mulud (1950), 110, 111–16, 188–9, 198
  Muslim–Jewish allyship, 150
  restoration of, 122–3, 153–4, 210–11
  support for, 169
Mohammed VI (Sultan of Morocco), 205
al-Mokri (Grand Vizier), 30
Moroccan Liberation Army, 125
Morocco, 4
  (Mohammed) Ben 'Arafa (Sultan), 121, 122
  Amazighité, 10
  caïdalisme/qa'idal system, 3, 8
  Casablanca terror attacks, 206
  collaboration (colonial period), 186–7, 237

colonialism, 8, 27, 29, 34, 36, 40, 81, 233
cultural pluralism, 219, 234
decolonising project, 175
economy, 64, 66–7, 98
foreign support, 205–6
French academic project, 36–7
Green March, 183
Hassan I (Sultan), 22–3, 24–6
history, erasing/forgetting, 175–7, 196–7
human rights, 205–6
independence, 100, 105, 109, 123, 169–70
Jews in, 142–3
journalism, 70–2, 205
legal system, 74–5, 170
map, 22f
maturity, 212, 219, 234
modernisation, 205–6
Mohammed VI (Sultan), 205
National Archives, 206
nationalism, 8, 64–5, 70, 88–9, 103, 107–8, 120, 127
rebellion/resistance/revolution, 27, 31, 65–6, 120, 122, 151, 170, 206–7, 237, 241
reform, 22–3, 25–6, 205–7
religion, 206
Second World War, 97–100
society, 34, 64, 83, 183
system of rule, 3
taxation, 3
trust in, 83
Years of Lead, 183
Youssef (Sultan), 31–2
'Abd al-Hafidh (Sultan), 28, 30–1
'Abd al-'Aziz (Sultan), 26–9, 100–1, 138
see also Hassan II (Sultan); Mohammed V (Sultan)
Morocco Since 1830 (Pennell, Richard), 238

Morocco That Was (Harris, Walter), 173, 179–80
Morocco under Colonial Rule (Bidwell, Robin), 184–5
Moulay Ighi (David Lachkar), 143
Mulud (1950), 110–16, 188–9, 198
al-Murakushi, Abdeljalil ben Muhamed al-Azidi, 179, 218–19
Muslim–Jewish allyship, 150–1
Muslims, the, 136–7, 142–3
    employment by Jews, 150
    Muslim–Jewish allyship, 150–1
    see also Islam
Mutafakkir, Ahmad
    Nuzum al-qawafi fi al-Basha al-Glawi: ibbana wala'ihi lil-'arsh al-'Alawi (Arranged Poems for al-Pasha al-Glaoui: During his Loyalty to the 'Alawi Throne), 212–13
mysterieuse Ouaouizert, chronique d'une colonne au Maroc, La (Mysterious Ouaouizert, Chronicle of a Column in Morocco) (Babin, Gustave), 60

national identity, 193–4
national indignity (*indignité nationale*), 103, 125–66
National Initiative for Human Development (L'Initiative nationale pour le dévelopement humain [INDH]), 206
nationalism, 8, 64–5, 70, 88–9, 103, 107–8, 120, 127
nationalist historiographies, 231, 232
newspapers, 70–4
Noguès, Charles, 88, 97
Nuzum al-qawafi fi al-Basha al-Glawi: ibbana wala'ihi lil-'arsh al-'Alawi (Arranged Poems for al-Pasha al-Glaoui: During his Loyalty to the 'Alawi Throne) (Mutafakkir, Ahmad), 212–13

L'Oeuvre, 136
L'Ombre du poète (The Shadow of the Poet) (Binebine, Mahi), 204–5
Orwell, George, 148, 178
    'Marrakesh', 178
otherness, 87
Oufkir, Mohamed, 199–200

Parti Communiste du Maroc (Communist Party of Morocco [PCM]), 103, 108
Passage to India, A (Forster, E. M.), 81–2
PCM (Parti Communiste du Maroc [Communist Party of Morocco]), 103, 108
Peets, Leonora
    Women of Marrakech, 178
Pennell, Richard
    Morocco Since 1830, 238
Péres, Gaston, 146
Pétain, Philippe, 51, 97, 98
Philippeville massacre, 122
Pinhas Ha-Cohen Azzogh, 144–5, 154–6, 157–8
politics of notables, 240
Ponsot, Henri, 77, 78
postcolonialism, 238
    historiographies, 231, 232–3
Power and Knowledge in Morocco (Eickelman, Dale), 65
press corporations, 72
prophecy discourse, 29, 121
Purim Katan/ Purim Sheni, 160

El Qadéry, Mustapha, 196, 200
qa'idal system, 3, 8, 10, 184–5, 196
    Hassan I, 23
    see also caïdalisme

qa'ids, the, 3, 23, 39–40, 46, 109, 198
  Amazigh, 198
  biographies, 213–15
  legal system, 75
  reconciliation, 224–5
Qanat dar l-khabar (The News Channel), 223
Qayd al-Qyyad: al-Basha al-Glawi (The Commander: The Pasha al-Glaoui) (Benhadar, Abdelilah), 216–19, 242
Qira'ton fi kitab al-Ustadh 'Abdessadeq al-Glawi 'an walidihi al-Basha Tuhami al-Glawi (Reading in the Book of Mr Abdessadeq El Glaoui about his Father the Pasha al-Thami al-Glaou) (Jebrou, Abdellatif), 211–12

racism, 54n, 82, 85, 188; *see also* anti-Semitism
ar-Rahman, 'Abd, 187
ralliement. Le Glaoui, mon père, Le (The Rallying: Glaoui, My Father) (al-Glaoui, Abdessadeq), 209–12
Rami, Ahmed, 185–6
Rashomon (Kurosawa, Akira), 110
Rashomon effect, 110, 115, 236
rebellion/resistance/revolution, 31, 65–6, 122, 170, 237
  Bouhmara Revolt, 27
  demonstrations, 206–7
  global, 241
  Jewish, 151
  strikes, 120
Reed Shaken by the Wind, A (Maxwell, Gavin), 168
religion, 136, 206
  Islam, 64–5, 136–7, 142–3, 150–1, 206
  see also, Jews, the

rescue discourse, 21, 32–4, 35, 81, 233
Réveil du Moghreb, Le, 73
Rif War, 49, 51
Ring of Bright Water (Maxwell, Gavin), 168
Rogers, Joel Augustus, 107
  World's Great Men of Color, 107
Roosevelt, Theodore, 100
rwaya, 5

Saduq, Ibrahim, 218
Salvatore, Giuliano, 168
Schoen, Paul, 16, 37–9, 234–5
  al-Glaoui, Thami, criticism of, 90
  Marrakesh rescue, 32–3
Schroeter, Daniel, 150
Second World War, 97–100, 149
Segonzac, René de, 32
Semtob, Ohana, 106
Service des liaisons Nord-Africaines (North African Liaison Service), 38
Son Excellence. En réponse à une campagne infâme: quelques documents (In Response to a Scandalous Campaign) (al-Glaoui, Thami), 74, 82–3
Son Excellence: le Maroc sans Masque (His Excellency: Morocco without a Mask) (Babin, Gustave), 12, 69–70, 71–2, 82, 147, 171, 181, 207, 235
Spain, 31, 101, 109, 135
Statut des Juifs (1940), 149
Steeg, Théodore, 51–2, 86–7
stories/storytelling, 6–7
  biographies, 13–14, 213–15
  concurrent realities, 110–16
  conspiracy theories, 100–3
  evolution of, 229
  'Freytag's pyramid' organisation, 236

stories/storytelling (cont.)
  history–story link, 5–6, 230–1
  imperial storytellers, 61–2
  in legal cases, 211
  literary formats/genres, 235–6
  mission civilisatrice, 233
  myths, 236
  order in, 6
  Rashomon effect, 110, 115, 236
  truth in, 110
  see also al-Glaoui, Thami, stories of
Story Makes History, Theory Makes Story (Fernandez, Juan), 6
Street in Marrakech, A (Fernea, Elizabeth), 176–7, 178
strikes, 120
Sultan, Fortuné, 108

Tamazight, 195
Tangier, 100–1, 135, 136
taxation, 3, 31, 54n
Telout
  castle of, 2f
  Jewish population, 143
terrorism, 206
Tizi n' Telouet, 21, 22f
Tolédano, Joseph, 150, 151
trade, 144
tradition, 5
traitor discourse, 177, 184, 210, 216, 218, 234

treason, 237
Treaty of Fes, 31, 123
Trouillot, Michel-Rolph, 175
truth or loyalty debate, 80–4

Uzri, Abdelwahed, 217–18

Vaffier, Ernest, 28f
violence, 120, 122, 124
Voices of Marrakesh, The (Canetti, Elias), 153, 178
Vyssotsky, Victor, 238–9

warrior discourse, 39–47, 233–4
wars, 40, 49, 51, 97–100, 122, 149, 241
Women of Marrakech (Peets, Leonora), 178
World's Great Men of Color (Rogers, Joel Augustus), 107

Year in Marrakesh, A (Mayne, Peter), 178
Years of Lead, 183
Yogurta, 199
Youssef (Sultan of Morocco), 31–2
YouTube, 221–3

Zebib, Najib, 188–9, 235
Zineb, Lalla, 30, 47, 126, 208

EU representative:
Easy Access System Europe
Mustamäe tee 50, 10621 Tallinn, Estonia
Gpsr.requests@easproject.com

www.ingramcontent.com/pod-product-compliance
Lightning Source LLC
Chambersburg PA
CBHW050209240426
43671CB00013B/2270